HISTORY
OF
THEOLOGY

HISTORY

OF

THEOLOGY

Bengt Hägglund

TRANSLATED BY GENE J. LUND

CONCORDIA PUBLISHING HOUSE

SAINT LOUIS · LONDON

Original title: *Teologins Historia*

Copyright 1966 3rd edition by AB CWK Gleerup Bokförlag
Lund, Sweden
for the Swedish edition

Copyright 1968 by Concordia Publishing House, St. Louis, Missouri
for the English edition

Translator: Gene J. Lund

Library of Congress Catalog Card No. 68-13365

Concordia Publishing House, St. Louis, Missouri

Concordia Publishing House Ltd., London, E. C. 1

MANUFACTURED IN THE UNITED STATES OF AMERICA

From the Foreword to the Second Edition

This presentation of the history of theology is designed to provide an introduction to Christian dogmatic literature and to describe its stages of development. The history of theology is, therefore, a branch of the history of ideas; it deals with the sources of the Christian tradition and examines the development of ideas reflected therein.

In continental theology a distinction has sometimes been made between "the history of dogma," referring to doctrinal developments prior to the Reformation, and "the history of theology," referring to post-Reformation developments. This division, which has scant factual basis, nevertheless shows quite clearly that the expression "the history of dogma" is hardly a satisfactory label for this particular area of research. With the present-day division of theological disciplines in mind, the expression "the history of theology" might also appear improper in this context. But when the word "theology" is also used to designate the interpretation of the Christian faith, both in its prescientific and in its modern forms, one can justifiably use the term "the history of theology."

The older presentations in the history of dogma — e. g., the three justly famous works by Adolph von Harnack, Reinhold Seeberg, and Friedrich Loofs — defined dogma as doctrines which had been officially accepted by the church. Harnack looked upon them as a secondary, scientific reworking of the doctrines of faith, or, in his own words, as "the result of the Greek spirit at work on the soil of the Gospel." He considered this a limited epoch in the history of the church, largely overcome by the Reformation, and he sought to criticize dogma on the basis of the criteria he claimed to have found in the original Gospel. Seeberg also thought of the formation of dogma as having taken place in a certain period of time, which was concluded for Protestants with the Formula of Concord and the Synod of Dort. But he also felt that dogma is an expression of Christian faith, and he discovered the basis of criticism in the dogmas themselves, insofar as they gave expression to the fundamental truths of the salvation wrought in Christ. It should be emphasized, however, that these major works do not as a matter of fact deal only with dogma in a definitive sense but with Christian theology in general. The more modern developments, however, were not considered a part of the history of dogma as seen from the point of view represented at that time.

In contemporary discussions there is no unanimity concerning the meaning of the term "dogma." In general, however, it has a far wider significance than in the definition mentioned above, for it also includes modern theological developments. Dogma is not only looked upon as something inherited from the past; it is also considered to be a contemporary reality, closely related to the proclamation of the Word. In some instances it is conceived of as a transcendent principle of revelation (as in Karl Barth, e. g.), in others as the scientific complement of the preached message of the church. Under such circumstances, it is easy to see how difficult it is to provide a clear-cut description of the sphere and of the task of the historian of dogma on the basis of contemporary premises.

But in spite of these difficulties, it is above all important to trace the history of theological thought through the years simply as a part of the realm of ideas, without judging and without employing any preconceived "critique of dogma" of one kind or another. If one desires to find a basic common element or a guiding principle to use in conducting research of this kind, it would seem to be preferable to proceed on the basis of the original Christian confession than on the basis of an ambiguous concept of what dogma really is. This confession, the Christian "rule of faith," has been a fixed reality from the very beginning, not with respect to form but with respect to substance (cf. Kelly, *Early Christian Doctrines*, 1958, p. 37: "a condensed summary, fluid in its wording but fixed in content, setting out the key-points of the Christian revelation in the form of a rule"). This rule of faith was reflected in the current symbols, but it could also be expressed in other doctrinal formulations. It stands out in the writings of the early church not as gradually developed dogma but as an expression of the originally given truths of faith and as a summary of the content of Scripture. The theology of the church is set forth as an explication of the original rule of faith or of that which was considered essential therein.

6

On this basis, the history of theology develops into a presentation of how the Christian rule of faith has been interpreted in history and within different groups. That such a point of view is neither arbitrary nor externally coerced can be seen in the fact that in one way or another the various theological schools have always sought, above all, to interpret the Christian confession.

As far as the theology of the church fathers is concerned, the point of view here referred to has usually manifested itself in the presentation of the history of dogma either consciously or otherwise. This is so because the literary efforts of the church fathers are closely related to the main issues involved in the rule of faith. In the case of medieval and contemporary theology, it is only natural that this material should be examined from other vantage points as well. The relationship to philosophy and contemporary intellectual presuppositions has been given a good share of attention in these attempts to see the various theological schools in all of their uniqueness. It is of great value, in delineating the history of theology, to take proper note of these facets of the overall picture. More work remains to be done in this area. If one intends to describe the way in which the rule of faith was interpreted in the medieval period (and later), and to study the interaction between theology and confession which has constantly gone on in the history of theology, many new research tasks must be undertaken. . . .

In this new edition of *The History of Theology* the text has been revised at a number of points, and at others it has been expanded on the basis of new or formerly unknown literature. Some chapters or sections have been entirely rewritten. The addition of a brief summary of English theology — beginning with the Reformation — represents the biggest change. . . . In response to a number of requests an index has been added to this edition. . . .

Bengt Hägglund

Lund, Sweden,
February 1963.

Foreword to the Third Edition

In this edition I have added a section on the theology of 19th-century revivalism. I have also brought the discussion up to the present time at a number of points by the addition of Ch. 34, "The Theology of the Early 20th Century; Contemporary Trends." The reader must not expect, however, to find a comprehensive or detailed survey of 20th-century developments in this chapter. The purpose of this closing presentation is simply to shed some light on certain of the more important ideas which have been broached in recent years and to clarify some of the essential problems involved in contemporary theological discussion.

For helpful assistance in the preparation of this third edition I am particularly grateful to Bo Ahlberg, Sven Ingebrand, Göran Malmeström, David Lagergren, Torsten Nilsson, Sven Hemrin, and Olle Sigstedt, among others.

Bengt Hägglund

Lund, Sweden,
August 1966.

Contents

PART III

The Modern Period
From the Reformation to the Present

PART I

The Age
of the Church Fathers

CHAPTER 1

The Apostolic Fathers

When we speak of the Apostolic Fathers, we usually have reference to a number of Christian authors whose writings have come down to us from the end of the first century and the beginning of the second. These writings — of an incidental nature for the most part (letters, homilies) — are of value to us because, next to the New Testament, they are the oldest sources we have that testify to the Christian faith. These writings, however, do not claim to be doctrinal presentations in the strict sense of the word, and as a result we could hardly expect to derive from them a complete picture of the articles of faith. And while they have contributed relatively little to the development of theology, they have done much to shed light on the concept of faith and the church customs that prevailed in the earliest congregations.

The most important of these writings are the following:

— The First Epistle of Clement, written in Rome about 95.

— The Epistles of Ignatius; seven letters to various addresses, written about 115 during Ignatius' journey to Rome and his anticipated martyr's death.

— The Epistle of Polycarp, written in Smyrna about 110.

— The Epistle of Barnabas, probably written in Egypt sometime around 130.

— The Second Epistle of Clement, written in Rome or Corinth about 140.

— The Shepherd of Hermas, written in Rome about 150.

— Fragments from Papias, written in Hierapolis of Phrygia about 150, cited in the works of Eusebius and Irenaeus (among others).

— The Didache ("The Teaching of the Twelve Apostles"), written in the first half of the second century, probably in Syria.

GENERAL CHARACTERISTICS

Although the writings of the Apostolic Fathers stand close to the apostles and the New Testament in a chronological sense, the difference between these sources is strikingly obvious, with respect to both form and content. Some of these writings were included for a time in the New Testament canon, but it is no accident that they were ultimately excluded. The difference between the New Testament books and the writings of the Apostolic Fathers is manifest in many respects. Attempts have been made to determine which of the apostles (Peter or Paul, for example) influenced the men who produced these writings. But this has been proved to be an unnecessary search. The theology of the Apostolic Fathers cannot be assigned to any particular member of the apostolic band; it rather reflects the faith of the typical congregation in the first years of Christian history. The similarities between these writings and the New Testament need not depend on the fact that the Apostolic Fathers borrowed in a direct way from one canonical author or the other; they rather reflect the fact that both sources deal with the same faith.

In comparison with the New Testament the Apostolic Fathers are distinctive chiefly because of their emphasis on what is generally called *moralism*. (Anders Nygren uses the word "nomism"; in English literature the term "legalism" is employed.) The proclamation of the Law has a prominent place in the writings of the Apostolic Fathers. This is true in part because these writings are hortatory in style and also because they were directed to the new congregations whose members had recently emerged from a pagan background. It was necessary to replace their old habits with Christian order and customs. In order to accomplish this, the Jewish manner of preaching the Law was used to some extent, together with other Jewish congregational practices, despite the fact that there was a great deal of opposition to Judaism and the ceremonial law. The Gospel was presented as a new law that Christ taught and by which He showed the way to salvation. The old law was said to be abolished, obsolete, but in the teaching of Christ there was a new law. The Christian life was said to consist, above all, in obedience to this new law.

16

Moralism was found not in the proclamation of the Law as such but in the manner this was done. There was a strong tendency among the Apostolic Fathers to emphasize obedience to the Law, as well as the imitation of Christ, as the way to salvation and the essential content of the Christian life. Christ's death and resurrection were pointed to as the basis of man's salvation. Because of Christ's work man can receive the forgiveness of sin, the gift of life, immortality, and release from the powers of corruption. But even in the context in which such matters were discussed it was not unusual for the Apostolic Fathers to place a strong emphasis on the Law and the new way of life. An analysis of some of the most frequently mentioned fundamentals will throw more light on this tendency.

Righteousness, as a general rule, was described not as a gift of God bestowed on men of faith (cf. Rom. 3:21 ff.) but rather in terms of proper Christian behavior. It was often presented as the power of Christ which enables man to do what is right and good, but at the same time it was also said in a rather one-sided way that the new obedience is the prerequisite of forgiveness and salvation. The latter was looked upon not as a gift of grace alone, given here and now to those who believe, but as something bestowed after this life, primarily as a reward for obedience to Christ. With the exception of First Clement, the writings of the Apostolic Fathers have very little in common with Paul's emphasis on justification by faith. It is not unmerited grace that stands at the center of this teaching but rather the new way of life that Christ taught and which He empowers. It must be remembered, however, that the character of these writings, as well as the objective the authors had in mind, was in part responsible for this emphasis. Furthermore, the fact that these were incidental writings, which made no claim to completeness, is another facet of the story. These writings presumed that those who read them also heard an oral proclamation in which other aspects of the Christian faith would be properly stressed.

Salvation is presented more often in terms of immortality and indestructibility than in terms of the forgiveness of sin. Another strongly emphasized facet in this connection is knowledge. Christ has brought us the knowledge of the truth. He is the Revealer sent by God so that we might know the true God and thereby be freed from the thralldom of idolatry and the false old covenant. The Apostolic Fathers did not say, however, that Christ is merely a teacher; they taught that He is God, the One through whose death and resurrection the gift of immortality is bestowed.

Sin is described as corruption, evil desire, and captivity to the power of death, plus error and ignorance; the idea of guilt is not strongly emphasized. We note here a counterpart to that which was said about salvation; the Apostolic Fathers looked upon this as immortality or as the enlightenment that results from the truth as it is in Christ. The relationship between salvation and forgiveness or atonement is also to be found here — especially in Barnabas — but it does not have the same place as in Paul or, for example, in the Protestant tradition. Salvation is associated with the physical life, in terms of freedom from death and corruption. Light and life, which form its content, are related to the Law. The way of obedience is the way to life.

The moralistic tendency in the Apostolic Fathers appears most conspicuously in their concept of *grace*. In the New Testament grace is the love of God revealed in Christ. It is related to God Himself, therefore, and to the work of redemption carried out by Christ. Man is justified by grace, not on the strength of his own works. Among the Apostolic Fathers this New Testament concept of grace was replaced by another, in which grace is looked upon as a gift that God bestows on man through Christ. This gift, which is sometimes placed in the same category with the knowledge that has come to us through Christ, is thought of as inner power associated with the Holy Spirit, by which man can strive after righteousness and walk in the way of the new obedience. Grace is therefore the prerequisite of salvation, but not in the New Testament sense — that righteousness is a gift of God bestowed on those who believe in Christ. The Apostolic Fathers rather say this, that grace conveys the power by which man can attain to righteousness and ultimately be saved.

The trend of thought here set forth clearly indicates the relationship between the medieval concept of grace, with its emphasis upon "good works," and the pattern previously established in this earlier tradition (cf. Torrance, *The Doctrine of Grace in the Apostolic Fathers*, 1948). There are at the same time, however, expressions that are more closely related to the Pauline doctrine of justification. Furthermore, one must also observe in this connection that we are dealing here with hortatory literature, designed to train people in the new life, strongly emphasizing the call to obey Christ's commands. This emphasis was made in order to provide a counterbalancing influence to the pagan morality that dominated the environment in which the people addressed in these writings lived. As a result one dare not use the writings of the Apostolic Fathers to draw far-reaching conclusions in regard to the entire Christian proclamation of that period.

CONCEPT OF THE BIBLE

As was true with the New Testament, it was thought that the books of the Old Testament possessed their own intrinsic authority. The fact that the Apostolic Fathers quoted the Old Testament as much as they did is all the more striking when we remember that their writings were directed, for the most part, to Christians who had come from a pagan background.

The church was thought of as the New Israel, and as such the heir of the writings associated with the old covenant. The true purpose of the Law and the Prophets was spiritual in nature, a fact that was revealed through Christ's words and deeds. The Epistle of Barnabas, which dealt with this problem in a special way, does not make any obvious distinction between what came to be known later as a typological interpretation and a free allegorical interpretation. It was assumed from the very beginning that the law of Moses had a deeper purpose. When, for example, the law of Moses forbids the eating of unclean animals, it is thought to mean that the Law thereby condemns the sins which such animals symbolize. References to Christ and the New Testament were found even in the most insignificant details (cf., e. g., Barnabas IX, 8). Behind all this was the conviction that Scripture was verbally inspired by the Holy Spirit; even external details were thought to conceal spiritual wisdom of some kind, which the Jews with their method of literal interpretation were unable to find.

The Apostolic Fathers also testify in no uncertain terms to the fact that the four gospels and the writings of the apostles were coming to be recognized as Holy Scripture with the same authority as the Old Testament, even though the New Testament had not yet taken its final form in their time. Nearly all of the books that came to be included in our New Testament are cited or referred to in the Apostolic Fathers. The oral tradition which originated with the apostles was also considered to

19

possess a decisive authority for congregational faith and practice. According to Ignatius the bishop was the bearer of this authoritative tradition.

THE DOCTRINE OF GOD; CHRISTOLOGY

The Apostolic Fathers shared a Biblical concept of the nature of God, based on the idea of God found in the Old Testament. They thought of God as the almighty One who created the world and made His will, His righteousness, and His grace known to man. As is said in the Shepherd of Hermas: "Believe above all that God is *one*, He who has created and ordered all things and formed all that exists out of nothing." Faith in the one true God is emphasized. The doctrine of the Triune God was not yet fully developed, but the Trinitarian formula was employed, for example, in Baptism, and faith in the Trinity was, quite naturally, implied. The explication of the manner in which the three Persons of the Godhead are related to one another belongs, however, to a later period.

The divinity of Christ is strongly emphasized in the Apostolic Fathers. As Pliny the Younger remarked in a well-known phrase included in a letter to Emperor Trajan, the Christians "sing to Christ as they sing to God." Christ was thought of as the preexistent Son of God, who participated in the work of creation; He is the Lord of heaven, who shall appear as the judge of the living and the dead. Christ is specifically referred to as God, particularly in the epistles of Ignatius. "Our God, Jesus Christ, born of Mary according to God's decree, truly of the seed of David, but also of the Holy Spirit," he wrote in his Epistle to the Ephesians. (XVIII, 2)

Christ was said to be present in the congregation as its Lord, and Christian people are united to Him as participants in His death and resurrection. This oneness with Christ is prominently set forth by Ignatius. He wrote to the Christians in Smyrna: "I have been told that you are established in an untroubled faith, firmly attached to the cross of Christ in both body and soul, steadfast in love through the blood of Christ, and convinced that our Lord is in truth of David's seed according to the flesh, and God's Son according to God's will and power." (First Epistle to the Smyrneans)

We also find in Ignatius a number of statements directed against (or elicited by) the Jewish-Christian Gnostics, in which he emphasizes the true humanity of Christ. Jesus' actual earthly life is asserted in opposition to those who held that Christ merely appeared to exist in human form, that He only seemed to suffer on the cross, and that after the Resurrection He returned to a nonphysical spiritual existence. This point of view is known as *Docetism* (from the Greek δοκεῖν). The struggle against Docetism was one of the more significant facets of early Christian theology, since Docetism contradicted what was basic in the apostolic proclamation, the veritable death and resurrection of Christ. Salvation resulted from this, which actually happened within the context of history, and to which the apostles were eyewitnesses. When Docetism explained away the death and resurrection of Christ, salvation was related to an abstract teaching and not to what God accomplished in Christ. Docetism assumed various forms: either it denied the claim of Christ's true humanity with the use of a theory about a ghostlike body, or else it selected certain aspects of Christ's earthly life as being potentially true, while the remainder of the Gospel account was explained away. A Gnostic by the name of Cerinthus, a resident of Asia Minor, was of the opinion that Jesus was united with Christ, the Son of God, at the time of His baptism, and that Christ left the earthly Jesus before He was crucified. It was thought that the suffering and death of Jesus was incompatible with the divinity of Christ. Another Docetic theory, associated with Basilides, suggested that a mistake took place, that Simon of Cyrene was crucified in place of Christ, and that Jesus thereby escaped the death on the cross.

According to Irenaeus, the Gospel of John was written for this purpose, among others, to refute the Gnostic Cerinthus mentioned above. The latter's point of view was characterized by the sharp distinction he made between the man Jesus and the heavenly spiritual being, Christ, who could have made His abode in Jesus for a brief time only. In opposition to this, the Gospel of John tells us that "the Word became flesh"; similarly, the First Epistle of John asserts that "Jesus Christ has come in the flesh." (2:22; 4:2-3)

Opposition of this same kind can be discerned in Ignatius' struggle against Docetism. Against those who said that Christ only appeared to suffer, Ignatius expressed the conviction that Christ was truly born of Mary, that He was actually crucified, and that He resuscitated Himself. Christ was "in the flesh" even after His resurrection, said Ignatius; He was not a "nonphysical spirit."

21

CONCEPT OF THE CHURCH

We can tell from the writings of the Apostolic Fathers that ecclesiastical regulations were being consolidated at that time. The office of bishop developed to the point where it was distinct from the college of elders. According to Ignatius, the bishop was the symbol of Christian unity and bearer of the apostolic tradition. The congregations were therefore admonished to hold fast to their bishop and to be obedient to him. Unity was said to consist primarily of a common doctrinal corpus, and the dominant position of the bishop in the congregation was explained on the basis of the fact that he was the representative of the true doctrine. This harmony which centered on the bishops was emphasized as a protection against heresy, which threatened to destroy the unity of the church. Originally the elders and the bishops were on the same level, but by this time the bishops occupied a position which was elevated above the presbyterial rank. This so-called monarchical episcopate first appeared in Asia Minor and is clearly pointed to in the epistles of Ignatius, while First Clement and the Shepherd of Hermas, which were written in Rome, do not mention an office superior to the college of elders. But First Clement also emphasizes the significance of the bishop's office and insists that those who hold this office are the successors of the apostles. The idea of apostolic succession developed out of a Jewish prototype. Two things are implied: first, the bishops received the true teaching from the apostles, just as the prophets learned from Moses (doctrinal succession), and second, they had been appointed by the apostles and their successors in an unbroken line, just as the family of Aaron alone had the right to appoint priests in Israel (ordination succession).

As a result a more specific type of congregational order, with ecclesiastical jurisdiction, developed within the early Christian church. This development has been evaluated in a variety of ways. The well-known legal historian Rudolph Sohm has put forth the idea that every church law is in opposition to the essence of the church. It is the Holy Spirit alone who rules in the church, and because of this the emergence of ecclesiastical "institutions" denotes a departure from the original spirit of Christianity (*Kirchenrecht*, I, 1892). Others have denied this thesis, however, by pointing out that ordinances are necessary. This development is not a later accretion; its origins take us back to the time of the apostles themselves. What happened later was the stricter application of existing forms and the acceptance of new ones (Seeberg). It has also been said in this context, and properly so, that the Holy Spirit and ecclesiastical offices are not contrary to one another; they rather belong together. The fact that the church is a creation of the Holy Spirit does not preclude the development of regulations, offices, and traditions. The services and offices of the church are related to the work of the Holy Spirit. (Linton, *Das Problem der Urkirche in der neueren Forschung,* 1932)

ESCHATOLOGY

The eschatology of the Apostolic Fathers included the idea that the end of time was imminent, and some of them (Papias, Barnabas) also upheld the doctrine of an earthly millennium. Barnabas accepted the Jewish idea that the world would exist for 6,000 years, as foreshadowed in the six days of creation. And thereupon, it was said, would follow the seventh millennium, in which Christ will visibly reign on earth with the assistance of His faithful (cf. Rev. 20). This is to be followed by the eighth day, eternity, which has its prototype in Sunday. Papias, too, supported the doctrine of an earthly millennium, and he described the blissful condition which will prevail during that time. This point of view ("millennialism" or "chiliasm") has been largely discredited in more recent times. In fact, Eusebius did this in his evaluation of the writings of Papias. (*Ecclesiastical History,* III, 39)

CHAPTER 2

The Apologists

The authors of the second century who sought above all to defend Christianity against current allegations from Greek and Jewish sources are commonly remembered as the Apologists. To these men Christianity was the only true philosophy, a perfect replacement for the philosophy of the Greeks and the religion of the Jews, which could do no more than present unsatisfactory answers to man's searching questions.

Chief among the Apologists was Justin, called "the martyr," whose two "apologies" date from the middle of the second century. His *Dialogue with Trypho the Jew* was written at about the same time. Among the others was Aristides, who wrote the oldest "apology" now extant, Tatian (*Oratio ad Graecos*, a pamphlet directed against Greek culture, ca. 165), and Athenagoras (*De resurrectione mortuorum* and *Supplicatio pro Christianis*, both written about 170). The following might also be included in this group: Theophilus of Antioch (*Ad Autolycum libri tres*, 169–182), and the Epistle to Diognetus, whose author is unknown, and the similarly anonymous *Cohortatio ad Graecos*, which appeared just before the middle of the third century. The last-named work has been erroneously ascribed to Justin. The Apologists wrote other pieces too, which are now lost and known only by name. (Cf., e. g., Eusebius' *Ecclesiastical History*, IV, 3)

GENERAL STATEMENT

The Apologists occupy a significant niche in the history of dogma, partly as a result of their description of Christianity as the true philosophy and partly as a result of their attempt to elucidate theological teachings with the help of contemporary philosophical terminology (for example, in the so-called "Logos Christology"). What we find here, therefore, is the first attempt to define, in a logical manner, the content of the Christian faith, as well as the first connection between theology and science, between Christianity and Greek philosophy.

The Apologists refuted the allegations directed against the Christians. Athenagoras (in his *Supplicatio*) discussed three main criticisms: godlessness, unnatural habits, and enmity toward the state. In response they directed an attack on Greek culture which was at times quite severe (Tatian, *Oratio ad Graecos*; Theophilus). But their most important contribution, as seen from the point of view of the history of dogma, was the positive way in which they presented Christianity as the true philosophy.

CHRISTIANITY AND PHILOSOPHY

The manner in which the Apologists conceived of the relationship between Christianity and philosophy is reflected in Justin's autobiographical work, *Dialogue with Trypho the Jew*. Justin presents himself as a man who thinks very highly of philosophy and who has sought for satisfactory answers to philosophical questions in one philosophical system after another. The purpose of philosophy, according to Justin, is to provide true knowledge of God and existence and, in so doing, to promote a sense of well-being in human minds. Philosophy is designed to bring God and man together. Justin investigated the Stoics, the Peripatetics, and the Pythagoreans, but they had left him unmoved. At last he became a Platonist and thought that he could find the truth there. Then he met an old man, unknown to him, who directed his attention to the Old Testament prophets, insisting that they alone had seen and proclaimed the truth. "They have only taught that which they have heard and seen with the help of the Holy Spirit." The testimony of this old man convinced Justin that Christianity was true. "My soul began immediately to burn, and I longed for the love of the prophets and the friends of Christ. I reflected upon their teachings, and found therein the only dependable and useful philosophy. It was in this way, and on this basis, that I became a philosopher." (VII, VIII)

The fact that Christianity is the only true philosophy implies, therefore, that it alone has the right answers to philosophical questions. Philosophy also involves, in this sense, the religious question concerning the true knowledge of God. Christianity alone can provide this knowledge; philosophy seeks for it but is unable to find it. This trend of thought does not, in itself, imply that Christianity is dependent on and subordinate to philosophy, as is sometimes suggested. Christianity is based on revelation, and the Apologists did not believe that revelation can be replaced by rational deliberations. In this respect Christianity is opposed to all philosophy. Its truth is not based on reason; it has a divine origin. "No one but the prophets can instruct us about God and the true religion, for they teach on strength of divine inspiration" (the closing words of *Cohortatio ad Graecos*).

At the same time, however, the way the Apologists approached Christian truth involved the tendency to intellectualize its content. Reason (λόγος) was the most prominent concept in their writings, and great stress was placed on the communication of truth.

Philosophy is evaluated in a variety of ways. Some of the Apologists were particularly critical of Greek philosophy. All pagan wisdom was to be replaced by revelation. Justin, on the other hand, had a more positive attitude toward the Greeks. It must be made clear, however, that the truth which can be discerned in such philosophers as Homer, Socrates, and Plato was basically derived from revelation. One related idea was that some of the wise men of Greece had visited Egypt and there became acquainted with the work of the prophets of Israel. Another idea suggested that the pagan philosophers shared in the λόγος σπερματικός, which is implanted in all men. Even human wisdom thus is dependent on revelation — scattered beams of the divine reason which has shined forth in full clarity from Christ. Philosophers have certain fragments of truth. In Christ truth is fully present, for He is Himself God's reason, the Logos who became man.

LOGOS CHRISTOLOGY

The Logos concept, derived from contemporary philosophy, especially Stoicism with its doctrine of universal reason, was used by the Apologists to explain how Christ was related to God the Father. Something of the Logos, they said, is to be found in all men. Reason, like an embryo, is implanted within them (λόγος σπερματικός). But the Apologists, unlike the Stoics, did not say that this was some kind of a general, pantheistically conceived universal reason. They rather equated the Logos with Christ. On this basis they could say that Plato and Socrates were Christians too, to the extent that they gave expression to reason. Their wisdom came to them from Christ via the prophets or a general revelation.

The Greek *logos* means both "reason" and "word." The Logos has been with God, as His own reason, from all eternity (λόγος ἐνδιάθετος). Subsequently this reason proceeded out of the essence of God, according to God's own decision, as the λόγος προφορικός, the Word which originated with God. This was done at the time of the creation of the world. God created the world according to His reason and through the Word, which proceeded from Him. In this way Christ was involved in the creation of the world. He is the Word, born of the Father, through which all has come into being. "In the fulness of time" this same divine reason clad Himself in a physical form and became man.

In this application of the Logos concept the Apologists found a way of describing the relationship of the Son to the Father in the Godhead by using recognized philosophical terms. Christ is truly God, but God is nevertheless not divided. Just as the word proceeds from reason, or — to use another analogy — as the light streams forth from the lamp, so has the Son come forth from the Father as the Firstborn without diminishing God or destroying the unity of the Godhead. This Logos Christology was an attempt to answer the Christian faith's most difficult question in the language of the day. The Apologists selected a concept from contemporary philosophy and used it to describe what to the Greek mind was absurd — that Christ is God but that the unity of the Godhead is not thereby denied.

It is implicit in this way of thinking, that even though the Logos has always been a part of the divine essence as the indwelling reason, it did not proceed from the Deity until the time of the creation of the world. Christ, therefore, would have been generated in time, or at the beginning of time. This philosophical Logos doctrine would also seem to suggest that Christ occupies a subordinate position relative to the Father. The Christology of the Apologists has often been labeled "subordinationist" as a result. It may well appear thus as seen from the point of view of a later time. The idea of the Son's generation in time, for example, has been opposed (Origen, see below), as well as the use of the philosophical Logos doctrine in the field of Christology (Irenaeus). But we must also remember that the Apologists posited the preexistence of the Logos in no uncertain terms, even though its appearance as "the Son" was thought to have taken place initially at the time of the creation. Furthermore, we should not forget that at the time of the Apologists the terminology employed to express the differences between the

"Persons" of the Trinity had not yet been devised. In the light of this, therefore, it is not fair to infer that the Apologists specifically taught that the Son is subordinate to the Father. (Cf. Kelly, *Early Christian Doctrines,* pp. 100 f.)

If Christ is presented as Logos, the divine reason, it is natural to conceive of His work primarily in pedagogical terms. He presents us with the true knowledge of God and instructs us in the new law, which guides us on the way to life. Salvation is interpreted in intellectual and moralistic categories. Sin is equated with ignorance. Man is thought to be free to do what is good, but only Christ can show him the true way to righteousness and life. The necessity of living according to the Law is emphasized, and in this respect the Apologists' view of the Christian life is in agreement with that of the Apostolic Fathers. As seen from the point of view of the historical development of dogma, the chief contribution of the Apologists was their attempt to combine Christianity and Greek learning, an attempt which found its chief expression in the Logos doctrine and its application to Christology.

CHAPTER 3

Jewish Christianity
and Gnosticism

JEWISH CHRISTIANITY

The term "Jewish Christianity" means many different things, and it is used in various ways by those engaged in research. It can refer to the Palestinian Christianity of the post-Ascension period, that is, the Christians of Jewish birth, who lived in Palestine and had their center in the congregation at Jerusalem — in contrast to the Christians who came out of a pagan background. On some occasions, however, the term is used to identify certain sectarian groups which emanated from the Jerusalem congregation after the Christian community there was driven into the area east of the Jordan about the year 66. It is in this sense that the term will be used here. One of the prime characteristics of this heretical Jewish Christianity, which is also known as "Ebionism" (after the Old Testament term *evjonim,* "the poor," originally a name honoring the Christians of Jerusalem), was their confusion of Jewish and Christian elements. According to what has been reported, the Jewish Christians may have assimilated the Essene monks, who have become well known in recent years through the discovery of the Dead Sea scrolls. The history of Ebionism is, for the most part, cloaked in darkness. Neither the fragments of literature which have been preserved, nor the references found in the church fathers provide us with a detailed picture of the ideas and customs of this group. Certain main lines of thought can, however, be reconstructed.

The Ebionites held fast to the validity of the law of Moses; one faction held that this applied only to them, but another, more militant faction insisted that Christians who came out of a pagan background were also obligated to the law of Moses. Another prominent idea associated

31

with the Ebionites was that they expected a Messianic kingdom to be established with its center in Jerusalem. This reflects their identification of Judaism and Christianity.

It is certainly true that the universal church considers itself to be a continuation of the Old Testament community, the true Israel, but this does not prevent a strong denial of "Jewishness" and the Jewish interpretation of the Law. Paul, for example, fought against those who wished to reintroduce circumcision (cf. Gal. 5), and he demonstrated how freedom in Christ excluded adherence to the way of righteousness which depended on the Law. The Ebionites, who held fast to Jewish precepts and considered them valid for congregational life, repudiated Paul's interpretation of the Law, as a result, and refused to accept his epistles.

In the writings of the Jewish Christians (the most important of which is the so-called "Pseudo-Clement," which contains, among other things, "The Preaching of Peter," plus a number of apocryphal gospels) Christ is put on the same level as the prophets of the Old Testament. He is here described as a new form of revelation of "the true Prophet," who appeared earlier in Adam and Moses, among others. The concept of Christ as the new Moses expressed the unity of Judaism and Christianity which was prominently emphasized in Ebionism. Christ was said to be "a man born of men" (cf. Justin, *Dialogue with Trypho the Jew*, p. 48), or, as it was often put later on, "simply and only a man." The Ebionites therefore denied the preexistence of Christ; some of them also denied the Incarnation and the Virgin Birth. They assumed that Jesus received the Holy Spirit at the time of His baptism and was thereby chosen to be the Messiah and the Son of God. Salvation was not associated with Christ's death and resurrection; it was rather thought that it would first become a reality at the time of Christ's second coming, when, according to expectations, an earthly millennium would begin.

On the basis of these ideas, Ebionism provided the prototype of a Christology which conceived of Christ in purely human terms and which assumed that He was not the Son of God until he was "adopted as such at the time of His baptism or resurrection" (the "adoptionist Christology"). Christ's divine attributes were thereby rejected.

As seen in the light of history, Jewish Christianity did not exert a great influence on the development of Christian theology. It was divided into various groups, and rather soon died out. In all likelihood it did not exist for more than 350 years at the most. On the other hand, however, it exerted a strong influence on Mohammedanism, in which some of its ideas reappeared in a new form. One of these was the concept of the "true prophet"; another was the parallel between Moses and Jesus.

If Jewish Christianity represents a confusion of Jewish and Christian elements, Gnosticism involved a combination of Hellenistic religion and Christianity. Ebionism was quite different from Gnosticism, therefore; it was particularly opposed to Marcion and his repudiation of the Law (see the next section). In spite of this, however, we can see in certain areas a combination of Gnostic and Jewish Christian ideas. This is true, for example, among the Elkesaites, who were probably named for a certain Elkesai, who might have been the author of a document which bears his name. Another example involves the adversaries mentioned in Col. 2, who also seem to have united Gnostic and Jewish ideas (cf. the reference here to "philosophy and empty deceit" (v. 8) and "an appearance of wisdom in promoting rigor of devotion" (v. 23). It would not be correct, however, to say that the main concepts of Jewish Christianity were Gnostic in form and origin. (Schoeps, *Theologie und Geschichte des Judenchristentums,* 1949)

GNOSTICISM

Gnosticism is the common name applied to a number of different schools of thought which developed in the first centuries of the Christian era. Insofar as the Christian "gnosis" is concerned, this refers to an attempt to include Christianity in a general religio-philosophical system. The most important elements in this system were certain mystic and cosmological speculations, plus a distinct dualism between the world of the spirit and the material world. Its doctrine of salvation emphasized the freeing of the spirit from its bondage in the material realm. This cult came equipped with its own mysteries and sacramental ceremonies, in addition to an ethic which was either ascetic or libertine.

Origins. The question of the origin of Gnosticism has been discussed at great length, and there does not seem to be any simple answer. Most of the Gnostic literature has been lost. However, some of it has been preserved in a Coptic translation in Egypt, e. g., the "Pistis Sophia," the "Gospel of Thomas," and the "Gospel of Truth." The two last-named writings were included in the significant manuscript discovery made at the village of Nag Hammadi (near Luxor) in 1946. Among the items found there, in an earthenware jug preserved in the sand, were 13 codices, including no less than 48 writings, all of Gnostic origin. This discovery has not yet been completely evaluated or made available to researchers. For the most part, our knowledge of Gnosticism has come down to us from the writings of the church fathers. They cite Gnostic authors, or refer to their teachings from time to time in their polemical sections.

The church fathers agreed that Gnosticism began with Simon Magus (Acts 8), but apart from this their reports vary. According to a certain Hegesippus, who was quoted by Eusebius (IV, 22), Gnosticism began among certain Jewish sects. The later church fathers (Irenaeus, Tertullian, Hippolytus), on the other hand, were of the opinion that Greek philosophy (Plato, Aristotle, Pythagoras, Zeno) was the chief source of the Gnostic heresy. If we are asking here about the Gnosticism which developed on Christian soil, these accounts need not be in hopeless contradiction. For this type of Gnosticism was a syncretistic system which combined widely disparate streams of thought.

When we speak of Gnosticism, we usually have in mind the system which developed in the Christian period, the "Gnostic heresy" which the church fathers opposed so strenuously. But Gnosticism was already present when Christian history began; it was then a rather vague religious phenomenon, a speculative doctrine of salvation with contributions from a number of different religious traditions. It came from the Orient, where it was influenced by the religions of Babylonia and Persia. The cosmological myths testify to its Babylonian origins, while its thoroughgoing dualism relates it to the religion of Persia. Mandaeanism is an example of a Gnostic religious formation in the Persian area. Subsequently Gnosticism appeared in Syria and on Jewish soil, particularly in Samaria, and there absorbed a Jewish coloration. It was this form of Gnosticism which existed at the beginning of the Christian era, and the apostles encountered it in Simon Magus, who was present in Samaria. From that point on a Gnostic school began to develop in the Christian sphere, with elements derived from Christianity. Because of this similarity, Gnosticism did not appear as an enemy of Christianity. It rather intended to blend Christianity and the other speculative elements already present within it into some kind of a universal religious system. It was in this form that Gnosticism appeared in the second century, with its chief exponents in Syria (Saturninus), Egypt (Basilides), and Rome (Valentinus). This later system was also deeply influenced by Greek religious philosophy. For a long time Gnosticism was Christianity's most dangerous opponent. The Christian polemic against Gnosticism was accompanied by a development of theological thought which had no parallel within the history of the church up to that point.

Tendencies. As we have already noted, many different tendencies were found within Gnosticism. The mythologies and systems which appeared under its general auspices were numerous and disparate.

According to Acts 8:9-24 Simon Magus appeared in Samaria, where Gnosticism had one of its roots. Simon identified himself as the "power of God" and pretended, therefore, to be a Messiah-figure. He also proclaimed freedom from the Law. He taught that salvation came, not through good works but through faith in him. According to the church fathers Simon Magus' teaching was the prototype of all heresy.

Saturninus appeared in Syria in the early years of the second century. His Gnostic system betrays an oriental influence.

Basilides worked in Egypt around the year 125. His Gnosticism was more philosophical in nature, and the Greek influence was stronger.

Valentinus, who was active in Rome from 135 to 160, has provided us with the classical presentation of the Gnostic system. The Greek contribution is also prominent in his work.

Marcion was included among the Gnostics by the church fathers. His teaching is similar to Gnosticism at many points. He was at the same time, however, the founder of his own unique school of thought, and his system was, in many respects, his own creation. As we shall see more clearly in what follows, the theological position held by Marcion and the Gnostics was frequently identical. But there is a difference, as Adolf von Harnack emphasized in his *History of Dogma*. For while Gnosticism is a religious potpourri, in which Christianity and Greek philosophy are blended together, Marcion attempted a radical reorganization of Christianity on the basis of certain ideas gleaned from Paul plus the elimination of all Jewish elements.

Chief concepts. Apart from Marcion, Gnosticism contains certain major concepts held in common by all of the schools and systems associated with it, even though the mythology and the cultic customs vary.

Gnosticism's fundamental metaphysics, which was defined most specifically in the work of Valentinus, has been described by the church father Irenaeus (*Adversus haereses*, I) and others. It is presented in mythological form under the hypostatization of a number of abstract concepts such as truth, wisdom, and reason. The basic point of view is dualistic in nature, which is to say that it proceeds from a contrast between the world of the spirit and the material world, together with a contrast between good and evil and between a higher and a lower sphere.

Because of this dualism, Gnosticism distinguished between the highest God and a lower deity, and it was the latter, they said, who created the world. The highest God was conceived in completely abstract terms as the ultimate spiritual essence; attempts to describe this God more specifically were not made, and He was not associated with any revelation. He was thought to be as far away from the world as possible. The Gnostics also insisted that this God could not have created the world. The world is evil, after all, and therefore it must have its origin in an inferior spiritual essence, in which evil is to be found. This creator god, or demiurge, was said to be the God of the Old Testament — the Jewish God. Gnosticism was antagonistic toward the Old Testament; it also rejected the Law, insisting that man could acquire superior insights which would free him of dependence on it. It was for this reason, above all, that the church fathers fought against Gnosticism — to defend the Christian belief in the one God who created the world and revealed Himself to the prophets.

Gnosticism's doctrine of God was related to high-flown speculations concerning the spirit world on the one hand and the origins of the material world on the other (the so-called "eon" doctrine). Valentinus, for example, estimated that 30 eons had proceeded out of the deity in a theogonic process. The material world was derived from the lowest of the eons as a result of a fall. The highest God, or the Progenitor, formed the first eon, which was also known as βυθός (abyss). Out of the "abyss" came "the silence," or "the idea" (σιγή or ἔννοια), and from these two, "the spirit" and "the truth" (νοῦς and ἀλήθεια). From the last-named, in turn, came "reason" and "life" (λόγος and ζωή), and from these "man" and "the church" and 10 other eons appeared. "Man" and "the church" together produced 12 eons, the last of these being "wisdom" (σοφία). The eons, working in concert, formed the world of the spirit, the Pleroma, which contains the archetype of the material world. The last of the eons fell from the Pleroma as a result of a seizure of passion and anxiety, and it was because of this fall that the material world came into being. The demiurge who created the world came forth from this fallen eon.

Christ and the Holy Spirit originated in one of the highest eons. Christ's task is to restore the fallen eon to the Pleroma, and, at the same time, to free the souls of men from their captivity in the material world and to bring them back into the world of the spirit. It was on this basis that the Gnostic concept of salvation developed. Salvation was said to consist in the release of the soul from the material world so that it could be cleansed and brought back to the divine sphere from whence it came. As is true in Neoplatonism, which had much in common with the system of Valentinus, the history of the world was thought of in cyclical terms. The soul of man was drawn into this cyclical process. Man fell from the world of light and was held captive in the material world. His salvation consists of release from the material world so that he can ascend once again into the spirit world, the world of light, from which he came.

According to Gnosticism, salvation of this kind was possible because of the higher insight (γνῶσις, "gnosis") available to the Gnostics; this insight was a form of mystery-wisdom which provided knowledge concerning the Pleroma and the way which led thence. But not everyone could attain this salvation; only the so-called "pneumatics," who were equipped with the necessary power to receive this knowledge, were able to do so. All other men, whom the Gnostics called the "materialists," were unable to utilize this knowledge. The Gnostics occasionally referred to a category between the pneumatics and the materialists, the so-called "psychics," in which category the Christians were commonly placed. It was thought possible that the psychics could obtain the knowledge needed for salvation. Gnosticism therefore taught a form of predestination: only the pneumatics could be saved. This separation of men into different classes was opposed by the church fathers. They also repudiated the Gnostic concept of a higher knowledge, which was elevated above the level of faith and pretended to elevate man into the sphere of divinity.

Gnosticism did borrow certain elements from Christianity and introduce them into its general concept of salvation. Christ, for example, is referred to in Gnosticism as the Savior, inasmuch as He was said to be the one who brought the saving knowledge into the world. But this is not the Christ of the Bible; the Christ of Gnosticism was a spiritual essence who emerged from out of the eons. This Christ could not have taken on the form of man. When He appeared on earth, said the Gnostics, He only seemed to have a physical body. At the same time the Gnostics also taught that this Christ did not suffer and die. Gnosticism, in other words, proclaimed a Docetic Christology.

The suffering and death of Christ was of no importance to Gnosticism; what He did to enlighten men, on the other hand, was emphasized to the exclusion of all else. He was the conveyor of that knowledge which man needs in order to be able to launch forth on the journey back to the world of light, "the journey to the Pleroma."

Gnosticism taught that salvation came to man by means of the mysteries which were characteristic of the Gnostic approach. Chief among these mysteries were Baptism and the Lord's Supper (distortions of the Christian sacraments) plus a number of additional sacred rites of similar nature. Through these the Gnostics were provided with the secrets of salvation resident in the higher knowledge. The mystical formulae thus acquired protected them against the powers which stood watch on the way through the spirit world. Furthermore, by virtue of their participation in the mysteries, the Gnostics received an inner strength (provided in a purely physical sense through tthe sacraments), and it was this which enabled them to conquer evil and ascend to the Pleroma.

The ethics of Gnosticism were related to its basic dualism. If salvation consists of the release of the spirit from the material world, it is natural that the ethical ideal should be conceived in ascetic terms. Certain sects preached a very strict form of abstinence, as, for example, the so-called Encratites (cf. Eusebius, *Ecclesiastical History*, IV, 28–29). But the very opposite point of view was also supported by some. In view of the fact that the spirit had nothing to do with the material, it was thought that external deeds were of no importance. Some said that independence from the material could be won only if one gave free rein to the lusts of the flesh (libertinism).

Gnosticism's thoroughgoing dualism (between the spiritual and the material) reflected its relationship to Greek thought. The latter was characterized by a deistic concept of God, and Gnosticism assimilated this too. In the light of these convictions, we can understand why Gnosticism was unable to accept the claim that Christ is both God and man (cf. the Ebionites). Gnosticism wanted to transform Christianity into a mythological speculation. Its doctrine of salvation implied a denial of that which is most essential to the Christian faith. The simple faith of Christianity was to be superseded by the higher knowledge of the Gnostics, which took the form of a personal conviction concerning the realities of the spiritual world. With this, for all practical purposes, Gnosticism became a religio-philosophical form of speculation, which either rejected or reinterpreted the basic content of Christianity. Gnosticism opposed the Christian belief in a divine creation: the creator, it said, was not the most high God, and the creation itself was looked upon as something base and evil *(blasphemia creatoris)*. The Second Article of the Creed was rejected or reinterpreted by the Gnostics on the basis of their Docetic Christology, which denied Christ's earthly existence and His atonement. Christ was looked upon as the transmitter of gnosis, while His suffering and death were dismissed as inconsequential. The purification which came through the mysteries was based on a mythological foundation. The Gnostics also repudiated the content of the Third Article of the Creed. The Holy Spirit was inserted into their mythology as a spiritual essence which had emerged from out of one of the eons. Irenaeus said of the Gnostics that they never received the gifts of the Holy Spirit and that they had contempt for the prophets (*Epideixis*, 99 f.). They also denied the resurrection of the body, on the basis of the idea that everything physical or material is evil and unspiritual. Gnosticism was, therefore, an idealistic reinterpretation of Christianity, which they sought to insert into a syncretistic system. This is particularly clear in their *blasphemia creatoris,* their Docetic Christology, and their denial of the resurrection of the body. Gnosticism had no eschatology: Instead of accepting the fulfillment of life in terms of the second coming of Christ, they spoke of the soul's ascent into the Pleroma.

Many Gnostic ideas reappeared later on in the form of Neoplatonism and other related idealistic schools of thought. In addition to this, certain theological concepts which were strongly influenced by Greek philosophy reveal tendencies which remind us of Gnosticism.

Marcion's contemporaries thought of him as a Gnostic, and so far as basic points of view (*blasphemia creatoris,* Docetism, denial of the resurrection of the body) are concerned, Marcion was in agreement with the Gnostics. But in other respects, he was an independent thinker, and he propounded many ideas which did not correspond with Gnosticism. Marcion was not syncretistic, for example; he wanted to reform Christianity by discarding everything which in his opinion did not belong in the Gospel. Furthermore, Marcion did not accept any of the mythological speculations which were characteristic of Gnosticism. Neither did he allude to any particular gnosis which was accessible only to the so-called pneumatics. All he wanted to do was to proclaim a very simple faith. He said nothing about the division of mankind into different classes. The points at which Marcion differed from the Gnostics have recently been given much critical attention (especially by Adolf von Harnack), and he has now been clearly distinguished from the Gnostics. He is now looked upon as a reformer, who rediscovered the otherwise forgotten Paul and who proclaimed salvation by faith alone in an age when moralism was a pervasive tendency in theology.

When the church fathers say that Marcion was the most difficult of all heretics, we sense that other facets of his theology, such as his doctrine of God and Christ, plus his radical separation of Law and Gospel, were most prominent in their estimation. It was in these areas that Marcion was linked with the Gnostics, and this suggested a denial of the church's basic teachings. Both sides of the story have their place in a presentation of Marcion's theological position, and those aspects which mark him off from the Gnostics impel us to consider him on his own merits.

At the outset Marcion embraced the faith of the church, but then he came under the influence of a Syrian Gnostic named Kerdo, and thus began the process of forming his own unique theology. He arrived in Rome about 140; when he was expelled by the congregation there, he started his own church, which soon became quite large. Vestiges of this organization were to be found in various places as late as the sixth century.

The basic point of departure in Marcion's theology is to be found in the distinction he made between Law and Gospel, between the Old Covenant and the New. Paul spoke of the Christian's freedom from the Law, and Marcion interpreted that to mean that the Law had been vanquished and that the Gospel was to be preached without any reference to the Law. The Law, he said, had been replaced by a new order. The

Gospel, to him, was a new, previously unknown message, which not only replaced the Law but stood in opposition to it. Tertullian characterized this attitude in the following words: "The separation of the Law and the Gospel is the characteristic and principal work of Marcion." (*Contra Marcionem*, 1, 19)

This trend of thought related Marcion to the Gnostic teaching of the two Gods. In Marcion — and this was characteristic of him — the creator God of the Old Testament was the God of the Law, whom he thought of as a God of severity and wrath, who took revenge on His enemies and kept His followers in thrall under the Law. The Most High God, as Marcion conceived of Him, was not so much an abstract spiritual essence, an infinitely transcendent God; He was rather the unknown God who revealed Himself to the world in Christ. Marcion thought of Him as the God of grace and mercy, the God of pure love. This God, said Marcion, fought against and conquered the God of law and justice and, out of pure grace, saved those who had faith in Him. This facet of Marcion's theology was a biased (or one-sided) and therefore distorted interpretation of Paul's concept of justification. According to Marcion, the God of love had nothing at all to do with the Law. He made a radical distinction between justice and mercy, between wrath and grace.

Christ was the one who proclaimed the Gospel of the God of love. As a matter of fact, He was truly this God Himself, who manifested Himself here on earth during the reign of Tiberius Caesar. He appeared, however, as a ghostly figure. Because He was different from the Creator God, He could not have assumed the mantle of human flesh. Marcion's Christology was Docetic, and yet he believed in the redemptive significance of Christ's suffering and death. This, of course, is a contradiction of his Docetic Christology, but it also marked him off from the Gnostics. This was observed by Irenaeus: "How could He have been crucified, and how could blood and water have flowed from His pierced side if He were not truly man but only apparently a man?" (*Adversus haereses*)

Marcion's God was a God whom the faithful did not have to fear, inasmuch as He was thought of as pure goodness. In view of this, one might expect that Marcion would have been completely indifferent with respect to morality. Quite the opposite was true, however, for in this matter Marcion, like the Gnostics, was strongly ascetic. He felt, for example, that marriage was something evil. Marcion taught that an as-

41

cetic code of ethics could help free man from the Demiurge, the Creator God, the God of law.

Marcion is also remembered for his radical alteration of the canon. He rejected the Old Testament on the ground that it was the proclamation of the God of law, the Jewish God, alone. The Messiah of the Jews had nothing in common with Christ. Marcion would not even permit an allegorical interpretation. With respect to the New Testament, Marcion desired that everything associated with Judaism or the Law be discarded. He retained only 10 of the epistles of Paul (the Pastoral Epistles were rejected) and a truncated version of the Gospel according to Luke. In so doing, Marcion made a radical attempt to determine, on the basis of his own understanding of the essence of Christianity, which writings should be normative.

The opposition of the church fathers to Marcion involved the same points of doctrine as the struggle with Gnosticism in general. They opposed him for denying that God created the world and for teaching that there was a God other than the God who created the heavens and the earth. Marcion's rejection of the Incarnation, based on his Docetic Christology, was another point at issue. Furthermore, the fact that he denied the resurrection of the body was strongly challenged. Marcion believed that only the soul could be saved; the body, which belongs to the material world, could not be.

CHAPTER 4

The Anti-Gnostic Fathers

The struggle against Gnosticism left its mark in a variety of ways on the theology developed by the church fathers in the first several centuries. The presentation of the Christian faith which we find in the so-called anti-Gnostic fathers must be understood against the background of this polemical situation. For these theologians of the early church, belief in the divine creation occupied a central place in a way which was not true in the later Western tradition, where the doctrine of salvation was often emphasized at the expense of other facets of Christianity. It was Gnostic idealism, with its denial of creation, which impelled the church fathers to treat the doctrine of God and creation, together with the problem of man, the Incarnation, and the resurrection of the body, in such great detail. Another obvious characteristic was the nomistic point of view which can be seen, for example, in Tertullian. This can also be explained in part against the background of Gnosticism, with its proclamation of freedom from the Law and its antinomian misinterpretation of the Pauline concept of justification.

IRENAEUS

Irenaeus came from Asia Minor, where as a child he had seen and been influenced by Polycarp of Smyrna, who, in turn, was a disciple of John. His theology, moreover, is representative of the Johannine tradition which is associated with Asia Minor. Most of his work, however, was done in the West. He became bishop of Lyons about 177, and he remained there until the time of his death (early in the second century).

Only two of Irenaeus' writings are still extant. The one is his comprehensive refutation of the Gnostics, *Adversus haereses*, of which a fragment of the Greek original and a Latin translation remain. The second, *Epideixis*, is a presentation of the basic teachings of the "apostolic proclamation." This was known only by name for a long time, but it was rediscovered in an Armenian translation in 1904.

What Irenaeus sought to do above all in his theological work was to defend the apostolic faith against Gnostic innovations. The gnosis of Valentinus was the chief threat to Christianity, in his estimation, inasmuch as it imperiled church unity on the one hand and sought to destroy the distinction between Christianity and pagan religious speculation on the other.

Irenaeus has been called the father of Catholic dogmatics. There is some truth in that expression, insofar as he was the first to attempt to provide a uniform summary of the whole of Scripture. Irenaeus rejected the Apologists' view of Christianity as the true philosophy. He refused to employ the assistance of Greek speculation, and he did not agree with those who said that the content of revelation was simply a new and better philosophy. For him the Biblical tradition was the only source of faith.

Irenaeus was, therefore, a Biblical theologian in a pronounced sense of the term. While the Gnostics sought for revelation in a hidden knowledge that was at least in part independent of the Bible, in myths and in mystery-wisdom, Irenaeus held forth the Scriptures as the only basis of faith. The Old and New Testaments were the means whereby revelation and the original tradition reach us. Beyond the Old Testament, which he thought of above all as the foundation of the doctrine of faith, Irenaeus referred to a collection of New Testament writings which he considered to be similarly authoritative and which was largely the same as our present canon. The word "testament" was not, of course, used in this context. The canon had not yet been formally established at that time. Some of the New Testament writings were thought to be too controversial; they were accepted as canonical in some circles, while in others their apostolic authority was challenged. For the most part, however, the scope of the New Testament canon was established even prior to Irenaeus' time. His own use of the New Testament writings is, to some degree, an obvious demonstration of this fact.

Irenaeus said nothing about the distinction between Scripture and tradition which appeared later on in the field of dogmatics. The oral tradition which he cited as having decisive authority was the teaching of the apostles and the prophets, which was entrusted to the church and perpetuated by those in the church who received the Gospel from the apostles. As far as content was concerned, this was nothing other than the proclamation deposited in written form in the Old and New Testaments. The Gnostics, on the other hand, distorted the teachings of the Bible by relying on traditions which did not originate with the apostles. In a well-known passage (*Adversus haereses*, III, 3, 3) Irenaeus referred to the unbroken line of Roman bishops, beginning with the time of the apostles, to demonstrate the fact that it was the church — and not the heretics — which preserved the correct tradition. It would be wrong, however, to read into this text the concept of apostolic succession which developed later. Irenaeus, after all, was primarily concerned about doctrinal content and not about ordination.

On some occasions Irenaeus spoke of doctrinal authority in terms of *regula veritatis*, "the rule of truth." In similar fashion, the church fathers frequently made mention of *regula fidei*, "the rule of faith," as the determining factor in questions regarding Christian teachings. The significance of these concepts has been widely discussed; some have professed to see in them a reference to the formal baptismal confession which was worked out in the struggle with Gnosticism, while others have interpreted the rule of faith to refer to the Holy Scriptures. That "truth" which, according to Irenaeus, was the "rule" (the Greek word κανών [canon] was used in this connection) was the revealed order of salvation which is witnessed to in the Bible and summarized in the baptismal confession. "The rule of truth" was not, therefore, fixed in a specific formula; neither did it designate the Scriptures as a doctrinal codex. It rather referred to revealed truth as this was reflected not only in the baptismal confession and the Scriptures but also in the preaching of the church. It was this revealed truth that Irenaeus used to combat the Gnostics, and it was this that he sought to interpret and describe in a manner consistent with the genuine apostolic tradition.

Irenaeus therefore derived his theology from the Scriptures. What he desired to do, above all, was to present God's order of salvation from the creation to the fulfillment (οἰκονομία *salutis*). Time, in his estimation, was a limited epoch; it began with creation and will end with the fulfillment. It is surrounded at both ends by eternity. It is within the context of time that the salvation event takes place. Within this context God has carried out the deeds to which Scripture bears witness and on which man's salvation depends. To the Gnostics salvation was not something accomplished within history; it was an idea, a speculative scheme which claimed that the soul could be elevated over the temporal and reunited with its divine origins through the instrumentality of gnosis. To Irenaeus all of this was actual history, with the fulfillment expected at the end of time. The difference between the Greek view of the world and the Christian concept of time is plain to see in these opposing points of view.

Creation was a part of the divine order of salvation. God's Son, the Savior, was present before the beginning of time in His preexistent state. Man was created so that the Savior should not be alone, so that there should be someone to save (cf. Gustav Wingren, *Man and the Incarnation According to Irenaeus*, 1947, p. 28). Everything was created through the Son and for the Son. Salvation was accomplished for the same reason that God created: that man might be like God. Man was created in the image of God, but as a result of the Fall this similarity was lost. The meaning of salvation is that man might realize his destiny once again, that man might become the image of God according to the prototype discernible in Christ. Man stands at the center of creation. Everything else has been created for man's use. But man was created for Christ and to become like Christ, who is the Center of all existence, the One who sums up everything in heaven and on earth. (Cf. *Adversus haereses*, V, 16, 2)

As seen from this point of view, creation and salvation are joined together because there is but one God who both creates and saves. The Gnostic teaching of the two gods blasphemed the Creator. It also implied that salvation was impossible. For if God did not create, neither can creation be saved. If God was not the Creator, neither would He save creation. But this is the goal of the entire order of salvation.

To the Gnostics salvation consisted of deliverance from creation, from the material world, and a return to pure spirituality. To Irenaeus, on the other hand, salvation meant that creation itself would be restored to its original state, that creation would finally achieve its God-given destiny. Salvation to Irenaeus did not mean, in other words, that the spirit of man would be released from its material bondage, but rather that the whole man, with body and soul, would be freed from the devil's dominion, returned to his original purity, and become like God.

Man was created, according to Gen. 1:26, in God's "image" and "likeness." It has often been said that Irenaeus was the first to introduce the idea (widely accepted later on) which held that these concepts pointed to two distinct qualities in man. This, however, is not correct. For Irenaeus frequently used both of these concepts to express the same matter, and these passages would seem to be decisive. (Cf. Wingren)

When it is said that man was created *in* the image of God, this, according to Irenaeus, is indicative of man's true destiny. It does not mean that man *is* the image of God but rather that he was created to become that. Christ, who is God Himself, is the image of God after which man was created. Man's destiny, therefore, is to become like Christ. This is the goal of salvation and of the work of the Holy Spirit.

At the time of creation, man was a child; he was not then fully developed, but he was created to grow. If man had lived in accordance with the will of God he would have grown, and through the creative power of God he would have achieved his destiny — complete Godlikeness. Irenaeus understood growth, not as an inner development but as the result of God's continued creativity.

But man departed from the way of obedience, having been tempted by the devil, one of the angels who, overcome by their envy of man, fell away from God. Thus it was that man came under the dominion of the devil. Man is caught up in the struggle between God and Satan.

The intent of the order of salvation, therefore, is to free from the clutches of the devil those whom he has wrongfully seized. This is the work of redemption, which was carried out through Christ. He has conquered the devil and thereby accomplished man's release. But in spite of this, the struggle continues. It must be said, however, that it entered a new phase after the resurrection of Christ. As a result, the decisive battle has been fought out. What happens is that men are drawn into the victory of Christ and thereby receive the life which was lost through Adam's fall.

This order of salvation can be pictured in various ways, such as release from bondage or as victory after struggle (see above). It can also be described in legalistic terms: *naturalia praecepta — lex Mosaica —* Christ, the new covenant, the restoration of the original law. The original law, having been given at the time of creation, expresses God's will for man. Man's destiny is to live in a manner consistent with this law, in obedience to God's command. In so doing, man receives life and righteousness from the hand of God and goes forward toward the goal of perfection and Godlikeness. This law was written in the heart, and man is free to follow it or to break it. But when man goes contrary to God's command, he comes under the dominion of sin. Thus it was that God entered into a new covenant with man, through the Israelites, and gave man the Mosaic law. The purpose of this law was to discipline man, to reveal sin and keep it in its place, and to maintain order in an external way until the coming of Christ. As seen in this context, Christ's task was to abrogate the Mosaic law and to restore the law which was given at the time of creation and which had been obscured by the Pharisaic regulations. Christ frees from the thralldom of the Law through His Spirit, which regenerates man and fulfills the law within him. The Holy Spirit restores obedience, and man is thereby regenerated according to the law which was given at the time of creation. This original law was an expression of that which constituted man's Godlikeness. There is, therefore, a parallel between the assertion that man was created in the image of God and that which is said about natural law.

Life and death are related to the Law, and Irenaeus described the order of salvation in these categories as well. Life and obedience to the Law go together. When man obeys God's commands, he receives life from God, but when he falls into disobedience, he comes under the power of death. For disobedience to God is the equivalent of death. It was because of disobedience that the stream of life was broken, and when this was done death appeared in the world of men. Death, therefore, is not associated with the body and created life in an *eo ipso* manner; it is rather something that has been imposed upon man because of sin. This is reflected in Gen. 2:17: "For in the day you eat of it you shall die." Salvation implies that life has been restored through Christ's victory over death. By believing in Christ, man can recover the life that was lost through the Fall. Salvation bestows the gift of immortality. The body will certainly die because of sin, in order that the power of sin might be reduced. The new life in the Spirit is activated by faith, and it reaches fulfillment after death. Then there will no longer be anything in man that belongs to death. The man who has been restored has realized the destiny for which he was created — to become like God and to live without dying.

The basic idea in Irenaeus' presentation of the order of salvation is that the work of creation has been restored and recapitulated in the salvation wrought through Christ. In opposition to the Gnostics, who taught that salvation consists of the release of the spirit from the material world, Irenaeus insisted that God and man, body and soul, heaven and earth are able to overcome the split occasioned by the incursion of sin and to be reunited once again. This, for Irenaeus, was the meaning of salvation.

Christ is the second Adam, a counterpart of the first Adam. The latter brought death and ruin into creation because of his disobedience. Christ, through His obedience, restores creation to its pure state. Adam yielded to the temptation of the serpent and thus came under the dominion of the devil. Christ overcame temptation and thus vanquished the tempter's power over mankind. He epitomizes the entire human race, just as the first Adam did. On the strength of His obedience and work of atonement, He became the fountainhead of a new humanity. He has perfected that which was spoiled through Adam's fall. Through Him humanity continues to grow toward the goal of perfection. Creation is restored, and its destiny is realized. Christ's redemptive work began with His birth of the virgin Mary and will be completed at the time of the general resurrection, when all enemies will have been subjugated to Christ, and God will be all in all.

Irenaeus described this entire *oeconomia salutis* in a single concept: *recapitulatio* (ἀνακεφαλαίωσις). This word means "recapitulation"; it also connotes "restoration." This concept is derived from Eph. 1:10, where mention is made of God's decree concerning "a plan for the fullness of time, to unite all things in Him, things in heaven and things on earth."

For Irenaeus, therefore, "recapitulation" was a designation for all of Christ's redemptive activity, from the time of His birth to the Day of Judgment. In carrying out this work Christ repeated that which happened at the time of creation, even though this was done, so to speak, in the reverse sequence. "He has recapitulated the first creation in Himself. For just as sin entered the world through one man's disobedience, and death through sin, so also has righteousness come into the world through one man's obedience, bringing life to those who formerly were dead." (*Adversus haereses*, III, 21, 9-10)

Recapitulation also implies perfection, or completion. That which was given through Christ, and which comes into being through His obedience, is superior to that which was given at the time of creation. Man was still a "child" at that time. Because of the salvation which has been wrought, man can grow up to complete Godlikeness, as represented in the person of Christ.

Irenaeus developed his Christology in opposition to the Docetic point of view championed by Gnosticism. The work of salvation presupposes that Christ is both true man and true God. "If the enemies of man had not been overcome by man, they could not have been truly overcome; furthermore, if our salvation is not from God, we cannot be sure that we are saved. And if man has not been united with God, it would not be possible for him to share in immortality" (III, 18, 7; cf. Gustav Aulen, *History of Dogma*, p. 32). Here we find a strong emphasis on Christ's humanity: a real man had to walk the way of obedience so that the order which was shattered by Adam's disobedience might be restored. At the same time, it was God alone who could carry out the work of redemption. Christ is truly man and truly God *(vere homo, vere deus)*.

The Son has existed with the Father from all eternity. But how the Son came from the Father is not revealed. As a result, man can know nothing about that. Irenaeus rejected the Logos speculations of the Apologists, in which the birth of the Son was compared to the way in which the Word proceeded out of reason. "Should it be asked, 'How was the Son brought forth out of the Father?' this is our answer: 'Concerning His generation, or birth, or manifestation, or revelation, or however one will express His ineffable birth, no one knows; not Marcion, not Valentinus, not Saturninus, not Basilides. Only the Father, who brought forth, and the Son, who was born, know about this'" (II, 28, 6). The Apologists said that a birth took place in time (the Word proceeded from the divine reason at the time of creation). Irenaeus, on the other hand, seems to have contemplated the possibility of a birth in eternity, but he did not express himself in a specific way on this point.

It was typical of Irenaeus that he refused to explain more precisely how it was that Christ came forth from the Father; the same was true with respect to the relationship between God and man in Christ. He sought to set forth the content of Scripture without the assistance of philosophy and to hold fast to the rule of faith without giving way to mere speculation. In *Adversus haereses*, I, 10, 1 Irenaeus provided a brief summary of the faith which had been handed down from the apostles: "The church extends throughout the entire world, to the uttermost ends of the earth. It has received its faith from the apostles and their followers. This faith is in the one God, Father almighty, who made the heavens and the earth and the seas and all within them; and in Christ Jesus, God's Son, who, to redeem us, took human form; and in the Holy Spirit, who, through the prophets, has proclaimed God's order of salvation, the Lord's twofold advent, His birth of a virgin, His suffering, His resurrection from the dead, His physical ascension into heaven, and His return from heaven in the glory of the Father. Christ shall return in order to 'restore all things' and to reawaken all flesh in the entire human race, so that all knees shall bow before and all tongues shall praise Jesus Christ, who, according to the invisible Father's pleasure, is our Savior and King."

There is in the theology of Irenaeus a parallel to the millennial doctrine, but he avoids speaking of the "1,000 years." He rather refers to a "kingdom of the Son," in which the dominion of Christ will be manifested in a visible way on earth. Furthermore, the Antichrist will be vanquished, nature will be renewed, and the faithful will reign with Christ in this "kingdom of the Son." This will precede the second resurrection and the Day of Judgment. Eternity will begin after the judgment is complete, when the Son shall deliver up the Kingdom to the Father, and God will then be "all in all." (Cf. Wingren, pp. 212 ff.)

TERTULLIAN

In a long series of learned and incisive writings, Tertullian involved himself in the ecclesiastical controversies of his time in order to defend the Christian faith and to instruct the faithful. He was the first of the church fathers with a typically "Western style," and in many respects he was the founder of the Western theological tradition.

Tertullian was born at Carthage in the middle of the second century; originally a pagan, he was converted to Christianity as a mature man. He practiced law in Rome for a time, but after his conversion he returned to private life in Carthage, where he devoted himself to studying and writing. His literary activity was confined approximately to the period between 195 and 220. In about the year 207 Tertullian associated himself with the Montanist movement, which later manifested sectarian tendencies.

As an author, Tertullian was very distinctive. In contrast to the earlier writers, he employed a formal style. He was prominent in the field of rhetoric, and his fund of knowledge was broad and deep. He was not a philosopher, however; he was more interested in social matters, and he had a good grasp of the law. He was a critical observer of life in general, and his writings manifest his strongly individualistic point of view. His deep interest in practical matters and his firm attachment to reality are characteristic of the Western point of view. As Karl Holl has written of Tertullian, "In him the Western spirit spoke clearly for the first time." (*Gesammelte Aufsätze*, III, 2)

Passionate enthusiasm and an ingenious dialectic characterized Tertullian's polemical writings. Because of his uneven, paradoxical and terse style, Tertullian is sometimes hard to understand.

The theological writings of Tertullian have exerted a widespread and significant influence. This has been true chiefly because he produced certain formulations that came into current usage and coined some theological terminology that has been a part of theological literature ever since (in the Latin language which he used). Furthermore, some of his concepts have provided the prototype for later developments in the field of theology. This was true, for example, with respect to the doctrine of the Trinity, Christology, and original sin. Tertullian was the precursor of Cyprian, who became his disciple, and of Augustine.

Tertullian's contributions to the age in which he lived were found in his polemical writings as well as in his pronouncements concerning practical ecclesiastical problems. Like the Apologists, he fought against paganism (cf. *Apologeticum*). Gnosticism was to him, as to Irenaeus, the chief opponent (cf. *Adversus Marcionem; De praescriptione haereticorum*). Finally, he also turned against Modalism (cf. *Adversus Praxean*). Tertullian wrote a number of books in order to develop his doctrinal convictions and to express himself with respect to practical congregational questions.

Tertullian's theology was, to a large extent, conditioned by his struggle with the Gnostics. His well-known rejections of philosophy must be seen in this context, for in his estimation philosophy was the source of the Gnostic heresy. Valentinus learned from Plato, Marcion from the Stoics, and as a result they transformed Christianity into a pagan philosophy of religion. Wrote Tertullian: "The philosophers and the heretics discuss the same subjects, and they employ the same involved argumentation. Poor Aristotle! It was you who taught them dialectics, to become champions at building up and tearing down. They are so cunning in their theories, so labored in their inferences, so sure about their evidence, so officious in their debates, which become burdensome by virtue of the fact that they deal with everything in such a way that, in the final analysis, nothing has been dealt with. What does Athens have to do with Jerusalem? What does the academy have to do with the church? What do heretics have to do with Christians? Our doctrine stems from Solomon's hall of pillars, from him who had learned that man must seek for the Lord with a heart of innocence. For all I care, one can, if he pleases, bring forth a Stoic and Platonic and dialectic Christianity. Since the Gospel of Christ has been proclaimed to us, we no longer need to inquire, or to examine into such things. If we have faith, we have no desire for anything beyond faith. For this is the first principle of our faith: There is nothing beyond this faith which we must believe" (*De praescript.*, 7). If one seeks for something beyond faith, he thereby reveals the fact that he does not really have faith. Such a man rather has faith in that for which he is seeking (ibid., 11). The Gnostics go beyond faith in their wisdom. The Christian, on the other hand, holds fast to the simple faith which is revealed in the Scriptures and preserved in the apostolic tradition. "To know nothing in opposition to the rule [of faith] is to know all things." (Ibid., 14)

Tertullian's rejection of philosophy was, therefore, involved in his struggle against the heretics. "The philosophers are the fathers of the heretics," he wrote (*Adversus Hermogenem*, 8). But this rejection can also be explained thus, that Tertullian recognized a fundamental distinction between faith and reason in epistemology. That which a man believes cannot be comprehended with his reason. The knowledge of faith is different from the knowledge of reason. The former possesses its own wisdom, which has nothing to do with rational evidence. Concerning the resurrection of Christ, Tertullian said: "It is certain because it is impossible" (*De carne Christi*, 5; cf. *De baptismo*, 2). It is this kind of "irrationalism" which is usually characterized with the expression *credo quia absurdum* ("I believe because it is absurd"). This phrase is not to be found in Tertullian, but it certainly does express his thoughts on this point.

What has just been quoted, however, is representative of but one side of Tertullian's understanding of faith and reason. Other passages in his writings set forth his more positive opinion concerning human reason. He does this without calling upon philosophy to bolster his arguments. In this matter Tertullian does not make the same strict demands upon theology as does Irenaeus.

It has sometimes been said that there is a rationalistic strain in Tertullian's so-called natural theology. He did say on occasion that the non-Christian has a natural understanding of the one God; the soul of man is *naturaliter Christiana.* Tertullian also propounded the cosmological proof of the existence of God: the beauty and order of creation is proof of the Creator's presence in the world, said he. These and similar thoughts were, however, intended to demonstrate the universality of Christianity and to support the Christian belief in a divine creation. As a result, one cannot justifiably accuse Tertullian of rationalism.

Even though he severely criticized philosophy, Tertullian frequently employed philosophical ideas and formulations. In opposing the spiritualism which was characteristic of Gnosticism, for example, he borrowed certain thought patterns from the Stoics, which were then shaped into a "realistic" theory. It is this realism which, to a certain degree at least, distinguishes Western thought from Greek thought. But Tertullian carried this to an extreme: theology, he said, must be connected with manifest reality at every point. The physical body provides the pattern for all reality. "Everything that is is a body of some kind; nothing is incorporeal except that which does not exist" (*De carne Christi,* 11). As a consequence of this thesis, Tertullian even ascribed corporeality to God, and he also contemplated the possibility that the soul has an invisible body. His theory concerning the origin of the soul was related to this; the soul, according to Tertullian, is transmitted by natural birth from one generation to the next. This concept is known as traducianism. The other theory concerning the origin of the soul is called creationism, which holds that the soul of each man is a new creation, direct from the hand of God. (Cf. Karpp, *Probleme altchristlicher Anthropologie,* 1950)

The doctrine of the Trinity occupies an important position in Tertullian's theology. In working with this facet of his theology, Tertullian adopted the Logos concepts of the Apologists and developed them further. His formulations provided the basis for the Trinitarian formulas and the Christology which were accepted later on.

Tertullian applied the Logos concept in the manner of the Apologists. Christ, he said, is the divine Word, which proceeded from out of God's reason at the time of creation. When God said, "Let there be light," the Word was born. Christ is one with God, and yet He is distinct from the Father. He has come forth from the essence of God as the rays emerge from the sun, as plants from their roots, or a river from its source. Therefore the Son is subordinate to the Father. He is the one who has revealed God, while God Himself is invisible. Like the Apologists, Tertullian used the expression "subordinationism." He strongly emphasized that the Son and the Holy Spirit are one with the Father but at the same time somewhat different from the Father. "The Father is not the Son; He is greater than the Son; for the one who gives birth is different from the one who is born; the one who sends out is different from the one who is sent" (*Adversus Praxean,* 9). In order to express the relationship between the Father, the Son, and the Holy Spirit, Tertullian coined the term *persona,* which eventually became the accepted term in this context. The Son, as an independent person, has come forth from the Father. The Logos has an independent existence. And yet the three persons are one, just as the sun's rays are one with the sun. To express this unity, Tertullian used the term *substantia,* which parallels the Greek word οὐσία, "essence" or "substance." This term, too, came to be commonly accepted in the formulation of the doctrine of the Trinity.

The three persons preexisted in God. But when they proceeded from God and into time, this took place in accordance with the order of salvation. The Son went forth from the Father in order to declare the order of salvation. The three persons denote different stages in God's revelation, but they are nevertheless one — just as the root brings forth a plant, and the plant bears fruit, while together they form one and the same plant. This view of the Trinity is usually referred to as an "economic" doctrine of the Trinity. The difference between the persons is described on the basis of their activity in the order of salvation.

Tertullian developed his Christology in opposition to modalism (of which more will be said later on). He drew a sharp distinction between the divine and human qualities in Christ. They have reference to two different substances, said he, which were united in one person, Christ, but not combined. When Christ said, "My God, My God, why hast Thou forsaken Me?" it was not God the Father who cried out ("For if so, to which God did He cry?") — it was the man, the Son, who cried to the Father. Christ suffered only as the Son, Tertullian asserted, and thereby rejected patripassionism (Praxeas), which so confused God and Christ that it claimed that it was the Father who suffered. It must also be pointed out, however, that Tertullian used such expressions as *Deus mortuus* and *Deus crucifixus,* which need not contradict what was said above. But he said nothing specific about the relationship between the divine and human qualities. The Logos appeared in the flesh, clad in a corporeal form, but was not changed into flesh. The subsequent doctrine of Christ's two natures was based on Tertullian. His terminology can be presented schematically in the following manner:

One substance (οὐσία) — three persons (ὑποστάσεις): Father, Son, Holy Spirit.

The person of Christ — divine and human nature (the substance of the Creator and human substance).

Irenaeus presented Christ as the Savior from the power of sin, who, through His Spirit, redeems man from the corruption of sin so that man can be restored to his original purity. Salvation was described, in other words, in terms of the recovery of health and wholeness. In Tertullian a different point of view comes to the fore: he presented Christ as the teacher who proclaims a new law *(nova lex)*, thereby strengthening man's free will so that he can live according to God's commands. To live in a manner consistent with God's law is set forth as the goal of salvation. This is achieved through instruction in the Law. The concept of merit is dominant. God rewards or punishes on the basis of merit. The relationship between God and man is seen in the contest of a judicial system. If God did not avenge and punish, there would be no reason to fear Him and to do what is right. Salvation, said Tertullian, is given as a reward for human merit. Good deeds as well as evil must be recompensed by God. This interpretation is clearly antithetical to that of Marcion, who so emphasized the love of God that all considerations of retribution and wrath were denied.

Tertullian's doctrine of grace was also introduced into this scheme. It is grace which saves — by which Tertullian meant to say that grace takes away the corruption which has adhered to human nature as a result of the incursion of sin. The idea that this corruption is to be found in nature itself, and is transmitted through birth, is to be found in Tertullian. This is where the doctrine of original sin began to take form. Through grace man can receive the power needed to live the new life. Grace is conceived as a power which is bestowed upon man and thus enables him to live a meritorious life. On the basis of this doctrine of sin — grace — merit, which Tertullian developed in the course of his controversy with Marcion (who stressed God's love), the foundation was laid for the doctrine of salvation which dominated Western medieval theology and, later on, Roman Catholicism.

As noted above, Tertullian joined the Montanist movement, partly as a result of the church's lax practice with respect to penance. The Montanist sect originated in Asia Minor in the middle of the second century, and spread from there to Rome and North Africa. It was remarkable for its strong emphasis on prophecy and the free gifts of the Spirit, for its belief that the end of the world was near, and for its rigid asceticism and strict practice of penance.

Because of his association with the Montanists, Tertullian is remembered as having been something of a schismatic, but at the same time he was also one of the chief opponents of heresy, as well as one of the foremost architects of orthodox Western theology.

HIPPOLYTUS

Hippolytus, who was a bishop in Rome and an opponent of Pope Calixtus (whose attitude with regard to penance he sharply disapproved), was banished to Sardinia during a persecution (ca. 235), and he died in exile. He wrote a number of books (in Greek), some of which are still extant, in which he continued the defense of Christian doctrine against Greek philosophy and ecclesiastical heresy. His best-known work is entitled *Philosophoumena* (or *The Refutation of All Heresy*), which is actually an encyclopedic survey of the philosophical ideas which stemmed from the Greek natural philosophers, of the various magical and religious concepts prevalent in his day, as well as of the ecclesiastical heresies which, according to Hippolytus, had their roots in Greek philosophy. This work testifies to the author's extensive learning and provides valuable knowledge concerning the various schools of thought which Hippolytus here describes. The polemical material, on the other hand, which was directed primarily at the Gnostics and the modalists, does not possess the same originality and power as do the polemics of Irenaeus and Tertullian.

CHAPTER 5

Alexandrian Theology

Christian theology developed in opposition to Greek philosophy and heretical tendencies. The Apologists turned back the objections of the pagan world and presented Christianity as the true philosophy; the anti-Gnostic fathers developed, on the basis of Scripture and tradition, a theology designed to protect orthodoxy from the speculations of Gnosticism and Greek philosophy. But what the Alexandrians offered as a substitute was a systematic world view based on philosophical insight, into which Christianity was inserted and upheld as the highest wisdom.

This was the first attempt to produce an actual synthesis between Christianity and Greek philosophy. Unlike the Apologists, the Alexandrians were not content simply to present the Christian tradition as a superior counterpart to philosophy. And unlike the Gnostics, they did not seek to replace Christianity with a syncretistic doctrine of salvation that abandoned some of the fundamental elements of the Christian faith.

The Alexandrian theologians wanted to preserve the Christian tradition in a faithful manner, and to do so they stood firmly on the Scriptures. At the same time they also possessed a consistent philosophical point of view, into the context of which they sought to insert the content of revelation in such a way as to create a new theological system. They used contemporary philosophy in this manner with the intent that the reality of faith could be set forth as a uniform and comprehensive world view. The purpose of this was not to mix Christianity and philosophy but only to present Christianity as the highest truth. Origen was one of the foremost Biblical theologians of all time, and he wanted to do nothing other than to set forth and interpret the meaning of Scripture. But as a result of his philosophical background he had a tendency to read philosophical and speculative implications into Scripture passages as their deepest meaning. This was done with the assistance of the allegorical method. Because of this, Origen's system came to bear the imprint of the Greek philosophy that had developed in his time (and previously) at Alexandria, which was the chief center of Greek education in that period. It was, therefore, the basic element of this philosophy which significantly conditioned Alexandrian theology as it was developed by Clement and Origen.

THE PLATONISM OF ALEXANDRIA

It is usually said that the philosophical background discernible in the theology of Origen is Neoplatonic. This is not completely correct. The actual founder of the Neoplatonic school was Plotinus, a younger contemporary of Origen. This school was founded in 244, after Alexandrian theology had come into being. Most properly, therefore, it must be said that Neoplatonism was a philosophical parallel to the Alexandrian theological system. But Plotinus and Origen both had the same teacher — Ammonios Sakkos. Through him Origen came under the influence of embryonic Neoplatonism. Later research (E. de Faye; Hal Koch, *Pronoia und Paideusis*) has shown, however, that this influence was not as great as has been supposed. As a matter of fact, Origen was an eclectic. But as far as philosophical schools are concerned, he stood closest to the Platonism which burgeoned forth in Alexandria during the first centuries of the Christian era and which is commonly referred to as Middle-Platonism. This was a continuation of the ancient Academy, but it had transformed classical Platonism into a comprehensive world system in which religion rather than theoretical knowledge was the distinguishing component. The world of ideas as set forth here was not simply the conceptual world, but above all the spiritual world that emerged out of divinity. The fundamental aspects of this system turned up again in both Neoplatonism and the Alexandrian theologians.

"The Alexandrian world scheme" (cf. Anders Nygren's *Agape and Eros*, trans. Philip S. Watson [London: SPCK, 1953], I, 186–89; the term is from Heinemann's *Plotinus* of 1921) was based on the old Platonism, inasmuch as it proceeds from the antithesis between mind and matter, between the world of ideas and the empirical world. This antithesis was fundamental.

Within this "world scheme" God was conceived of as the only One, transcendent over all else. The intelligible world emanated from God in an eternal process. Thought (νοῦς) was the first stage; the subsequent one was the world soul, which is the lowest within the spirit world. As the result of a fall which took place in the spirit world, the human soul was detached and united with the material. The world event is striving to fulfill this purpose, that the intelligent beings which to a greater or lesser degree had fallen away from their original state might, through training and cleansing, arise into the presence of divinity and thus be freed from the shackles of the material world. The goal, in other words, was to bring about an ecstatic reunion with God (ὁμοίωσις θεῷ) via this ongoing process of training and cleansing.

This cyclical scheme, which had already appeared in another form among the Gnostics, was fully developed in Alexandrian Platonism and formed the background for the theology of Origen and Clement. They employed this same scheme with certain alterations and additions. Within its frame the doctrine of salvation was set forth.

CLEMENT

In Alexandria, about whose first Christian congregation we know very little, a catechetical school came into being in the middle of the second century, the first Christian institution for higher education. Towards the end of the second century this school experienced an unusual growth and became the matrix of Alexandrian theology. The first well-known theologian associated with the catechetical school in Alexandria was Pantaenus, who was soon overshadowed by his pupil Clement (ca. 150–215), who, in turn, taught Origen. The main features of the theological system proper were developed by Clement, but it was Origen's utilization of this system which brought it into prominence.

The fundamental aspect of the theology of Clement is the idea of God's pedagogy. In order that the fallen spirit of man shall be able to ascend to and be reunited with the divine, education is required. This is done through discipline and punishment, through admonition and instruction. This training is the very purpose of the existence of the material world. Clement made this clear in his major books, such as *Admonition to the Greeks, The Instructor,* and *The Miscellanies.*

The education of man is accomplished through the Logos, who revealed Himself in a final and definitive way within Christianity. But there was also a preparatory stage, prior to the coming of Christianity, and the same Logos who was manifested in Christ also exerted a pedagogical influence on men in that period. Among the Jews He proclaimed the Law, and among the Greeks it was philosophy which in a comparable fashion prepared the way for the coming of Christ. Greek philosophy, in other words, was a phase in God's pedagogy, similar to the law of the Jews. Both helped to prepare men for the Incarnation and came out of the same source, the Logos, who appeared to men even before the birth of Christ. As seen from this point of view, philosophy, like the Law, is a vanquished position, inasmuch as Christ has come with the saving knowledge whereby men are brought to faith.

What has now been said is a partial explanation of Clement's view of Christianity and philosophy. Christianity and philosophy, according to Clement, are not antithetical. Philosophy rather gives expression to the same revelation which was completed later on in Christianity. Therefore philosophy, according to Clement, is able to serve as "a kind of preparatory school for those who obtain faith through proof."

But the influence of philosophy on Clement was expressed particularly in this, that it led him to conclude that "knowledge" is on a higher level than faith. He therefore distinguished between πίστις and γνῶσις. The former, according to Clement, is the simple authoritarian Christian faith, quite literal in nature, and concerned about the fear of punishment and the hope of reward. The latter, on the other hand, is considered to be the higher form of knowledge, which does not believe on the basis of authority but rather evaluates and accepts the content of faith in the light of its own inner convictions. "Knowledge" leads to love, and love impels deeds which would not result from fear. Clement strongly emphasized the claim that knowledge is the higher level on which faith is brought to perfection. Only the "gnostic" could be a perfect Christian. Nevertheless, the difference between faith and knowledge was not considered to be identical with the Gnostic division of mankind into the hylics and the pneumatics. Clement did not think of men as being predestined to the one category or the other. Neither did he conceive of the knowledge to be derived on the higher level as being of a different kind from that which is found in faith. Faith was said to contain everything to a degree. But an external faith is unable to grasp the real meaning of faith, inasmuch as it accepts dogma simply on the basis of authority. "The gnostic," on the other hand, is able to grasp the meaning of faith, having assimilated it internally. Clement's challenge to the Christian, therefore, was to proceed from faith to knowledge. Knowledge leads to the vision of God and to a life of love toward one's neighbor. Clement desired to replace the false gnosis of Gnosticism with the true, Scriptural gnosis of Christianity. The higher knowledge which he taught did not conflict with the external faith based on authority. But Clement's development of the Christian gnosis was strongly influenced by Platonic philosophy, which formed his base of operation and which served, as he saw it, as a preparatory school to Christianity for those who were to proceed from "naked faith" to the deeper understanding of faith.

The main ideas in the Christian gnosis, as developed by Clement, recurred in the theological system of Origen, and for that reason will not be discussed further at this point.

ORIGEN

The circumstances of Origen's life are rather well known, particularly as a result of the work of Eusebius (*Ecclesiastical History,* VI). Born in Alexandria in 185, of Christian parents, he revealed enthusiasm for the Christian cause at an early age. In fact, while still a young man he almost died a martyr's death, as did his father. In the year 203 he succeeded Clement as the head of the catechetical school in Alexandria, and he served there for many years. He enjoyed unusual success as a teacher, but the opposition of the bishop of Alexandria forced him into exile. He went to Palestine, where he founded a school in Caesarea similar to the one in Alexandria and continued his activity. He died in Caesarea in 251 — or, according to another source, in Tyre in 254.

As a writer in the field of theology, Origen's productivity was enormous. Only a portion of his writings have been preserved. His exegetical works consist of commentaries, homilies, and editions of texts. Origen had access to a number of manuscripts which have since been lost. In his greatest work, the *Hexapla* ("the Sixfold"), Origen placed six different versions of the Old Testament in parallel columns in an effort to determine the correct text. But only a small part of the *Hexapla* is still extant, and the same is true of his numerous homilies and commentaries. Origen's theological point of view was expressed most clearly in his great literary battle with Celsus *(Contra Celsum)* as well as in the work in which he sought to set forth a comprehensive presentation of the Christian faith. The latter has been preserved in a Latin translation by

Rufinus *(De principiis)*. It is difficult to imagine the original scope of Origen's production. Jerome estimated that he produced as many as 2,000 writings.

Early in his career Origen encountered opposition from those who charged him with teaching false doctrine. There were a number of unique points of view embodied in his theology, which was, in a general way, strongly influenced by Greek philosophy. For this reason Origen's theology became increasingly controversial, and it was finally condemned as heretical by the Fifth Ecumenical Council (553). In spite of this, however, Origen has proved to be an extremely influential theologian. It can be said, as a matter of fact, that he was the founder of the Eastern theological tradition, just as Tertullian was the founder of the Western tradition.

Origen was a Biblical theologian, but as the result of his use of the allegorical method (borrowed from the Platonic tradition) his interpretation of the Bible also permitted the acceptance of the world view which was developed within the philosophical school of Alexandria.

It must be pointed out, however, that Origen did not only allegorize. As the outstanding exegete that he was, he also manifested an understanding of the historical meaning of the texts he worked with. His typological interpretations must also be distinguished from the allegorizing tendency. The former involved the exposition of Old Testament material within the framework of the history of salvation; Origen interpreted this eschatologically, Christologically, and sacramentally. The mystical interpretation, which refers to the Christian's inner experience, also belongs in this category. These ways of interpreting Scripture have been employed to some extent throughout the entire Christian tradition. What was unusual about Origen was that he also used the allegorical method. This method had been used previously by the Jewish philosopher of religion Philo of Alexandria, who read Platonic philosophy into the Old Testament. On principle, this method is related to the Platonic point of view. It distinguishes between letter and spirit in the same way that Platonism generally distinguishes between substance and idea.

In Origen, allegory is based on the understanding that there is a spiritual meaning in the background of every passage of Scripture. Just as man consists of body, soul, and spirit, so Scripture possesses a literal (or "somatic"), a moralistic (or "psychic"), and a spiritual (or "pneumatic" significance. The latter is always present, and when the literal interpretation appears unreasonable, one must hold strictly to the spiritual.

Furthermore, the allegorical method assumes that all the details in Scripture are symbolic of great, universal spiritual realities, for example, the powers of the soul and cosmological events. The allegorizer, therefore, takes leave of solid historical ground and conceives of Scriptural pronouncements as purely spiritual or idealistic phenomena. This marks the difference between allegory and typology. It is plain that this method was well suited to elicit from Scripture the cosmological ideas which are present in Origen's theological system. The allegorical method enabled him to create a synthesis between his system's Christian and Hellenistic ideas.

The rule of faith, according to Origen, is identical with the content of Scripture. He provided a summary in the first part of his *De principiis*, in which work his theological system is most clearly presented. Here he inserted ideas from the Christian tradition into the framework of the Alexandrian world scheme. Three major themes are found here:

1) Concerning God and the transcendental world;

2) Concerning the fall into sin and the empirical world;

3) Concerning salvation and the restoration of the finite spirits.

A characteristic motif in Origen's theology has to do with the education of fallen rational creatures through divine providence. The three following basic ideas were presupposed: (a) the course of the world is guided by divine providence; it had its origin in God, and all things from the movements of the heavenly bodies to man's earthly relationships are governed by a divine power. (b) The goal of God's providential care of the world (in which man is central) is to restore the rational creatures who are here imprisoned in their bodies to their divine origin. (c) This restoration will take place as a result of education (παίδευσις) — which is to say that it is not a natural phenomenon, neither is any coercion employed, but it is to be accomplished by influencing man's free will. That man has a free will was, for Origen, a fact established by the rule of faith itself. On this Origen constructed his theological system, and as a result his concept of salvation was presented in terms of education. As was true with Clement, the idea of God's providential pedagogy was basic in Origen's system.

1. Origen described God as the highest spiritual being, as far removed from the material and the physical as is possible. In the light of this, the anthropomorphisms in the Bible must be reinterpreted. They have no literal significance. Corporeality is incompatible with the concept of God. In this Origen is diametrically opposed to Tertullian.

God, out of goodness and love, created an intelligible world of a purely spiritual kind. This spirit world comes forth from God through all eternity. The Logos, Christ, is a part of this world. Origen rejected the idea that the Logos appeared first of all at the time of creation (cf. the Apologists and Tertullian). In place of this, he asserted that the Logos preexisted eternally in an independent way ("There never was a time when He was not"). The Logos was not created in time; He was born of God in eternity. As Origen conceived it, this birth of the Son in eternity was an emanation analogous to the emergence of the spirit world from divinity (cf. Irenaeus, who presented the same idea apart from this philosophical background). This gave rise to the question: How is the Son related to the Father? On the basis of his teaching of the birth of the Son in eternity, Origen said (a) that the Logos is of the same essence as the Father (ὁμοούσιος), but also (b) that the Son is nevertheless different from the Father and subordinate to Him. The Son is "the second God." The Father alone is "not born" (ἀγέννητος). Both the *homoousios* concept and subordinationism are therefore found in the theology of Origen.

2. The spiritual beings experienced a fall, whereby some of them were further removed from their origin than were others. They "cooled off" (ψῦχος, cold), so to speak, and became rational creatures, ψυχαί (plural of ψυχή, soul). Thus it was that angels, men, and demons came into existence. The visible world was created as a consequence of the fall, in order to punish and purify man. The world provides the place and the conditions in and by which the divine instruction can take place. Origen, therefore, did not look upon creation as something evil (as did the Gnostics). He actually asserted that God created the visible world, but only for the purpose that man might receive instruction within it. The creation has no independent significance. Existence in the material world is, in part, punishment for rational spirits, but that is not all. For as Origen saw it, earthly things are symbolic of heavenly realities, and in contemplating them, it is hoped that man can be elevated to

the heavenly level. Thus it was that the material world was also involved in the providential instruction of the human spirit.

3. Origen conceived of salvation in the following manner. Man is a spirit which has fallen from the intelligible world and has been ingrafted into a body which is animated by a soul. To be saved, man must rise again into the spirit world, there to be reunited with God. This salvation is accomplished through Christ, the Logos who became man. Christ's soul did not fall from its pure state. His soul entered His body, and thus the divine and human natures were united. But, said Origen, the physical side of Christ was progressively absorbed by the divine so that He ceased being man (cf. Ignatius, who held that Christ remained in the flesh even after the Resurrection).

Origen did teach a doctrine of atonement, but inasmuch as this redemption was important chiefly to those who find themselves on the lower level of faith, as he saw it, the major emphasis was placed on the instruction which Christ imparts relative to the mysteries of the faith. Salvation is not completed until after death. The process of purification continues after death, and as a result of this men are brought to perfection and are reunited with God — first the good men, but also, at last, the evil ones. Everything shall be reunited with its origins (ἀποκατάστασις πάντων). But any resurrection of the body is out of the question. Matter will no longer be found, neither will there be men anymore; all shall be brought back to a state of pure spirituality ("You are gods; you are all sons of the Most High"). Another fall, and the creation of new worlds, is a possibility. Here we note the influence of the Greek concept of the cyclical nature of history.

In Origen's system, typical Platonic ideas were combined with the Christian tradition. Some aspects of this system are completely Hellenistic in nature, and thus have no relation to the Biblical proclamation. This is true, for example, of the idea of the intelligible world's emanation from out of divinity, of the eventual restoration of all things, and of the cessation of all that is material and physical. In other cases, the Biblical tradition is faithfully preserved. Origen frequently did this, however, by bringing these two points of view into such intimate association that it is impossible to distinguish the Christian element from the Hellenistic. Origen's method evolved into a uniform, systematic pattern of thought which was both Christian and Hellenistic. The pedagogy concept, for example, is a Greek idea, but Origen used it at the same time to express his Christian convictions. He deliberately chose to present a uniform description of the content of the rule of faith and at the same time provide an answer to the philosophical questions about life which were current in his day.

CHAPTER 6

Monarchianism: The Trinitarian Problem

During the closing years of the second century, two unusual theological developments came to the fore, both of which received the same designation: Monarchianism. Both of these caused serious strife within the church, and both were ultimately rejected as being heretical. This strife, which continued throughout the greater part of the third century, had a significant influence on the development of the history of dogma. It was in the background when the church gave shape to the doctrine of the Trinity. The views which were rejected at that time have served as prototypes for many similar aberrations and heresies down through the years, e. g., the Unitarian point of view, which has emerged time after time in the history of theology as a rationalistic interpretation of Christianity.

The "monarchical" concept, from which both of these schools took their name, appeared in the writings of Tertullian, who used it with reference to the unity in the Godhead. Monarchianism denied the Trinitarian concept, for it held that this was opposed to faith in the one God. Its adherents repudiated the idea of "economy," according to which God, who is certainly one, revealed Himself in such a way that He appeared as the Son and as the Holy Spirit.

The Monarchian rejection of the three Persons in the Godhead was influenced by the Greek concept of God, which elevated God over all material considerations, including change and diversity. In the light of this, the Greek point of view was unable to accept the claim that God appeared and acted in this world. Whenever men have repudiated the concept of the divine "economy," that is, the distinction between the Persons of the Godhead as conditioned by the order of salvation, the presupposition has been provided by a deistic view of God, in which the Biblical teaching of God is replaced by an abstract idea of God.

Monarchianism, therefore, possessed a common presupposition and a common basic idea: the difficulty of combining faith in one God with the Christian faith in the Father, the Son, and the Holy Spirit. Because they were not satisfied with the solution provided by the Logos doctrine, nor with the teaching of the three Persons (hypostases), nor with the "economy" concept, they sought for new ways to solve the problem — whereby they eliminated essential elements of the Christian faith and arrived at a rationalistic or Docetic position.

In a sense the term "Monarchianism" is an artificial designation. It does not suggest a uniform point of view; it rather indicates a feature which was held in common by two streams of thought which appeared at approximately the same time. For the most part these two streams of thought were diametrically opposed.

The one form of Monarchianism was called dynamic (or adoptionistic), and the other was called modalistic.

DYNAMIC MONARCHIANISM

The first representative of this point of view was the tanner Theodotus, who came to Rome from Byzantium in the year 190 as the result of a persecution. He was opposed to the Logos Christology and in general denied the divinity of Christ. He rather believed that Christ was merely a man (the Ebionite position). He was born of a virgin, said Theodotus, but was nevertheless an ordinary man. He was superior to other men only with respect to His righteousness (Tertullian, *Adversus omnes haereses,* 8). More specifically, Theodotus conceived of the relationship between Christ and the man Jesus in the following manner: Jesus had lived as other men; at the time of His baptism, however, Christ came over Him as a power and was active within Him from that point on. The belief that the divine element in Christ was a power bestowed on Jesus at His baptism gave "dynamic" Monarchianism its name. Jesus was thought of as a prophet who did not become God, even though He was equipped with divine powers at a given time. He was not united with God until after His resurrection. Theodotus was excommunicated by Bishop Victor of Rome.

The foremost proponent of Dynamic Monarchianism was Paul of Samosata, bishop of Antioch about 260. He carried on in the tradition of the Ebionites and Theodotus, and taught that Christ was only a man equipped with divine powers. He did not reject the Logos idea, but in his thinking the Logos was equated with reason or wisdom, in the sense that these qualities can be ascribed to a man. According to him the Logos was not an independent hypostasis. God's wisdom dwelt in the man Jesus, but only as a divine power; it did not form an independent person within Him. The personal element involved was that of the man Jesus only. In saying this, Paul repudiated Tertullian's teaching about the Logos as *persona* and Origen's doctrine of the Logos as an independent hypostasis.

Paul of Samosata was declared heretical by a synod in Antioch in the year 268. His point of view was Unitarian in nature: "The Son" was merely a man, he said, and the Holy Spirit was the grace infused into the apostles. This rationalistic interpretation of the Christian faith in God was the first clearly formulated example of a point of view which has appeared in many different forms. In more recent times it has appeared in Socinianism and other Unitarian schools, as well as in neology and in certain branches of liberal theology.

MODALISM

The second form of Monarchianism appeared first in Asia Minor, but Noetus and his disciples carried it to Rome. There it was that Praxeas lived, the modalistic representative against whom Tertullian wrote. The major spokesman for this school was Sabellius, who taught in Rome beginning about the year 215.

Noetus did not accept the "economy" concept with respect to the doctrine of the Trinity; neither did he approve the Logos Christology and the subordinationist tendencies implicit therein. To Noetus the Father alone is God, and even though He is hidden to man's sight, He has come forth and made Himself known according to His own pleasure. God is not subject to suffering and death, but He can suffer and die if He chooses to do so. In saying this, Noetus sought to emphasize God's oneness. The Father and Son are not only of the same essence; they are also the same God under a different name and form. Noetus refused to differentiate between the three Persons of the Godhead. As

71

he saw it, one could as well say that the Father suffered as to say that Christ suffered. Praxeas mitigated this opinion somewhat; he said that the Father suffered *with* the Son — but his position was also rejected. Tertullian referred to this as "patripassianism."

More than any other man, it was Sabellius who gave form to the modalistic point of view. He asserted that Father, Son, and Holy Spirit are one; they are of one substance, that is, and can be distinguished from one another only by name. He attempted to describe his position in a variety of ways: As man consists of body, soul, and spirit (for example), so are there also three facets to the divine essence; again, the three Persons are related in the way that the sun and its warmth and light are. The Father is the sun, while the Son is the illuminating rays and the Spirit is the warming power which proceeds from the sun. The Son and the Spirit are merely the forms which divinity assumed when it appeared in the world (at the time of its "expansion"). Sabellius is supposed to have said that "God, with respect to hypostasis, is only one, but He has been personified in Scripture in various ways according to the current need" (Basilius, Epistle 214). It was assumed, therefore, that God appeared in different forms at different times, first in a general way in nature, then as the Son, and finally as the Holy Spirit. It is from this pattern of thought that modalism received its name: the three Persons are the different ways *(modi)* in which the one God revealed Himself. It was characteristic of Sabellius that he not only believed that the divine substance is one; he also believed that the three Persons in the Godhead are one and the same.

What Sabellius said about the different forms of revelation was comparable to the "economy" concept of the Trinity, but it was unlike it in that (according to Sabellius) the Son and the Spirit appear after one another at different times. God is not Father, Son, and Spirit at the same time. Sabellius also refused to distinguish between the Persons; there is no real Trinity. In the "economy" concept it was thought that the three forms of revelation were independent hypostases. In opposition to Dynamic Monarchianism, modalism strongly emphasized the fact that Father and Son are one with respect to their substance. As a result, however, modalism was unable to do justice to Christ's humanity. We find here, as in Dynamic Monarchianism, a rationalistic tendency in which revelation is replaced by metaphysical speculation. Modalism — or Sabellianism, as it is often called — was rejected as heretical when Sabellius' teachings were condemned in 261.

THE ATTITUDE OF THE CHURCH

The theology of the church opposed Monarchianism in a particular way at the following points: the doctrine of the Son's consubstantiality with the Father (contra dynamism), the doctrine of the three Persons in the Godhead (contra modalism), and the doctrine of the Son's birth in eternity (contra both).

Dynamism either denied the divinity of Christ or interpreted it as a mere power which had been bestowed upon the man Jesus. The Alexandrian theologians (and Tertullian, too) described the divinity of Christ in terms of His consubstantiality with the Father. According to Clement and Origen, the Logos emanated from the Deity and is, therefore, of the same substance (ὁμοούσιος) as the Father. According to Tertullian, Father, Son, and Spirit are of the same substance.

Modalism rejected the distinction between the Persons and identified the Son with the Father, and the Spirit with the Son and the Father. Tertullian, with the assistance of the Logos doctrine, developed the concept of the three Persons, which are not only forms of revelation but three independent hypostases.

Both kinds of Monarchianism transformed the doctrine of Christ in a rationalistic direction: in the one case, Christ is merely a man; in the other, He is merely a form by which God revealed Himself. The preexistence of the Son is denied by both. The Son did not emerge as an independent entity until the appearance of Christ. And while the subordinationist theology simply taught that the Logos preexisted within the one divine essence, as God's "reason," Origen developed his doctrine of the Son's birth in eternity: the Son proceeded from the Father in eternity and existed as the Son, as an independent hypostasis, before all time.

Among those who opposed Monarchianism and contributed to the theological development within the church at the end of the third century were Novatian and Methodius.

Novatian, who was a presbyter in Rome ca. 250, was closely related to Tertullian's theological position. He stressed, on the one hand, the divinity of Christ and the fact that He is consubstantial with the Father (contra dynamism), and on the other, Christ's true humanity and the distinction between the Persons in the Godhead (contra modalism).

Methodius of Olympus (d. 311) continued in Origen's theological tradition, but he rejected the latter's teachings about the eternal creation, the preexistence of the soul, and the restoration of all things.

CHAPTER 7

Arianism:
The Council of Nicaea

The challenge of Monarchianism returned in a more acute form in the violent ecclesiastical controversies of the fourth century. It was then that the threat of Arianism was combated and that the church's Trinitarian formula was established at the ecumenical councils held in Nicaea (325) and Constantinople (381).

There is also a purely historical connection between Arius, the fourth century's most embattled heretic, and Dynamic Monarchianism. Arius, who was a presbyter in Alexandria ca. 310, was a disciple of Lucian of Antioch, who, in turn, was a follower of Paul of Samosata.

Like the Monarchians, Arius proceeded on the basis of a philosophical concept of God. God could not possibly impart His essence to anyone else, in view of the fact that He is one and indivisible. It is inconceivable that either the Logos or the Son could have come to be apart from an act of creation. Thus, as Arius said it, Christ could not be God in the true sense of the term; He must rather be a part of creation. As a result, Arius thought of Christ as a "middle being," as less than God and more than man. He also said that Christ was a created being, having been created either in time or before time. Arius therefore denied the preexistence of the Son in all eternity and attributed divine attributes to Him only in an honorary sense, based on the special grace Christ shared and the righteousness He manifested. "The Son was not always, for when all things emerged out of nothingness and all created essence came into being, then it was that God's Logos also came forth out of nothing. There was a time when He was not (ἦν ποτε ὅτε οὐκ ἦν), and He was not until He was brought forth, for even He had a beginning, when He was created. For God was alone, and at that time there was neither Logos nor Wisdom. When God decided to create us, He first produced someone whom He called Logos and Wisdom and Son, and we were created through Him." (Athanasius, *Orationes contra Arianos*, I, 5)

Arius' own bishop, Alexander, came out against him and excommunicated him on the ground of heresy ca. 320. The conflict soon enveloped the entire East, and Arius received support from Eusebius of Nicomedia, among others. In view of the fact that this struggle jeopardized the unity of the entire church and, at the same time, the inner strength of the Roman Empire, Emperor Constantine decided to involve himself in it in an effort to get the matter settled. First he sent his court bishop, Hosius, to Alexandria to act as a mediator, and when that strategem failed he called a general council to be held in Nicaea in the year 325. Bishops from all over the empire were invited to attend.

Three different points of view were presented at the Council of Nicaea. There were, in the first place, a small number of pure Arians (led by Eusebius of Nicomedia). In the second place there were those who opposed Arianism, chief among whom was Bishop Alexander of Alexandria and his deacon Athanasius. The above-named Hosius of Cordova also belonged to this party. Finally, there was a mediating group, represented in particular by Eusebius of Caesarea. The formula which the council finally accepted was presented by him. But after this formula was approved, it was altered in such a way that it became more specifically anti-Arian. Thus it was, for example, that the expression ὁμοούσιος (of the same substance) was inserted into the formula through the intervention of Hosius. This was done in order to emphasize the opposition to Arius. The Nicene formula was constructed, primarily, on the basis of a symbol then in current use. It is possible that this symbol was the baptismal formula then used in Caesarea, to which new facets, conditioned by the polemical situation, were added. A final addition was an anathema against all of Arius' teachings. The so-called Nicene Creed is not identical with the formula accepted at the Council of Nicaea, but it was given its final form before the end of the fourth century. It was approved by the Council of Constantinople (381) and the Council of Chalcedon (451). The Nicene Creed was also based on an older baptismal formula, and it includes a number of the anti-Arian expressions found in the Nicene decision.

Opposition to Arius was based partly on his doctrine of God and, in connection with this, partly on his doctrine of Christ. Two particular criticisms were directed at Arius: one, he introduced polytheistic ideas and the worship of creation; two, he destroyed the basis of salvation by denying the divinity of Christ.

Arius assigned the Logos to the category of created beings. Because he also felt that the Logos should be worshiped as a divine being, it was possible to criticize Arius for introducing idolatry. Creation was placed side by side with the Creator and worshiped as divine. If Christ is different from God, but nevertheless is God, this implies the worship of two Gods. Arius also spoke of other semidivine beings.

Christ, according to Arius, was a created being whose existence began in time or before time. He thereby rejected the teaching of the divinity of Christ and His birth in eternity. The Christ whom Arius proclaimed could not have created the world; neither can He be the Lord of creation. Arius' Christology thereby repudiated Christ's work of redemption, and this became the main point at issue between Arius and his opponents. If Christ is not of the same substance as God the Father, He can neither possess nor transmit the full knowledge of God. And salvation consists, among other things, in this, that Christ has presented us with this true knowledge of God. If He is not one with God, He could not do this.

If Christ is not the Lord of creation, neither could He carry out the work of redemption. If He is not God, He cannot make man divine. The real meaning of salvation is that it brings life and immortality to man. God's Son in human form could have conquered death, made atonement for guilty man, and restored man to life and immortality only if He is of God's own essence.

This Christology, which was hammered out during the struggle against Arianism, has been summarized in the Nicene formula, above all in the following sentences about Christ: "the only-begotten . . . begotten of His father . . . God of God, Light of Light, Very God of Very God; begotten, not made; being of one substance with the Father." The final anathema against Arius contained these pertinent words: "Those who say that there was a time when He was not, and before He was generated He was not, and that He came forth from that which is not, or who say of Him that He is of another hypostasis or essence, or say that God's Son is created or changeable, all such are condemned by the universal church."

An overzealous defender of the Nicene point of view was Marcellus of Ancyra (d. 374). He taught that the Logos, who was of the same substance as God, could be called "Son" only from the time of the Incarnation. He also believed that Christ's Sonship will cease at a certain time and that the Logos will then be reincorporated into the Father. The words "whose kingdom shall have no end" were inserted into the Nicene Creed in order to counterbalance the teaching of Marcellus at this point. He championed an "economy" concept of the Trinity with his conception of an "expansion" of divinity to the Son and the Spirit. The Arians, who opposed him, criticized him for being Sabellian, but in contrast to the modalists he drew a sharp line of distinction between the Logos and Him from whom the Logos came.

One of Marcellus' disciples, Photinus of Sirmium (d. 376), drew inferences from Marcellus' theology which made it appear as though he (Photinus) supported the adoptionist, or dynamistic, Christology. Thus it was that the older polemical literature often referred to "Photianism" as a designation for this point of view. Photinus thought of the Logos as being identical with the Father, while Christ was considered to be Mary's son — and no more.

Long theological controversies followed the Council of Nicaea (325). At the outset the Nicene decision met with strong opposition. The original Arian group, which subsequently adopted a mediating position and which formed around Eusebius of Nicomedia, grew increasingly influential. Even the emperor went over to this point of view; Athanasius was forced to leave his bishop's office. In the middle of the fourth century (at the Synod of Ancyra, 358) a new mediating party, which derived its name from the Greek ὁμοιούσιος (of similar substance), appeared. But a number of theologians who were active during the last part of the century, chief among them the so-called "Cappadocians" (about whom more will be said later), came out strongly in favor of the Nicene decision and developed it even further (the proto-Nicene orthodoxy). Some of the "similar substance" proponents went over to this position, from which they were not far removed even before they took this step. And thus it was that the ground was prepared for the final victory at the Council of Constantinople in 381 (later referred to as the Second Ecumenical Council), where the Nicene decision was confirmed anew.

CHAPTER 8

Athanasius:
The Formation of the
Trinitarian Doctrine

The staunchest defender of the faith in the church's struggle with Arianism and the imperial power which supported the heretics for a long time was Athanasius, whose name was mentioned in connection with the Council of Nicaea. After the death of Alexander in 328, Athanasius became the patriarch of Alexandria. But as the result of his steadfast allegiance to the Nicene decision, he was subjected to one persecution after another. He had to flee from his episcopal see no less than five times, and he spent a total of nearly 20 years in exile. When he died in 373, the Arian controversy was still in progress, but as a result of his contributions, the way was prepared for the final victory of the Nicene theology at the Council of Constantinople, 381.

Among the writings of Athanasius our particular attention is called to the following: *Oratio contra Gentes* and *Oratio de incarnatione Verbi* (written about 318), and his magnum opus, *Orationes contra Arianos* (written about 335 — or, according to another theory, in 356 and thereafter). Athanasius' *Epistolae* are also significant as theological documents, above all his letter to Serapion.

Unlike the older Alexandrian theologians (Clement, Origen), Athanasius did not insert the Christian faith into a closed, philosophical system. On the contrary, he rejected the resources of philosophy in the development of Christian doctrine; the Bible was his sole source. For him, as for Clement, the rule of faith and the content of Scripture were identical. Tradition, according to Athanasius, is authoritative only if it is in agreement with Scripture. As he made clear in his Easter letter of 367, the New Testament canon is definitive.

From what has been said, it is clear that Athanasius worked with a consistent Biblical principle. At the same time, he insisted that the Bible should not be interpreted legalistically; it must rather be understood in the light of its own center, which is Christ and the salvation wrought by Him. Athanasius' conception of the Bible reminds us of the words of Luther: "What proclaims Christ is God's Word."

In the fight against Arianism, Athanasius developed the church's doctrine of the Trinity and the Logos. Some of his major arguments went as follows: (1) If Arius was right in saying that Christ is just a created being, and not of the same substance as the Father, salvation would not be possible. For God alone can save, and He has come down to our level in order to raise us up to His. (2) Arius' teachings involve the worship of creation or faith in more than one god.

As the first argument makes clear, Athanasius was concerned about combining the doctrine of the Trinity with the salvation wrought by Christ, which is the center of all theology as he saw it. Because of this, he continued to point out that the Arian heresy did not simply touch upon isolated points of doctrine; it rather subverted the entire Christian faith. The atomistic or doctrinaire style which often characterized theological polemics in Athanasius' time is not to be found in his writings.

We must not conclude, however — in analogy with modern thought — that the Logos doctrine was of significance to Athanasius only in its relation to the concept of salvation. In his estimation this doctrine was quite simply one of the fundamentals of the Christian faith, and therefore it was the elementary insistence of truth itself which prompted Athanasius to defend the Nicene doctrine of the Trinity against Arianism. The second argument listed above indicates this.

Like Irenaeus, Athanasius described a distinct order of salvation, beginning with the creation and pointing forward to the fulfillment. This *ordo salutis* provided the background for his polemic against Arius, just as Irenaeus developed his polemic against the Gnostics on a corresponding train of thought.

Salvation and creation belong together, as Athanasius saw it. It was the almighty Creator Himself who carried out the work of salvation, so that the fallen creation might be restored to its original destiny. This implies that God's purpose with creation is being realized and that a new creation is coming into being. This refers, in a special way, to man.

Man was created "in God's image," but as a result of the incursion of sin, he fell away from God and was given over to death and corruption. Salvation was achieved when God's Son, the Logos, personally involved Himself in humanity and thereby restored man to his likeness to God. "This could not have happened, however, if death and corruption had not been destroyed. Therefore, as a matter of course, He assumed to Himself a mortal body, so that death might be destroyed in Him, and so that man, created in God's image, might be renewed. He who came in the Father's image was alone equal to this task." (*Oratio de incarnatione Verbi*, 13, 8-9)

The primary meaning of the salvatory work of Christ is to be found in this, that the curse of sin and death has been taken away. This was done when the Logos, who is God's own Son, took upon Himself the conditions of human existence, bore man's sins, and subjected Himself to death. It was thus that these powers were overcome, for in view of the fact that Christ is of the essence of God, they were unable to conquer Him. He freed Himself from the bonds of sin and death, and in so doing He also freed all human nature from these powers. It was for this purpose that God's Son became man. If the Logos had not really become man, He could not have freed man, He could not have overcome the power of sin and death which held human nature in thrall.

In the second place, the salvatory work of Christ implies that man, who has been freed from the power of sin and death through the Atonement, can be renewed and deified. The same Christ who conquered death has sent His Spirit, through whom He re-creates man and enables man to share in the divine life which was lost to him through the Fall. Man thus comes to possess immortality and to live again as he did originally — in the image of God. This deification of man is the goal of salvation. The stronger emphasis on this aspect of salvation, rather than on the forgiveness of sin, was typical of the Fathers of the early church. It can be said, however, that Athanasius, more than the others, also stressed the need of forgiveness; he recognized that sin brought guilt and that the atoning work of Christ was a sacrifice for sin. But above all, salvation is associated with immortality. Sin and death, after all, go together. If sin had not brought death, said Athanasius, it could have been overcome quite easily by repentance. But in view of the fact that sin did result in mortality, salvation could be won only if death were overcome. And thus, since the power of sin has been overcome, the work of the Holy Spirit is to give life to man and to make man like God. This is possible only if Christ is actually of the same essence as God. Because He is God Himself, He first deified His own human nature, and as a result of this, He can do the same for those who believe in Him and who share, by faith, in His death and resurrection.

In the light of this, the message of salvation as taught by Arius, who said that the Logos was a created being and not as God Himself, had to be repudiated. "The truth reveals that the Logos is not one of the created things; He is, rather, their Creator. For He has taken upon Himself the created, human body of man, in order that He, likewise a Creator, could renew this body and deify it in Himself, so that man, on the strength of his identity with Christ, might enter the kingdom of heaven. But man, who is a part of creation, could never become like God if the Son were not truly God. . . . Likewise, man would not have been freed from sin and damnation if the Logos had not taken upon Himself our natural, human flesh. Neither could man have become Godlike if the Word which became flesh had not come from the Father — if He had not been His own true Word." (*Orationes contra Arianos*, II, 70)

Athanasius also emphasized another facet of Christ's work of redemption: Christ, he said, came to reveal that He is God's Son, who reigns over all creation; in so doing, He restored the true worship of God, which man in his ignorance and blindness had forgotten. In one passage Athanasius summarized the work of Christ in the following manner: "The incarnate Savior revealed His goodness to us in two ways: by the fact that He took away the sting of death and renewed us, and by the fact that He, who is in Himself hidden and invisible, revealed Himself through His work so that we might know Him as the Father's Logos, the Ruler and King of the entire universe." (*Oratio de incarnatione Verbi*, 16)

Christ's work was a manifestation of His power, a demonstration of the fact that He is the Lord of all things, while idols and demons are as nothing. The idea that Christ restored the true worship of God by revealing Himself as the true God was (as already noted) also one of the major arguments employed in the struggle with Arianism. Arius introduced a pagan type of worship, complete with faith in several gods and the worship of creation rather than the Creator. This resulted from his denial of the divinity of Christ and from the claim that the Logos is a created being.

In his doctrine of the Trinity, which was directed particularly against Arianism, Athanasius strongly emphasized the claim that the Son is of the same substance as the Father. This conviction was not simply elicited from the key word of the Nicene decision, *homoousios*, itself; Athanasius felt free to accept other terms too, including the otherwise suspicious word *homoios*. Athanasius' belief that the Son is consubstantial with the Father was rather based on the facts themselves. The Logos is not a part of creation; it rather shares in the same divinity as the Father Himself. Athanasius also overcame the earlier subordinationist point of view. The Logos is not another God, and does not stand lower than the Father, as a spiritual being which emanated from the Father. The Father and the Son comprise one Deity. The Father is the one who defines Himself and generates; the Son is the one who is thus generated. The Father is, in Himself, the divine essence; the Son is God in external activity, as He appears in God's work. "The Son is not another God. . . . For if He is also something other, even to the point that He was generated, He is nevertheless the same as God; He and the Father are one through the unique nature which they share in common, and through the identity of the one divinity." (*Orationes contra Arianos*, III, 4)

Athanasius did not speak about "Persons" in the Godhead; he rather articulated the relationship between the Father and the Son in a different way. He held to the Father-Son concept, or spoke of the difference between them as being conditioned by God's activity. The Father is the source, the Son is God in His external activity. Then there is also the Holy Spirit, who carries out God's work in the individual. Athanasius taught that the Holy Spirit, too, is "of the same substance." He is a part of the same divine essence and is not a created spirit. Man becomes Godlike through the work of the Spirit. Renewal would not be a genuine act of salvation if the Holy Spirit were not of God's own essence. The external activity of the Triune God is not divided; that is to say that Father, Son, and Holy Spirit all work together. It was in his letter to Serapion that Athanasius first developed the thought that the Holy Spirit is of the same essence as the Father and the Son. This was one of his greatest and most independent contributions to theology.

THE THREE CAPPADOCIANS

Even though Athanasius' presentation of Nicene orthodoxy was fundamental to its subsequent development, his formulations were not strictly adhered to in the church-sanctioned doctrine of the Trinity. For this, ideas were also derived from (among others) Origen and Tertullian — for example, the teaching of the three Persons in the Godhead. But Athanasius' convictions in this matter were not forgotten. Those who carried on his work, and who did more than anyone else to give the doctrine of the Trinity its final form, were the so-called "Three Cappadocians."

Basil the Great (d. 379, archbishop of Caesarea) was the chief architect of the so-called proto-Nicene theology, which finally conquered Arianism. His younger brother, Gregory of Nyssa (d. about 394), developed the same orthodox point of view in a rather more speculative manner, and Gregory of Nazianzus (d. about 390) interpreted this in a rhetorical way in his *Orationes*.

It was largely due to the influence of the three Cappadocians that the Nicene theology finally won out as the true mediating position between Arianism and modalism. Furthermore, the basis of future developments in Eastern theology was prepared at this time. The three Cappadocians were more specifically "Eastern" in their theology than was Athanasius. This is to be seen, for example, in the fact that they interpreted Athanasius in the spirit of Origen, as well as in the fact that they associated the Nicene orthodoxy with ideas from the older Alexandrian school of thought.

While Athanasius strongly emphasized the idea of the "one substance" and proceeded from that point in his description of the Trinity, the Cappadocians proceeded from the idea of the "three distinct Persons" and developed a terminology which was descriptive of both unity and trinity. In so doing, they accepted the earlier Greek theology which conceived of the three Persons as different levels in the Divine Being (Origen).

It was at this time that a precise distinction was made between the two concepts expressed in the Greek words οὐσία and ὑπόστασις. The first of these was used to denote the indivisible nature of the divine essence, while the latter was placed in juxtaposition with the word πρόσωπον (person). Basil illustrated this distinction in the following

84

wav: The concept "man" refers to that which is common to all men. But individual men, such as Paul or John, possess distinctive characteristics which mark them off from other individuals. Both Paul and John exist independently, but they also have something in common: they are men; they belong in the general category of "man." So while they share a common essence (οὐσία), they are also individual persons with an independent existence (ὑπόστασις). The hypostasis is, therefore, the special form of existence, the unique characteristics, whereby that which is held in common is given concrete expression. It is that which exists in the individual and not in anyone else.

When the hypostasis concept is employed in the doctrine of the Trinity, it is thereby indicated that the three Persons possess their own peculiar qualities and attributes, whereby they distinguish themselves from one another and appear each in His own special form of existence. At the same time, they all share in the one divine essence. This presentation of the doctrine of the Trinity is usually summarized in the words, "one essence, three Persons."

When asked what it is that distinguishes the three hypostases, the Cappadocians answered by referring to the relationship which exists between them. The Father is ἀγέννητος (not generated); the Son is generated of the Father; the Spirit proceeds from the Father through the Son (Gregory of Nazianzus, *Orationes*, 25, 16). That which characterizes the Persons in relation to one another was also described with reference to the divine activity: the Father is the source (αἴτιος), the Son is the one who carries out the work (δημιουργός), and the Spirit is the one who brings it to completion (τελειοποιός). (Gregory of Nazianzus, *Orationes*, 28, 1)

The point at which the Cappadocians went beyond Athanasius had to do, in particular, with the distinction between *ousia* and hypostasis. In drawing this distinction, the Cappadocians sought (with the aid of philosophical terminology) to describe what it is that characterizes the divine nature and the three Persons in and of themselves, independent of the Trinity's external activity. The only result of this was a number of formal distinctions, which, in the light of the Christian faith, appear to be necessary consequences. What these men were trying to do here was to elucidate that which goes beyond the limits of human knowledge, and which, therefore, cannot be more clearly expounded.

85

AUGUSTINE'S DOCTRINE OF THE TRINITY;
THE ATHANASIAN CREED

As far as Eastern theology is concerned, the Cappadocians brought the doctrine of the Trinity to a certain degree of completeness. A corresponding development also took place in the West, partly as a result of the influence of Eastern theology. Above all, it was Augustine who shaped the Western position on this matter, particularly in his book *De Trinitate*. Augustine's theology provided the basis for the Trinitarian position found in the Athanasian Creed, the last of the three Ecumenical Creeds.

The three Cappadocians emphasized the three hypostases in particular, and their major problem was therefore associated with the unity of the divine essence. This was characteristic of the Eastern point of view, with its more static, abstract concept of God. The problem, of course, was this: How could the entire divine essence be found in three distinct existences? This problem gave rise to the old subordinationist theology, and the Cappadocian contribution was precisely this, that they arrived at the "one substance" position (as did Athanasius and the Nicene Creed) at the same time that they also strongly proclaimed the distinction between the three Persons.

Augustine, who represented the Western point of view, developed his Trinitarian position on the basis of the one divine essence. What he sought to make clear was that the divine unity is so constituted that it includes the three Persons, and that the "threeness" of God is implicit in this unity. He described the triunity as an internally necessary relationship between the three facets of the one divine essence. This, to Augustine, was an unfathomable mystery, which man in this life can never completely comprehend, much less describe in conceptual terms.

But Augustine did employ analogies drawn from human relationships in an effort to demonstrate a comparable relationship of three things within one and the same entity. Certain human phenomena, particularly the structure of the soul of man, were used to symbolize (though very imperfectly) the inner-Trinitarian reality. Thus Augustine said, for example, that love implies a relationship between the one who loves and the object of love. This suggests a relationship between the three following: the one who loves (*amans*), that which is loved (*quod amatur*), and love itself (*amor*). A corresponding relationship is to be

86

found in the Godhead between Father, Son, and Spirit. What is peculiar about this relationship is the fact that both subject and object are present within the same indivisible essence. The Father generates the Son, the Father loves the Son, etc. According to Augustine, there is an analogy to this in man's spiritual life. The very act of observation involves three elements which are necessarily related to one another: there is the object observed (*res*), the sight itself (*visio*), and the attentiveness of the will (*intentio voluntatis*). The same relationship is said to exist between thought, intellect, and will in the act of knowing. Thought content is present, in some way, in the soul; this, in turn, is considered and given form by one's intellectual ability, which directs itself to the object by the power of the will (*memoria — interna visio — voluntas*). The life of the soul in its entirety includes a corresponding "threeness": memory, intelligence, and will. And here we can see the same oneness between subject and object that Augustine found within the inner-Trinitarian relationships. The soul is aware of itself, has knowledge of itself, and loves itself; in other words, the object of its activity is found, in part, within itself. It is, simultaneously, both subject and object in self-conscious and self-loving acts.

Augustine did not say that these analogies are perfect — that they clear up all of the mysteries associated with the Trinitarian concept. To a large extent, his presentation was developed in the form of speculations about the inner-Trinitarian reality. Thus it was that a new stage of development came into being which went beyond the "economy" concept of the Trinity which provided the original form of the doctrine of the "three in one." Augustine strongly emphasized the oneness of the Divine Being and attempted to show that the threeness was implicit in the oneness and vice versa. This fundamental conviction is also found in the Athanasian Creed, which is actually based on the theology of Augustine, even though it was, by degrees, invested with the authority of Athanasius. This creed is a hymnlike statement, and it was probably drawn up sometime during the fifth or sixth centuries, conceivably by a disciple of Augustine. It is a good summary of the doctrine of the Trinity as this was enunciated by the early church. The historical development of Christian dogma as it has been sketched out up to this point provides the background for this creed, which in brief and concise sentences summarizes the position the church reached during the Trinitarian and Christological controversies.

This *Symbolum quicunque* (as it is called, after its opening words) presents, in its first section, an interpretation of the doctrine of the Trinity: "And the Catholic faith is this, that we worship one God in Trinity, and Trinity in Unity; neither confounding the Persons, nor dividing the substance." The distinction between the Persons is stressed in part: "For there is one Person of the Father, another of the Son, and another of the Holy Spirit." And so is the unity of the divine essence: "But the Godhead of the Father, of the Son, and of the Holy Spirit is all one: the glory equal, the majesty coeternal." All three Persons share in the divine essence and its qualities: "uncreated" — "incomprehensible" — "eternal." And yet there are not three uncreated, incomprehensible, and eternal beings; neither are there three Gods; there is only one God. Each Person must be recognized as God and Lord, but this does not mean that there are three Gods or three Lords.

The following formula describes the relationship which exists between the Persons: the Father is not made, not created, not born of anyone; the Son is begotten of the Father alone; the Spirit proceeds from the Father and the Son.

The last part of this creed deals with Christology.

CHAPTER 9

The Christological Problem

The real problem of Christology is reflected in this question: How is the divinity of Christ related to the humanity of Christ? How can He who is true God also be man at the same time? How could He live under human conditions and appear in human form?

Such questions came to the fore in the earliest period of church history, particularly in the struggle with the Docetists and in the rejection of the Ebionites. The heretical tendencies implicit in these schools of thought reappeared in new forms during the so-called Christological controversies, which had a prominent place in the development of dogma beginning with the middle of the fourth century.

APOLLINARIS

The fact that the Christological question reappeared at this time must be seen against the background of the rejection of Arianism and the confirmation of the *homoousios* formula. How could the fact that the Logos is of one substance with the Father be combined with the fact that the Logos appeared in human form? That was the major question involved in the theological discussions of the time.

The man who first posed the problem in this form, and motivated the ongoing theological reworking of the answer, was Apollinaris of Laodicea, who appeared on the scene sometime after the middle of the fourth century. And while he was actually a member of the "Nicene party," he nevertheless dealt with the Christological problem in a way that was repudiated by the church.

Apollinaris was not satisfied to accept the idea that the Logos (i. e., Christ) was, with respect to His divine nature, of the same substance as the Father. The main problem, as he saw it, was this: How can man conceive of Christ's human existence? According to Apollinaris, Christ's human nature had to possess a divine quality. If this were not the case, Christ's life and death could not have wrought man's salvation. It would appear, therefore, that Apollinaris taught as follows: God in Christ was transmuted into flesh, and this flesh was then transmuted into something by nature divine. According to this point of view, Christ did not receive His human nature, His flesh, from the Virgin Mary; He rather brought with Him, from heaven, a heavenly kind of flesh. The womb of Mary simply served as a passageway. (Cf. Schoeps, *Vom himmlischen Fleisch Christi*, 1951, p. 9 ff., and Kelly, *Early Christian Doctrines*, p. 294)

As Apollinaris understood Christ, therefore, He has only one nature and one hypostasis. This nature is the nature of the Logos, which in Christ was transmuted into flesh. The latter, in turn, assumed a divine quality at the same time. Apollinaris strongly opposed the idea that the divine and human elements in Christ were combined, that the Logos simply arrayed Himself in human nature and was connected with it in a spiritual manner.

One of Apollinaris' characteristic tendencies is to be seen in the way he developed his idea about how the Logos became man. To accomplish this, he proceeded from the distinction between flesh and spirit, or between body, soul, and spirit. Man is constituted of these components, and it is the spirit (or the reasonable soul) which makes man what he is — which provides his true essence. Christ's reason or spirit did not consist of human reason; it consisted of God's Logos. God and man are therefore united in Christ as body and soul are in man, inasmuch as the human soul was replaced by God's Logos.

This unity of Logos and flesh has had the result that the flesh is thought of as a divine or heavenly flesh. For it is the spirit or reason which molds the physical so that, together, they form one nature. In Christ, however, as Apollinaris saw it, this one nature is of a divine variety.

It is obvious that Apollinaris emphasized the divinity of Christ to such a degree that he lost sight of His true humanity. Christ, according to Apollinaris, does not have a human soul. He has but one nature, the incarnate nature of the divine Logos. Because of this point of view, Apollinaris was not far removed from the old modalism. There was a strain of Docetism in his theology.

90

Opposition to Apollinaris came chiefly from the Cappadocians and from the school in Antioch. In contending with him, the opposition emphasized that Christ's true humanity must mean that He not only had a human body but also a human soul, for it is body and soul together which provide the essence of humanity. Apart from human reason, man is no longer man. Apollinaris' detractors were also repulsed by his assertion that God Himself would be fleshly, or that He submitted Himself to suffering.

ANTIOCH AND ALEXANDRIA

The so-called school of Antioch was very sharply opposed to Apollinaris. Its foremost representatives were Diodorus of Tarsus (d. 394), Theodore of Mopsuestia (d. 428), and Theodoretus. The famous preacher John Chrysostom (d. 407) can also be included in this list, as well as Nestorius, whose teachings were later rejected as being heretical. When Nestorius' theology was repudiated, the influence of this school diminished considerably. But it was nevertheless very significant for the development of doctrine, and it distinguished itself particularly for its consistent scientific approach.

The Antiochene exegetes refused to employ the allegorical method; instead, they worked out a historical-grammatical mode of interpretation. Scripture, they said, must be interpreted in a literal sense, in a manner consistent with its original meaning.

The Christology which developed in Antioch was also related to this basic historical approach. The primary emphasis was placed on the humanity of Christ. Christ, they said, had both a human soul and a human body; furthermore, He underwent a process of development. It was thus that He became more closely united to God, until the process was completed at the time of the Resurrection.

The Antiochenes also held fast to the Nicene decision regarding the *homoousios*. According to His divine nature, Christ was actually of the same substance as the Father. The Logos, however, was not transmuted into a man; instead, He retained His divine nature, took upon Himself a human form, and united Himself to human nature. This union was conceived of thus by the Antiochenes: the Logos employed human nature as an organ; He worked through it. At the same time, however, the two natures remained distinct; each was an independent entity, and they were united only by their activity and by their unity of purpose. It was,

91

then, a question concerning spiritual and moral unity; it was not a physical problem, as it was for Apollinaris.

As a result of such opinions, the Antiochene theologians also opposed Apollinaris on Christological grounds. Each of the two natures in Christ must be preserved intact. The divine and human natures were not changed in such a way that the one was merged into the other. Christ possessed the true divine nature, but at the same time He was also a real man with a human body and soul. To Apollinaris, Christ had but one nature: the divine. The Antiochenes asserted that we must distinguish between the Logos and the human nature which He assumed. The Logos combined Himself with man and dwelt in him as in a temple. This does not mean that the one nature was merged into the other. The natures were not transformed in such a way that they became identical. When we read in John 1:14 that "the Word became flesh," the "became" (ἐγένετο) must be interpreted in a figurative sense, said Theodore. The Logos took flesh upon Himself, but He did not become flesh. "For when it says that 'He took' the form of a servant (Phil. 2:7), that means that it actually happened thus; it was not a pretense. But when we read that 'He became,' that must not be taken literally, for He was not transmuted into flesh." (*De incarnatione,* 9)

The Antiochenes therefore emphasized the difference between the two natures and insisted that each retained its own unique qualities. There was a complete divine nature, that of God's Logos, and a complete human nature. At the same time, however, the original Antiochenes also asserted the unity of the person. And it was this aspect of the Christological problem which was decisive for the school of Antioch. It was on this point, for example, that Nestorius was accused of heresy. His predecessors had emphasized the fact that Christ is *one* person, with *one* will, and a single independent existence. "We do not say that there are two sons; we properly believe in but one Son. For the distinction between the two natures must be upheld unconditionally, and the unity of the person perpetually maintained." (Theodore, *De incarnatione,* 12)

In the struggle which involved the Antiochenes and Apollinaris was reflected the persistent opposition of the two leading theological schools of that period, the one in Antioch and the other in Alexandria. This opposition was based on two different points of view regarding the entire field of theology. The Antiochene school emphasized the historical aspect, rejected the use of allegory, and put particular stress on Jesus' earthly, human existence, His development and historicity. The Alexandrian school, on the other hand, was deeply influenced by Greek philosophy, with its emphasis on the metaphysical, on the spiritual, divine realities, as well as its sharp antithesis between the divine and the human. The divine element in Christ was emphasized in such a way that the human element was not always properly recognized.

Parallels to both of these points of view can be seen in two diverse tendencies in the New Testament. The Incarnation is described in John in terms of Christ "becoming man" ("the Word became flesh," 1:14), and in Philippians we read that Christ "took the form of a servant, being born in the likeness of men." (2:7)

In the Antiochene school the attempt was made to do justice to both the divine element and the historical, human element in Christ. The unity between the two was described as being of a moral nature, a unity of will. The believer, of course, worships the *one* Christ — a subjective form of unity. In reality there are two essences or natures.

The Alexandrian point of view was based on the fundamental distinction between the divine and the human, which coincides, of course, with the attitude of idealism. The Incarnation was set forth as a transmutation of the Deity into human nature. But in view of the fact that the divine essence is unchangeable, this meant that human nature was elevated to the level of divinity, transmuted into divine nature. Conceived of thus, unity was thought to involve not only activity and will, but substance itself. It was, in other words, a substantial, physical unity, in which the qualities of human nature disappeared.

NESTORIUS AND CYRIL

The opposition between the Alexandrians and the Antiochenes provided the background for the bitter struggle which took place between Nestorius and Cyril at the beginning of the fifth century. It must be said, however, that church politics and personal ambition also entered the picture. Alexandria was in competition with Antioch, and particularly with Constantinople, for ecclesiastical domination in the East, and theological questions became involved in this fight for power. The Synod of Ephesus (431) decided in favor of the Alexandrian theology, and Nestorius, who upheld the opposing position, was declared heretical and driven into exile. When this was done, the entire Nestorian party separated itself from the rest of the church. The Nestorians then organized their own church body in Persia, and spread throughout Asia, but they were doomed to an isolated existence. Small Nestorian congregations have remained, however, right down to the present time (cf. The Marthoma Church in India).

Nestorius, who became patriarch of Constantinople in 428, was in general a representative of the Antiochene school of theology. The verdict of history on Nestorius and his works has changed radically. Because of the anathema hurled at him by his contemporaries, it has been generally concluded that he carried the Antiochene point of view a bit too far and that he came up with a false Christology as a result. It has been thought that he set forth a doctrine of "two Christs," one divine and one human, and thereby invalidated the Christian faith. Thus it was that the "heretic" label has been attached to Nestorius, and he has been held up as the prototype of a point of view which presents a false antithesis between the divine and the human.

During the time of the Reformation, for example, the Roman Catholic Church was accused of having a Nestorian Christology. In our own time, one could point to the attitude which often forms the basis for the scientific approach to theology; it is marked by a bifurcated view of theology, one using history as a point of departure, the other using religious experience. A similar distinction is made between the historical Jesus and Christ, the Son of God. These attempts to solve the question of the relationship between theology and science remind us in a way of Nestorius and the basic elements in his Christology.

Modern research has presented us with an evaluation of Nestorius which is completely at variance with the older tradition. Improved access to primary sources has made this reconsideration possible. It is now being heard that Nestorius was misunderstood and wrongly interpreted by his opponent, Cyril, and that it was this, together with church politics, which provoked the struggle between them. The fact of the matter, it is said, is that Nestorius' theology was similar to the old Antiochene school of thought and that he had no heretical tendencies. According to Seeberg, "None of the great 'heretics' of the history of dogma have borne this name so unjustly as Nestorius" (*Lehrbuch der Dogmengeschichte*, II, 2d ed., 204). Seeberg and Loofs have done more than any others to rehabilitate Nestorius.

It must be said in this connection, however, that these two historians of dogma represent a theological point of view which is much more closely related to Nestorius and the Antiochene school than it is to the Alexandrian. The Antiochene Christology, with its emphasis on the historical Christ and on the moral union of the divine and human elements, has been found more tenable, as seen from the scientific point of view, than the Alexandrian Christology with its emphasis on the physical union of Christ's two natures or the deifying of the flesh. The Antiochene Christology is better adapted to the modern scientific point of view, and it is this which explains, in part at least, the altered verdict on Nestorius. It is obvious, however, that his teachings were misinterpreted by his opponents in the heat of their struggle, and also that the fight against him was not motivated entirely by theological considerations. The difference between Nestorius' theology and the theology of the older Antiochenes was not as great as his opponents claimed it to be.

The basis of Nestorius' Christology was the same as that of the earlier Antiochene theologians; all insisted that the divine and human natures in Christ must not be confused, that they must be thought of as completely distinct. The immediate point in question between Nestorius and his opponents was related to this fundamental teaching, though in itself it would appear that this point was no more than an insignificant detail. The Alexandrian theologians had begun to refer to Mary as θεοτόκος (the mother of God). If there was in Christ a physical union of God and man, then, it was argued, the man Christ who was born of Mary must be called God, and Mary must be called "the mother of God." This conclusion was in harmony with the adoration of Mary which was increasing at that time. Other things contributed to this same development. It was said, for example, that Mary was untouched by the taint of original sin; it was also held that she remained a virgin throughout her life.

But Nestorius was opposed to the expression θεοτόκος. Mary, he said, gave birth to David's son, in whom the Logos had taken residence. The divine element in Christ was not to be found in His human nature; it was present only because the Logos had united Himself to this man. This union, according to Nestorius, took place at the time of Christ's birth. In saying this, Nestorius contradicted the Dynamic Monarchians, who held that this union was not accomplished until the time of Christ's baptism. Because he felt as he did about these matters, it was impossible for Nestorius to refer to Mary as θεοτόκος. At most, he claimed, one might refer to her as χριστοτόκος (the mother of Christ).

As a result of this, Nestorius was accused of denying the divinity of Christ. If Christ lived and suffered and died only as a man, then the salvation He wrought is of no avail. The older Antiochene theology held that the human element was united to the divine in Christ in a moral, spiritual fashion, so that He was truly one person. But how did Nestorius feel about this? He, too, spoke of Christ as being one person, but he had a tendency to distinguish between the natures in such a way that there was no actual oneness in the person of Christ. He said, for example, "I distinguish between the natures, but I worship but one [Christ]." This does not imply a real unity in Christ Himself. To say "I worship but one [Christ]" rather implies a subjective unity on the part of the believer.

Whether or not it is fully just to say that Nestorius was a heretic, it is nevertheless true that his trend of thought made it difficult to make a clear statement on the unity of Christ's person. The divine and human natures stood starkly side by side. Nestorius can be quoted as saying that certain characteristics and events in Jesus' earthly life were purely human, while in others the divine powers came to the fore. But on the basis of what he believed, it was impossible to express in an adequate manner the simultaneous union of the divine and human elements in Christ.

As we have already noted, Nestorius' chief opponent was Cyril, the patriarch of Alexandria, who was also his competitor for the greatest ecclesiastical power in the Eastern Church. Cyril was a representative of the Alexandrian school of theology, but he was not as one-sided about this as was Apollinaris. He sought, above all, to combine the basic concepts of the Antiochene theology with those that were typically Alexandrian. But he was ruthless in his opposition to Nestorius, and he published a statement against Nestorius which included a dozen anathemas. At the Council of Ephesus his position emerged victorious. It was there that the Alexandrian θεοτόκος concept was accepted, while the Nestorian point of view was rejected.

In contrast to Apollinaris, Cyril emphasized that Christ is completely man, with a human soul. Both natures are found in Him, each retaining its own qualities. With the Antiochenes, Cyril therefore stressed that there are two complete natures in Christ and that they are not changed into or confused with one another.

But in contrast to Nestorius, Cyril insisted that there is a real, substantial union between the two natures in Christ. He rejected the idea of a moral or devotional union. One of his anathemas against Nestorius goes as follows: "He who does not confess that the Logos came forth from God the Father to unite Himself hypostatically with flesh, to form with the flesh *one* Christ, God and man, he shall be damned." If it was not God Himself who appeared in Christ's earthly life, so that God Himself thus suffered and died, He cannot be our Savior. Nestorius' point of view made Christ's true divinity an impossibility, and thereby also salvation through Him.

Cyril described the unity between God and man as a physical or substantial unity. The heart of the matter is found in his words "unity with respect to the hypostasis." This expression may appear to correspond to the doctrine of the personal union, *unio personalis*. But in the writings of Cyril the word "hypostasis" does not denote "person," as in the doctrine of the Trinity; it is rather used as a synonym for *ousia*. This expression, therefore, suggests the same as the words "unity with respect to the essence." What Cyril is trying to say here is that this is a question of a real union, which is implicit in the nature of the matter itself, in Christ Himself, and not simply in our worship of Him. Cyril, in other words, borrowed from Apollinaris, who said, "God's Logos has but one nature, that which became flesh."

Because Cyril asserted, at the same time, that the two natures must retain their separate identity, a contradiction developed within his Christology. He placed the Antiochene teaching of the two distinct natures (complete with an emphasis on Christ's true humanity) side by side with the Alexandrian idea of a physical unity. The same paradox is to be found in the Christological formula which was finally fixed and accepted as definitive, but in Cyril this concept is not as sharply delineated. His point of view has been recognized as fully orthodox, but at the same time it was also possible for the later Monophysites to accept certain of his formulations.

In the doctrinal controversy which preceded the Council of Chalcedon in 451, it was the Nestorian and Cyrillic points of view which constantly contended for domination. A third important element involved in this struggle was the Western Christological position, which was developed by Hilary, Ambrose, and Augustine. Their ideas, and the way in which they were presented, exerted a decisive influence on the eventual formation of the official ecclesiastical point of view. Even Tertullian had spoken of Christ as having two natures in the one person. Western theology developed this concept by saying that it is the Logos who constitutes the person of Christ itself, who took up human nature and united Himself with it and acted through it. Christ, therefore, is but one person, and this person bears the stamp of divine nature. Such ideas are similar to the Alexandrian point of view. At the same time, however, the distinction between the natures was emphasized.

EUTYCHES; THE COUNCIL OF CHALCEDON

Eutyches, who was the archimandrate of a cloister in Constantinople, was in general agreement with the Alexandrian school of theology and was definitely opposed to the Antiochene Christology. He claimed that after Christ became man He had but one nature. His humanity, however, was not of the same essence as ours. On the basis of these beliefs, Eutyches was excommunicated in Constantinople. The matter was finally brought before Pope Leo I. A general synod was called to meet in Ephesus in 449, and it was here, with the assistance of the Alexandrian party, that Eutyches was reinstated into his office. The papal attitude in this matter, which was conveyed in a letter to Bishop Flavian of Constantinople, was not even discussed. This is the synod which is remembered in church history as the "robber synod." It has been given this name because of its stormy proceedings, and it never received recognition as an ecumenical council.

As a sequel to the "robber synod," Pope Leo's above-mentioned letter came to the fore as the center of interest. It was Leo's intention to call into being a new meeting which would undo the decisions taken at Ephesus. Hence it was that another synod was held in 451, this one in Chalcedon. By that time the situation had been altered to the pope's advantage, and his letter served as the basis for the proceedings at Chalcedon. Here it was that the Alexandrian point of view was sharply repudiated, while Leo's Western position was commended. The pope's letter was not expressly approved by the council, however; it rather decided to write a new formula which was clearly Western in tenor. This formula rejected not only Nestorius but also Eutyches, which is to say that it repudiated both pronounced Dyophysitism and pronounced Monophysitism. On the one hand, Chalcedon condemned those who proclaimed "two sons," and on the other, those who assumed that there were "two natures before the union but only one after the union."

The Chalcedonian decision marks the conclusion reached as the result of the various controversies which arose in the early church, and it provides the confessional summary of the thought processes which flourished within the Christological sphere. A glance at a number of the decisive sentences in the formula will reveal how Chalcedon was related to the earlier points of view, and how the different controversies were settled: "We confess one and the same Son [against Nestorius, who so distinguished between David's son and God's Son that he was believed to teach that there were 'two sons'], our Lord Jesus Christ, who is perfect in His divinity [against dynamism, Arius, and Nestorius] and perfect in humanity . . . with a reasonable soul and a body [against Apollinaris, who replaced Christ's human soul with the Logos and taught that the Logos assumed a "heavenly flesh"], of one essence with the Father according to divinity [cf. the Nicene Creed] and of the same essence as we according to humanity [against Eutyches], like us in all things save that He was without sin; who according to His divinity was generated by the Father before all time, and who according to His humanity was born of the Virgin Mary, the mother of God [Cyril vs. Nestorius; cf. Ephesus, 431], for our salvation: one and the same Christ, Son, Lord, Only-begotten, revealed in two natures [the Western Christology] without confusion, without change [against Eutyches — and earlier opinions such as that of Apollinaris], indivisibly, inseparably, the distinction of natures being by no means taken away by the union, the property of each nature being preserved, and concurring in one person and one hypostasis, not parted or divided into two persons, but one and the same Son and only begotten God, Logos, the Lord Jesus Christ."

The significance of the Council of Chalcedon was extremely great. The intention of the decision reached there was to combine the Alexandrian and Antiochene positions. Nestorius was condemned, but none of the other Antiochenes was. Eutyches' teachings were repudiated, but Cyril's were recognized as orthodox. The men gathered at Chalcedon also had a loftier goal in mind: the combining of Eastern and Western points of view in connection with these dogmatic questions. Pope Leo I, who gave the development of Christology a Western touch, exerted a great influence on the decision reached at Chalcedon. Here it was, therefore, that ideas from Rome, Alexandria, and Antioch were combined in a common, orthodox doctrinal formulation.

SEVERUS; MONOPHYSITISM

Long-standing doctrinal controversies arose in the wake of the Council of Chalcedon. These were conditioned in part by political motives, but the theological position sanctioned at Chalcedon also helped to ignite the flames. Numerous groups, particularly in the area of the Eastern Church, opposed certain expressions in the Chalcedonian formula. It was thought that Chalcedon made concessions to Nestorius' teaching of the two persons in Christ and thereby denied the unity of the person of Jesus. Some went so far as to say that the Christ described in the Chalcedonian formula was an "idol with two faces."

As a result of this opposition, the so-called Monophysite school arose, which can be divided into two main groups. One of these represented a more moderate position and deviated but little from the orthodox Christology, even though it refused to recognize the Chalcedonian decision. Its chief spokesman was Severus of Antioch, whose theological position was close to that of Cyril of Alexandria. The formula cited above (p. 97) which states that "God's Logos has but one nature, that which became flesh," was interpreted by Severus in such a way that the word "nature" corresponds more nearly to the hypostasis concept, or "person," than to the Chalcedonian use of "nature" (which signified "essence," or "substance"). As a result, Severus' understanding did not exclude what the church taught concerning two natures. He also held fast to the belief that Christ is true man.

In the other Monophysite branch we find a trend of thought which reminds us of Apollinaris of Laodicea or of the Eutychianism which was rejected by the Council of Chalcedon. Those who upheld this Monophysite position began with the idea that Christ in His manhood could not have the same nature as we; they rather believed that He transmuted His human nature to conform with the divine nature. They were unable, apparently, to do justice to Christ's true humanity without thinking of the flesh as having been deified in one way or another. Thus, according to one theory, Christ's body was glorified and exalted to a state of incorruptibility from the outset of the Incarnation. In other words, Christ's body was the same before the Resurrection as it was after this took place. This point of view, frequently referred to as Incorruptible Docetism, was upheld by Julian of Halikarnassus, among others.

The Monophysites criticized the Chalcedonian decision on the basis that it would be unreasonable to speak of the two natures in Christ and yet maintain that there is but one person, or hypostasis. Nature or essence must also include an independent hypostasis. One could not speak of a perfect human nature without also thinking of it as an independent personal existence. If one assumed that there are two natures, this would imply (said the Monophysites), as a matter of fact, that one also was thinking of two persons.

This criticism had its effect on the interpretation of the Chalcedonian formula. For one thing, in the years that followed there was a tendency to strengthen the emphasis on the unity of Christ's person. Thus it was that the Chalcedonian decision regained its domination; the Monophysite position failed to win the victory. It was nevertheless true, to a certain extent at least, that the problem raised by the Monophysites was not completely resolved. The question still remained: How can a belief in the two natures be combined with a belief in one person, or hypostasis?

LEONTIUS OF BYZANTIUM;
THE MONOTHELITE CONTROVERSY

One answer to the chief problem involved in the Monophysite struggle was provided by Leontius of Byzantium (d. 543). He derived some assistance from the philosophy of Aristotle; in fact, he was one of the first theologians to do this. In his Christology, however, he borrowed the terminology of the three Cappadocians, for the most part, and contributed the idea of the "enhypostasis" as a solution to the contradiction between the Monophysite and Dyophysite points of view.

He began with the old concepts employed in the doctrine of the Trinity, φύσις (= οὐσία) and ὑπόστασις (= πρόσωπον). Φύσις indicates a thing's "beingness" — that it is, and that it is constituted in a certain way. It refers to that which makes a thing what it is. The hypostasis concept denotes that something exists for itself, as an independent subject. These concepts were in current use previously. In the Christological formulation, therefore, Christ was presented as two natures (essences) in one hypostasis (person). The problem, therefore, is this: Can there be a "nature" which is perfect with respect to its own kind and which is nevertheless not an independent hypostasis? Leontius sought to solve this problem by the use of the ἐνυποστασία concept. It is conceivable that there is a nature which does not have an independent existence but rather exists in something else. There is in Christ but one hypostasis, and this is the hypostasis of the Logos, which has existed from eternity and which, in time, took upon itself human nature. Therefore the Logos became the hypostasis of the man Christ as well, so that Christ's human nature has its hypostasis in the Logos. Christ's human nature is not without a hypostasis; it rather has its hypostasis in something other, viz., in the Logos (ἐν-υπόστατος).

This type of Christology suggested an approach to the Monophysite position. It is the Logos which constitutes the person of Christ, which provides the hypostasis even for the human nature. This human nature does have an independent existence, but it is incorporated, so to speak, into the Logos. This does not deny, however, that Christ's human nature is complete, consisting of both body and soul.

This "enhypostasis" theology was endorsed by the Fifth Ecumenical Council (held in Constantinople, 553) and judged to be a correct interpretation of the Chalcedonian decision. As a result of this, the Monophysites obtained a certain degree of support for their views. They still were not satisfied, however, with the solution set forth by Leontius. His position was presented in a purely logical manner, while the Monophysites desired to give expression to a physical union. Subsequent to this, the Monophysites went their own way and organized their own church body, which was found, for the most part, in Syria, Palestine, and Egypt. A number of national churches in the East came to have a Monophysite character: the Armenian, the Syrian-Jacobite, the Egyptian (Coptic), and later the church in Abyssinia. In general it was the more moderate branch of Monophysitism (that represented by Severus) which influenced the churches in these areas.

After the Monophysite controversy had run its course, the so-called Monothelite struggle arose. The major question involved here was this: Does Christ have one will or two? It is worthy of note, in this connection, that the Christological problem (as reflected in this struggle) had moved away from purely metaphysical considerations; concrete psychological factors were now being injected. This did not, however, result in greater clarity. The Monothelites accepted the teaching of the two natures, but they insisted that Christ had but one will — that of the divine Logos. They sought thus to do justice to the psychological unity which characterizes the Biblical picture of Christ. The will, they maintained, belongs to the person and forms one facet of its essence. The Dyothelites said, on the other hand, that such a position came very close to Docetism. If one believes that Christ possesses a complete human nature, this presupposes that He also has a purely human will, just as His divine nature has a divine will. Those who held this position also believed, however, that that divine will dominates and works through the human will, so that there is no gulf between them. Such a point of view was developed by Maximus the Confessor (d. 662) and was accepted by the church at the Sixth Ecumenical Council (also held in Constantinople, 680–81), the so-called Trullan Synod. An attempt was made at this council to combine Dyothelitism with the enhypostasis idea, thus emphasizing the independence of both natures as well as the existence of the human nature *in* the divine. This decision was not clear-cut, however, and it was not recognized by the Reformers of the 16th century.

JOHN OF DAMASCUS

The Christological position of the early church attained a degree of completeness in the work of John of Damascus, who lived in the eighth century (the years of his birth and death are unknown). More than anyone else, he summarized the tradition which subsequently became the norm in the Greek Orthodox Church. He also exerted a profound influence in the West. John reechoed the theology of the early church fathers and presented it in a standardized form with the assistance of the philosophical apparatus he employed. His magnum opus is entitled *The Source of Knowledge*, and it consists of three different parts. The first section is dialectic in form and discusses nothing but the philosophical questions; the second section deals with heresy; while the third is the dogmatic section, "An Exposition of the Orthodox Faith." This last section eventually came to serve as the dogmatic norm of the Greek Church.

John was well acquainted with Aristotelian and Neoplatonic philosophy, and he borrowed concepts and thought forms from both. These were used as the foundation of his theological system. In other words, he employed a scholastic methodology; he was the first to do so in the field of dogmatics. For the most part he collected the ideas of the past and gave them a more specific form without pretending to be original. His scholastic adaptations are his chief contribution. In the extended presentation of his Christological position he associated himself with Leontius of Byzantium and Maximus the Confessor.

John of Damascus strongly emphasized the unity of the person of Christ: "The hypostasis of God's Logos is perpetually one." This one hypostasis is, at the same time, the hypostasis of the Logos and of the human soul and body. He believed, in other words, that the human nature exists in the divine and does not have an independent personal existence.

At the same time John also emphasized the difference between the two natures and assumed the Dyothelite point of view. He gave careful consideration to the question of the relationship of the two natures to one another and contributed some new ideas in this area. Because of the unity of the person, a "mutual penetration" takes place, by which the Logos takes up the human nature and then imparts His qualities to it. Thus it can be said, for example, that "the Lord of glory" was crucified or, on the other hand, that the man Jesus is uncreated and infinite. In this way both natures retain their uniqueness and distinction.

John also gave very strong expression to something which at times would seem to contradict what he said about the idea of "mutual penetration." For he went on record as believing that it was the divine nature alone which penetrated the human, and not vice versa. He did this to give point to the fact that divinity, as such, must remain unchanged, untouched by suffering and death. The rays of the sun which shine upon a tree are not affected by the fact that the tree is cut down. So it is with God; He is above the suffering which Christ experienced. If one asks about the natures in an abstract sense (as "divinity" and "humanity"), they must be sharply distinguished; the divine does not become human, the human does not become divine. But if one looks upon Christ as an actual person, the unity of the natures is apparent. He is wholly and completely God and at the same time wholly and completely man — as far as the identity and unity of His person are concerned. That which accomplishes this unity, therefore, is the hypostasis of the Word, which also becomes the hypostasis of the human nature manifested in Christ. The picture of Christ which we find in the scholastic formulations of John of Damascus is also reflected, in a way, in the iconography of the Orthodox Church, in which our Lord's transcendent and majestic qualities clearly shine forth.

The role of symbolism is consistent with the degree to which the absolute transcendence of divinity is emphasized. It was not sheer coincidence that the theology of John of Damascus came to the defense of the "worship of pictures" (this did not imply worship in its true sense; it rather suggested adoration and veneration). Symbols serve to mediate divinity; they are accessible to the senses and represent that which is invisible, heavenly. Pictures do, in a real sense, represent the divine, and as such they might become the object of adoration. After a long struggle between the opposing parties in the Eastern (Byzantine) Church (some were strongly opposed to the adoration of pictures), it was decided at the Council of Nicaea in 787 that this practice was acceptable (see below, p. 153).

CHAPTER 10

The Development of the Concept of the Church

As we have seen, theology in general took form in the struggle with heretical or divergent points of view. And so it was with the concept of the church; it developed, in part at least, as a result of opposition from Gnosticism and other foreign schools of thought.

The development which took place in this area during the first period of church history signified that a more distinct pattern of ecclesiastical organization was emerging and also that ideas designed to justify and support this external consolidation of congregational life were being brought to perfection. At the same time different conceptions of the church's essence, its holiness, and its relation to the external organization were contending with one another.

Ignatius, who was put to death by the Romans early in the second century, emphasized the importance of the episcopal office as the rallying force within the church. The Gnostics, with their false teachings, threatened to destroy the faith and unity of the church. Therefore the faithful were called upon to close ranks around the bishops, who succeeded the apostles as the leaders of the congregations. The bishops assumed this position because they represented the apostolic tradition and thereby guaranteed purity of doctrine and an unbroken connection with the apostles. It is by divine ordinance that each congregation is united under a single head, as the apostles were united around Christ. The church is one, holy, and universal because it preserves the true apostolic tradition. And this unity is embodied in the bishops. Another idea attributed to Ignatius is that the unity of the church is explained by the fact that it is the one and only administrator of the means of grace. The sacraments constitute the church as well as the Word, the pure teaching, and these make it necessary for the faithful to hold together around the episcopal office. Other theologians expressed these same ideas, which represent the early Eastern tradition (e. g., Irenaeus).

The Roman concept of the church, on the other hand, was developed later and chiefly on Western soil. The question of the church assumed a central position in the West, too, but for a different reason than in the East. The development of the church concept in the West was conditioned by and joined together with a number of different problems relative to both ecclesiastical theory and practice. The Roman concept took form as the result of long-standing discussions concerning such matters as penance, the holiness of the church, and the validity of heretical baptism.

The basic aspects of the theory and practice of *penance* which characterized the early church reappeared in the writings of Tertullian. It must be pointed out that this concept of penance is different from that which is held by Protestants. The older Protestant tradition described penance as the work of Law and Gospel, whereby man is crushed by the Law and raised up by the Gospel. Penance was thus defined in terms of contrition and faith. As Tertullian saw it, penance is the way for man to regain peace with God. God becomes angry with the sinner, and He punishes sin according to His norm of justice. But in His grace He has made it possible for man to receive forgiveness and to live again in a right relationship with God. This "way out" is the act of penance, which is looked upon, to a certain degree, as a work of merit, appeasing the wrath of God. It consists of contrition, confession, and satisfaction. The first penance is associated with Baptism, which is a confirmation of the forgiveness of sin. After they are baptized, Christians are to avoid obvious sins. If they should fall, however, they can be restored on the strength of a second act of penance. It was thought that there could be but one more act of penance subsequent to baptism. Originally Tertullian held that a second penance might be possible even for mortal sins, but when he became a Montanist he insisted that those who committed mortal sin after baptism could not perform an act of penance. In fact, it was the lax position of the church on this problem that prompted Tertullian to join the Montanists.

The thorniest problem related to the practice of penance had to do with the possibility of a second act of penance. Penance was compared by some to a plank in the water which Christians, after making shipwreck of their faith, could take hold of. But others adopted the stricter view of Tertullian and held that penance for such mortal sins as idolatry, murder, and adultery was excluded.

It was in this situation that Bishop Calixtus of Rome (217–22) issued an ordinance which permitted a second penance even in cases of mortal sin. In view of the fact that Christ had mercy on the adulteress, he felt that the clergy could continue to give absolution for grave sins (though not for murder and idolatry). Calixtus claimed that the bishops had the right to assume responsibility for the practice of penance and to make the necessary related decisions. Penance came to be looked upon, therefore, as something over which the church had jurisdiction, and it was placed in the hands of the bishops.

But Calixtus was opposed by Tertullian and Hippolytus, both of whom demanded a stricter interpretation. They said that only God could forgive sins, and they rejected the opinion that the bishops (as the successors of Peter) had such power. The older, original tradition is reflected in this criticism by those who opposed the embryonic hierarchical tendencies and sought at the same time to maintain a more rigorous concept of penance.

It was Cyprian, bishop of Carthage (d. 258), who continued to develop the doctrine of penance and to lay the foundation for the Roman concept of the church. The Decian persecution of the middle of the third century brought a serious problem to the fore in this connection: Could those who fell away under the pressure of persecution be received back into the church again? Those who were able to produce a statement from a fellow church member who remained firm in the faith and yet escaped death (the so-called "confessors") were received back into congregational fellowship. The confessors were accorded a special place in the church at that time; it was thought that the Holy Spirit dwelt within them to an unusual degree. This custom threatened to degenerate, and Cyprian asserted that the bishops alone were in a position to render judgment in such matters. Arbitrary decisions, arrived at without episcopal consent, could do harm to the church. The authority of the law and ecclesiastical ordinances took precedence over the purely spiritual authority of the martyrs.

Prominent among those who opposed Cyprian was Novatian in Rome. He insisted on a stricter practice of penance and did not wish to receive back into the church those who had fallen away. As Novatian saw it, the church was to be composed of those who were, without question, holy. The holiness of the church was to be found not only in the sacraments but also in the holiness of its members. He finally broke away from the church, but the organization he founded never became very significant.

A synod of bishops in Carthage accepted Cyprian's point of view as the correct one. It was agreed here that the bishops had the right to decide whether or not the lapsed should be readmitted into the church and be given absolution. It was in connection with this question that Cyprian developed his doctrine of the church. The new element in his thought is not to be found in what he said about penance; it is rather this, that he assigned a higher authority to the bishops than to the confessors and thereby contributed powerfully to the centralization of the church around the episcopal office. Cyprian could see no difference between the authority of this office and that of the Holy Spirit; to him, the bishops are the bearers of the Spirit. Spirit and office belong together, and those who are truly spiritual will subordinate themselves to those in the episcopal office. Cyprian looked upon this office as the basis of the church.

Cyprian also supported the hierarchical tendency which conceived of the *Lord's Supper* as a sacrificial act, with the bishop offering the sacrifice to God in place of Christ.

The bishop, therefore, stands at the head of the congregation as Christ's representative. Cyprian also believed, in consequence of the foregoing, that each congregation should have but one bishop, inasmuch as this office represents the unity of the church. "There is one man for the time priest in the church, and for the time judge in the stead of Christ" (Epistle 59 [54], 5). He did not mean by this that one bishop could dominate all of the others; he simply meant that each congregation was to be united under a single bishop. The whole of the church of Christ is to be found in each congregation. As it turned out, however, his ideas contributed to the assumption of "primacy" on the part of the bishops of Rome. This claim began to be made in Cyprian's era, and it subsequently resulted in the papal doctrine — that the pope is the vicar of Christ on earth.

Cyprian looked upon Peter as the symbol of the church's unity (cf. Matt. 16:18). But he also felt that the other apostles possessed the same degree of authority. And in opposing those who asserted the Roman primacy, he referred (among other things) to Gal. 2, where we are told that Paul stood up to Peter and rebuked him.

But one of Cyprian's contemporaries, Bishop Stephen of Rome (254–57), concluded that the bishop of Rome, who was the successor of Peter, the chief apostle, thereby had supremacy over all of the other bishops. He assumed this power for himself and dramatized his claim by demanding obedience from the other bishops and by personally appointing bishops in Gaul and Spain. He claimed "the chair of Peter" on the ground of succession, and he spoke of the "primacy" of the bishop of Rome.

Cyprian and others opposed this claim, but Stephen won out. Cyprian believed that the bishop was supreme in the church; not, however, simply on the strength of an external succession but also as the bearer of the Spirit. The bishop represented the church, and all Christians were to subject themselves to this office. Those who were outside this fellowship could not be Christian, even if they were martyrs or otherwise renowned for their faith, "because there is no salvation outside of the church" (Epistle 73 [72], 21) and because "He who does not have the church as his mother cannot have God as his Father." (*De ecclesiae unitate*, 6)

The validity of the baptism given by heretics was another question of significance in this connection. Were those baptized by heretics properly baptized, or should they be rebaptized if they returned to the fellowship of the church? Different opinions prevailed within Christendom. Cyprian concluded, on the basis of his concept of the church, that the baptism given by heretics was not valid and that persons so baptized should be rebaptized upon returning to the church. The spirit of regeneration, which Baptism confers, can be provided only by the bishop who possesses the gifts of the Spirit. A heretical baptism is not a work of the Spirit; it is a "sordid and profane dipping." (Epistle 73 [72], 6)

Stephen of Rome, and others, held a contradictory point of view. They felt that baptism given by a heretic is valid, provided it is done in the name of the Triune God. The use of water and Christ's words of institution are the essentials of Baptism. Where Christ's name and water are used, the baptismal act is effective, regardless of the attitude of the one who performs the rite.

In the one case, the emphasis was placed on the Spirit-emphasized episcopacy as the church's unifying element; in the other, on the institution and the office as such. This latter position was more agreeable to the concept of the church which gradually became dominant. The question of heretical baptism arose later on in a different context — in the struggle between Augustine and the Donatists.

CHAPTER 11

Augustine

GENERAL COMMENT

Augustine's name has a place not only in the history of dogma but also in the general history of culture. In addition to theology, the fields of philosophy, literature, church government, and juridics have also been influenced by his writings.

Better than any other "Latin," Augustine summarized the culture of antiquity and blended this heritage with Christian theology. He brought about, therefore, a synthesis of the philosophical heritage of antiquity and Christianity, but he also contributed something new and distinctive from out of his own personality. At the same time that he was deeply anchored in antiquity and the Christian tradition, he also exercised a creative impact upon both theology and philosophy. He represented a culture that was passing away — the Roman — but at the same time his ideas served as a basis for the age that was coming. In the centuries that followed, theologians have continued to wrestle with the problems Augustine set forth, to cultivate his ideas, or to use his work as source material. Both scholastic and mystic, both papal church politics and the reform tendencies of the Middle Ages found seminal suggestions in the thought world of Augustine of Hippo.

The first thing to do in this connection is to try to understand Augustine's basic concept of Christianity, together with his significance in the development of the history of dogma.

Augustine's theological position was linked up with that of the early church, which he brought to completion — at least as far as the "Western" portion is concerned. He assembled and articulated the Christian tradition. But at the same time he also contributed something new.

As seen from the philosophical point of view, Augustine was a Neo-platonist. This school of thought exerted a decisive influence on him, and he never ceased to present his Christian beliefs in categories derived from it. He related Christianity to the ideas of his own period, which were colored to a large extent by Neoplatonism. As perceived in a formal sense, Augustine's theology is a synthesis of Neoplatonic and Christian thought forms, and the basic concept which characterizes his theology bears the imprint of this synthesis.

Augustine was a man of the West, and the most prominent facets of his theology are those which are found at the center of Western theology. The question of the church as well as the anthropological questions, for example, were answered by Augustine in such a way that his answers became basic to theological thought in the centuries that followed — and this was true even when Augustine's position was not completely accepted.

There are four different elements in Augustine's theology which are of particular interest in this context. These are his doctrine of the Trinity (treated above), his basic concept of Christianity (Neoplatonism and Christianity), his doctrine of the church (developed in his struggle with Donatism), and his doctrine of sin and grace (developed in his struggle with Pelagius).

AUGUSTINE'S PERSONAL DEVELOPMENT

In order to understand Augustine's theology, it is important to know something about the course of his life and his inner development, which influenced the formation of his position. The best source of information is his well-known book *Confessions,* written about the year 400.

Augustine was born in Tagaste, Numidia, in 354. His father was a pagan, but his mother was a Christian, so he was introduced to Christianity at an early age. He was sent to Carthage in 371 to be educated. While there he lived a completely worldly existence until he read Cicero's *Hortensius,* which created a love of philosophy within him. A desire for truth replaced the desire for wealth and fame. In later years he recognized this change of mind as a step on the way to Christianity. "O truth, truth, how ardently my soul sighed for thee from this time!" From the very beginning it was to some extent clear to Augustine that the truth could not be reached apart from Christ. What prevented him from believing was the unphilosophical and (as he saw it) barbarous language of the Bible. Neither could he bring himself to submit to the authority of the Bible, which faith presupposes.

A short time after the above-mentioned incident Augustine joined with the Manichaeans, a sect which was fairly widespread in Africa. This group, which was founded by a Persian, Mani, in the third century, had much in common with Gnosticism. But its dualism was even more radical; it was not simply a dualism between God and the world, but above all between God and evil. Evil was thought of by the Manichaeans as an original principle side by side with God, an independent power which limited God's dominion and against which God struggled. Their system of salvation is reminiscent of the Gnostic plan, and in general this provided Manichaeism with a comprehensive, speculative explanation of the world. Manichaeism was also characterized by a strict, ascetic code of ethics, which often devolved into the exact opposite — libertinism — among its members. Augustine was attracted to Manichaeism by its rational explanation of the world, as well as by its ascetic code, which temporarily provided a solution to his problems. But the deceitfulness of the Manichaean position became progressively more obvious to him, and after 9 years he departed its ranks.

In that same year, 383, Augustine went across the sea to Italy. He lived in Milan, where he came in contact with the famous theologian and churchman Ambrose, who exerted a decisive influence on him. Ambrose was a representative of the Western theological position, but he had also been deeply impressed by the theology of the East, as well as by Greek philosophy. Among other things, he had appropriated the allegorical method of interpretation from Philo and Origen. This method came to have great significance for Augustine, inasmuch as it enabled him to set aside some of the passages of Scripture which he found objectionable. In his preaching, Ambrose strongly emphasized the Pauline concept of justification through the forgiveness of sins, and this too was of great significance for Augustine.

First of all, however, Augustine turned to Neoplatonism. It was largely this school of thought which led him away from Manichaeism. The Neoplatonic concept of God was diametrically opposed to the Manichaean concept. The former viewed God as the absolute, the unchangeably good, elevated above all change, the source of all that is. Such a view was incompatible with the idea that evil is an independent principle and with the assumption that God struggled with evil and would be to that extent changeable, exposed to the variations of existence. Evil cannot be something independent, a creative and effective principle. In the Neoplatonic context, evil was thought of as a negative quality, nonbeing, lacking the good. Augustine accepted this definition of evil, and it formed the background of his diagnosis of the nature of sin. The impact of Neoplatonic thought upon Augustine is clearly presented in this passage from his *Confessions:* "But having then read those books of the Platonists, and thence been taught to search for incorporeal truth, I saw Thy invisible things, understood by those things that are made. . . . Then I was sure that Thou art, and art infinite . . . and that Thou truly art, who art the same ever, varying in no part or motion; and that all other things are from Thee, on this most sure ground alone, that they are. . . . And afterwards, when my spirits were subdued through Thy Bible . . . I learned to distinguish between presumption and confession — between those who saw whither they were to go, yet saw not the way, and the way that leads not only to behold but to dwell in the blessed country." (VII, 20)

As it turned out, however, it was a passage from Paul's Letter to the Romans which destroyed the last vestiges of resistance and facilitated Augustine's conversion to Christianity. These were the decisive words: "Let us conduct ourselves becomingly as in the day, not in reveling and drunkenness, not in debauchery and licentiousness, not in quarreling and jealousy. But put on the Lord Jesus Christ, and make no provision for the flesh, to gratify its desires." (13:13-14)

These words impelled Augustine to depart from his worldly ways; they directed his desire toward the transcendental, not for temporal advantage but in order that he might understand and behold God. His will was broken, but it became whole again as a result.

Augustine's conversion meant that he had to give up his ambition to become a famous rhetorician. Formerly he was held in thrall by worldly desires, but this now eased, and his thoughts were turned to spiritual things. At the same time, he submitted to the teachings and the authority of the church. It was faith in Christ which made the transcendental a living reality to Augustine.

After his conversion, Augustine and a few other faithful Christians retired to a place called Cassiciacum, outside of Milan, and after some time he was baptized there in 387. In the following year he returned to Carthage. While he was on the way, his mother died — an event which affected him for a long time.

After living in Carthage for a number of years, Augustine was elected to serve as presbyter in the church at Hippo. Later he became bishop in this same city (395). And there he stayed until his death, which took place when the Vandals invaded the area and laid siege to Hippo in 430.

Many interpretations of the meaning of Augustine's conversion have been given. A number of Protestant researchers, including Harnack, have claimed that his conversion did not signify a break with his former position. They feel that he remained a Platonist even after his conversion. Such postconversion writings as his *Soliloquies* are cited as evidence. On the basis of this book (written at Cassiciacum), the significance of his conversion has been minimized — which is quite the opposite of what Augustine himself says of this experience. Catholic researchers support the claim made in the *Confessions* and point to the conversion as a genuine transformation, as a result of which Augustine came to possess the Christian faith and submitted to the teachings of the church. As a result of the investigations of Nörregaard and Holl, the latter interpretation is now commonly accepted. Holl has shown that Augustine's philosophical studies, which he obviously continued after his conversion, then had a different orientation.

AUGUSTINE'S BASIC CONCEPT OF CHRISTIANITY

In his *Confessions* Augustine describes his pilgrimage to the Christian faith. He tells how he wandered, blindly, on the paths of error. All the while, however, he was subject to the drawing power of grace and was more and more attracted by the love of truth, until finally, through his conversion, this love became permanent and his desires were directed toward spiritual reality. Prior to this, he was able only to glimpse the truth in the distance, and his love for it was too evanescent to enable him to overcome his love for the world. The kaleidoscopic nature of secular interests held him captive and exerted a divisive influence upon his desires. He knew no peace until he came to have faith in Christ, until he submitted to Scriptural truth. Only then did he find that for which he had been groping in vain. This was the experience Augustine summarized in these well-known words: "Thou hast made us for Thyself, and our hearts are restless till they find rest in Thee." (*Fecisti nos ad te et inquietum est cor nostrum, donec requiescat in te. Confessions,* I, 1)

As we have already noted, Augustine did submit to the authority of the church and did acccept the teachings of Scripture subsequent to his conversion. His baptism and his choice of a new way of life testify to the decisive nature of this change. In his writings, however, we can see a certain amount of continuity; what he wrote after his conversion is to some extent related to what he wrote before. Even the things he wrote immediately after his conversion (the *Soliloquies*, e. g.) are obviously influenced by Neoplatonism. As time went on, he did turn more and more to the Christian tradition, but he never broke completely with Neoplatonism (as he did, for example, with Manichaeism). As he saw it, Christianity and Neoplatonism were not mutually exclusive. He rather believed that Neoplatonic ideas had enabled him to find the way to Christianity and to understand its profoundest implications. As a result, the fundamentals of his theological position were always in part determined by Neoplatonic presuppositions.

Augustine's basic attitude toward philosophical speculation did, however, alter after his conversion. Prior to this, philosophy had held out to Augustine the possibility of finding the truth via rational means, through the use of speculation. After his conversion Augustine understood the relationship between theology and philosophy in accordance with the formula, "I believe in order that I may understand" *(credo ut intelligam)*. Submission to authority now held first place in his life. He no longer held that philosophical speculation was the way to the goal. He now believed that one could truly come to know God only by faith, by accepting revealed truth. He did not thereby conclude, however, that the possibility of considering faith in rational terms was precluded; he felt that the truth of faith could also be the object of comprehension, at least to some extent. But philosophical thought no longer enjoyed pride of place in Augustine's life; it had been replaced by faith and by submission to the authority of Scripture.

For Augustine, logical thought based on faith (the *intelligere*) and related to submission to the teachings of the church took the form of a synthesis between Christianity and Neoplatonism. As he saw it, these two were in harmony with each other; they were not mutually exclusive. That is not to say that Augustine looked upon Neoplatonism as a religion on the same level as Christianity. Quite the contrary; he considered the latter the only source of truth. But they were related in his mind in the sense that Christianity alone can provide the proper answers to the questions posed by Neoplatonism or philosophy in general. Philosophers seek the truth, but they cannot find it. They recognize the goal, but they don't know the way that leads to it. So when Christianity provides its answers to the deep questions asked by philosophy (the only valid answers to be found), it finds itself in a bifurcated relationship to philosophy. On the one hand, the attitude of faith reveals the falseness of philosophy by exposing its emptiness, its inability to satisfy man's deepest longings. On the other hand, Christianity accepts the questions raised by philosophy, and thereby recognizes the basic attitude toward life which is characteristic of philosophy. This bifurcation is typical of Augustine's understanding of Christianity. On the one hand, he acknowledged the truth of revelation and the Christian tradition in opposition to reason and philosophy. On the other, he presented Christianity in the categories implicit in the philosophical presuppositions which he accepted. Augustine created a synthesis which involved both Christian and Neoplatonic elements in mutual interaction. These lines of thought can be isolated and distinguished one from the other, but in Augustine's mind they formed a unitary point of view, simultaneously Christian and Platonic.

Neoplatonism taught that the most elementary tendency to be found in man is his search for happiness, and it is this idea, above all, which connects Augustine with it. As he saw it, the basic presupposition of all human striving is to be found in man's concentration upon an objective which promises to bring him certain benefits. "We certainly all wish to live happily." (*De moribus ecclesiae catholicae*, I, 3, 4)

Furthermore, Augustine desired to prove that this concentration of the human will is not simply confined to casual and temporal goals. What man longs for above all other things is the highest good *(summum bonum)*, and even though he might satisfy his desire for temporal advantages, this will not satisfy him completely. This is revealed by the fact that man is constantly directing his attention toward new goals. He is not satisfied with that which is only partly good, which offers values of an inferior variety. That which fully corresponds to human destiny and toward which his deepest aspirations are directed must be the highest good, something of absolute worth, not qualified by anything higher. Augustine also believed that if a man strives for and reaches a certain level of achievemant, his longing will not be stilled, for he must always live in fear of losing what he has gained. For the

119

good he has won is changeable and perishable. Only what is enduringly and unchangeably good can satisfy the heart of man. And it is God alone who is such a *summum et incommutabile bonum.* Hence there is in all men a natural longing for God, the highest good. This desire expresses itself even in perverted forms of love. "God, who is loved by everything that is able to love, either knowingly or unknowingly. . . ." (*Soliloquies,* I, 1, 2)

There is a eudemonism in Augustine, but it is not the philosophical eudemonism which holds that the satisfaction of desire or the fulfillment of one's own pleasure is the loftiest goal. According to Augustine, the loftiest goal is union with the highest good, with something transcendent, not to be found in the human sphere. "For me the good is to cling to God" (Sermon 156, 7). The vision of God is the supreme objective. When all of one's spiritual powers are directed toward God and eternity, then it is that one's mind is properly disposed, that one's soul can experience peace and clarity. This kind of love is the highest command, which embraces all the others. "Love, and do what you will." (*Dilige, et quod vis, fac. In epistolam Joannis,* VII, 8)

Augustine distinguished between love for the highest good, *caritas,* and love for the world — the desire, that is, which seeks the good in the temporal. This later came to be known as *cupiditas.* These are related to each other as good and evil. *Caritas* is the only true form of love; *cupiditas* is a false, perverted form. It can be said, therefore, that the power of desire is itself the same in both cases. In the natural man it is directed toward the world, toward the sensual and the variable. When conversion takes place, this striving is replaced; the Christian man is directed toward the heavenly and eternal. His life has been changed by the fact that his love for God has been awakened, and this love gradually overcomes his love of the world.

Augustine thought of love (*amor*) particularly as that which coincides with man's inner will. This might either be directed upward towards God and the eternal (*ascendit*), or downward (*descendit*) towards that which is subject to the will — creation, the temporal order. The former is *caritas,* the latter *cupiditas.* Man can attain his destiny and come to know peace only after his love is wholly directed towards God. In one passage Augustine compares love (*amor*) to a stream of water which, instead of running down into a sewer where it can do no good, ought to be sprayed on the garden to refresh all that is there. As

120

he understood it, the element of striving is essentially the same in both *caritas* and *cupiditas*. The love which is lavished on the things of the world ought to be directed towards God instead, for He is the highest good, the enduring good.

It might appear, in the light of this, as though man should break his relationship with the world and devote himself exclusively to that which is eternal. Such, however, is not the case. Augustine did place a high estimate on a life of seclusion, and he gladly conceived of the religious relationship as an intimate fellowship of the soul with God — a vision of God which is a foretaste of eternal blessedness. But Augustine did not disdain life in this world in itself. It is only when the temporal is given first place in a man's heart that it becomes objectionable. God's creation is good, and man has been put here to care for the gifts God has made available to us. But how then is man's position in the world related to his fellowship with God? Augustine answered that question by drawing a distinction between *uti* and *frui*, to use and to enjoy. Even that which is created can be the object of love in its own way, but man must not find his ultimate goal therein. These things should only be used as means in the service of the higher form of love. God alone should be the object of that love which rests, without question, in the loved one. Such love is perpetual absorption in God — *fruitio Dei*. The difference between *frui* and *uti* is the difference between loving because of a thing itself *(diligere propter se)* and loving because of something else *(diligere propter aliud)*.

Man's life can be compared to a pilgrim's journey to the fatherland. The goal of his wanderings is that land which alone offers him true joy. In his journey he must use ships and wagons to reach his goal. If he were to search for his joy in the pleasures of the journey, that which ought merely be a means would thereby become the goal. In the same way, the world in which the Christian lives should be used, but it must not become the object of joy. That love which uses the things of the world but finds its true joy nowhere but in the heavenly fatherland, is *caritas*. That love which seeks for satisfaction in the world, by using God as a means of temporal enjoyment, is *cupiditas*. "The good use the world that they may enjoy God; the wicked, on the contrary, wish to use God that they may enjoy the world." (*The City of God*, XV, 7)

The distinction between *uti* and *frui* provided the basis for a comprehensive system respecting man's deportment vis-à-vis God and the world. This is thought of as being arranged according to a scale of values where everything has the place it deserves, depending on its own value and depending on its nearness to or distance from that which is of absolute value. Love is to be adjusted according to this scale of values, and thus becomes an *ordinata dilectio.* A well-ordered love is one which loves God as He deserves, and loves the world only because of its relation to the highest good, only because it is a means of attaining to that which is of supreme value.

Augustine did not thereby deny, however, that the creation, too, could be the object of love. But such love must be adjusted according to the value of the thing in question, which is determined not by what it does for us here but by the fact that it points ahead to the highest good. Even self-love *(amor sui)* has its place according to Augustine. For when we are told, "You shall love your neighbor as yourself," this suggests that man is also to love himself. Augustine introduced this idea into the *dilectio ordinata* doctrine. One should love his own life according to its worth in the scale of value.

But the *amor sui* concept also meant other things to Augustine. It might be used as a synonym for love in general, inasmuch as all love is basically *amor sui* — a concentration upon one's own welfare or upon the highest destiny. It was in this sense that Augustine said that proper self-love is to love God and deny oneself.

But *amor sui* can also be used to designate a false kind of self-love, in which man seeks only his own pleasure, and loves himself instead of God. Such love is one facet of human *cupiditas,* and as such it is opposed to the true form of love. In Augustine's writings, therefore, *amor sui* can be understood in three different ways: as legitimate, "well-ordered" self-love; as concentration upon the highest destiny (in this sense the term is synonymous with *amor Dei*); or as a false self-love.

The decisive contrast is to be found between *caritas* and *cupiditas.* As a created being, man is obliged to seek for his good outside of himself. In his corrupt condition, he seeks for it in the world, in temporal things and pleasures. Sin is precisely this, that the deepest concentration of the human will is diverted from God to the world, so that man loves the creation instead of the Creator. The change which takes place in conversion is that *cupiditas,* the improper love of the world, is transformed into *caritas.* Such a man is saturated with the love of God.

Man is unable to bring about this change by himself. He is captive to his desire for temporal good. If the love of God is to be awakened within him, it must come to him from the outside as a gift. It must be "infused" into him *(infusio caritatis)*, an expression which Augustine derived from Rom. 5:5: "God's love has been poured into our hearts through the Holy Spirit, who has been given to us." Man can overcome his love of the world only after the love of God has been given to him.

Did Augustine understand this infusion of love in a physical sense, as the conferring of a power? He has been interpreted in this way, chiefly by the liberal school of theology, which generally proceeds on the basis of the physical-ethical antithesis. But this conclusion is not correct. Grace and love are poured into man's life, but this is done through the Holy Spirit, not in any magical way. In fact, it can be said that the *caritas* which is bestowed on man is coincident with the Holy Spirit. It is God who gives Himself to man, and it is through His presence that man is filled with the kind of love which enables him to overcome evil desires.

In later Roman Catholic theology this infused grace is conceived of as an inner power, which is conferred through the sacraments. As a result, this is frequently thought of as a magical, supernatural occurrence. But it cannot be said that the personal, ethical way of looking at things is lacking in the writings of Augustine. Grace is looked upon as a real transforming power, and this power is God Himself, the Spirit who is given through faith in Christ.

The Incarnation was necessary for salvation. The Cross of Christ tells us that God debased Himself even to death for man's sake. It is this alone which can break human pride *(superbia)*. Pride holds us captive in ourselves, and this is the cause of our misfortune and unhappiness. Nothing can break these bonds except the humility of Christ, which provides us with an example and a remedy for our *superbia.*

Augustine brought two lines of thought together into a synthesis: salvation results from God's work, His prevenient grace, and His coming down to us in the incarnation of Christ; this is the one major idea. The other is characterized by the *caritas-cupiditas* dialectic: the striving after the highest good, which is hidden in every man. This striving is corrupted by an improper love of the world and the self, and it must, as a result, be redirected to its highest goal and so find satisfaction in the

Christian love of God. Thus it was that Augustine combined a basic Neoplatonic concept (the *eros* doctrine) with the Christian doctrine of salvation in an attempt to provide answers to man's deepest questions and at the same time to summarize the content of the Christian Gospel. (Cf. Anders Nygren's *Eros and Agape,* trans. Philip S. Watson [London: SPCK, 1953], II, 449–562)

AUGUSTINE'S DOCTRINE OF THE CHURCH

With respect to the doctrine of the church, Augustine continued to develop the Western tradition which had originated, above all, with Cyprian. It has been possible to interpret Augustine's position in a variety of ways. This can be illustrated by the fact that both the hierarchical concept and the antipapal tendencies of the Middle Ages found support in Augustine's ecclesiology.

What prompted Augustine to develop his concept of the church more carefully was the Donatist controversy, which had had a divisive influence on the church in North Africa ever since the end of the third century. It might be said that Donatism was the first significant "free church" movement. Some of its ideas are remindful of Cyprian and Novatian (see above), as well as of the more ancient separatist tendencies.

This schism, which took its name from Donatus the Great, bishop of Carthage (d. 332), began during the Diocletian persecution. Certain practical questions related to the persecution formed the basis of the difficulty. For example: should copies of the Scriptures be surrendered to the heathen? The stricter party said no, that the Scriptures should not be so surrendered. Others took a milder view and said that such an action could not be called treachery. But when this latter opinion was injected into an episcopal election in Carthage, the opposing group rallied their forces and elected their own bishop. The schism continued from that point, and eventually the entire church in North Africa was divided. At times more than half of the bishops in that area belonged to the Donatist party. Donatus was one of the bishops of Carthage who upheld the stricter point of view.

Originally this controversy also involved a personal question: a bishop of Carthage had been consecrated by one who had surrendered the Scriptures during a period of persecution. The stricter party was of the opinion that such an act was invalid. Subsequently the controversy was expanded to include the question of valid baptism, of the holiness of the church, etc. The Donatists formed their own church body, which they held to be the only true church. This group grew extensively in North Africa, but only there. Augustine, too, became involved in this controversy. In a series of writings he refuted the Donatist point of view and went so far as to say that the secular powers ought to assist in forcing the Donatists back into the church. Discussions were held with the Donatists in Carthage in the year 411, and from that point on the movement began to diminish in numbers and influence. Finally it died out altogether. But essentially the same attitude as that held by the Donatists has come up time after time in the history of the church. Sectarian or free-church points of view are generally based on a Donatistic ecclesiology. For this reason the struggle between Augustine and the Donatists is of great significance also from the point of view of principle.

The Donatists perpetuated the old pneumatic tradition: the only valid incumbents are those who possess the gifts of the Spirit. Like Cyprian, they associated the office and the Spirit, and concluded that the bishop's office possesses the gifts of the Spirit. They recognized as true bishops only those who demonstrated by their blameless lives and their gifts that they were bearers of the Spirit. This position, in itself, need not have given rise to a schism. But later on it was also concluded that the pastoral acts of an unworthy bishop are invalid. Those ordained by such a man could not, as a result, be true bishops. Those baptized by an unworthy, heretical incumbent are not properly baptized, inasmuch as such pastors do not have the gifts of the Spirit. Donatism therefore represented a point of view which used to be called *theologia regenitorum:* the spiritual influence of (for example) the sacraments was thought to depend on the holiness of the officiating clergy. (The opposite: *theologia irregenitorum)*

The position of the Donatists as reflected in the above-mentioned practical questions was related to their concept of the church. They conceived of the church as a fellowship of saints. And inasmuch as the existing church tolerated hypocrites and those who had once fallen away or had a milder view about penance, it was necessary to sever connections with this church. The Donatists insisted that those who left the existing church to affiliate with their own organization had to be rebaptized. Only the ordination given by approved bishops was held to be valid. Like Cyprian, the Donatists emphasized the importance of the

Spirit-filled episcopacy, but since they also agreed with Novatian in thinking of the church as a fellowship of pure saints, they became separatistic.

One of Augustine's predecessors in the fight against Donatism was Optatus of Mileve, to whom he dedicated one of his polemical writings. In a number of writings produced around the year 400 (e. g., *De baptismo*), Augustine set forth his major ideas on the question of the church and the sacraments in opposition to Donatistic doctrines.

The chief problem in this controversy had to do with the validity of baptism and ordination. As noted above, the Donatists insisted on rebaptizing those who joined their church. They argued, in this connection, that only one who was truly holy could provide a valid and effective baptism; only thus could the baptized be sanctified. In opposition to this, Augustine maintained that the church had to recognize as valid even the baptism performed by a schismatic. For baptism is, in itself, a sacred act, and it is not dependent upon the holiness of the one who gives it. "There is a great difference between an apostle and a drunkard; but there is no difference at all between a Christian baptism performed by an apostle and a Christian baptism performed by a drunkard. . . . There is no difference between a Christian baptism performed by an apostle and that performed by a heretic" (Epistle 93, 48). "The water used in a heretical baptism is not adulterated; for God's creation is not in itself evil, and the Gospel's Word ought not be faulted by any false teacher." (*De baptismo,* IV, 24)

Through baptism a man is marked as belonging to Christ; he receives a *character dominicus,* just as slaves and cattle are marked to show that they are the property of a certain individual. In the same sense, baptism implies that a man belongs to Christ. This mark is — in the medieval term — indelible *(character indelebilis)*. The same holds true for the ordination of pastors and the consecration of bishops. Therefore, according to this point of view, rebaptism is never necessary, and neither is reordination. Augustine, therefore, was a representative of a *theologia irregenitorum* (see above).

In this respect Augustine was at odds with Cyprian. The latter held that only a baptism performed within the church, where the Spirit is to be found, could be effective for salvation. And therefore a heretical baptism would not be valid, and those who came to the church from a heretical background must be rebaptized.

Is it true, then, that Augustine made no distinction between a schismatic baptism and a baptism performed in the church? He definitely believed that both baptismal acts were equally valid, but, like Cyprian, he also felt that only the church's baptism had a redemptive influence. Baptism confers the forgiveness of sin and regeneration only where men adhere to the one church. For it is only within the church that the Holy Spirit is given, and with Him the gift of love (*caritas*). Augustine solved the problem of combining these two thoughts by distinguishing between the sacrament itself and the efficacy of the sacrament (something which Cyprian did not do). "The sacrament is one thing; the efficacy of the sacrament is another thing." The effect of the sacrament, which can be found only where the unity of the church is preserved, is love. "No one has the love of God who does not love the unity of the church, and because of this it is correct to say that one can receive the Holy Spirit only in the Catholic Church" (*De baptismo*, III, 21). But the sacrament itself exists even if its efficacy does not: "The baptized person does not lose the sacrament of Baptism if he separates himself from the unity of the church. By the same token, an ordained man does not lose the sacrament to administer Baptism if he separates himself from the unity of the church" (*De baptismo*, I, 2). Baptized heretics receive Baptism in the same way as the righteous; but they do not have love.

Augustine used the word "sacrament" in a wider sense than we do. He did agree, however, that Baptism and the Lord's Supper are the chief sacraments. They have come to us from Christ, and with the Word they form the basis of the church (cf. John 19:34). Augustine drew a sharp line of distinction between the external signs, or elements, used in the sacraments and their spiritual meaning. In the same way, he also distinguished between the external Word and the Spirit who speaks in the Word. The external signs are symbols that point to the spiritual realities. Augustine conceived of spiritual efficacy as being parallel to the external reality. They belong together as a result of God's command, but at the same time, they are distinct. This "symbolical" conception in Augustine's thinking was derived from his Neoplatonic background. External things were clearly separated from the spiritual, and yet they could serve as symbols pointing to the divine, the means by which the divine comes near to us. The sacraments are external signs which contain a spiritual content. But they are not necessarily attached to these signs.

Opposition to Donatism also involved the concept of the church in general. As already mentioned, the Donatists thought of the church as consisting of perfect saints, a description which fits their group alone. Augustine objected by saying that they thereby restricted the church to Africa. As he saw it, the entire church of Christ is found in the entire world. This is the church based on the Word of Christ, in which His sacraments are administered. The ungodly and the hypocrites cannot be cast out of this group by other men. Those who belong to this church in an external sense must be considered a part of it, even though the Spirit or love are lacking in some. These do not belong to the communion of saints, to the church in the true sense of the term. According to Augustine, the true church is composed of the pious, those in whom the Spirit of God is at work and in whom He has ignited the flame of love, *caritas*. They are bound together by an inner, invisible fellowship, "the unity of the Spirit in the bond of peace." By virtue of their mutual concern, they give expression to the love poured out through the Spirit of Christ, and as a result they form a spiritual unity in Christ. They are the body of Christ. This inner church, held together by the invisible bonds of love, is not the equivalent of the external church organization — Christendom on earth. This, too, forms a community, a community of all who confess the name of Christ and partake of the sacraments. This external ecclesiastical community is constituted by the sacraments and is sanctified through Word and Sacrament. Its holiness does not consist in the holiness of the members or in the charisma of the clergy. In this church true Christians and hypocrites are found side by side, and they live together just as the weeds and the wheat grow together until the time of the harvest.

The church, therefore, meant two things to Augustine: the external organization and the communion of saints (or the community of true believers). These are not the same, for there are many who belong to the church in an external sense who are not numbered among the true believers. But they are nevertheless related, inasmuch as the communion of saints is always present within the external organization. The true faith can be found only where men live in churchly unity. Apart from this communion there is no salvation, for the Spirit of Christ is not to be found apart from it, and neither is love.

On occasions Augustine also referred to a third definition of the church, when he spoke of it as the *numerus praedestinatorum*. This group of believers coincides neither with the external organization nor with the communion of saints. It is not identical with Christendom either, for one can conceive of the fact that God may elect even those who are outside of the church (Job, who was not an Israelite, is mentioned here as an example) or who do not receive the sacraments (such as the penitent thief). Neither are the elect precisely the same as those who now belong to the community of believers. For it is possible that some of these will fall away in the future, inasmuch as they do not possess the gift of perseverance. The elect are those who have shared in grace and remained faithful to the end. That no man is able to see or judge who it is that belongs to the group of predestined is explained by the very nature of the case. Augustine's threefold concept of the church can be illustrated in the following manner:

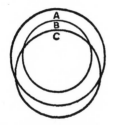

A. The external institution of salvation, Christendom.

B. The communion of saints, the bride of Christ, the invisible fellowship of love.

C. The predestined.

Augustine's doctrine of the church was significant not only in relation to the Donatist controversy but also for his description of the kingdom of God and the kingdom of the world presented in his famous volume *The City of God*. Its 22 books, completed during the years 413 to 426, were written particularly as an apology directed against the heathen who blamed Christians for the misfortunes of society. It is also a description of world history, envisioned by Augustine as a struggle between two states or communities represented by heathendom and Christendom. "The city of God" and "the city of the world" are not presented here as two administrative units, whose power is to be regulated vis-à-vis one another, but rather as two societies, which have contended with each other from the beginning of time. This contention has determined the course of history and has formed its inner continuity. Both societies are held together by the bonds of love: in the one case there are persons who love God even to the point of self-contempt, and in the other, persons who love themselves to the point where they despise God. This difference was found even in the world of the angels (there were good angels and bad), and this same difference took form in the world of men beginning with Cain and Abel. We are told that Cain built a city, while Abel lived as a stranger on the earth. Through Christ, the godly society took concrete form in the church, the fellowship of believers, just as the earthly society has appeared in the form of the Roman Empire and other heathen states.

It would not be proper, therefore, to compare Augustine's "city of God" and "city of the world" with the modern contrast between church and state. Augustine's view was broader. He spoke of two lines of development, of two societies, which are active in the events of history. He was not simply referring to external powers or communities.

"The city of God" is not the external ecclesiastical organization or hierarchy, but above all the communion of saints, the inner church, which is hidden and yet concretely present in the external organization. "For the commonwealth of the saints is above, even though it provides citizens here below, who dwell here as strangers until the dominion of the heavenly commonwealth is manifested." (*The City of God,* XV, 1)

By the same token, "the earthly city" is not identical with the state; it rather designates the society of evil and godless men, who have been the driving force behind the formation of the pagan state.

Augustine wrote this book primarily to defend the communion of saints against the pagan Roman state. This antithesis is of fundamental significance. The godly society is a spiritual fellowship of the pious believers. The earthly society is a fellowship of evil men, all the enemies of God. This did not mean, however, that Augustine was completely opposed to the secular state. He recognized, for example, that even an evil, pagan state, which in itself embodies the earthly city, is of value, inasmuch as it supports external order and thus provides certain benefits. He also referred to the Christian state as the ideal, for it not only provides the external structure but also serves at the same time as a means by which the kingdom of God can grow and advance. The goal of such a state is found in the kingdom of God; in itself it is but a means of promoting the Kingdom. It is therefore in principle subordinate to the kingdom of God and is obligated to obey its laws.

It can be seen from the foregoing that the relation between "the city of God" and "the earthly city" is the same as that between *caritas* and *cupiditas. Cupiditas* is something evil, for it loves only the world and forgets God. This does not mean, however, that all love for temporal things is reprehensible. But this love must be subordinated to the higher love, and it must use temporal things as a means for reaching the higher level. In the same sense, the earthly state is not evil in itself but it may become so. For if the state becomes an end in itself, or if it becomes the only society in which men are involved, or if it is directed only toward earthly advantage — then it becomes evil. If, on the other hand, a state is controlled by Christian laws and is subordinate to the fellowship of believers as its highest goal, for the achievement of which it serves as a means — then it fulfills its God-given function. Then the state assumes the position designed for it, and is good and useful both in the service of secular purposes and for the growth and development of the kingdom of God.

"The city of God" is not, therefore, the equivalent of the external church, but neither did Augustine conceive of these entities as being antithetical. Those who believe in Christ, who are filled with His Spirit and who live in God's love, share in a spiritual fellowship. It is through this group of faithful that Christ brings His kingdom to victory. As such, this group is representative of Christ's dominion on earth. And while this inner community is invisible, it is at the same time a tangible association, a "life of the saints together." "The city of God" can also be identified with the kingdom of God, in so far as this has been realized here on earth. But this "city" will at some time in the future blend into the eternal kingdom, which lies beyond the boundaries of time and which involves the perfection of the communion of saints.

As far as the relationship between the godly state and the earthly state are concerned, Augustine maintained that the latter ought to be subject to the former. This is consistent with the general presuppositions. The earthly state has been designed only to serve earthly objectives. It exists for the sake of external order. In addition to this, the earthly state ought also support the community which includes God's elect, the holy ones. The kingdom of God is the objective of the entire human race. And the earthly state should serve this purpose too, in the depths of its being, if it is to be a truly Christian state. This trend of thought does not, in itself, imply that the state should be subject to the church (the external ecclesiastical structure, that is), for Augustine is speaking here of the communities themselves and their inner purposes. During the Middle Ages, however, Augustine's thought was interpreted to mean that the state is subject to the church, and *The City of God* did

form the basis of the doctrine of papal supremacy over secular authority. Emperors and kings were said to have received their power from
the pope, and it was the pope's privilege, therefore, to establish them in
their offices. Augustine did not endorse this concept of ecclesiastical
rule, but there was nothing to prevent such a development. Augustine
did, as a matter of fact, feel that the fellowship of believers is manifested
in the external ecclesiastical clergy and organization, and he drew no
specific line of demarcation between "the city of God," the inner spiritual community, and the external structure of the church. The former
presupposes the latter. The hierarchical concept therefore represents a
reinterpretation of Augustine's point of view, but it is at the same time
a logical extension of certain facets of his theology.

AUGUSTINE'S DOCTRINE OF SIN AND GRACE

There is a certain inner analogy between, on the one hand, the Trinitarian and the Christological controversies which raged in the East
during the fourth and fifth centuries and, on the other, the Pelagian
controversy in the West during the fifth century. Both involved the
same question: What is the basis of our salvation? Subsequent to the repudiation of Arianism and the monarchical heresies, the following argument came to the fore: If Christ is not true God, He cannot save man;
if He is not true God and true man in one person, He cannot free man
from the dominion of sin and death. In a similar manner, Augustine asserted, in opposition to Pelagius, that salvation is God's own work; it is
not of human origin. In the one controversy, the major question was
concerned about the relationship between the divine and human natures in Christ; in the other, about the relationship between God's grace
and man's free will (cf. Ragnar Bring, *Kristendomstolkningar,* 1950,
p. 230 f.). Just as Athanasius taught that Christ is truly God, so that the
work which He carried out is God's own work, so also did Augustine
teach that it is the grace of God alone which can accomplish man's salvation. But for Augustine this was not a purely theological question; it
also had anthropological overtones. In Western theology the doctrine of
sin and grace, like the doctrine of the church, came to occupy the center of interest.

Pelagius, a native of Ireland, appeared in Rome shortly before the
year 400 as a very strict preacher of penitence. Later he worked in
North Africa also. Caelestius was one of his disciples, and somewhat

later Julian of Eclanum became the foremost representative of Pelagian-ism. Pelagianism was widely accepted, but it also elicited strong opposi-tion, especially in Augustine, who wrote against it. The Eastern theolo-gians were also persuaded to reject Pelagius, and at the Council of Ephesus in 431 (where Nestorianism was condemned) the Pelagian point of view was repudiated as heretical.

In his preaching, Pelagius appealed to man's free will. He assumed that man of himself has the ability to choose between good and evil. He felt that if man did not believe that he was able to carry out God's commands he never would be able to do so, and as a result would never change for the better. It would be futile to expect man to do what appears impossible.

In the theology of the early church the idea of the freedom of the will was a basic presupposition both in the West and among the Greeks. The preaching of the Law was done with this in mind; so also with the process of rearing and educating. Apart from this freedom one could not hold man responsible for his acts; neither could his transgres-sions incur guilt.

But in the controversy between Augustine and Pelagius this entire question of the freedom of the will entered a new stage and became one of the main issues in the question of salvation itself — the problem of sin and grace. In the mind of Pelagius, the freedom of the will was given much more significance than in the earlier tradition. To him it was not simply man's ability to choose and act in freedom (not simply a formal or psychological freedom, to use more modern terminology). It also implied, as far as Pelagius was concerned, that man was free to choose between good and evil; if confronted by a number of alterna-tives, he might choose the right way to act as well as the evil way.

In other words, man has the possibility and the freedom to decide in favor of the good. Sin, according to Pelagius, consists only in isolated acts of the will. If a man wills what is evil, he sins. But there is nothing to prevent him from choosing the good, thereby avoiding sin. Pelagius rejected the idea that sin should be thought of in terms of man's nature or character. Sin is not a fault of nature but of the will. As a result, he also refused to accept the teaching of original sin. Sin consists only of what man does, and because of this it cannot be transmitted by hered-ity, it cannot be implicit in nature. Pelagius was able to assert human responsibility only on these terms; he could envision man's improvement only against such a background. Small children, who are unable consciously to choose that which is evil, are therefore free of sin, according to Pelagius. As a result, Baptism need not imply deliverance from sin.

Pelagius also contended that man, generally speaking, can advance toward sinlessness, that one can increasingly avoid evil and choose the good. How then did he explain the universality of sin? Why does free man so often choose what is evil? Confronted by such questions, Pelagius referred to mankind's long-standing habit of sinning *(longa consuetudo vitiorum)*. Because of repeated acts of the will, man's propensity to sin has been increased.

But man is nevertheless able to choose the good by an act of the will. Does he then have no need of the grace of God? No, not even Pelagius would say that; he, too, spoke of grace, although not in the same way as Augustine. To the latter, grace is something that alters the will of man, which fills him with love for God and thereby changes the entire direction of his will. To Pelagius, God's grace means that man has been equipped from the beginning with a will that is free to choose the good. The work of grace is a benefit of nature *(bonum naturae)*. Furthermore, God's grace facilitates the choosing process and enables man to attain that which is good. This assistance is provided through the preaching of the Law and through the example of Christ, as well as by the forgiveness of sin, which enables a man to continue his course without being encumbered by the past. It is necessary, therefore, that man's will be supported by God's grace. But at the same time man is able to choose the good of and by himself.

Augustine was sharply opposed to such ideas. His concept of freedom and of sin and grace was presented in a number of writings directed against Pelagianism (cf. *De spiritu et littera*, 412; *De natura et gratia*, 415; and *Contra Julianum*, 421). The controversy was concerned for the most part with the following points: the freedom of the will, original sin, the acquisition of salvation, grace and predestination.

As seen from one point of view, this entire facet of Augustine's theology constitutes a description of man and of man's position relative to God. At the same time, however, Augustine's theological anthropology was also inserted into his teaching of the order of salvation. Chief attention is given to God's dealings with man and to man's varied conditions in the course of that event which is known as God's plan of salvation for the world. Statements concerning the freedom of the will and the work of grace are conditioned by the different stages in which man has found himself in his development from creation to perfection. Augustine distinguishes four such stages, inasmuch as he speaks of man *ante legem, sub lege, sub gratia,* and *in pace* (or, in more recent terminology, "before the fall," "after the fall," "after conversion" and "in perfection").

In the so-called original state, i. e., at the time when the first man was created, man possessed a full measure of freedom. His will was then free not only in the realm of action; it was also able to choose between good and evil. In other words, man then possessed freedom in the formal sense as well as the ability to choose the good. This kind of freedom implied, therefore, the ability to refrain from sin *(posse non peccare).* This ability was not man's because of his natural endowment; it was his only because of the assistance of divine grace. It was *prima gratia* alone which gave man the freedom to choose the good.

But freedom also contains the possibility of a fall, and the first sin was occasioned by free will. The Fall implies that man, in a spirit of arrogance, turned himself away from God and set himself in the direction of evil. *Caritas* was replaced with *cupiditas* in man's life. Man thereby lost the gift of grace, and with it the freedom which constituted the ability to choose the good. For when grace was lost, human nature was altered. Reason and will no longer control the baser powers of the soul; on the other hand, these powers have assumed a dominating position, and man, as a result, has been ensnared in the toils of desire and driven by concupiscence. This is a condition which he is powerless to change. In isolated instances the will can overcome concupiscence, but the direction of the will nevertheless remains the same. Man is unable to overthrow the thralldom of concupiscence, because in this condition the world is the ultimate objective of his will, and God.

The Fall, therefore, means that man has lost the freedom to choose the good. In place of this, man now has a compulsion to sin *(necessitas peccandi).* His *posse non peccare* has been changed to *non posse non peccare.* Here is Augustine's opposition to Pelagius. Augustine denied that man, after the Fall, continued to have a free will in the true sense, the freedom to choose the good, that is. He rather stands under compulsion to sin, which is to say that he acts in such a way that corruption is inevitable. Isolated good deeds can be carried out, but these do not change the evil intent of his will. At the same time, however, Augustine did not deny freedom in a formal sense. His concept is not deterministic. Man acts freely. But his condition being what it is, man is free only to sin. In other words, his freedom is sharply limited, or distorted. Man's tendency to choose the evil determines the course of his conduct and prevents him from doing the good. To be sure, man is free as far as individual acts of the will are concerned. At the same time, however, his basic attitude, shaped by his will, is something he cannot change — and to that extent he is not free.

Man's evil volitional tendencies express themselves as concupiscence, or desire. But at the same time, the first sin was an offense (*culpa*) which incurred guilt before God. For this reason, original sin implies a perpetual condition of guilt (*reatus*). It is this guilt which is the essence of sin, or that which makes sin sin (its *formale*). Inherited guilt is removed by Baptism, so that original sin is no longer counted as sin. Nevertheless, one's sinful condition remains even after Baptism; concupiscence, attributable to the influence of original sin, is still there. The nature of man itself is injured by the corruption implicit in original sin; it is, as a result, a "nature vitiated by sin." Sin is not simply a series of isolated willful acts; it is a real corruption of nature, resulting from the fact that the direction of the will has itself been distorted. Luther emphasized this by saying that sin not only refers to outward acts; unbelief and enmity to God form its essence. In a similar manner, Augustine described sin as a perversion of the will. In this we see the main point at issue between him and Pelagius.

The claim that sin is implicit in human nature is suggested by the very idea that corruption is inherited. The first false step resulted from man's free will. But the entire human race was involved in Adam's fall. The Biblical Adam is "man" in general; all are epitomized in him, so that all of his descendants form a unity in him. As a result, all share in Adam's guilt, even though the presence of original sin in the individual is not dependent on an act of the will; it is there before the will begins to exert itself. The condition of guilt is inherited, and is removed from the individual through Baptism.

And so with human depravity; it, too, is inherited as a result of Adam's disobedience. That is to say, that it is propagated in a real way from one generation to the next. Augustine believed that in and with natural propagation evil desire was also passed on from one generation to the next. In this way, mankind has become a *massa perditionis*. The entire race is in thrall to desire and afflicted by the corruption which results from it.

Furthermore, as Augustine understood it, our inherited sinful condition also makes us guilty before God; on the basis of original sin man is worthy of divine condemnation. In the light of this, Augustine concluded that unbaptized children are liable to damnation. Later Roman Catholic theology mitigated this assertion in various ways, and even Augustine suggested that the prayers of the family could in some cases replace Baptism. The concept of inherited sinfulness has often been misunderstood. Naturally enough it does not suggest a denial of childish innocence as seen from a purely human point of view. It is not a question of actual sin; it rather points to a condition in which man finds himself as a result of the perversion of his will. The doctrine of original sin also presupposes the unity of the human race in Adam. For how else could guilt or responsibility be ascribed to an individual for something he did not do? The Augustinian position in this matter does not distinguish between children and adults; the same offense applies to all. To think of original sin as imposing guilt is equally difficult in both cases. It must be assumed, in this connection, that original sin as such lies beyond the boundaries of empirical knowledge and therefore cannot be appraised from the point of view of the experience which reason has at its command.

In his doctrine of original sin Augustine describes sin as a condition which involves the entire man; it is not just isolated acts. Sin is the turning away of the will from God (*perversitas voluntatis a summa substantia*). This intimates that evil is something negative, lacking in substance, and cut off from God's fellowship, but at the same time something that implies guilt and produces depravity in no uncertain terms.

In connection with this concept of sin, it is logical to conclude that after the Fall man's will has been incapable of the good. To be sure, man can occasionally do that which is good and useful here on earth. But as long as the perversion of the will holds sway, this cannot be something truly good, for man himself remains evil and his actions are directed at that which leads to corruption. This doctrine of the unfree will (which should not be confused with determinism) implies that man is unable to cooperate in the interest of his salvation.

137

That which is the only source of man's salvation, the grace of God, was revealed in the work of Christ. He made atonement for our sins, and through faith in Him man can share in grace. This is the only road to right living: "What the Law commands, faith accomplishes" (*Quod lex imperat, fides impetrat. De spiritu et littera*, 13, 22). The function of grace consists partly in the forgiveness of sin, partly in regeneration.

Through the work of mediation carried out by Christ, the broken fellowship with God has been restored. Guilt is removed through the forgiveness of sin, and man recovers the spiritual life which was lost through the Fall. As Augustine understood it, salvation is found in the forgiveness of sin, and grace is the loving will of God which works this forgiveness.

But grace does not only remove sin; it also brings about man's regeneration. Human nature is actually depraved by sin. This injury can be healed only by grace (*gratia sanans*). Life returns when man's relationship to God is restored. Grace creates a new will in man. This implies an "infusion of love" (*infusio caritatis*). The evil will, oriented toward the world, is replaced by a good will, by *caritas*. As a result, man can obey God's commands; formerly, he was unable to do so. His freedom, i. e., his ability to do good, is restored (*libertas restituta*). As long as earthly life lasts, this freedom is merely beginning. For in this life man must fight against desire and is restored only by degrees. What can bring about the good in man? Only love, the new will. Without the assistance of grace, man can never do that which is good. As a result, the fulfilling of the Law, which God requires, is possible only as God Himself supplies the power. "Give what you command, and command what you will" (*Da quod jubes, et jube quod vis. Confessions*, X, 29). Such love goes together with faith. To believe in God is to love Him and to hope one day to see Him. Faith, hope, and love belong together; they are the essentials of Christianity.

Salvation results from the forgiveness of sin, by faith, quite apart from human merit. There is nothing that man can do by himself to bring about this salvation. This was Augustine's main argument against Pelagius; Augustine took this basic idea from Paul, whose teaching of justification by faith had a decisive influence on Augustine. Man's will is incapable of good, and therefore salvation must be God's own work. But for Augustine grace includes the regeneration of man. Man's will is altered, love is poured into him; as a result of this, man can truly do that which is good and can become God's co-worker in faith. As seen from certain points of view, Augustine appears to say that this regeneration is the goal. God's love (caritas) is the presupposition of man's salvation. This interpretation of Paul is somewhat different from that of the Reformers. According to Luther and the Lutheran tradition, it is only faith in Christ and His merits which justifies man; human works do not enter in. Augustine, too, said that man is saved by faith, but this faith also does that which is good; it is connected with and expresses itself in caritas. Deeds that originate in love are thought of as being meritorious and will eventually be rewarded. But Augustine also emphasized at the same time that such merit can be won only by grace. Said he, "When God rewards our merits, He is actually rewarding His own gifts." (Epistle 194, 19)

Augustine did not say, however, that forgiving grace is the only cause and presupposition of salvation; he also recognized the importance of the love which God pours into man's heart. The actual basis of salvation is grace alone (not man's free will), but that which is of note in the work of grace is not so much the "alien" righteousness of Christ which is imputed to us but rather the change which takes place in the life of the newborn individual because of the love of God which has been poured into him.

Augustine's opposition to Pelagius was expressed most strongly in his doctrine of predestination. The grace which is the sole source of man's salvation is God's loving will; it is, at the same time, almighty. The omnipotence of this grace implies that a man's salvation depends solely on God's will and decree. God in eternity chose certain men to be snatched out of the corrupted masses and to share in His salvation. The work of grace in the order of salvation is therefore the execution in time of God's eternal, hidden decree. Augustine based this conclusion on Rom. 8:30: "And those whom He predestined He also called; and those whom He called He also justified; and those whom He justified He also glorified."

The ultimate basis of human salvation, therefore, is not to be found in our merits or free will but rather in the will of God. To Augustine, this meant that those who have been chosen will one day be saved. Those who once come to believe cannot conceivably fall away. Grace supplies them not only with faith but also with the gift of perseverance (donum perseverantiae). This trend of thought has given rise to a consid-

139

eration of what is called "irresistible grace" (*gratia irresistibilis;* the term itself was not used until later). Augustine even believed that the predestined can be found outside of the church. Such persons, he maintained, would be saved by the power of grace operating apart from the available means. (Cf. above, p. 129)

Augustine also concluded in this connection that if one is not saved, this too has its basis in the will of God; God did not will salvation for such a person. For nothing can be done apart from God's will and power. How can this idea be related to the claim that "God is love"? Such questions cannot be answered. The words in 1 Tim. 2:4, God "desires all men to be saved" (which have been difficult for all who teach double predestination), were interpreted by Augustine to refer only to all "classes" or "kinds" of men.

Augustine's doctrine of predestination represents the ultimate consequence of what he believed about grace as the sole basis of man's salvation. Later theology has not usually followed him in drawing such conclusions. The teachings of irresistible grace and double predestination have been more often than not rejected. These ideas have continued to provide sharp competition for Pelagian tendencies, however, and they have often been accepted by theologians who have wanted to be consistently faithful to Augustine on this point.

PART II

The Middle Ages
From Augustine to Luther

CHAPTER 12

The Controversy
on Augustinianism
to the Synod of Orange, 529

Augustine's doctrine of grace and predestination prompted widespread controversy even before he died, and it continued to occupy the center of theological discussion throughout the Middle Ages and even, in part, into the post-Reformation period. The following problems came to stand in the foreground: the scope of free will, the function of grace in man's conversion and regeneration, and the meaning of predestination.

A group of monks in the city of Hadrumetum (south of Carthage) began a dispute about Augustine's doctrine of grace during his lifetime. Some interpreted it to mean that men lack freedom of the will and that their works would therefore have no significance for the final judgment. But others disagreed by saying that grace supports the free will, thereby enabling man to do what is good; each will be judged by his own works. Augustine became involved in this dispute himself, and this motivated him to explain his position with great care in *De gratia et libero arbitrio* and *De corruptione et gratia*.

The so-called "Semi-Pelagian" school of thought also arose in opposition to Augustine; this was particularly widespread in Gaul. Augustine's doctrine of predestination, which was interpreted as fatalism by the Semi-Pelagians, was the chief cause of this opposition. The idea that the will is incapable of faith and good works in general was also found to be objectionable. Augustine, who was informed of this attack by his disciples Prosper and Hilary, replied by writing *De praedestinatione sanctorum* and *De dono perseverantiae*.

The main architect of the Semi-Pelagian position was John Cassianus (d. 430/435), the founder of the cloister of St. Victor in Marseilles.

It must be noted that Semi-Pelagianism was not an offshoot of Pelagian theology; it rather referred back to the pre-Augustinian tradition in the East. The Semi-Pelagians felt that the Pelagian heresy could be avoided without using the extreme ideas imbedded in Augustine's doctrine of grace. John Cassianus, who saw things from the point of view of a monk, recognized the reality of sinful depravity, but he also maintained that man can live a moral life. Sin is inherited from Adam insofar as the entire human race participates in his transgression. Because of this, man cannot be saved or live a virtuous life without the help of grace. But the seeds of good, which need only be brought alive by grace, are present in human life. By the exercise of free will, man can either reject grace or pursue it. When man is converted it is sometimes God who takes the initiative, but on other occasions He waits for us to decide, so that our will anticipates God's will. God does not will any man's damnation. When this happens, it is done against His will.

It is obvious from what has been said that while Cassianus accepted Augustine's concept of original sin, he rejected the idea of the omnipotence of grace. On the other hand, he believed that conversion and regeneration result from the cooperation of grace and free will. Rejection does not have its basis in the will of God.

In the years that followed, this theological position was widely accepted in Gaul. Additional forms of opposition came into being. Prosper of Aquitaine sought to promote the pure Augustinian point of view, while Faustus of Riez (in Provence; d. ca. 490/500) opposed him by going even further than Cassianus in the direction of Pelagianism. Vincent of Lerins, who coined the well-known principle which holds that the only valid tradition consists of that which is taught "everywhere, always, and by all," thought that Augustine's doctrine of grace was an unfounded novelty which did not satisfy the questions involved.

Faustus agreed with Cassianus in saying that the divine and human wills cooperate. But he did not believe that grace is an inner, life-giving power; as he saw it, grace is merely the enlightenment and awakening which comes by preaching, or the revelation of Scripture. The drawing power of grace and the consent of the will combine to produce conversion. Predestination is based solely on the foreknowledge of human merit.

For a time Semi-Pelagianism was very successful; it was confirmed by a synod in Arles in 473, for example. But it never won out conclusively. The popes in Rome were not much interested in the theological disputes of Gaul, and they gave most of their support to the Augustinian position. The fear of pure Pelagianism was a contributing factor in this.

Chief among Augustine's disciples (after Prosper) was Fulgentius of Ruspe (d. 533), perhaps the most prominent theologian of his period. He was active as a bishop in North Africa, but he spent a long time in Sardinia, having been driven there by the Vandals. His greatest work, *Contra Faustum*, has been lost, but it is clear from his writings which are still extant that he strongly upheld the Augustinian doctrine of predestination. He, too, taught that no one who had been chosen from eternity could go lost, and also that no one who had not been predestined to salvation could be saved. Fulgentius therefore accepted a *duplex praedestinatio*, as well as God's particular will to save. He interpreted the Augustinian position in a presentation of masterful clarity. Because of a similarity of styles it has been thought by some that Fulgentius was the author of the Athanasian Creed, but this has not been proved beyond all doubt. (See above, p. 87)

At this time Caesarius of Arles (d. 542) was promoting the Augustinian viewpoint in Gaul. Opposition was aroused, and Caesarius' theology was rejected by a provincial synod in Valencia. Subsequently, however, Caesarius won the attention of the pope, and at the Synod of Orange (529) he succeeded in bringing into being a confession which dealt with original sin, grace, and predestination. The Semi-Pelagian position was repudiated in this confession, while the Augustinian doctrine of grace was implemented. This decision was confirmed in the following year by Pope Boniface II and subsequently received almost canonical prestige. This marked the end of the Semi-Pelagian controversy and further implied that a modified Augustinianism was recognized as the norm in questions concerning the doctrine of predestination.

The Synod of Orange, whose 25 canons were drawn for the most part from a collection of quotations from Augustine prepared by Prosper, sanctioned Augustine's teaching of original sin. The synod agreed that as a result of original sin the entire man is changed for the worse, both in body and soul, and that the free will is not undamaged. Both sin and death have come to the entire human race through one man. Furthermore, the anticipatory activity of grace was strongly emphasized: the very prayers in which we pray for grace are themselves stimulated by grace. By ourselves we are unable to take the first step to receive grace. God does not wait until man wills to be cleansed from sin; He rather works through the Spirit to implant this desire within us. Neither is the longing for wholeness, or the beginning of faith, or the feeling of faith something that is a part of man by nature. When a man consents to the preaching of the Gospel, this must be attributed to the enlightenment and inspiration of the Holy Spirit. Man is not good in himself; God must work all good within him. Even the regenerate must pray to God for help in order to persevere in doing good.

The canons of the Synod of Orange also touched upon the relation between grace and merit. It was agreed that merit does not precede grace. Good works deserve reward, but good works are possible only by virtue of unmerited grace. The love of God is a gift of God; it is poured into our hearts by the Holy Spirit. The final conclusion therefore was (as it says in the appendage written by Caesarius) that neither faith nor love nor good works result from the activity of the free will; they must be preceded by the divine grace of a merciful God. This grace is received through Baptism. If they are earnest about it, all of the baptized can — with Christ's help — fulfill that which relates to the salvation of the soul. In this connection the idea of double predestination was rejected; those who taught that some are predestined to hell were condemned by the Synod of Orange.

Because man's will for and striving after the good has its origin in grace, the latter is the source of all good in man. And grace is an inner power, not merely the influence of an external revelation. As seen from one point of view, Canon 22 of the Synod of Orange summarizes the content of the entire confession: "Of himself, no man is anything but lies and sins. If one does possess something of truth and righteousness, it comes from that fountain after which we ought to thirst in this desert, so that, sprinkled, as it were, by some of its drops, we might not succumb on the way."

Properly speaking, the Synod of Orange marks the end of the controversy over Augustinianism. But the problems involved in the vortex of this controversy continued to elicit long-standing disputes; they also gave rise to complex speculations in the minds of medieval theologians. Some of these same questions also arose again in the post-Reformation debates, and even then the ideas which came into being during the Pelagian and Semi-Pelagian controversies were discussed anew.

CHAPTER 13

The Transition from the Early Period to the Medieval Period; Gregory the Great

During the tumultuous period when the western Roman Empire fell apart, and when political domination was assumed by the Germanic peoples, the more important theological questions got less and less attention from the leaders of the church. Nevertheless, the foundation of the later scholastic theology, as well as of medieval culture in general, was laid during this time. An important contribution was made by those who acted to preserve the heritage of antiquity for the medieval period that was coming into being.

Among these was Boethius, a Christian philosopher and an official under Emperor Theodoric. Accused of having connections with the Eastern Roman Empire, Boethius was arrested and finally executed in Pavia in 525. He is remembered as both the "last Roman" and the "first scholastic." Through his own writings, as well as by his translations of Aristotle's books on logic, he transmitted the knowledge of Aristotelian logic to the Middle Ages. His scientific system also served as a prototype for medieval university education.

The writings attributed to Dionysius the Areopagite also belong to this period. In four treatises entitled *The Divine Name, The Heavenly Hierarchy, The Ecclesiastical Hierarchy,* and *The Mystical Theology* he set forth a world system based on Neoplatonic patterns. He dealt here, among other things, with the angels, whom he divided into nine choruses, each in its turn divided into three triads. In the two latter treatises Dionysius presented his views on the sacraments and offices of the church, as well as on the soul's way of salvation according to the postulates of mysticism. These writings plus 10 letters by the same author falsely claimed to be the work of Paul's disciple Dionysius. The prolonged discussion of the origins of these writings was finally settled at the end of the last century, when it was demonstrated that parts of these writings were based on the work of Proclus (d. 485), a Neoplatonic philosopher. Inasmuch as they were quoted by theologians in the second decade of the sixth century, they can be dated somewhere between 485 and 515. They were probably written in Syria. And even though the subject matter involved lies on the periphery of theology, these writings played an important role throughout the Middle Ages. Knowledge of the world view and the religious system of Neoplatonism was transmitted to medieval Europe via these writings. These "pseudo-Dionysian" writings were translated into Latin by the philosopher John Scotus Erigena.

Cassiodorus (died ca. 583), like Boethius a statesman in the kingdom of the Ostrogoths, made his reputation as a collector and encyclopedist. A contemporary whose name is associated not so much with the history of dogma as with general church history was Benedict of Nursia (d. 547), the famous monk whose monastic rule dominated Western cloisters until the 12th century. By virtue of his recommendations about study and writing in the monasteries, Benedict made an outstanding contribution to the enrichment of spiritual life during the Middle Ages.

Isidore of Seville appeared somewhat later (d. 636), but more than anyone else he collected the scientific and theological knowledge of that era and made it accessible for coming generations.

In a time of serious religious decline and material need, a former municipal prefect and monk (in Rome) was elected pope in 590. His name was Gregory. This is his own description of the church he was chosen to lead: "It is an old ship, hard beset by the waves, pressed about on all sides by heavy seas; the screeching of the rotting planks warns us of shipwreck ahead" (Epistle I, 4). In the history of dogma the pontificate of Gregory is usually considered the dividing line between the early church and the Middle Ages. The foundation of the medieval papacy was laid to a large extent during the years of his powerful reign. But Gregory's contributions were of fundamental significance in the field of theology as well.

Gregory accepted Augustine's doctrine of grace, in a simplified and unsophisticated form, and he passed this on to the Middle Ages. He taught that God's love and grace precede man. Merit does not precede grace, inasmuch as the human will is incapable of good. Preparatory grace transforms the will. In the execution of that which is good, grace cooperates with the free will. Good can therefore be ascribed both to God and man, to "God because of His prevenient grace, and to man because of his obedient free will." The object of grace is to produce good works, which can be rewarded (in the form of man's regeneration and salvation). The idea of merit and reward is a fundamental presupposition here, as it is in medieval theology in general.

The rejection of all merit *prior* to grace gives rise to the idea of predestination. God has called some, but left the others in their corruption. The concept of foreknowledge is, in a sense, denied: for as far as God is concerned, there is no distinction between present and future; that which is coming is, to God, the present. Hence the question concerns knowledge rather than foreknowledge.

Gregory's presentation of the doctrine of the Atonement also served as a model for a number of medieval theologians, among them Anselm and Abelard. Gregory set Christ forth as an example for men, as well as the one who presented the substitutionary and atoning sacrifice to God for the sins of men. He is the mediator between God and man, who Himself bore the punishment for man's guilt. The death of Christ is also described in this way: the devil overreached himself. The divine nature is likened to a fishhook hidden in Christ's body, which the devil swallowed without taking note of who it was that he attacked.

The sacrificial aspect of the doctrine of the Atonement was associated with the idea of the Lord's Supper as a sacrifice, in which the death of Christ is mysteriously repeated for us. "If He is resurrected to die no more, so that death no longer has any dominion over Him, He is nevertheless brought to us anew in His immortal and incorruptible life through the mystery of the holy sacrifice. His body is thereby given and received for man's salvation, and His blood is poured out, not now at the hands of unbelievers but in the mouths of the faithful" (Dialogue IV, 58). The sacrificial nature of the Lord's Supper is also described in terms of the sacrifice of contrite hearts on the part of the faithful.

Among Gregory's most important writings is his interpretation of the Book of Job, entitled *Moralia,* which in many respects laid the foundation for the medieval view of life, including the ethical aspect. In his *Dialogues,* a collection of the miraculous deeds performed by holy men,

Gregory did much to awaken and encourage the strong faith in miracles which was characteristic of medieval Christianity. He emphasized, among other things, the ability of the Lord's Supper to influence even man's temporal welfare. It was said, for example, that men were saved from shipwreck or imprisonment because others received the Lord's Supper on their behalf (Dialogue IV, 57). The large number of Gregory's letters which have been preserved deal chiefly with practical ecclesiastical matters.

In his teaching of penance, Gregory developed the concept of satisfaction as a means whereby eternal punishment could be mitigated or taken away; he also presented his ideas about purgatory in this connection. It was characteristic of Gregory, generally speaking, to combine the very best theological tradition (which he tried to preserve) with elements drawn from popular piety. Some of these were of a rather crass or vulgar nature, but even these were sanctioned by Gregory. In spite of this, however, Gregory the Great must be ranked without question among the most important of those who laid the foundation for medieval theology and for medieval culture in general.

CHAPTER 14

Carolingian Theology

The span of time between Gregory the Great and the beginning of the scholastic era (from 600 to 1050, in other words) was not distinguished for developments in the field of theology. Nevertheless, one thing about this period was remarkable: the enthusiasm with which the newly Christianized peoples devoted themselves to the cultural resources made available by Christianity and antiquity. The era of the Carolingian Empire was the golden age in this respect. This era also included a number of important theologians, such as Alcuin (d. 804), Rabanus Maurus (d. 856), Radbertus (d. 865), Ratramnus (d. after 868), and Hincmar of Reims (d. 882). But their activity did not take the form of a new orientation of theological thought; they rather collected and reproduced the older tradition. Among the church fathers, they referred particularly to Augustine and Gregory. Even the study of Scripture was pursued in the traditional way. In the so-called *catenae* (chain commentaries) these men compared the patristic interpretations of various Bible passages. Of greatest importance to the future was the commentary usually ascribed to Walafrid Strabo — the so-called *Glossa ordinaria*. In this work, quotations from the church fathers are applied to various facets of the doctrine of faith. These quotations proved to be a valuable source for theological activity in subsequent years. Two significant Anglo-Saxon theologians who were active in this period were Theodore of Canterbury (d. 690) and the Venerable Bede (d. 735). The latter is best remembered for his *Ecclesiastical History of the English People.*

The theology of this period formed the basis for subsequent developments by preserving the heritage of the patristic age and of antiquity. Dogmatic discussions did arise on certain points, some of which deserve closer attention.

151

The adoptionist controversy was a reecho of the Christological debates of the early church; it involved, in a special way, the interpretation of the Formula of Chalcedon. A Spanish theologian, Elipandus of Toledo, set forth the idea that the man Jesus was united with the Son of God, the Second Person of the Trinity, in such a way that He could be called *Filius adoptivus*. By virtue of God's prior decision and will, He had been chosen to be called God's Son. By saying this, Elipandus desired to do justice to the idea that Christ is as one of us. The word *adoptivus* itself was taken from the "Mozarabic" liturgy. The chief opponent of this Christology was Alcuin. He compared the adoption concept to the Nestorian idea of two persons in Christ. Elipandus' mode of expression made it necessary to think of "two sons" (according to Alcuin): the divine Logos, who was God's Son according to His essence, and the man Jesus, who was adopted as Son.

Adoptionism was condemned by a number of Frankish synods (Regensburg, 792; Frankfurt, 794; Aachen, 799). As a result, the way was prepared for the acceptance of the Byzantine Christology in the West as well. As was true of Leontius or John of Damascus, Western theologians came to think of the divine Logos as the bearer of the personal unity, having taken the human nature up into His person. As Alcuin put it: "When God assumed fleshly form, the human person disappeared, but not the human nature." (*Migne*, PL 101, 156)

The "Filioque" controversy and the picture controversy. One of the earliest additions made to the Niceno-Constantinopolitan Creed in the West was the word *Filioque:* "The Holy Spirit . . . proceeds from the Father *and the Son.*" The Frankish theologians deliberately supported this alteration, and sought to justify it theologically. The above-named Ratramnus was among those who defended this usage in the face of opposition from Patriarch Photius. Ratramnus found support for his stand in ideas derived from Athanasius and Augustine. The Eastern point of view was considered Arian with respect to the Holy Spirit. In the Greek Church it was thought that the divinity of the Father was superior to that of the Son and the Spirit and formed the source of the divine essence. As a result, the Holy Spirit could proceed only from the Father. The question of authority was also involved; the Greeks argued that changing the creed in this way was unwarranted. Rome adopted a wait-and-see policy for a long time, but when the Nicene Creed was inserted into the Mass in the 11th century, the use of the *Filioque* was approved.

The Frankish theologians were also involved in another controversy with the Eastern Church. The Seventh Ecumenical Council, held in Nicaea in 787, had consented to the reverent adoration (προσκύνησις) of pictures of Christ and the saints. The explanation given was that such adoration is directed not to the pictures themselves but to those represented by the pictures. The actual worship (λατρεία) of pictures was repudiated. Nevertheless, at the synod held in Frankfurt in 794 the Frankish Church rejected this decision. Charlemagne and his theologians maintained that pictures should not be the object of any kind of adoration. They should rather be thought of merely as decorative objects or as pedagogical devices. In this matter the point of view of the Frankish Church was not universally upheld in the West. Rome never rejected this Nicene decree, and later on (e. g., at the Council of Constantinople held in 870) the Church of Rome recognized the adoration of pictures in the same sense as the Council of Nicaea. (See above, p. 105)

The predestination controversy. A Saxon monk named Gottschalk, who after reluctantly entering monastic life resided at the cloister of Orbais in France, concluded that it was his responsibility to proclaim double predestination in its strictest form. He claimed (with some justification) that he found support for his teaching in the writings of Augustine, and he accentuated his point of view by avoiding all mention of human freedom. Predestination is based on God's unchanging nature. Gottschalk did not say, however, that certain persons are predestined to evil. What is rather decided beforehand is that the ungodly will receive the punishment which they deserve, just as the righteous will receive eternal life. In both cases, therefore, the right thing is done. But rejection has its cause in the eternal decree of God. The atonement wrought by Christ applies only to those elected to eternal life. The following quote from Gottschalk's confession summarizes his message: "For just as the unchangeable God, prior to the creation of the world, by His free grace unchangeably predestined all of His elect to eternal life, so has this unchangeable God in the same way unchangeably predestined all of the rejected, who shall be condemned to eternal death for their evil deeds on judgment day according to His justice and as they deserve." (*Migne,* PL 121, 368 A).

Gottschalk presented his doctrine at a religious conference in Mainz, where he was opposed by Rabanus Maurus, one of the leading theologians of that period. At a synod held in Chiersy in 849, Bishop Hincmar of Reims, in whose diocese the cloister of Orbais was located, condemned Gottschalk to house arrest in the monastery. Certain contemporary theologians sought to defend Gottschalk, even though they did not agree with him on all points, but his teachings were officially condemned. Gottschalk lived as a prisoner in the monastery for 20 years, all the while insisting that his position was correct. Some of the poems which he wrote during this time have been preserved. In an age when Gregory's interpretation of Augustine, with its emphasis on freedom of the will and cooperation with grace, strongly influenced the theological climate, Gottschalk stood, for the most part, alone.

CHAPTER 15

The Lord's Supper in the Early Middle Ages

As noted above, the idea that the Lord's Supper is a repetition of Christ's atoning sacrifice (the sacrifice of the Mass) began to take form in the time of Gregory the Great. The bread and wine are Christ's body and blood. Exactly how should this be understood? Speculations about this question occupied several Frankish theologians during the first half of the ninth century. As a result of their efforts, the ground was laid for the later medieval doctrine of the Lord's Supper. It must be noted that at this time the Lord's Supper was by no means interpreted only in terms of the sacrifice of the Mass. This idea was but one of the elements involved in the concept of the Lord's Supper in the early Middle Ages. The idea of participation was emphasized with equal enthusiasm. But in the one case as in the other, the question of the Real Presence assumed a central position.

The teaching of the Real Presence, as such, was elevated above all doubt. But the question which arose was this: Should the Real Presence of Christ be understood symbolically or literally? Augustine's interpretation of the Lord's Supper contributed much to the way that question was answered. Augustine's concept was, for all practical purposes, "symbolic": the sacrament is, he said, a sign *(signum)*, which is to say that the external, visible elements are the bearers of a reality which is invisible and exists only in the realm of the spirit. Augustine sought to solve the problem involved by distinguishing between *res* and *signum,* or between *sacramentum* and *virtus sacramenti.* The difficulty which occupied theologians in subsequent generations was chiefly this: How can we combine the Augustinian point of view with the common assumption of faith which holds that the bread and wine are more than signs,

that they are in reality identical with the body and blood of Christ?
(See p. 127 above)

Paschasius Radbertus gave this question a thorough investigation in
his book *De corpore et sanguine Domini*. He set forth the doctrine of
the Real Presence in no uncertain terms: after the consecration, there is
nothing other than the body and blood of Christ, albeit under the form
of bread and wine. The body which is imparted in the Lord's Supper is
identical with that which was born of the Virgin Mary, which suffered
on the cross and arose from the dead. The change which occurs in the
elements results from the creative power of the almighty word. Just as
Almighty God was able to create *ex nihilo,* and to bring forth Christ's
body in the Virgin's womb, so also can He by His word present Christ's
body and blood under the form of bread and wine. It is obvious, however, that this is accomplished in a mysterious and, to a certain extent,
figurative manner, inasmuch as the elements retain their external form.
Hence the question for Paschasius was this: How can the sacramental
event be both figurative (symbolic) and in the truest sense actual at
one and the same time?

As Paschasius came to believe, the symbolic aspect is restricted to
that which is perceptible in the purely external sense: the visible elements and their reception by the communicant. But that which is perceived inwardly, the giving of Christ's body and blood, is a reality *(veritas).* Through the influence of the word and the Spirit, the bread becomes the body of Christ and the wine becomes the blood of Christ.
"What is perceived externally is a figure or mark, but what is perceived
internally is entirely reality and no figure at all; and therefore nothing
else is here revealed but reality and the sacrament of the body itself — the true body of Christ, which was crucified and buried, surely
the sacrament of His body, which is divinely consecrated by the priest
above the altar with the word of Christ through the Spirit: whence the
Lord Himself exclaims, "This is My body' (Luke 22:19)." (*Migne,* PL
120, 1279 B)

Paschasius did not altogether reject the Augustinian position with its
symbolic interpretation; he rather retained it as an obvious presupposition. At the same time, however, he emphasized the real change in the
elements as the essential aspect. Paschasius Radbertus' ideas concerning
the Lord's Supper formed an important link in the theological chain
which led forward to the dogma of transubstantiation.

But while he lived, Paschasius' position on the Lord's Supper elicited a variety of contradictions from theologians who wished to emphasize more strongly the symbolic interpretation of Augustine. The Frankish theologian Ratramnus, for example, wrote a book with the same title as that written by Radbertus (see above), in which he replied to the questions posed by Radbertus. Ratramnus interpreted the Lord's Supper symbolically. The body and blood of Christ are actually received. But this is done in a figurative manner: the external elements are symbolic of an inner reality which can be perceived only by faith. "They are figures according to their visible appearance, but indeed according to the invisible substance, i. e., the power of the divine Word, they are the true body and blood of Christ." (*De corp. et sang.*, 49; Seeberg, III, 75)

What has just been cited could in itself have been said also by Paschasius. But the difference between the two men was that whereas Paschasius restricted the figurative aspect to the externals, Ratramnus extended it even to the designation "the body and blood of Christ." The latter maintained that the bread could be referred to as the body of Christ only in a figurative sense — only in the sense that Christ spoke of Himself as the Bread of Life or as the True Vine. The words of institution are not to be taken literally, he said. When the Bible speaks of Christ's birth of a virgin, and of His suffering and death and burial, these passages must be read literally. In such cases we are dealing with a direct, nonfigurative form of expression. But in the Lord's Supper the actual significance of the Sacrament — the reception of spiritual or heavenly gifts — is enshrouded in the veil of the external symbols.

What other theologians objected to above all in Radbertus' position was that he identified Christ's historical body with the host presented in the Sacrament of the Altar (see above). According to Ratramnus, the body received in the Lord's Supper is not the earthly, human body but a heavenly, spiritual body which can be received only by faith, in a spiritual way. "The external appearance, therefore, is not the thing itself but its image — that which is perceived and understood by the mind as the truth of a thing" (*De corp. et sang.*, 77, 88; Seeberg, III, 75). "Christ's body must not be understood physically but spiritually" (ibid., 74; Seeberg, ibid.). This position is very close to Augustine's: the Lord's Supper is the external symbol of the internal reception of heavenly gifts, something which can be realized only in faith.

It was for the most part the ideas of Radbertus which were further developed to form the basis of the theory of the Lord's Supper which came to dominate the Middle Ages. The Augustinian position was gradually pushed side and replaced by the teaching of transubstantiation.

CHAPTER 16

The Doctrine of Penance in the Early Middle Ages

During the time of the early church, penance implied the readmission into the fellowship of the church of those who had fallen into open sin after baptism. This was a public act, which could take place but *one* time. There were various opinions about the extent of application. It was thought originally that such grave sins as adultery or murder or apostasy were excluded, but eventually its validity was extended to cover such sins as well. This form of penance was maintained up to the end of the sixth century. In Spain, for example, the idea of repeated acts of penance with priestly absolution was long rejected. But as time went on, the public act of penance gradually lost its meaning. In its place, other forms began to take shape, and thus it was that the foundation of the far-reaching medieval practice of penance was laid. The roots of this development can be traced back to the Celtic and Anglo-Saxon churches.

Within the Celtic Church, which in many respects preserved a unique character, the public form of penance was not known. On the other hand, a private form, consisting of confession to the priest, satisfaction, and readmission into the fellowship of the church, came into being. Church manuals dating from the sixth century, which carefully describe the manner of doing penance for various kinds of sin and also set the time factor involved in each case, have been preserved. One such manual is entitled *Poenitentiale*. Doing penance could involve fasting and prayer, giving alms, living a life of abstinence, and so on. The strictest form was permanent exile *(peregrinatio perennis)*. Some of the protracted forms of doing penance could be reduced if the penitent would keep a vigil, recite the Psalms endlessly, or do something else of a difficult nature. The possibility of "redemption" was also recognized:

one form of punishment could be exchanged for another, or one person could even purchase the services of another who would do penance for him.

In this context, penance did not only concern mortal sins; lesser offenses were also involved. Private confession was a combination of public penance in church and the pastoral penance practiced in cloisters and among pious laymen. It came to fulfill the same function as public penance did in the early church, viz., to reinstate individuals into the fellowship of the congregation. In the early Middle Ages, however, it was extended to cover also secret sins.

Celtic and Anglo-Saxon missionaries brought this form of penance over to the continent, where it was gradually accepted without any opposition. French confessional manuals dating from the later part of the eighth century have adopted the Celtic regulations.

At the beginning of the ninth century, the so-called Carolingian reform of penance sought to reestablish the old public form of penance and to abolish the confessional manuals. But this effort did not succeed; the newer forms continued to be used.

By the year 800 the public form of penance had virtually disappeared. It remained, in vestigial form, in the following tradition (the *poenitentia solemnis*): in the case of gross, public sin, an act of reconciliation in church was prescribed. Thomas Aquinas wrote: "Sometimes those who have become contaminated by and have become guilty of gross and public sins ought to have public and solemn penance imposed on them, for their own good and as an example to others." (*Summa theologica*, suppl., qu. 28, art. 1)

The Celtic form of penance kept growing in popularity, and it came to form the basis of the practice of penance in the Roman Catholic Church. This new form was different from the older in that it recognized that penance could be and ought to be repeated, and also because it was concerned with lesser, private sins. This new form was not public, but neither was it purely private, inasmuch as confession was made to a priest and prescribed forms of making satisfaction were involved.

Penance in this new form implied *contritio cordis, confessio oris,* and *satisfactio operis. Contrition* was always emphasized, but *confession* before a priest also became necessary — in part so that the proper form of *satisfaction* could be levied on the individual. The public act of reconciliation was replaced in the confessional by the priestly *absolution,* which was given even before the completion of the satisfactions. The regular confession of even the lesser (venial) sins gradually became a universal obligation in the church. The Fourth Lateran Council of 1215 prescribed that confession must be made at least once a year.

From the very outset, the use of the confessional was related to the office of the priest and its power to bind and to loose. The priest could "bind" a person either by excommunicating him or by prescribing another kind of penance; the priest "loosed" a person by granting absolution. As a result of this, the confessional became the church's primary means of exercising discipline, and the strongest tie between priest and people. A general absolution, given to the entire congregation without prior auricular confession, was used on certain occasions, but it never replaced the regular practice of confession.

The demand to make satisfaction and to "do penance" was strictly enforced at this time. One could do penance either by giving alms or by fasting. Other common satisfactions were going on a pilgrimage, scourging oneself, or entering a cloister. The stricter forms of obligations could in many cases be replaced by assuming milder or briefer but more intensive penalties. This was called *redemptio,* the same method already noted in the Celtic confessional manuals. Fasting could be replaced by the giving of alms, for example, or a long fast could be shortened by scourging or by continuous reading of the Psalms.

CHAPTER 17

The Older Scholasticism

GENERAL INFORMATION

Within the context of the history of dogma, scholasticism refers to the theology which took form in the Western universities beginning in the middle of the 11th century, reached its culmination in the 13th century, deteriorated in the late Middle Ages, and was finally destroyed by humanism and the Reformation.

The distinguishing characteristic of scholasticism was its use of the philosophic method. The scholastics employed the dialectical system which was inherited from antiquity and was introduced into the philosophy taught in the schools and universities which flourished in the Middle Ages under the protection of the church and the cloisters. The scholastic approach developed when men began to subject the traditional material to an independent dialectical treatment. In addition to the Scriptures and tradition, the positions adopted by various teachers ("doctors") also came to play an important role. Other persons commented on their writings, around which separate "schools" were formed, and one system succeeded another. The dialectical method led by degrees to an endless division of theological problems; speculation was carried further and further, even to peripheral details.

Such expressions as "scholastic" and "scholastical" have often been used to designate a formalistic, sterile kind of theology, the presentation of which is confused and encumbered by the inclusion of unnecessary distinctions and empty rationalizing. As a general evaluation of medieval scholasticism, however, this is misleading. Medieval scholasticism was frequently degenerate, to be sure, but at its best it represented a serious activity, in which theological problems were skillfully and energetically studied. One cannot deny that this tradition possessed a plethora of ideas and observations, presented with logical discernment.

But why has scholastic theology been so hard to understand? The chief reason for this, perhaps, is that the philosophical tradition on which medieval university education was constructed has been replaced in more recent times by other presuppositions. As a result, our knowledge of the older forms of thought, which were dependent on antiquity, has to a large extent disappeared.

The usual estimate of scholasticism has frequently been influenced by the criticisms of humanism and the Reformation. Because of this, it is fairly easy to think of scholasticism as a uniform school of thought. But this is not the case. Many different schools were represented in this category. At the same time, scholasticism experienced a long and varied development, from the original form to the complicated and in many respects degenerate speculations of the late Middle Ages.

Two factors above all contributed to the development of scholasticism: church renewal on the one hand, which expressed itself in monastic reform (cf. the Cluny reform, e. g.), and on the other hand the increased association with the philosophical education of the time. The cloister and cathedral schools of this era, like the universities which later grew out of them, developed a form of instruction which was based on the educational heritage of antiquity. As a result of this, theological material, too, was studied in accordance with philosophical methods and thought forms. At the outset, logic was looked upon as the basic science. The writings of Aristotle in the field of logic were made available through Boethius (see above). The Aristotelian metaphysics was not used in theological instruction until later on, but once introduced it served as one of the most important presuppositions for the construction of the "high scholastic" systems.

THE LORD'S SUPPER

A doctrinal controversy which to a certain extent represented a continuation of the dispute concerning the Lord's Supper in the Carolingian period arose in the middle of the 11th century. Berengar of Tours (d. 1088) protested against the increased acceptance of the idea that the elements are changed by the words of consecration. This theological position, which was developed by Radbertus, was frequently combined with the superficial and naive idea that the body of Christ is divided into just as many pieces as the host consisted of, etc. Berengar defended the Augustinian position, as Ratramnus had, and he rejected the idea of a change as being unreasonable. The consecration means only that the elements are given a new, spiritual meaning. For the faithful, the elements are signs *(signa)* or pledges *(pignora)* of the receiving of the heavenly Christ. The substance of the elements does not change, said Berengar, but they do become a "sacrament," the bearers of an invisible gift.

Berengar's position, which was officially condemned at a number of synods, and which he himself was forced to deny many times, was opposed by Lanfranc (d. 1089, Archbishop of Canterbury). Lanfranc and other theologians developed the idea that the elements actually change, even though their external characteristics remain the same. The whole of Christ was said to be present in every part of the host, and is received by both believers and unbelievers. These men also rejected the mediating position which is called impanation or consubstantiation. This idea held that the elements retain not only their external characteristics but also their own natural substance, while at the same time serving as the bearers of the presence of Christ as a new, heavenly substance. This theory was later adopted by the nominalists in the late Middle Ages.

The doctrine of transubstantiation (an expression coined by the early scholastics) was subsequently established by Pope Innocent III at the Fourth Lateran Council of 1215. It was decreed there that "the bread in the Lord's Supper is changed by the power of God into the body of Christ, and the wine into the blood of Christ." (Cf. below, pp. 193–94)

THE CONTROVERSY BETWEEN NOMINALISM AND REALISM

Anselm of Canterbury (d. 1109, abbot of the cloister at Bec in Normandy, from 1093 archbishop of Canterbury) is remembered as the renewer of the Augustinian tradition and the founder of scholasticism. In his book *De fide Trinitatis* Anselm opposed the point of view which was called nominalism and which was supported by a number of contemporary dialecticians, among them Roscellinus. Nominalism held that man's universal concepts are nothing more than word pictures or names, which we use to identify what is common to various objects in the same category. Anselm maintained that concepts which are not perceived by the senses but which are formed by our rational powers are nevertheless representative of something real, a reality of a higher variety, comprehensible only to reason *(universalia sunt res)*. This point of view, in opposition to the former, was called realism. The philosophical debate in which Anselm thus became involved had a great influence on church doctrine as he saw it. For in his opinion the nominalist position contradicted the church's doctrine of the Trinity, as well as its Christology, inasmuch as it subverted the very foundation on which these doctrines were based. The thought was this: If one cannot distinguish between an object and its qualities, neither can one distinguish between God and His relations. The doctrine of the Trinity presupposes a distinction between God's substance and the three Persons in the Godhead, and thus it follows that reality is ascribed to the substance itself. The nominalists assumed that reality could be ascribed only to that which is particular. As a result, the three Persons could be conceived of only as three substances. This would mean that nominalism presented either a tritheistic point of view or a monotheism which eliminated every distinction between Persons. In respect to the Christological question, Anselm argued along similar lines: If a person does not distinguish between the individual man and the universal concept of "man," how can he believe that the Son of God took upon Himself human *nature?* For Christ did not assume a human person but only human nature.

At the same time, an extreme point of view developed side by side with Anselm's more moderate realism. The extremists emphasized the reality of the universals in such a way that individual objects became nothing more than modifications of the common substance, thus losing their independent reality (cf. William of Champeaux). But this school of thought, as well as extreme nominalism, was opposed by one of the most famous theologians of the age, Peter Abelard (d. 1142, active in Paris and elsewhere).

Abelard was a highly controversial figure in the theological arena, who was more than once accused of heresy. But in the dispute about the reality of the universals, he developed a mediating position which was generally accepted, even by the high scholastics. Abelard distinguished between concepts as merely a complex of sounds on the one hand *(voces)* and as designations of reality on the other *(signa)*. Entities for which concepts serve as signs do not exist apart from things as independent substances. But at the same time, definite reality can be ascribed to universal concepts: they exist *prior* to things, as the pattern of design in the mind of God. Furthermore, they exist *in* individual ob-

166

jects as their form or substance. And as designations of that which is common to various individuals they exist in our consciousness. This modified realism was subsequently adapted by Thomas Aquinas, who expressed his position in the formula "universals before things, in things, and after things" *(universalia ante res, in rebus et post res).*

THE DEVELOPMENT OF THE THEOLOGICAL METHOD

As seen from one point of view, scholasticism was an independent treatment of the doctrinal tradition inherited from the past. As already noted, this new theological presentation was made with the assistance of philosophy, used in one way or another. There was no parallel to this in the Eastern Church, which was for the most part content to preserve the dogmatic decisions made by the church fathers.

The man who was above all responsible for the scholastic development of the inherited tradition was Anselm of Canterbury. He did not himself produce a comprehensive study of dogmatics, but in a large number of modest books and meditations he demonstrated his sagacity with respect to individual points of doctrine. His point of departure for theological thought was a living, experiential faith. "Whoever has not believed will not understand. For whoever has not believed will not gain experience; and whoever has not gained experience will not understand." Meditation and theological speculation belong together. Anselm sought to advance from faith to a knowledge of faith's mysteries *(fides quaerens intellectum).* He desired to use the powers of reason as much as possible in his examination of the rational bases *(rationes necessariae)* of revealed truth. This method did not by any means suggest contempt for authority (Scripture and tradition); it was rather an attempt to utilize all available means to investigate and establish the truth of faith. As nearly as we can tell from the content of his point of view, Anselm was a faithful follower of Augustine.

Peter Abelard also exerted a powerful influence on the formation of the theological method. It was he who introduced the dialectical method, which was a bold attempt to combine authority and reason, faith and free scholarship. In his book *Sic et non* he posited propositions from the Christian tradition, to which he appended other statements, also drawn from Christian sources, which appeared to contradict them. He then proceeded to reconcile these opposed points of view. As he saw it, this can be done in three ways: (1) by scrutinizing these statements critically in the light of history, in order to determine their relationship; (2) by grading them on the basis of authority: the Bible is alone infallible, while the church fathers could be in error; (3) by throwing light on traditional truth by using reason and universal rational principles.

Abelard proceeded on the basis that faith and reason cannot contradict each other, since they issue from the same source — divine truth. Because this is so, he felt, one can subject the truth of faith to the test of reason without any danger. But why do this? In order not only to repeat that which is authoritative but to elucidate it.

The two Victorines, Hugo and Richard of St. Victor, who were in charge of the famous school in Paris that bore this name, went beyond Anselm in this direction. In their adaptation of tradition, they combined rational speculation with contemplative involvement. In his book *De sacramentis Christianae fidei* Hugo of St. Victor gave us scholasticism's first comprehensive treatment of dogmatics. (He used the word "sacrament" to refer to sacred things in general, to all aspects of the Christian faith.) The plan of the book followed the history of salvation. Richard's magnum opus was a discussion of the doctrine of the Trinity (in six volumes).

Hugo distinguished between meditation and contemplation. And while such distinctions are quite foreign to our way of thinking today, this was characteristic of the theological method of his time. *Meditation*, which was closely related to prayer, implied a search for truth; its objective was to enkindle the love of God in human hearts. *Contemplation* presupposed the overcoming of desire, and the illumination of the soul by the light of the truth. There were two kinds of contemplation: *speculation*, the dispassionate and scrupulous considering of the truth, and *contemplation proper*, the highest form of dedication to knowledge, the comprehensive view, which presupposes that the soul is filled with joy and peace, that it rests in the truth, and that it has attained to the perfect love of God.

Peter Lombard (d. 1160) combined the meditative adaptation of tradition provided by Anselm and the Victorines with Abelard's dialectic method. His well-known magnum opus, *Libri quattuor sententiarum*, encompassed the entire field of dogmatics. Its great significance can be attributed above all to the fact that it provided an orderly and lucid account of traditional doctrine. The volume is divided into four books:

(I) "Concerning the Trinitarian Mystery"; (II) "Concerning Creation"; (III) "Concerning the Incarnation of the Word and the Restoration of the Human Race"; (IV) "Concerning the Doctrine of Signs."

With respect to the various questions of detail which are quoted pro and con out of the Bible and the church fathers, Lombard sought with the aid of the dialectical method to show how such contradictory statements could be brought into agreement. His own position was very moderate. He acknowledged that philosophy could be of some help in providing solutions to the questions at hand, but he appealed to the recognized authorities (above all, the Scriptures) as being decisive in such matters.

Lombard's *Sentences* — as his work is often called — were of fundamental importance for theological instruction in the Middle Ages, right up to the time of the Reformation. A huge number of commentaries and expositions based on this book have been preserved, many of them only in manuscript form.

FAITH AND REASON

Anselm, like Augustine before him, represented that position with respect to faith and reason which was customarily characterized by the expression, "I believe in order that I may understand" *(credo ut intelligam).* Basing their opinion on the words found in Is. 7:9 (Vulgate), "If you do not believe, you will not understand," those who follow this line emphasize that faith is the presupposition of a rational insight into revealed truth. As Augustine put it, understanding is the reward of faith.

Anselm developed this position in more detail, among other places, in his *Proslogion.* It is clearly expressed, for example, in the following passage: "I do not attempt, Lord, to penetrate Thy depth, for by no means do I compare my intellect with it; but I desire to understand, to a degree, Thy truth, which my heart believes and loves. For I do not seek to understand in order that I may believe, but I believe in order that I may understand." (Ch. 1)

A similar statement appears in another work by Anselm, *Cur Deus homo:* "As it is the proper order that we should believe the deep things of the Christian faith before we presume to discuss them by reason, so it seems negligent to me if, after we have been established in the faith, we do not seek to understand what we believe." (I, Ch. 2)

The *credo ut intelligam* concept presupposes that theology and philosophy can be harmonized. That which forms the content of faith, and which man comprehends by faith, can also be understood by reason — at least to some extent. Faith and the principles of reason are not antithetical. It is the task of theology to present the content of faith in such a way that it can be understood and comprehended. For this reason, according to Anselm, theology must follow philosophical principles and use the assistance of logic. It is faith, however, which has the primacy, for man does not come to faith through reason; but on the contrary understanding comes by faith. The role of reason is simply to make clear, a posteriori, that the truths of faith are necessary even as seen from the point of view of logic and reason. For it is only after one has grasped revealed truth in faith that he is able, through rational discussion and meditation, to perceive that that which he believes is also agreeable to reason.

A good example of Anselm's argumentation is to be found in the so-called ontological proof of the existence of God, presented in his *Proslogion*. Faith conceives of God as the highest and most perfect being. This concept can be grasped intellectually even by those who deny the existence of God (cf. Ps. 14:1). That which is the highest conceivable cannot, however, exist only in the intellect. For then that which does actually exist — which is a condition superior to existing only as an idea — would be elevated above the highest conceivable, which would be unreasonable. Therefore one must assume that there is a highest being which exists both in the intellect and in reality.

The ontological proof was subject to various kinds of criticism even during the Middle Ages. Thomas Aquinas did not accept it; he rather held to the cosmological proof. He criticized Anselm's thought in this way: Assuming that God is the highest conceivable, and that a real existence is superior to one that is merely imagined — this does not prove the existence of God. The only conclusion one can draw is that if God is the highest conceivable, He must *be thought* to exist in reality. But reality cannot be verified in this manner, for it is not a quality which can be ascribed to an object in the same way as other qualities. Reality cannot be verified as a logical necessity, inasmuch as it does not belong to the sphere of logic.

To Anselm faith implied attachment to the revealed truth. But this was not simply an intellectual attachment; neither was it, therefore, merely an assumption, as some have thought. As far as Anselm was concerned, faith is related to love. Faith thus involves a volitional aspect — the concentration of the will on the object in which one has faith.

According to Hugo of St. Victor, faith is part cognition, part affection. Basically, as he saw it, faith is an act of the will, a volitional grasping of the content of faith involving three distinct stages. Hugo based these distinctions upon whether one was devoted to faith only on the basis of reverence *(sola pietate)*, or with the consent of reason *(cum approbatione rationis)*, or with an inner attraction and a certainty which comes from personal experience.

Abelard emphasized more strongly that faith is a form of knowledge. The will is motivated by the act of knowing, and to this extent there is a volitional aspect in faith. But it was of a secondary nature as far as Abelard was concerned, and in this he differed from Anselm and Hugo, who felt that faith is primarily an act of the will. Anselm and Hugo also believed that the content of faith is suprarational, whereas Abelard tended to look on faith as a form of necessary knowledge, analogous to philosophical knowledge.

ANSELM'S THEORY OF THE ATONEMENT

In his well-known book *Cur Deus homo* Anselm gave us a lucid exposition of the problem of the Atonement or, more correctly, of the Incarnation. This presentation, too, comes under the rubric *credo ut intelligam*. Anselm did not simply intend to provide a theological interpretation of the work of Christ but to demonstrate that the doctrines of the Incarnation and of the Atonement wrought through the death of Christ are borne up by a logical necessity. Anselm claimed that one could prove that this and nothing else had to happen, even apart from the testimony of revelation. As a result, he desired above all to serve those who already believe, but also to shame those who scoff at the faith.

The question which Anselm used as a point of departure was this: "On what basis or for which urgent reasons did God become man so that by His death, as we believe and confess, He thereby gave life to the world? Why did He do this, inasmuch as it could have been done either through some other person, angel or man, or simply by His will?" (I, Ch. 1)

Anselm's book is in the form of a dialog between himself and Boso, one of his disciples. Boso asks the questions, and Anselm answers them.

The teaching of satisfaction in Anselm's theory has its background in cosmology and in the history of salvation. Anselm believed that God, in His wisdom and love, had decided from eternity to establish a kingdom of rational beings, obedient to His royal will, dwelling under His dominion. When a fall took place in the angel world, thereby diminishing the number of spiritual beings who were to live in this kingdom, God created man to replace the fallen angels. Human destiny, therefore, is to live under God's dominion and to obey His will. When man fell away from God through an act of disobedience, the entire divine plan for the universe was disturbed, and God was deprived of His honor. This was not simply a personal insult; it was also a violation of God's majesty and of the plan He had ordained for the world. It was unthinkable that God's plan should go unfulfilled, or that God should have to endure this insult to His honor, occasioned by man's fall into sin. "*Anselm:* In the order of things, there is nothing less to be endured than that the creature should take away the honor due the Creator, and not restore what he has taken away. . . . Therefore the honor taken away must be repaid, or punishment must follow; otherwise, either God will not be just to Himself, or He will be weak in respect to both parties; and this it is impious even to think of. *Boso:* I think that nothing more reasonable can be said." (I, Ch. 13)

It was therefore necessary, as seen from the point of view of the plan God had willed for the world, that this wrong should either be remedied or punished. God could not surrender the plan He had established, and neither men nor angels could escape God's imperious or punishing will. It would be unreasonable and therefore impossible and contradictory to God's nature for the confusion and perversity brought about by sin to remain. Hence the famous conclusion: "It is necessary that either satisfaction or punishment follow every sin" (*necesse est, ut omne peccatum satisfactio aut poena sequatur.* I, Ch. 15). In view of the fact that punishment *(poena)* in this case implied the destruction of man and thereby the frustration of God's plan for a kingdom of rational beings who serve Him, the only remaining alternative was to provide a remedy *(satisfactio).*

Man is unable to make such satisfaction. For inasmuch as man is obligated to perfect obedience to God's will, nothing that he can do could be considered a fitting recompense for the wrong which was done. Anything that man might do is simply his appropriate duty. Sin is a greater evil than we can comprehend, since it is an insult to God's honor and a violation of the divine plan for the world. Because of this, an infinite compensation was required, greater than all that there is apart from God. Hence, no one can repay God for all that man owes Him because of sin, except one who is greater than all that there is apart from God, viz., God Himself. "*Anselm:* Therefore none but God can make this satisfaction. *Boso:* So it appears. *Anselm:* But none but a man ought to do this, otherwise man does not make the satisfaction. *Boso:* Nothing seems more just. *Anselm:* If it be necessary, therefore, as it appears, that the heavenly kingdom be made up of men, and this cannot be effected unless the aforesaid satisfaction be made, which none but God can make and none but man ought to make, it is necessary for the God-man to make it." (II, Ch. 6)

Christ, who is both God and man, is therefore the only one who could make amends for man's guilt. This satisfaction was made, according to Anselm, not through Christ's life, for His obedience was only that which He owed to God, but rather through His death. Christ was not subject to death, but He subjected Himself to it voluntarily and thereby acquired merit which shall forever redeem the sins of all men. By making this merit available for man as satisfaction for sin, Christ thereby repaired the broken plan, and man was reconciled to God. "Now you see how reason of necessity shows that the celestial state must be made up from men, and that this can only be by the forgiveness of sins, which man can never have but by man, who must be at the same time divine, and reconcile sinners to God by His own death." (II, Ch. 15)

Anselm's theory of the Atonement developed the juridical (or forensic) point of view: the Atonement is a *satsifactio vicaria,* which in a superabundant manner redeemed the guilt of all men and thereby restored God's offended honor. That the merit which Christ acquired through His voluntary death can be transferred to the human race is dependent on a divine decree. How this fits into the history of salvation is not clear, but this is consistent with the rational basis which, as noted above, involves the logical demonstration of the necessity of the Incarnation independent of the Bible.

To some extent Anselm found the model for his theory of the Atonement in the medieval practice of penance, with its careful weighing of offense and satisfaction. The deliberate one-sidedness of *Cur Deus homo* makes it necessary for us to conclude that this writing was not representative of scholasticism's doctrine of the Atonement taken as a whole. Thomas Aquinas, for example (who provides us with a suitable comparison), related satisfaction to the idea that Christ was the second Adam, the head of a new humanity. This description is more fully in agreement with Biblical categories. Christ is presented not only as the individual God-man, whose satisfaction has been transferred to man, but also as the head of the congregation which participates in His death and resurrection through faith and Baptism. This concept goes beyond the purely juridical evaluation of the merits won by someone else.

Abelard's understanding of the Atonement was very different from Anselm's. As he saw it, Christ's death has salvatory power only in the sense that it awakens reciprocal love in our lives and so destroys our sins. Christ's life and message were interpreted in a similar manner. Anselm's book *Cur Deus homo* does not tell us how the individual receives Christ's atonement, but Abelard provided an answer to this question. Said he, forgiveness is provided on the basis of the love awakened within us through Christ's example. Not many have agreed with Abelard on this point. The medieval era was dominated by the idea that the Atonement comes to us as an infused grace received through the sacraments.

THE QUESTION OF GRACE AND NATURE

The older scholasticism based its exposition of grace and justification (as well as many other things) on the Augustinian heritage. The fundamental distinction between grace and nature was not recognized at that time, as it was by the later scholastics, who began to use the concept of the supernatural *(supernaturalis)* to describe the way in which grace is related to nature. Such early scholastics as Anselm and Peter Lombard described the work of grace chiefly as the restoration of nature. They did not, therefore, think of it as elevating man above nature. The numerous questions which were treated in this context were usually answered on the anthropological level. This can be illustrated by the following typically Anselmian trend of thought:

Originally, by virtue of the grace bestowed on him at Creation, man possessed righteousness *(iustitia)*; this consisted of the proper attitude *(rectitudo)* of the will, and its ability to practice virtue. As a result of the Fall, man lost the *rectitudo* of his will, and he therefore lacks the possibility of being righteous on the strength of his own power. He cannot deal justly, for to do so presupposes the proper volitional qualities. Inasmuch as righteousness depends on the will's *rectitudo*, it cannot be achieved by an act of man's will. Neither can the perverseness of the will be altered by an external influence, i. e., from any created thing. Thus it is that man can be justified only by grace (*gratia praeveniens* or *operans*). Furthermore, if the proper attitude of the will is to be maintained once it has been restored, the assistance of grace is required. For man can retain righteousness only by willing it. And this proper attitude of the will is the work of grace. Hence it follows that righteousness can be preserved only by grace (*gratia subsequens* or *cooperans*).

Those who have followed the Augustinian line have usually juxtaposed operating and cooperating grace with living faith (*fides viva*). Merit does not precede grace. Because the will is bent in upon itself (*incurvitas*, the opposite of *rectitudo*), its lack of righteousness makes it impossible for the will to cooperate in bringing man to salvation. Faith and righteousness mutually condition one another: for to will what is right requires faith (the knowledge of the truth), and to have faith requires a "right will." Both of these are the product of grace, which repairs the ruin of nature and restores its original righteousness (*gratia sanans*). The order in which this is done is described, for example, in the following way: through the infusion of grace, which must come first, the will is turned toward a new objective, and new stirrings are awakened in man. He deplores his sin and thereby receives the forgiveness of sin.

It was not until early in the 13th century (a theologian named Philip the Chancellor marks the transition) that men began to speak of grace as a supernatural gift which elevates man above nature so that he can share in the divine (*gratia elevans*). As already pointed out, this idea was characteristic of the theology of "high scholasticism."

CHAPTER 18

High Scholasticism

GENERAL PRESUPPOSITIONS

The development of scholasticism reached its apex during the 13th century. The synthesis between the philosophical *Weltanschauung* of antiquity and the Christian faith, long anticipated in the West, was now brought to completion and established in fixed patterns. A general advance in science and learning formed the basis for the theological achievements of this age. The University of Paris, which became an international stronghold for theological education, replaced the Parisian cathedral schools in the 12th century. The two mendicant orders, the Dominican and the Franciscan, founded at the beginning of the 13th century, also did much to promote learned theological study. The major theologians of the time were associated with these orders. The increased knowledge of Neoplatonic and above all Aristotelian philosophy which then became available (partly with the assistance of such Arabian commentators as Averroes and Avicenna, partly through direct translations into Latin) contributed significantly to the doctrinal development of high scholasticism.

Prior to this, Western knowledge of Aristotle was confined to his work in the field of logic, but in the 13th century his other writings also came to light. In the sphere of general science the study of his natural philosophy led to a new interest in natural science. And in the field of theology Aristotelian premises gradually came into use — in spite of some opposition from ecclesiastical sources. Theologians discovered, above all in Aristotle's metaphysics and ethics, a number of viewpoints and definitions which could be useful in their scientific approach to doctrinal questions (e. g., Aristotle's distinction between form and substance, and between actuality and potentiality, his doctrine of causation, and his description of virtue). This new philosophical element

177

created a new attitude in the field of theology, and this in turn did much to prepare the way for the majestic synthesis of theology and philosophy and faith and reason which manifested itself in the theological systems of the 13th century.

Contemporary theological instruction consisted of lectures, chiefly on Biblical texts, and disputations on particular dogmatic problems. At this point, however, a new feature was added in the impressive form of the so-called theological summaries and sentence commentaries (wherein, above all, the scholastic heritage was preserved for posterity). The earlier "dialectical" treatment of the material was replaced by more radical methods, which often reflected the procedure of the disputations. The Biblical-Augustinian tradition was here inserted into a world view which was formed on the basis of Neoplatonic and Aristotelian metaphysics. The doctrinal propositions or sentences previously loosely joined together could thus be transformed into a firm and uniform system.

In high scholasticism, philosophy was accorded a position relative to the knowledge of faith which was different from that given it by the older scholasticism — depending, of course, on the extent to which the new scientific methods were followed. The older scholastics employed the dialectical method in discussing the truths of faith in order, so to speak, to demonstrate their logical necessity a posteriori. Under the high scholastics the rational adaptation became more independent in relation to faith. The metaphysical world view came to form the basis of the entire theological presentation. The Augustinian *credo ut intelligam* evolved into a system in which faith and reason were looked upon as two equal principles of knowledge, harmoniously working together, even though it was recognized at the same time that they represented two different worlds. The way now led from *intelligere* to *credere*. Faith formed the superstructure to the natural knowledge involved in the Aristotelian system of metaphysics.

AUGUSTINIANISM AND ARISTOTELIANISM

Even though the theology of high scholasticism did not as a rule cultivate a particular philosophical point of view, preferring instead to synthesize the elements found in various sources, one can nevertheless discern a number of major currents of thought, dominated by those of Augustinian and Aristotelian origin. (Neoplatonism, which also played

178

a significant role, was present to some extent in Augustinian ideas, but it exercised a direct influence as well, particularly in mysticism.)

The Augustinian-Neoplatonic line was represented above all by the older Franciscans (see below), while the theologians of the Dominican order were more closely related to the Aristotelian point of view. But there were no hard and fast lines of demarcation: those who perpetuated the Augustinian tradition also devoted themselves in some measure to the new Aristotelian concepts; at the same time, there were Dominicans who derived a great deal from the Augustinian heritage. Thomas Aquinas, the most prominent of the Dominican theologians, did as a matter of fact combine Augustinian and Aristotelian points of view — the inherited Christian doctrinal tradition and the contemporary philosophical structure. As a philosopher, however, Thomas was closer to Aristotle than to the pure Augustinian concepts.

The incorporation of Aristotelianism into Christian theology presupposed the rejection of certain concepts held by this pagan philosopher and his commentators, inasmuch as they were contradictory to Christianity. Among these, e. g., were Aristotle's idea concerning the eternal nature of the world, his belief that there is a universal soul rather than an individual soul, etc. At the same time, however, there was a group of theologians who accepted Aristotle without these limitations, just as he was made known to the West by the Arabian philosophers. To do this and simultaneously hold fast to the fundamentals of the Christian faith, these men took refuge in the theory of double truth: what is true in philosophy can be false in theology and vice versa. This school of thought, known as Latin Averroism, was represented, for example, by Siger of Brabant and Boethius of Dacia. Its views were condemned by ecclesiastical authorities (Paris, 1277), just as Aristotle's natural philosophy had been proscribed in order to prevent its initiation into theology. In its "Christianized" form, however, Aristotelian philosophy did provide (in future years) the scientific basis for scholastic theology.

It may be well at this point to mention some of the basic characteristics of the Augustinian-Neoplatonic and the Aristotelian thought forms. These distinctive philosophical points of view left their mark on the opposing theological schools within high scholasticism.

The Augustinian position with respect to epistemology was based on the idea that intellectual knowledge can essentially be derived from an immediate "enlightenment." Man participates in divine thought, and his

179

intellect therefore possesses within itself the ability to create insight. External things are not the direct cause of our knowledge; they only provide the impulses which cause the subject to form knowledge. This is called the illumination theory, and it also has significance for the understanding of faith. True faith is an immediate certainty, inwardly given, an infused or inspired faith *(fides inspirata)*. This is superior to all authority, and it implies an immediate certainty about divine things.

The Aristotelian epistemology, on the other hand, is based on the idea that the human subject receives knowledge from without. In its relationship to the world without, the intellect is passive, and it possesses the ability to receive the form of things as *species intelligibiles,* which are transformed from things to the intellect via sensual impressions. "There is nothing in the intellect which was not earlier in the senses." This position involves a stronger empirical interest and a pronounced sense of tangible reality. This is important also in theology. The Christian concept of creation is, in a sense, of decisive significance in this tradition. God is thought to stand in a direct relationship to external reality and to be active also in the temporal order. The high appreciation of the natural order as an expression of God's creation which has been characteristic of later Western theology, both within Lutheranism and Roman Catholicism, was promoted by the influence of Aristotelian philosophy. Its epistemology held, therefore, that knowledge is formed by external impressions. The soul is a blank slate *(tabula rasa),* which is able to receive these impressions and thus form logical knowledge. In the act of knowing, the soul is united with the form of the object which it perceives. Knowing involves the union of the intellect and the object of knowledge. The forms which provide the nature of things, and the forms which the intellect receives and absorbs into itself are identical. According to Thomas Aquinas the soul is, "in a way, all things" *(quodammodo omnia).* Faith is to be understood in an analogous manner. Faith is not so much inner enlightenment as it is a form of knowledge similar to others, although it has a different object. The truth of faith is not empirical but revealed. This revealed truth comes to man through the authorities (e. g., Scripture), but it has its origins in God's own truth. What we have here is a question of supernatural knowledge in contrast to natural knowledge.

The Augustinian and the Aristotelian schools also differed with respect to anthropology: in the one case the soul of man was thought of as an independent entity, while in the other soul and body were spoken of as a unit. But dualism is involved to some extent even in those forms of scholasticism which are otherwise Aristotelian in structure. Furthermore, the Franciscan school was voluntaristic, whereas Aristotelianism tended to be intellectual: within the former the will was seen to be the primary factor, ruling in a sovereign manner over one's actions; according to the latter point of view the intellect was thought to be of prime importance. The intellect, it was said, influences the will, so that the will desires that which the intellect considers to be good. This difference of opinion was of significance in the dispute between Thomism and Scotism (see below), just as it was later on in the controversy between the Thomists and the nominalists.

THE OLDER FRANCISCANS

Alexander of Hales (d. 1245, the first of the Franciscans to teach at the University of Paris) was the founder of bona fide high scholasticism. His book, *Summa universae theologiae,* was designed to be a commentary on Peter Lombard's *Sentences,* but it was at the same time the first and the most comprehensive of theological summaries. As such, it was of fundamental importance for Franciscan scholastic theology. The huge amount of material gathered in this book has not yet been thoroughly researched. It can be said in a general way, however, that Alexander represented the older Augustinian line from Anselm and Hugo of St. Victor but at the same time introduced certain categories derived from Aristotelian metaphysics and further developed the dialectical technique.

Alexander defined theology as a kind of wisdom *(sapientia).* Man comes to possess theological knowledge through direct inner enlightenment. The knowledge of God is with man from the outset (a congenital factor), while additional knowledge is imparted by grace later on. This enlightenment which comes by grace is identical with infused faith *(fides infusa)* and it is combined with a certainty *(certitudo)* which is independent of authority. As will be clear from what has been said, Alexander accepted Augustine's theory of illumination: all knowledge, both natural and revealed, presupposes the illumination of the soul by a divine light. Alexander's concept of faith was voluntaristic; he emphasized the practical, voluntary nature of faith. The Franciscan doctrine of grace will be dealt with later on.

Bonaventura (d. 1274, a contemporary of Thomas Aquinas and like him a teacher in Paris) was closely related to his predecessor, Alexander of Hales, and the Augustinian tradition. He too accepted the illumination theory of knowledge as well as the voluntaristic concept of faith. Bonaventura also placed great emphasis on the concept of exemplary ideas — a concept which did much to influence the scholastic view of the world. He said that the prototype of created things was to be found in God's thoughts. Created things retain an indelible impression of these divine thoughts (to a greater or lesser degree), and they are an expression of them. Those things which most remotely represent the divine are called "shadows" *(umbrae),* others are called "vestiges" thereof *(vestigia),* while some things — those that most clearly reflect it — can be called "images" *(imagines)* of the divine. In this last category, for example, we find the soul of man. This kind of thinking formed the background for the so-called doctrine of analogy: the created world is neither identical with nor absolutely distinct from the divine, but it is in some sense similar to it. There is an analogy between God and creation, and on the basis of this we can know something about God as a result of our knowledge of created things.

Bonaventura and his followers were to some extent opposed to Thomas Aquinas and the Thomists. They disagreed, for example, about the doctrine of grace (see below) and about epistemology and even with respect to the basic view of the relationship between God and creation. Bonaventura referred everything, even natural knowledge, to its divine origins, and he did this in such a way that the natural and the supernatural blended together into a comtemplative unity. Thomas, on the other hand, employing a closely related analogy concept, emphasized the lack of similarity and the fundamental distinction between God and the created world.

Bonaventura combined scholastic erudition with mystical contemplation. Among his many writings there is a sentence commentary — thought by some to be the best of its kind — and also a brief summary of dogmatics, entitled *Breviloquium.* But he also left behind a number of other works which are clearly of a mystical bent, chief among which is the well-known *Itinerarium mentis ad Deum* — an attempt to describe the ways in which the soul can raise itself to knowledge of God and to the vision which forms the highest stage of this knowledge.

THE DOMINICAN SCHOOL

Albertus Magnus (d. 1280, a native of Württemberg, active in Cologne and elsewhere) left behind an enormous amount of scholarly works, which testifies to his universal erudition. He was occupied with all the sciences known in his era. In the field of natural science, where his contributions are recognized even today, he demonstrated his ability to make independent observations and also his empirical point of view, which was different from the traditional method of perception. It was Albertus who, more than anyone else, made Aristotelian philosophy known and useful for contemporary science. In the field of theology it was he who prepared the way for the acceptance of the new principles; this was accomplished in part by transforming Aristotelianism in such a way that it harmonized with the doctrine of faith. As a result of this activity, Albertus laid the foundation for the work which was completed by his famous disciple Thomas Aquinas. As a theologian, Albertus followed the traditional Augustinian point of view for the most part.

Thomas Aquinas (d. 1274, when only 50 years old; teacher in Paris, and for a time at the papal curia and in Naples; son of a prominent Italian family) brought scholasticism to its highest point of development. He surpassed Albertus as a systematician, and he also succeeded in bringing the new Aristotelian concepts and the Christian tradition together in an organic union.

The following is a list of some of his better-known works in theology and philosophy: a sentence commentary, written at the beginning of his career; a number of Bible commentaries; *Summa contra gentiles*, an apologetic work which spans the entire field of theology; *Summa theologica*, begun in 1269 and not yet finished at the time of his death (the missing parts were supplied later by one of his followers, who used corresponding material taken from Thomas' sentence commentary); a group of minor works; and commentaries on most of the writings of Aristotle.

The *Summa theologica*, which was Thomas' magnum opus and the classical work of all scholasticism, and which is still the basic text for theological study in the Roman Catholic Church, consists of three parts: Part I deals with the divine Being and God's creative work; Part II concerns God as the goal of human activity; and Part III deals with Christ as the way to reach that goal, and with the sacraments and eternal life.

THOMAS' TEACHING ABOUT THE KNOWLEDGE OF GOD

Basic to the Thomistic system is the conviction that the human intellect is in accordance with things in their essential structure and that, in the process of knowing, the mind of man identifies with things and partakes of their essence. One can compare this to the expression referred to above, that the soul of man is *quodammodo omnia*. Man's ability to penetrate the very nature of things, and to know their cause and purpose, is the basis of metaphysical speculation. At the same time, however, there is some knowledge of God which is, so to speak, given, such as the knowledge that God is, that He is the highest, perfect Being, etc.

Thus it is that the possibility of man's knowledge of God as the highest Being and as the Ground of all reality is to be found in the ability of the intellect to comprehend the nature of things. Man cannot, of course, comprehend God's absolute nature, which is infinitely superior to created things. But there is nevertheless a connection between the absolute Being and the created world — they both exist. When the intellect grasps the nature of things, it can also draw the conclusion that God exists in a corresponding manner. Existence can be ascribed in an analogous way both to God and to created things (to employ a later term: *analogia entis*).

By virtue of our knowledge of the created world, therefore, we can arrive at some knowledge of God. Thomas presented five different ways in which this can happen. He developed these ideas on the basis of five important aspects of the created world, viz., movement, efficient causes, necessity, perfection, and the order of things. From these Thomas proceeded to speak of God as the first, unmoved Mover *(actus purus)*, the first Cause *(ens a se)*, the absolute Necessity, the absolute Perfection, and finally as the highest Intelligence. On the other hand, Thomas rejected the idea of an immediate, congenital knowledge of God.

Our natural knowledge of God is highly imperfect: it includes a general realization that God exists, but it cannot tell us what He is really like. There is, however, another way of knowing God, which is elevated above reason and cannot be reached by metaphysical speculation. This is the knowledge of God which comes to man through revelation. It is derived directly from God's own knowledge, and it is accessible to man through the light of grace *(per lumen gratiae)*.

It is this supernatural knowledge of God which is the proper subject of theology. This knowledge is received by faith and is clearly distinct from purely rational, verifiable knowledge. For the content of faith does not possess the kind of evidence that results from direct observance of the object of knowledge or from being able to understand why it is as it is. Faith is based on authority, on something that someone else has said. The certainty of revelation lies in this, that God has spoken. Yet such knowledge is itself basically of the same kind as that derived from natural sources. In this Thomas was opposed to the older Franciscans, who looked upon faith as an immediate illumination, complete with an axiomatic certainty inspired by God (see above). According to Thomas, faith is knowledge *(scientia)*, although its content is different from that which is derived from natural sources.

As a result of this view, Thomas' concept of faith was influenced by his theory of knowledge. There is an unbroken connection between ordinary conceptual knowledge and the supreme vision of the divine Being. That the intellect partakes of the nature of things is analogous to the fact that faith partakes of the divine.

If faith is to be perfect, it must be combined with love. Man is able to believe in God and truly share in His life only on the strength of the infused gifts of grace. The highest level of sharing is the beatific vision, which shall replace faith in eternity and which implies that man, by the light of glory *(per lumen gloriae)*, will there see God directly and thereby share in His being.

THEOLOGY AND SCIENCE ACCORDING TO THOMAS

As already noted, the Thomistic system involved the application of Aristotelian principles to the theological sphere. This was done in such a way that these philosophical concepts did not simply serve as incidental formulae or as principles of methodology; they rather molded the very structure of the system itself. The presupposition was that theology and science are in harmony, just as are faith and reason.

As Thomas understood it, theology is a science. At the same time, it is different from rational knowledge, inasmuch as the content of faith is inaccessible to reason and can come to man only through revelation and the light of grace. Reason is unable to perceive the basis of revealed truth, but faith accepts it on the basis of God's authority. This might be compared to a peasant hearing someone discuss philosophic truth. He does not recognize the principles which lie behind this truth, but he can nevertheless assume that it is so because he has confidence in the philosopher who is speaking, who does know the principles and why they act as they do. A similar relationship occurs in the sciences: one science will sometimes support its claims on the basis of propositions borrowed from another, without trying to prove them independently. The optometrist, e. g., borrows from geometry, and geometry in turn borrows from mathematics. In the same way, theology builds on borrowed propositions whose correctness it does not itself demonstrate. The higher "science" from which theology secures its principles is the supernatural world's own knowledge, the knowledge which God and the angels possess about divine matters. In this way theology is given a scientific character, even though it cannot itself prove or even fully comprehend the principles on which it bases its assertions. Complete insight and understanding belong to another world. Theology is the knowledge of God possessed by persons living in this world. It is based on faith, which finds its support on another's authority and which holds revelation to be true even though it lacks rational evidence.

On the basis of this unique idea — borrowing theological principles from a higher science — Thomas Aquinas succeeded in combining two contradictory scientific concepts: the Aristotelian and the Augustinian. The former held that science, in the strict sense of the term, involves only objects which can be rationally demonstrated. According to the latter, even the knowledge which comes by faith can afterwards be perceived and contemplated by our rational powers. Duns Scotus and the late medieval nominalists criticized this Thomistic compromise and — applying the Aristotelian concept more consistently — rejected the idea that theology is a *scientia*.

DUNS SCOTUS AND HIS UNDERSTANDING OF FAITH AND KNOWLEDGE

Duns Scotus (d. 1308, teacher at Oxford and Paris) was a Franciscan, and he continued the older Franciscan opposition to the solution suggested by Thomas to the problem of theology and science. Duns Scotus was considered the most astute of the scholastics (*doctor subtilis*), and it was he who carried the philosophical analysis of theological questions to its extreme. At the same time, Duns gave rise to new trends of thought which foreshadowed the dissolution of scholasticism and signaled the end of the harmonious relationship between theology and philosophy.

Duns, like Thomas, was an Aristotelian, but he was more empirical than Thomas. For Thomas, reality was to be found in the nature of things, i. e., in the universal. For Scotus, also individuality implied logical reality. He argued that individual qualities give a thing its form, while Thomas maintained that only matter is the basis of the division into individual things (matter is the *principium individuationis*). Scotus himself was a realist, but as a result of his emphasis on the subjective he anticipated the rise of nominalism, which associated all reality with individual things.

While Thomas stressed the relationship between theology and science with respect to knowledge, Scotus demonstrated that there is a cleavage between theological and scientific knowledge. The latter deals with the universal, with that which things have in common, with universal laws and principles. Theology, on the other hand, deals with God's revelation, which includes, among other things, the singular works of salvation, to which Scripture bears witness. This implies that its objects are somewhat "contingent" (the opposite of "necessary"). Because of this, a theological system cannot be constructed simply on a metaphysical basis, as was the case in Thomism, for when theology deals with supernatural truths it must refer only to the Scriptures and to ecclesiastical tradition. Scotus was unable to find the way which led from natural knowledge to faith; the latter, as he saw it, is supported only by authority.

Theology is not so much a question of theoretical knowledge. Faith is practical knowledge *(cognitio practica)*; it presupposes the surrender of man's will to God's, to authority. And its object is not theoretical knowledge; it is rather to change the human will so that it comes to agree with God's will. Faith finds its goal in love *(caritas)*. According to Thomas, a volitional aspect was also included in knowledge, which was supreme in his estimation. The goal of faith, as Thomas understood it, is the beatific vision, which can be understood in analogy to earthly knowledge.

As has been made clear from the foregoing, Scotus' point of view, like that of the older Franciscans, was voluntaristic. Fundamental to his theological position was the concept of God's sovereign will, against which the free will of man is set. The goal is that the latter shall be subjected to the former and be conformed to it.

When Scotus turned against Thomistic intellectualism, and to a certain extent undermined the harmony between theology and science to which Thomas gave expression, this did not mean that Scotus refused to use philosophy in the service of theology. On the contrary, he carried the scholastic method even further than his predecessors. But in principle Scotus looked upon philosophy as merely an aid (through logic, e. g.) in further explicating the doctrines of the church and in refuting false teachings.

DUNS SCOTUS AND THOMAS AQUINAS

As a result of the work of Duns Scotus, the contrast between the Franciscans and the Dominicans (which we have already touched upon) was accentuated.

With respect to *the doctrine of God,* the difference between the two schools can be explained as follows: Thomas thought of God as the highest Being, which meant that he conceived of God in intellectual categories. Scotus, on the other hand, emphasized God's sovereign will as the basis for the course of the world and for revelation. Scotus distinguished between God's *potentia absoluta* and *potentia ordinata.* According to the former, God is completely free and can act independently of all rules. Good is good because God wants it so *(perdeitas boni).* According to the latter, God acts in a manner consistent with the order of creation and the order of salvation, which is to say that He permits men to be saved through the work of Christ and the sacraments of the church. But it is conceivable that God (according to *potentia absoluta*) could act independently of this order. As Thomas saw it, on the other hand, God's will always coincides with the order which He established. God wants the good because it is good *(perseitas boni).*

Scotus also deviated from the prevailing scholastic position in respect to *Christology.* This was because he strongly emphasized the humanity of Christ. Scholasticism ordinarily conceived of the human nature as having been absorbed by the divine nature. The latter was "person forming," which was often tantamount to presenting a one-sided picture of Christ. Scotus' stress on Christ's humanity can be explained by his empirical point of view, as well as by his conception of the reality of the individual.

As was true of scholasticism in general, Thomas Aquinas associated *the doctrine of the Atonement* with the sacraments. Through His suffering, which included His entire earthly life and not just His death,

Christ has secured sufficient merit to counterbalance the sins of all men for all time. This merit is transferred to the faithful through the sacraments, which bring to us the gifts of grace. Scotus too connected salvation with the suffering of Christ, but this relationship, as he saw it, exists only because God has accepted Christ's sacrifice as a substitute for human compensation. All depends, in the final analysis, on God's free acceptance. Such a position is quite far removed from the idea of the rational necessity of the Atonement as set forth by Anselm.

The most important difference between the Franciscans and the Dominicans is to be seen in connection with the doctrine of grace and justification.

THE DOCTRINE OF GRACE IN HIGH SCHOLASTICISM

How can a man be justified and share in the blessings of salvation? The high scholastics had much to say in answer to this question (particularly the older Franciscans, who provided a detailed *ordo salutis*). For the most part they built on the inherited tradition. As a rule, however, the merit and reward ideas were emphasized more strongly than in the earlier Augustinian position, and a Semi-Pelagian tendency is clearly visible in Franciscan theology. Greater significance was attached to the sacraments as the agents of grace. Furthermore, the high scholastics distinguished between natural and supernatural operations of grace in a way that was not true previously. This led to a concept of grace in which it was asserted that man can be elevated above the level of nature. Besides this, the idea of the preparatory acts was inserted into the doctrine of justification itself. The major aspects of the *ordo salutis* developed by the older Franciscan theologians will be apparent from what is said next.

As a result of Christ's atoning work, God's plan of salvation for humanity has been put into effect. Through His predestination, God has selected those who believe in Christ to be freed from sin and to attain to blessedness and eternal life. This takes place in justification and in the course of the continued work of grace in man's life. Life in the church under the influence of the Word and of sacramental grace is, therefore, a continuation of Christ's atoning work, and the execution in time of predestination's eternal decree.

What is grace? This was thought to be in part the eternal loving will of God, or uncreated grace (*gratia increata*), and also to be that grace

189

which comes to man as a gift and therefore prepares the way for human salvation, or created grace *(gratia creata)*. The latter consists chiefly of the so-called infused grace (see below), which brings about justification and good works. But *gratia creata* also includes all of that which God gives to man for nothing. These gifts, and particularly those which prepare man for salvation, were summarized by the Franciscans under the term *gratia gratis data*, the grace given freely to man, without involving the question of merit (or, in other words, for nothing).

Some of the preliminaries to salvation can be discerned even in natural man. Among the heathen, for example, one encounters a certain longing for knowledge about God; in the reason and will of man there is a certain proclivity to devise and do what is good. But above all, *gratia gratis data* refers to that which specifically prepares the way for the reception of the higher grace: an embryonic faith *(fides informis)*, preliminary repentance, which results from the fear of punishment *(attritio)*, a lower form of fear *(timor servilis)*, and an indefinite hope *(spes informis)*. The call which comes through the Word *(vocatio)* also has its place here.

The proclamation of the Word, or the Gospel, has a relatively obscure place in the order of salvation. It merely provides the knowledge which is necessary if one is to receive sacramental grace, and with it justification. Chief emphasis is given to the sacraments. The Word has something of a legal character, telling us what to believe and do. The Gospel is presented as a new law *(nova lex)*, which not only commands but also provides the power necessary to carry out its commands. But this power is not provided through the Word itself; it comes via the sacraments instituted by Christ.

The gifts which are summed up in the *gratia gratis data* concept are related exclusively to the natural sphere. The question is: What must a man do in his own strength *(facere quod in se est)* to be prepared for the reception of grace? The baser forms of faith and repentance which are possible at this stage are not enough in themselves to justify man. But according to the Franciscans, they do constitute a *meritum de congruo*, or proportional merit. It is probable that God rewards these deeds, even though they are not truly meritorious in themselves. The reward they bring is that God provides the true grace *(gratia gratum faciens)*. It is this which justifies a man — makes him well-pleasing to God — and wipes out his guilt, at the same time that it makes available to human nature that superior equipment which is necessary to produce good works and to win *meritum de condigno*, genuine merit.

Justifying grace is an infused *habitus*, a *donum habituale*, provided through the sacraments, primarily through Baptism but also through penance and the Lord's Supper. Grace can be lost, and then regained through penance. This *habitus* elevates a man's nature to a higher level and replaces the *donum superadditum* which man lost as a result of the fall into sin. Infused grace alters the direction of man's will towards God and makes possible both a genuine faith *(fides infusa)* and a spirit of repentance which is motivated not by fear of punishment but by love for God *(contritio; timor filialis)*. Thus it is that genuine merit can be found, which will be rewarded with eternal life, the grace of glory *(gratia glorificationis)*.

Thomas Aquinas changed certain facets of this scheme. He emphasized the priority of grace in relation to man's free will, and he rejected the strong psychologizing which characterized the Franciscan position. According to Thomas, man is unable in his own strength to prepare himself to receive grace. We cannot take the initiative in creating faith; the beginning of faith coincides with the coming of grace. As a result, all talk of *facere quod in se est* must cease. A certain preparation can take place, but only with the assistance of grace, and this (according to Thomas) is not meritorious. It does not, of and by itself, lead to salvation. Justification is purely and simply a supernatural work, which can result only by virtue of infused grace. When a man comes to share in the *habitus* of grace — and this takes place in a moment — he is justified.

Among the older scholastics, as with Augustine, grace was understood as the making whole of human nature *(gratia sanans;* see above, pp. 174–75), which had been damaged by the Fall. But not so with the high scholastics, who conceived of grace as a supernatural gift which elevates the nature of man to a higher level *(gratia elevans)*. These gifts of grace were looked upon as being necessary, not only because man is a sinner but also because it was thought that man could attain the saving knowledge of God and the blessed vision of God only after these gifts were added to what is ours by nature.

Justifying grace coincides with infused love, which perfects a man and enables him to perform meritorious deeds. As a result of its influence, man's original righteousness is restored (because it equips man with the *habitus* of love), and his already converted will is supported in

191

its desire to do what is good (*gratia operans* and *gratia cooperans*). Grace is an inner power which enhances his natural qualifications and provides him with supernatural virtues. Hope becomes a firm trust, and faith becomes not simply a *fides informis* but an inner conviction molded by love. Fear becomes "filial fear" (*timor filialis*). When grace cooperates with man's natural powers, merits result. These are meritorious as the work of free will, but they become fully meritorious only with the assistance of grace. Merit is not required for man's justification; it is needed only in order that man might be able to retain the gifts of grace and attain to blessedness (*beatitudo*), which thus appears in part as a reward for his merits.

HIGH SCHOLASTICISM'S VIEW OF THE SACRAMENTS

Scholasticism gradually formulated the point of view which came to be accepted quite generally within the Roman Catholic Church. Beginning with Peter Lombard, it was thought that there are seven sacraments: Baptism, confirmation, the Lord's Supper, penance, extreme unction, ordination, and marriage. Thomas Aquinas conceived of the sacraments as "physical" signs, designed to protect and enhance the life of the spirit. Bodily life begins with birth and then requires growth and nourishment. So it is with spiritual life; it begins with the new birth of Baptism, receives strength to grow from confirmation and nourishment from the Lord's Supper. Spiritual life is further advanced through penance, which removes the sickness of sin, and by extreme unction, which takes care of the remnants of sin. The last two sacraments concern man in relation to society: ordination, which bestows the right to rule over others in the clerical office (and thus corresponds to political office in the civic sphere), and marriage, which is intended to increase the church numerically (and which is related both to spiritual life and civic life). Thus it was that the seven were justified. It was more difficult, however, to show that each of these had been instituted by Christ. And it was not easy, either, to demonstrate the claim that each sacrament consists in part of an external element (*materia*) and in part of an accompanying word, which provides its purpose and effect (*forma*). This was particularly difficult in the case of penance, ordination, and marriage.

All of the sacraments were looked upon as bearers of the grace which resulted from Christ's substitutionary suffering. The sacraments manifest this suffering in various ways, and they convey its healing and creative influence to the members of the church. This concept was given logical form in a variety of ways. The Franciscans, and especially Duns Scotus, associated themselves with the Augustinian, symbolic point of view, and they looked upon the communication of grace as an effect brought about directly by God, alongside the external use of the sacraments. In other words, the effect of grace is something which accompanies the external use of the sacraments. Thomas Aquinas, on the other hand, devised a theory in which he referred to the sacraments as instruments for the communication of grace. Thomas believed that grace is not only "morally" related to the external use of the sacraments, but that it is "physically" included within them. According to this theory, the sacraments are not simply signs of the grace which God bestows in an invisible manner, but they are in the real sense the cause of the communication of grace. It was thought, therefore, that the sacramental act is in itself effective, independent of accompanying faith in the words of promise. This conviction is expressed by saying that the sacraments work *ex opere operato.*

In addition to the elements *(materia)* and the accompanying words *(forma),* it was also maintained that the intention of the ministrant to execute the sacraments as the church intended is necessary to sacramental validity. On the other hand, the effect of the sacraments was not thought to be conditioned by whether the officiant has faith or not.

Finally, we shall point briefly to some of the questions discussed in connection with the various sacraments.

Water was the prescribed material to be used in *Baptism,* and its form was the words spoken by the officiant: *Ego te baptizo in nomine Patris, et Filii, et Spiritus Sancti.* Baptism, like confirmation and ordination, was thought to confer a *character indelebilis,* and because of this these sacraments were never repeated and lack of faith could not render them invalid. When it was asked what this *character indelebilis* was like, lengthy discussions resulted.

It was held that *confirmation* provided the power required for the Christian's spiritual struggle. Its *materia* is balsam oil, which is smeared on the confirmand's forehead while these words are spoken: *Consigno te signo crucis et confirmo te chrismate salutis in nomine Patris,* etc.

The Lord's Supper was looked upon as the most important sacrament, inasmuch as it is most closely related to the suffering of Christ. The doctrine of transubstantiation — which, as mentioned earlier, was ratified at the Fourth Lateran Council in 1215 — was interpreted by Thomas to mean that the substance of the bread and wine is changed by the consecration into the body and blood of Christ. On the other hand, the elements retain their accidents, their size, smell, taste, and so on. Nor should it be said that the substances of the elements are destroyed *(annihilatio)*, but rather that they are transformed into the substance of the body and blood of Christ.

Another theory was championed in particular by Duns Scotus. He believed that the bread retains its substance and that Christ's glorified body comes down into the bread through the consecration and is found there together with the natural substance of the bread, without quantity but whole and complete in every part of the sacramental bread. This is the so-called consubstantiation (or impanation) theory. Scotus attempted to reconcile this theory to the teaching prevalent in the church, but the two were incompatible. Scotus also considered the possibility that the substance of the bread is replaced by the body of Christ and is therefore destroyed. The impanation theory was subsequently adopted by the nominalists, but it was unable to replace the already sanctioned doctrine of transubstantiation.

Penance was thought of simply in terms of auricular confession to a priest, including the three acts which provide the suggested *materia* of this sacrament: the contrition of the heart, the confession made by the mouth, and the satisfaction prescribed by the priest. The latter consisted of prayer, fasting, and the giving of alms. The form of the sacrament is to be found in the words of absolution: *Ego te absolvo,* etc. In this form, penance presupposed that the power of the keys (the right to bind or loose a man with respect to sin) has been given to the priest. The so-called indulgences presented a special problem. It was believed that the power of the keys also included the right to exchange one form of satisfaction (corresponding to the sin involved) for another, easier one, or to excuse the need to make satisfaction altogether. The indulgence system was justified by the claim that the church possesses a treasury of surplus merits, acquired by Christ and the saints. The original intention was that an indulgence should be given only in connection with confession and that sincere repentance was a necessary prerequisite. But the practice was separated from genuine penance, and then it was that the gross misuse of the indulgence system, which aroused strong opposition even during the late Middle Ages, appeared.

Extreme unction was given only when it was assumed that death was near; then the sick person's various members were anointed with consecrated oil while prayer was said. This sacrament was looked upon as a complement to penance, and it was believed to result in the removal of the remnants of sin and — "where practical" — in the healing of the body. Biblical support for this act was found in James 5:14-15.

Ordination, or consecration into the various church offices, was also considered to be a sacrament, inasmuch as it provided sanctifying grace by means of a visible sign. The act itself, which in the case of a priest involved the presentation of chalice and paten with bread and wine, was not considered to bring grace as did the other sacraments; it was the officiating bishop who through his person provided the power of office. The act of ordination was therefore looked upon as symbolic, and not as effective in itself (Thomas, *Summa,* suppl. qu. 34, art. 5). Most persons believed that the bishops and the priests together form the "priestly office" *(sacerdotium),* while others thought of the episcopacy as a special office superior to the other (e. g., Duns Scotus).

Marriage, which has both civic and religious implications, was thought to receive its sacramental character from the fact that it symbolizes Christ's love for the congregation (Eph. 5). Mutual agreement *(mutuus consensus)* was considered to be the effective cause of marriage. The form of this sacrament was taken not from the priestly benediction but from the verbally expressed *consensus.* The indissolubility of marriage was regarded as the result of its sacramental nature. In view of the fact that marriage is illustrative of the love which Christ revealed in His suffering, it can be placed (despite the civic overtones) in the same category with the other sacraments — as a mediator of the grace which is a fruit of Christ's suffering and death.

At the Council of Constance (1414–18) the severe criticisms which John Hus and John Wyclif (see below) directed toward the sacramental system were repudiated. At the Council of Florence (1439) the tradition of the seven sacraments, which had been shaped by scholasticism, was formally accepted (the bull *Exultate Deo,* by Pope Eugenius IV).

CHAPTER 19

Late Scholasticism

OCCAMISM

Late medieval nominalism, which ought to be distinguished from the earlier school of the same name, was a unique phenomenon in the history of theology. At the same time that its representatives were sharply opposed to the entire range of previous scholastic thought and contested many of its fundamental principles, they nevertheless perpetuated the scholastic tradition and completed (sometimes in an extreme fashion) the dialectical reworking of theological material. Their profound interest in philosophy is witnessed to by the thorough treatment given to questions on the periphery of theology, and particularly to the problem concerning the relationship between theology and philosophy. (When they commented on Lombard's *Sentences,* they dealt chiefly with the Prolog and the first book.)

The originator and foremost representative of this school was William of Occam (teacher at Oxford; accused of heresy and summoned to Avignon, where he was held in custody for four years; later taught at Munich, where he was protected by the emperor, Louis of Bavaria; died in 1349). Chief among his many followers were Peter d'Ailly (d. 1420, cardinal, active in the reform councils) and Gabriel Biel (d. 1495, professor in Tübingen), whose *Collectorium* summarized the Occamist tradition in an exemplary manner. Biel's theology was basic for the instruction in a number of German universities, including Erfurt, where Luther was educated.

Occam took a fresh look at the problem of universals which had been prominently discussed by the first scholastics. Occam rejected the realism of Thomas Aquinas and revived the nominalist position, which held that only the individual possesses reality. He did not believe that there was any basis to the claim that universal concepts actually exist, either within or apart from things. Occam proceeded from the principle that one ought not assume the presence of more entities than is necessary. One need not assume that universal concepts exist apart from our thoughts *(extra animam)*. The realistic point of view must therefore be repudiated. Universals are only concepts which are formed in the mind of man to designate a number of individuals of the same kind. The task of science is to investigate concepts in their context and relationships. As a result, logic was the basic science as far as the Occamists were concerned, while metaphysics was to be abolished. In spite of certain tendencies in the direction of a more modern, more empirical method of observation, Occamism actually led to a much more abstract form of speculation than was true among the realists. This was partly because it was no longer believed that science was able to deal with things in their external reality but merely with terms and concepts as they appeared in man's mind or in verbal presentations.

Occam developed his epistemology primarily in order to deal with the problem of theological knowledge. His criticism was directed against the so-called proof of the existence of God. By denying the reality of the universals, the cosmological proof of Thomas Aquinas fell by the wayside. For this implied, as shown above, that we can attain insight into the existence of God by virtue of our knowledge of the universal element in the things we see. To Occam, God, in the most proper sense, is something individual *(res singularissima)*. Neither can one rationally prove that God is the first cause of all things. Metaphysics can, of course, demonstrate in other ways the existence of one or many gods, but such claims as the oneness of God, and His infinity, must be looked upon as confessions of faith and nothing else.

Still less can the doctrine of the Trinity be pondered in a rational manner. Occam conceded that it presupposes a realistic point of view, for it speaks of relationships which exist independently of our thought processes. While Occam otherwise denied the reality of such relationships, he was content to refer the question of the Trinity to the authority of Scripture, which cannot be invalidated by the principles of empirical knowledge — for such knowledge deals only with creation, not with God.

What has now been said illustrates Occam's understanding of the relationship between theology and philosophy. Unlike Thomas Aquinas, Occam did not consider theology a science. Its propositions cannot be elucidated by logical means; as articles of faith, they have their only support in the Scriptures. Occam felt that there is a radical difference between theology and philosophy. But that is only one side of the matter. The other is that he believed quite simply that theological concepts and propositions could be treated by logical and dialectical means. Indeed, he and his associates practiced this art with great virtuosity. The fact that Occam conceived of theology and philosophy as being radically different did not, therefore, prevent Occamist theology from being more highly colored by philosophical argumentation than was true of any other previous school of thought.

According to Occam, theology must be based on *fides infusa*. What did he mean by faith? Above all, an inclination to believe Biblical truth. He did not accept the older Franciscan idea of faith as an immediate experience of the divine. Faith is concurrence in or agreement with Biblical truth. Biel defined faith as follows: "One who reads the Bible (if he is a believer) immediately agrees with each and every thing recorded there, because he believes that all these things are revealed by God." (*Collectorium*, III, dist. 24, qu. unica, G)

The nominalists held, in principle, that Scripture is the sole authority. Some even attempted to cite its teachings in opposition to the pope and other ecclesiastical authorities. But in general practice the Bible and the doctrines of the church were blended together; ecclesiastical traditions were firmly supported even if they lacked Scriptural foundation. This was true, for example, of transubstantiation, which Occam accepted even though he felt that other theories were more Biblical in nature. The nominalists developed a theory of the immediate inspiration of Scripture. Canonical authority was based on the conviction that the words of the Bible were inspired in the writers by God Himself.

Not everyone can attain a firm faith in all of the Biblical truths. A distinction was therefore made between *fides implicita*, which accepts Biblical or doctrinal truth only in a general way, and *fides explicita*, which presupposes a knowledge of the individual articles of faith. The latter was required only of clergymen, while the former was considered sufficient for laymen in general.

As far as theological content was concerned, Occam for the most part accepted the older tradition. But he also altered it at a number of points and lodged criticisms which weakened its foundations.

An example can be found in his concept of sin and grace. Occam did not believe that original sin actually exists in man's nature. It is merely God's judgment of man, ascribing to man the guilt of Adam; it is not an actual corruption of human nature. In connection with the traditional view of sin, Occam also spoke of sin as *fomes*, an inclination in man to do what is evil.

One consequence of such a concept of sin would be that grace is looked upon merely as the forgiveness of sin, an exoneration from guilt. If sin is not thought of as habitual depravity, there is certainly little reason to think of grace as an infused *habitus*. Occam did make a concession to tradition in this case, however, for he spoke of grace as *gratia infusa* even though he was otherwise critical of the *habitus* concept.

Occam's understanding of the order of grace was influenced by Pelagian ideas. When a man has done all that he is able to do *(facit quod in se est)*, he is rewarded with gifts of grace. Man is able, of his own power, to produce merit of a lower order *(meritum de congruo)*. His natural powers can even enable him to love God above all things. These ideas were related to the belief that sin is not a corruption of nature but only separate volitional acts. It was the Occamist teaching about grace which was later criticized above all by the Reformers. (Cf. the Apology to the Augsburg Confession)

With respect to the question of predestination, Occam perpetuated the idea of voluntarism which went back to Duns Scotus. God is the Absolute Will. In His *potentia absoluta* He is independent of every law. If a man is to be saved, therefore, this depends exclusively on God's decree. Similarly, the decision as to whether or not an act of man is meritorious is also dependent on God's will. The old relationship between merit and grace was therefore sundered. *Caritas*, infused grace, was no longer thought to be a necessary prerequisite for meritorious deeds.

The entire Occamist ethic was marked by this same point of view. Good is good because God wills it. There are no eternal commands, and those which exist are valid because of the power of God's will. Nothing can prevent God from making other commands valid.

THE LATE MEDIEVAL OPPOSITION

As one could infer from what has already been said, nominalist theology was at many points critical of prevailing church doctrine in its scholastic configuration. This does not mean, however, that there was any overt opposition or deep skepticism involved (as some have tried to find in Occamism). The nominalist theologians adhered very strictly, as a general rule, to the dogmatic position of the church. The eventual heretical contradictions were avoided by their reference to ecclesiastical authority as the foundation of faith and to the cleavage between theological knowledge and rational knowledge. But a more pronounced criticism of the medieval church and its theology did come from other sources, as for example the Waldenses and such individual theologians as Wyclif and Hus.

John Wyclif (d. 1384) was sharply critical of papal authority. Christ alone is the head of the church, he said. Church and state form a unity under the dominion of Christ, with the Scriptures serving as law. Wyclif thus developed the idea of an independent national church.

Theologically speaking, Wyclif began his career as a nominalist, but he later adopted the realist position; he came to feel that the latter position was in closer agreement with the content of revelation. Wyclif found support for his opposition to the medieval church in the writings of Augustine. It was from this point of view that he criticized the doctrine of transubstantiation, which he felt was unbiblical. In opposition thereto he suggested a symbolic interpretation of the Lord's Supper, citing the Augustinian distinction between sacramental sign and spiritual meaning. Wyclif's far-ranging critique of church and dogma also included censure of the theory of penance and the indulgence system.

Wyclif's ideas were subsequently taken up by John Hus (d. 1415), whose activity led to widespread opposition movements in Bohemia.

Jean Gerson (d. 1429) was included among the medieval authors with whom Luther agreed in many things. He was a nominalist, but he criticized the scientific approach of scholasticism and emphasized instead the subjective experience of faith. In other words, Gerson combined the nominalist theological position with the mystical view of life.

The Protestant Reformation was not simply a continuation of the late medieval opposition to the Roman Catholic Church. It was rather a renewal of a much profounder nature and with far greater consequences. But it did not by any means come into being as a completely unexpected revolution; it had deep roots in the developments of the Middle Ages.

CHAPTER 20

The Medieval Mystics

Medieval mysticism had its origins in Augustinian theology and monkish piety. Bernard of Clairvaux (d. 1153) was the first medieval figure to develop mysticism as a unique theological position. Bernard based his theology on the belief that the man Jesus is Lord and King. Meditations on Christ's earthly life, and particularly on His sufferings, were at the center of Bernard's mysticism. Above all he was motivated by the concept of Jesus as the soul's Bridegroom, which he derived from the Song of Solomon. Among the first scholastics who perpetuated the mystical point of view were Hugo and Richard of St. Victor. They inserted mystical ideas into the scholastic theological system.

It has often been thought that mysticism and scholasticism are opposed to one another, but the actual relation between them defies this conclusion. Mysticism was not foreign to scholastic theology, nor was the latter foreign to mysticism. There were some scholastics who were pronounced dialecticians (as, for example, Abelard and Duns Scotus), while others blended scholastic theology and mysticism in their writings, such as the Victorines, who have already been mentioned. Thomas Aquinas provides us with another example of this. His books in the field of theology are expressive of mystical experiences and feelings. There are elements in scholastic thought which are related to mysticism. Franciscan theology speaks of the knowledge of God as coming directly to the soul of man. Thomas considered the beatific vision to be the perfection of theology, and he thought of knowledge as a preliminary to this vision. Mystical contemplation frequently formed the basis of scholastic activity. Thomas Aquinas once said that he learned more from his meditations before the cross of Christ than from the study of erudite books. A Franciscan theologian who combined mysticism and scholasticism to a high degree was, as mentioned earlier, Bonaventura.

During the late Middle Ages mystical forms of piety were encouraged by certain basic elements in the culture of the time. There was an increased interest in man, for example. The need for personal, experiential Christianity grew. Individual religious experience was emphasized in a way that was not common in the classical medieval culture. More extensive education increased the influence and the religious activity of the laity.

Late medieval mysticism was dominated by a school which is usually called German mysticism, because of its geographical range. In northern and western Germany a group known as *die Gottesfreunde* ("the friends of God") came into being. The most prominent of the German mystic authors belonged to this group. Most of them were from the Dominican school and were related in some respects to the theology of Thomas Aquinas.

One characteristic of mysticism was that it restricted the subject matter of theology much more than did scholasticism. The mystics were above all interested in the following subjects: the doctrine of God, the angels, the soul of man, and the significance of the sacraments and of the liturgical acts.

Chief among the late medieval mystics was Meister Eckhart of Hochheim (d. 1327; taught in Paris, Strasbourg, and Cologne). The most prominent of his followers was Johannes Tauler (d. 1361; active as a preacher in Strasbourg, Cologne, and Basel), who has enjoyed great respect, not least of all among Protestants. Heinrich Seuse (or Suso, d. 1366) and Jan van Ruysbroeck (d. 1381; of Flemish extraction) also belonged to this group. The anonymous *Theologia deutsch* also originated among "the friends of God."

Meister Eckhart was related theologically to Thomas Aquinas, but he wove the traditional Christian material together with a Neoplatonic mysticism. At the same time that he developed mystical ideas along theological lines, he also served as a preacher and lecturer. He used both Latin and German. Shortly after his death, 28 of the doctrinal propositions which he defended were declared heretical. Because of this, his name was largely unknown among theologians until the 19th century, when the Romantic Movement placed Eckhart in the foreground among the mystics. German idealism also adopted some of his basic concepts, though in an altered form. Late medieval and Renaissance philosophy was also influenced to some extent by Eckhart's point of view. Related ideas are found particularly in the works of the well-known philosopher Nicholas of Cusa (d. 1464).

According to Meister Eckhart, God is the absolute One, beyond the complexity of creation and even beyond the Trinity. He described the origins of the world partly as a creation, partly as an emanation. There is an absolute cleavage between God and creation. The soul of man alone occupies the middle ground. The soul includes a divine nucleus in the depths of its being, which is the foundation of the soul or the spark of the soul (scintilla animae). This foundation of the soul is identical with the absolute One, and it is the place where God is born in the soul. Eckhart did identify God and being, which sounds like pantheism, but this assumption is neutralized by the sharp distinction which he drew between God and the creation.

Christ, according to Eckhart, is the prototype of the union of God and man. As such He is the example for all the faithful. Eckhart did not place the Cross and the Resurrection at the center, but rather the Incarnation, in which this union was manifested.

Man is saved by dying away from the world and by entering into himself in such a way that he can be united with the divine. This is done in three stages: through purification, illumination, and union.

The first stage, purification, consists of repentance, a dying away from sinful pursuits, and a struggle against sensuousness.

The second stage, illumination, consists in the imitation of the sufferings and obedience of Christ. The best means for this are contemplation of Christ's sufferings, surrendering one's own will, and being absorbed in the will of God. It would be wrong to conclude that the mystic ideal is pure passivity. The fusion of God's will and man's can just as well take place in an active life. The object is to will and to do that which is good, according to God's desire, and to turn away from the evil which originates within us. Love of one's neighbor is the highest form of the love of God. Eckhart wrote: "If anyone should find himself enraptured in the way Paul once was, and then came to hear about a sick man who asked him for a bowl of soup, I believe it would be much better to forsake the rapturous love in order to serve God in a greater love." But above all, said Eckhart, it is suffering which promotes the dying away from one's self. "The quickest way to reach perfection is through suffering." Mystical meditations were often related to painful mortifications, as can be seen, for example, in the writings of Heinrich Suso.

The third and highest stage, the union of the soul with God, takes place when man becomes entirely free from created things and their allurements, as well as from himself. Christ is then born in the soul, and man desires what God wants and becomes one with Him. In some instances this experience was of an ecstatic nature, or else it produced visions, which constitute the very acme of the life of the pious. According to Thomas Aquinas, the vision of God can only take place in eternity, but the mystics sought for this perfect experience of the divine already here in this world.

According to German mysticism, God is the One, the only reality. Being is God, said Eckhart. Where then does creation fit into this monistic point of view? If God is the only reality, that would mean that created things are nothing. But they too have come forth from God. Must not a certain reality at the side of God be ascribed to them? The mystics replied to such questions by saying that the things of the world lack reality apart from God. They are like the rays of light which could not exist apart from the lamp. They are related to God as light is to the fire. Therefore one can speak of the creation as having originated with God and, nevertheless, as being nothing.

Man's task in life is to depart from the world and even from himself in order to find perfection, which is to say, to be absorbed by the One, to be united with God Himself and thereby to make contact with the only true reality. Man himself belongs to creation, which is nothing, dominated by evil. The primary cause of man's alienation from God is his own will, which has separated itself from God's will. Salvation consists of man's reunion with the divine, and this is accomplished through the three stages referred to above: purification, illumination, and union.

The mysticism of Meister Eckhart was different from that of Bernard of Clairvaux; it was less closely related to Christian doctrine and was more deeply influenced by Neoplatonic ideas. The "mystical union" was emphasized more by the former as the goal of the pious. Eckhart also used philosophical ideas more generally, whereas Bernard's mysticism centered upon meditations based on the life of Christ.

The other authors who are numbered among the "German mystics" were certainly influenced by Eckhart, but as a rule they were more faithful to the doctrinal tradition of the church. This was especially true of Johann Tauler and the *Theologia deutsch*.

Johann Tauler's sermons have come down to us in written form, and they have been read extensively also by Protestants. Tauler was more practical and also more popular than was Eckhart. There are many genuinely evangelical ideas in his writings, and Luther regarded him highly. Nevertheless he was a typical mystic. He accepted the teaching of the divine foundation of the soul within man, and he often placed the inner word above the external proclamation and the words of Scripture.

Another source which exerted a great influence on Luther was the modest little book *Theologia deutsch*. It was first published in 1516 — by Luther himself (it was, in fact, the first book Luther brought to press). In the Foreword to a later edition Luther said that "next to the Bible and St. Augustine, this book has taught me more than any other." The paper on which Luther submitted these words has been lost, but in the past century another version of this statement was found, bearing the title *Der Frankforter*. Luther believed that Tauler was the author of *Theologia deutsch*, but recent discoveries have shown that this is not true. The author of this book, which probably appeared toward the end of the 14th century, was a member of "the friends of God," but he remains anonymous. The major topic dealt with is "the perfect good" — union with God — and the way to reach this goal.

Another well-known book by a late medieval mystic was *De imitatione Christi*, by Thomas a Kempis. It appeared at the beginning of the 15th century. The author was initially a teacher at the famous monastic school at Deventer in Holland, but he spent most of his time writing at an Augustinian cloister in Germany. No book written by a mystic has been read more widely than this one. In fact, *The Imitation of Christ* is one of the most widely distributed books in the entire field of literature. It has been published in some 3,000 editions. The book was published anonymously, and the question of its authorship was long debated.

PART III

The Modern Period From the Reformation to the Present

CHAPTER 21

Luther

Luther's contribution to the Protestant Reformation forms the basis of the entire growth and development of Evangelical Lutheran theology. Furthermore, his writings have to a greater or lesser degree served as a direct source of inspiration for theological thought and the preaching of the Word throughout all of the epochs which have passed since the time of the Reformation. As a result, Luther's writings have assumed a central place in the history of theology.

What we intend to do in this chapter is merely to provide a survey of the major facets of Luther's theology, as seen against the background of previous and contemporary traditions.

LUTHER'S DEVELOPMENT TO THE DIET OF WORMS, 1521

In modern Luther research many have shown partiality to "the theology of the young Luther." This interest is based on the idea that the Reformation can be explained genetically by going back to the young Luther in order to see how his thinking developed. Furthermore, it is believed that significant parallels can be drawn between certain forms of modern theology and the young Luther and his earlier, relatively unknown world of thought. It ought to be remembered, however, that those who proceed on this basis look at the Reformer's theology from points of view different from those he himself referred to in his more mature years. He himself was very critical of his earlier development and concluded that he was then in error in many respects and that he did not then clearly recognize the degree to which he was at variance with the scholastic tradition in which he had been educated.

But apart from this, it is certainly important for our understanding of Luther's person and message to know something about his earlier development and the kind of education he received, for this forms the background for his appearance in public.

After preparatory schooling at Magdeburg and Eisenach, Martin Luther (1483–1546) enrolled in the year 1501 at the University of Erfurt, where he studied in the arts faculty and passed his master's examinations on Jan. 7, 1505. Here he learned Aristotelian philosophy according to the *via moderna,* which is to say, in the nominalist tradition. Representatives of this school, which then dominated several German universities, stood in opposition to Thomism *(via antiqua)* and claimed that they understood and interpreted the philosophy of Aristotle in a more correct way. Later this was at times reflected in Luther's polemics. He was known among his comrades as a "keen dialectician."

After taking his master's examination, Luther began to study law and at the same time to lecture in the arts faculty. But then the crisis occurred which in the summer of 1505 led him to decide to become a monk (the thunderstorm at Stotternheim, on July 2, 1505). Luther thus entered the cloister of the Augustinian eremites in Erfurt. After two years he was ordained as a priest (1507), and he studied theology in accordance with the study program of the cloister. During this time he became acquainted with the dogmatic position of the Occamists. Biel's *Collectorium* and Peter d'Ailly's and Occam's sentence commentaries were included among the works he studied. In 1509, after lecturing for a year at Wittenberg on Aristotelian ethics, Luther himself became a so-called *sententiarius,* which gave him the right to lecture on the *Sentences* of Peter Lombard. The notes he made for these lectures have been preserved throughout the years. He also began to study Hebrew at this time, something quite unusual in those days.

In 1510 Luther was sent to Rome to attend to a matter which concerned a dispute in the Augustinian order, and he, like many other Rome-pilgrims of the time, was disappointed at the degeneracy there. After his return to Germany, Luther was forced to leave Erfurt and go to Wittenberg, where Elector Frederick the Wise had organized a small university in 1502 and where the vicar-general of Luther's order, Johann von Staupitz, resided.

It was at the behest of Staupitz that Luther continued to devote himself to studying and preaching. In the following year (1512) Luther became doctor of theology and took a professorship, *lectura in biblia,* at the university.

At this time Luther was beset by anxiety, which could not be conquered even by an exaggerated use of the sacrament of penance. The

Occamist doctrine of grace did not satisfy him. This doctrine stated that if a person did all he could, using his own powers *(facere quod in se est)*, God would then also give him His grace. But how could one be sure that he had fulfilled all of the preliminaries? Occamist theology also calculated that man could, by his own natural powers, love God above all things. This prompted Luther to wonder whether or not he was one of the elect (predestination obsession).

In this situation Luther was helped to some extent by Staupitz, who was his confessor. Staupitz was a Thomist and a mystic, and therefore acted on the basis of a tradition different from Luther's. He recommended, among other things, that Luther contemplate the crucified Christ rather than worry about his election, and thus see trials and tribulations as signs of God's grace. On the strength of the new insights which Luther struggled to attain during this period, he acquired greater certainty and overcame his anxiety. Luther also later spoke of "temptations" — they occupy an important place in his theology. But in the question of their concrete background there is a difference between temptations during his time in the monastery and those he spoke of later on. The latter were more connected with difficulties in his life's calling: the resistance and indifference of the people, the persecution and opposition from the pope and the enthusiasts, the realization that he alone was responsible for the upheavals of the Reformation, etc. During his time in the monastery, on the other hand, the question of predestination stood in the foreground. Luther's temptations were also due to physical causes, but the assumption that his struggle in the monastery was a pathological depression is without valid foundation. This is proved, among other things, by his great capacity for work during this time.

From 1513 to 1517 Luther continued to work quietly — teaching, preaching, and disputing. During these years he lectured on the Psalms (1513–15), Romans (1515–16), Galatians (1516–17), and Hebrews (1517–18). Some of these lectures have been preserved, partly in notes taken by those who heard him and partly in Luther's own notes.

These early writings prepared the way for Luther's later appearance on a much larger stage and contributed to the mature Reformation point of view. With respect to the interpretation of Scripture, Luther here expressed the opinion that one can understand the Bible only from the vantage point of religious experience or, more properly, as a result of being practiced in faith.

Luther's dependence on Augustine was very great. In his early years Luther as a general rule identified his position with Augustine's. It was the latter's teaching of sin and grace that Luther desired to uphold in opposition to the scholastic teaching of justification. This was also decisive as far as Luther's relation to Occamism was concerned.

Many of the concepts derived from the nominalist tradition made a lasting impression on Luther's thought. One can point, for example, to the distinction between theology and science, the critique of the *habitus* doctrine, or the idea of the absolute and well-ordered power of God *(potentia Dei absoluta et ordinata).* In the essential questions, however, one can see how radically Luther broke with Occamist theology. His polemical thrusts were directed early and often at this position. Occamism's Pelagian doctrine of grace, and its blending of theology and philosophy were sharply attacked in a disputation against scholastic theology in 1517. Luther held that it was unreasonable to assert that man could of his own natural powers love God above all things and thereby prepare himself for the reception of grace. Rather, it is characteristic of natural man to love himself and the world and to be opposed to God. Grace precedes a good will, and to do good one must first be good. The Occamists spoke of a "logic of faith," applicable even in questions involving the mysteries of faith, but in doing so they had to bring theological propositions before the bar of reason and mix together theology and philosophy. It had been said during the Middle Ages that no one could be a theologian without the help of Aristotle. But Luther said that no one could be a theologian unless he rejected the help of Aristotle.

Luther's first appearances elicited small attention. But when he posted his *Ninety-five Theses* on Oct. 31, 1517, and thus took up arms against the flourishing misuse of the indulgence system, he aroused a storm which soon led to a complete break with the Church of Rome and its theology. A war of pamphlets ensued, involving among others Sylvester Prierias and Luther, and in 1518 the Roman curia, acting through Cardinal Cajetan, made a clumsy attempt to force Luther to recant (at Augsburg). A highly polemical debate between the Roman theologian Johann Eck and Luther, held in Leipzig in 1519, produced no great victory for either side.

As seen from the theological point of view, the disputation held when Luther visited in Heidelberg in 1518 was of greater significance.

This debate not only touched upon the pertinent question of indulgences but also concerned the problems of sin and grace, of man's inability to do good, of free will and faith. As the theses of 1517 had been directed against scholastic theology, the point of this disputation was directed against the theology and philosophy of Occamism. Luther also turned his back on the Occamist leaders at Erfurt. But as he did this, he won more and more respect from the younger generation. Wittenberg University flourished to such an extent during these years that it was soon able to compare itself with the greatest educational centers in all Germany.

A decisive event in Luther's life was the discovery that the "righteousness of God" as referred to in Romans is not a righteousness that judges and demands, but the righteousness given by God in grace. Luther mentioned this discovery in the Foreword to his collected works (1545), and he associated it with the preparation of his second commentary on the Psalms, written in 1518–19. In interpreting the passage in Ps. 30 which says (in the Vulgate version) *in tua justitia libera me,* Luther went to the words in Rom. 1:17, "For in it [the Gospel] the righteousness of God is revealed through faith for faith, etc.," and thereby achieved this insight after long deliberation. This discovery provided him with a key to the understanding of similar passages in the Bible, and he thus attained new clarity with respect to the point which became central in Reformation theology. The significance of this discovery (called *das Turmerlebnis*) has been the object of lively discussion in Luther research. If it happened at the same time as the Reformation breakthrough, it should most likely be assigned to an earlier year than Luther indicated, namely to the period 1511–14. Other scholars have tried to give another explanation while retaining Luther's own dating.

Some of Luther's most significant writings were published in the years 1519 and 1520. As evidence of his extraordinary productivity during these years one can point to the fact that in the second half of 1519 Luther published no less than 16 books. The 80-page (in the Weimar edition, 40) rejoinder directed against Sylvester Prierias was written in two days. Among other writings produced in these years were the minor *Lectures on Galatians* (1519); *A Treatise on Good Works;* and *On the Liberty of a Christian* (1520). In the same year appeared the *Address to the Christian Nobility of the German Nation,* with suggestions for reforms in education and in the church; also the controversial

tract *On the Babylonian Captivity of the Church,* in which Luther
made it clear that he had broken with the Roman concept of the sacraments, as well as with the monastic system. In so doing he also attacked
some of the most important foundations of medieval culture.

A bull of excommunication was drawn up by degrees in Rome, in
which Luther was accused of heresy on 41 points. These points did not
touch upon the major aspects of his theology, however; for the most
part they were of an inconsequential nature. The above-mentioned Dr.
Eck and papal nuncio Jerome Aleander took the bull up to Germany to
be made public. Among other things, the bull prescribed that Luther's
writings should be burned. Book burnings were organized in a number
of places, but they did not awaken any great response. Luther responded by permitting an auto-da-fé to be held outside Wittenberg on
Dec. 10, 1520, in which the canon law and certain other Romish books
were burned. He also threw the papal bull into the fire on that occasion, an act which apparently went unnoticed for the most part at that
time. What was more important in this event was Luther's repudiation
of canon law, which was symbolized by the burning of the same.

After negotiating at length, Elector Frederick of Saxony finally succeeded in bringing the Luther matter before the *Reichstag,* which met
in Worms in April 1521, with Emperor Charles V in attendance. Standing before the assembled diet, Luther was called upon to recant. His famous answer, which he presented after a day of deliberation, made it
clear that he could not recant unless he was convinced by Scripture or
by right reason. The discussions which followed between Luther and
the leading Catholic theologians present in Worms only served to show
more clearly that it was impossible for Luther to accept the Roman
Church and its theology.

LUTHER'S THEOLOGY IN RELATION TO OCCAMISM
AND LATE MEDIEVAL MYSTICISM

We have already noted the decisive break between Luther and Occamism, which was that aspect of scholasticism to which Luther stood
nearest. The criticism which led Luther to reject the Occamist doctrine
of grace has also been mentioned. According to Occamism, grace was a
new condition in man, a *habitus infusus,* imparted as a reward to those
who did all they could to prepare themselves for the reception of grace.
Luther, on the other hand, looked upon grace as the forgiveness of sin,

216

which can be received only by those who are in themselves sinful and as nothing before God. To ascribe to man a natural ability to love God or to prepare himself for grace is to render the Gospel null and void, said Luther.

There are those, however, especially in Roman Catholic quarters, who have tried to show that Luther was essentially dependent on the Occamist tradition on certain other points of doctrine. It is asserted that this was true, for example, of the imputation concept, as well as with respect to the relationship between theology and philosophy. Even at these points, however, it is possible to observe a difference in kind between Occamism and Lutheranism in spite of a certain similarity of thought.

Occamism appended the following to the accepted doctrine of justification: God, in His *potentia absoluta,* can make a sinner righteous without reference to any habitual grace and independently of the existing order of salvation. Justification takes place only by imputation or by divine acceptance. When Luther said, correspondingly, that God "declares" a sinner to be righteous, or that justification has its sole basis in God's free mercy, he was proceeding on an entirely different basis. Such acts do not presuppose a gratuitous disregard of sin or of the order of salvation; they rather do presuppose God's order of salvation, whereby sinners are justified for Christ's sake apart from all merit of their own. The basis of salvation is to be found not in arbitrary power exercised by God, but in Christ's substitutionary suffering and in the perfect merit which He won. So in spite of certain external similarities, Luther's concept of imputation was basically quite different from that of the nominalists.

With respect to the question of the relationship between theology and philosophy, nominalism destroyed the harmonious unity which was characteristic of high scholasticism. The truth of theology cannot be the object of "knowing" in the proper sense of the term, they maintained, inasmuch as it is not based on direct observation or rational axioms and therefore cannot be proved beyond all doubt. Theological knowledge presupposes revelation, and its certainty rests on external authority. In spite of this, however, Occamism assumed that there was a close relationship between the knowledge of faith and reason, and rational speculation was accepted without question as an aid in the interpretation of the articles of faith. As a result, theological knowledge was placed for all practical purposes on the same level as philosophical speculation.

In general, Luther agreed with the Occamist distinction between faith and reason, but at the same time he gave up on rational speculation and insisted that one could not judge or fathom revealed truth by the use of reason. The gulf between faith and reason as Luther understood it does not exist simply because the knowledge of faith is based on authority, but above all because reason has been blinded through the corruption of nature and as a result is unable to understand "what belongs to the Spirit of God." Luther therefore concluded that nominalist speculation concerning the questions of faith represented an inappropriate blending of theology and philosophy. The distinction which Luther himself drew between faith and reason did not rest merely on the plane of epistemological theory; for him it was a matter which concerned the basic theological questions. This distinction was related in Luther's theology to the purely theological contrast between flesh and Spirit and between Law and Gospel. As a result, there was no profound agreement between Luther and Occamism in this matter either. Rather, as seen on the theological level, there was the sharpest antithesis.

Luther's relationship to late medieval mysticism has also been discussed at length by scholars in the field of Luther research. There were a number of clear points of contact here — more important, perhaps, than those which united Luther with the nominalists — but nevertheless, there were also profound differences with respect to the basic questions.

Mysticism represented a personal, experiential kind of religion, which was in opposition not only to the Christianity of the institutional church but also to scholastic education. The mystics insisted that philosophic wisdom was unprofitable and deceitful. Luther, in his opposition to scholasticism, could go along with such tendencies to a certain degree, at the same time that he made this kind of criticism much more profound.

Religious anthropology was another point of contact. The mystics spoke of the "old man" as the egocentric will in opposition to God, and of the "new man" as the will which is united with God. This contrast reminds us of Luther's distinction between the old man and the new. Furthermore, the mystics strongly emphasized the significance of suffering and tribulation for the growth of the Christian. They also spoke of putting the egocentric will to death and of the contrast between the

218

"inner" and the "outer" man. This has its parallels in Luther. He adopted the mystic point of view in many respects and gave expression to similar experiences concerning communion between God and man.

At the same time, however, the decisive difference between Luther and the mystics is to be found in the theological view of man. They did not agree about sin, for example. Luther taught the doctrine of original sin, while the mystics held to the idea that there is an indestructible divine nucleus in man's innermost being. The mystic way is to turn away from all that is external, from all that belongs to the world. Even sin was looked upon at times as something external, something that does not touch the inner man. It amounts to this, that the world is looked upon as something unreal, immaterial, which the mystic must learn to disregard. But as Luther saw it, sin could not be ignored in such a manner, inasmuch as man is a sinner through and through. Man's self-knowledge consists precisely in that he comes to know himself as a sinner. For the mystic the object is to enter his own innermost being and thereby to experience liberation; for Luther conversion is to experience God's judgment upon oneself.

As can be seen from what has been said, Luther and the mystics also conceived of man's union with God in different ways. According to the mystics, this union takes place within man's soul, beyond sin and corruption. Luther also spoke of faith as a darkness in the soul of man, as something beyond all experience (or observation). But it is not an experience of the divine as something resident in our being, but an adherence to the external Word. Luther also believed that the fellowship between God and man is something real, but that it is a fellowship between God and sinful man. As seen from the human side, it is not absorption in the divine but a recognition of sin and a plea for grace.

Mysticism assumed so many different forms, however, that in comparing Luther with mysticism one cannot justly refer to the latter as an unambiguous quantity. Luther admitted that he thought very highly of the German mysticism which he found in Tauler and *Theologia deutsch*. He also appreciated the insights of Bernard of Clairvaux, although he was critical of some, while he categorically rejected the Platonic mysticism as presented in the writings of Dionysius the Areopagite (see above, pp. 147–48). In the sermons of Tauler, Luther found a concept of salvation which was free of the prevalent emphasis on merit and which conceived of Christian righteousness not only as "virtue" but as a supernatural participation in God's own being, as God's presence in the soul. In his critique of the scholastic concept of grace and merit, Luther therefore sensed a close kinship with this kind of mysticism, in spite of the distance between himself and the ideas that were typical of mysticism in general.

MAJOR ASPECTS OF LUTHER'S THEOLOGY

a. *Understanding of Scripture.* Luther's theology is a theology of the Word. "So faith comes from what is heard, and what is heard comes by the preaching of Christ" (Rom. 10:17). These Pauline words were of basic significance to the Protestant Reformation. The divine Word, which creates faith, stands out at the same time as the foundation of theology. The authority of Scripture had certainly been emphasized before this — and not least of all in the Occamist tradition — but when Luther referred to Scripture as the divine Word, brought to man through the apostles and prophets, he spoke with a new conviction concerning the primary position and the inalienable authority of the Word. What was new about Luther's attitude toward Scripture was chiefly his deeper insight into its content. Furthermore, Luther recognized that the authority of the Word was valid even where it was opposed by tradition; it is binding on the conscience. Finally, the principles of interpretation were also thoroughly transformed in Luther's exposition of the Bible.

Christ is at the center of the Bible. "Scripture ought to be understood *for* Christ, not against Him; yes, if it does not refer to Him it is not true Scripture." "Take Christ away from the Bible and what more do you find there?" Essential to understanding the Word is accepting the promises of the Gospel by faith. If this faith is lacking, the divine Word cannot be understood rightly. Luther thereby removed himself from a legalistic interpretation of the Bible, which finds in Scripture a collection of different doctrines and commands, and from a closely related "enthusiastic" concept which claims to possess the "inner Word" as a norm for the interpretation of the Bible. By clearly comprehending the fact that the message of the Gospel is the central facet of the content of Scripture, Luther possessed a certain freedom with respect to his view of the details of the Bible, a freedom which signified nothing else than that the central content (total context) of the Bible is the determining factor in the interpretation of the details. This was by no means a defiance of Scripture's canonical authority. Luther's position has sometimes been interpreted to mean this, but such conclusions are incorrect. Understanding in the deeper sense presupposes exactly what we mentioned — the obedience of faith before the external Word. Faith itself, therefore, is based on the unconditioned validity of the Word. Its authority is also justified by this, that we men, because of our weakness, must be bound to Scripture as an external, binding norm. "If the church is not to be destroyed, it is necessary for us to hold fast to the distinct commands and writings of the apostles." According to another of Luther's statements, the apostles are our infallible teachers by virtue of a special divine commission.

In our relationship to the Bible, therefore, both freedom and constraint hold sway. As seen from the point of view of faith as such, we are free with respect to the literal details. Faith is of primary importance in the interpretation of the Bible; this means that Scripture should be understood in the spirit of Christ and not legalistically. But as seen from the point of view of the conditions under which faith comes into being, we are bound to Scripture as an external authority.

Men have frequently pointed to Luther's so-called critique of the canon (to certain statements made about James, among others) as an example of his freedom vis-à-vis the authority of Scripture. But this is misleading. As a matter of fact, Luther did not feel that the New Testament canon was absolutely fixed. He looked upon four of the last books of the New Testament (Hebrews, James, Jude, and Revelation) as apocryphal, or as writings whose apostolic authority was debatable. According to Luther, evangelical character and apostolic authenticity are above all important in the determination of canonicity. Thus, for example, what is said in the Epistle of James about faith and works is interpreted as an indication that the epistle is neither apostolic nor canonical. (In the Protestant tradition, it was not until the time of Gerhard that also the so-called antilegomena among the New Testament writings began to be recognized as truly canonical.)

In spite of certain similarities, there is a great contrast between Luther's interpretation of the Bible and the modern, historical interpretation, but this contrast has frequently been overlooked. It is certainly true that Luther attached the greatest importance to what he called the literal or historical meaning of Scripture. But by this he did not mean a historical interpretation in the modern sense of the term; it was rather an understanding derived from within the context of faith. Luther believed, for example, that the Old Testament is a direct witness to Christ, and not simply that it contains some predictions about Him. The "history of religion" view of the Bible was unknown at that time.

Luther's understanding of the Old Testament corresponded to the ideas he went on to develop with respect to the relationship between Law and Gospel. The Mosaic law, in the jurisdictional sense, was abolished through Christ. It was for the Jews what the Saxon laws were for the Germans and is therefore valid only for a certain people and in a limited time. The Law has, however, received a higher fulfillment than the external execution of the commandments. It points forward to the Gospel and is brought to its fulfillment only through the proclamation of righteousness by faith in Christ. The Law is therefore preserved, and as God's commands, to which all men are bound, it is valid even in the era of the new covenant. At the same time, however, we can also see the Gospel in the Old Testament. Christ is there too, not only as the future Messiah, foretold in the Law and the Prophets, but also as the One who speaks directly in the Psalms and through the prophets.

The traditional medieval interpretation of the Bible held that Scripture has a fourfold meaning. It can be expounded literally, tropologically (i. e., with respect to the individual Christian), anagogically (i.e., with respect to eternity, and also allegorically, by which was meant that one could, for example, allow the Word to point to general realities in the world of faith or of the church.

Luther rejected this scheme. As far as he was concerned, Scripture has but one original and proper meaning, the grammatical or historical. He also recognized, as a matter of course, the figurative interpretation, which is to be found in the Bible itself, as for example in the parallels drawn between Christ and certain Old Testament figures (typology). Luther also spoke (especially in his early sermons) of a *sensus spiritualis* or *mysticus*, which points to a direct allegory. But this point of view was given a subordinate position. It lacked reliability, and it appeared in Luther's sermons only as a traditional embellishment of the exposition of Scripture. In later years Luther forsook this kind of Bible interpretation more and more.

In Luther's view of Scripture is the idea that the Bible can be understood from out of itself, each person acting as his own interpreter. The interpretations of tradition or of the clergy are not necessary for a

right understanding of the Bible (as Roman Catholic theologians have said). The Word possesses in itself an "external clarity" which it conveys and administers through the office of the ministry (in ministerio verbi). It is for this reason as well that Scripture — without the addition of human commands and doctrinal opinions — is the sole foundation of faith.

The "external clarity" of the Word must be distinguished from the so-called "inner clarity," which is the heart's understanding of the content of Scripture. This comes into being only through the Holy Spirit, who enlightens and instructs man internally. Luther also emphasized the significance of experience for the proper understanding of God's Word. Training in faith, plus the experience which is given through the application of faith and through tribulation of faith and through tribulation of various kinds, is necessary for a genuine insight into the Word (the school of the Holy Spirit).

It is characteristic of Reformation theology that the Word is placed in the center of things not only as a source of insight into a supernatural reality but also as an effective, creative, and life-giving Word, through which God judges and raises up. Faith is related to the Word itself, not simply to a metaphysical reality behind the Word, and there it finds salvation. In this we can see a fundamental contrast between Reformation theology and scholastic theology.

b. *Law and Gospel; evangelical penance.* According to one of Luther's well-known expressions, the proper division of Law and Gospel is the Christian's highest art. One can with good reason refer to the dialectic which Luther had in mind here as being fundamental to his entire theology.

It is possible to receive the impression from the many relevant statements which have been made that Law and Gospel are two distinct orders and that in the life of the Christian the order of the Law ought to be replaced by the order of the Gospel. Luther, however, was very much opposed to this interpretation (as he made clear in his dispute with the antinomians, for example). For just as the Law never reaches fulfillment apart from the Gospel, so also must the Gospel be preached together with the Law; the Law serves as background. Apart from the Law, the meaning of the Gospel would be lost. How could one proclaim the forgiveness of sin apart from the Law, which reveals sin and accuses the conscience? For as the Law unmasks sin and condemns man, it also drives him to seek the help of Christ (cf. Rom. 3:20; Gal. 3:19, 24). Thus it is that Law and Gospel are closely linked together in this tangible manner; they mutually condition one another. Nevertheless it is necessary (as said) clearly to distinguish the one from the other.

The Law tells us what we are to do, under the threat of punishment. The Gospel, on the other hand, promises and provides the forgiveness of sin. Just as one must differentiate between the righteousness which is acceptable before men and that which is acceptable before God, so one must also distinguish between the preaching of the Law and that of the Gospel. One task of the Law is to compel men to act, to promote the good and prevent the evil. As such it therefore includes all public order and activity on the different levels of life. Luther called this the civil use of the Law *(usus legis civilis)*. But when it comes to a man's relation to God — his righteousness in a higher sense — the task of the Law is completely different. The Law cannot produce a single good work, and man is here referred to the Word of the Gospel, which offers him forgiveness of sin for the sake of Christ. In this context the function of the Law is simply to reveal sin and to make the threat of wrath real — the wrath under which man stands because of his sinful nature. Luther called this the theological or the spiritual use of the Law *(usus theologicus seu spiritualis)*.

Law and Gospel characterize two kinds of preaching, which simultaneously exert their effect: the Law accuses and judges, while the Gospel awakens faith in the heart and thereby raises man up and re-creates him so that he can begin to love God and his neighbor — i. e., so that he can live in the frame of mind which the command of love demands.

It was obedience to Law and Gospel which produced the evangelical form of penance. In Luther's theology this form gradually replaced the institutional system of penance developed during the Middle Ages, the misuse of which Luther attacked as early as in the *Ninety-five Theses* of 1517. Some of the major aspects of his critique of the Roman doctrine of penance will be apparent from what follows.

Repentance in the New Testament sense (μετάνοια) is not simply a temporary penitential act, as in the Roman Catholic system; it is rather a lifelong conversion accomplished by the death of the old man and by participation in Christ's substitutionary satisfaction. This fundamental discovery, testified to already in the *Ninety-five Theses* (cf., e. g., Thesis

1), gradually brought with it a radical transformation of the entire doctrine of penance.

The proper kind of contrition is not that which is merely concerned about isolated offenses, but is rather to be found in the brokenheartedness which the Law brings about through the insight that all men stand under the curse of sin. As a result, contrition is not a meritorious activity but is a passive acceptance of the accusation of the Law, which presupposes faith in the judgment God's Word pronounces over sinful men.

As a consequence of this, the confession of sin is something other than a recitation of all of one's faults in the confessional, which is an impossible demand. But in addition to this, sin does not consist of isolated offenses; it is the corruption of one's entire nature, which is not recognized until the Word of God is proclaimed. At the same time, however, Luther continued to emphasize the great usefulness of private confession. But he refused to believe that the granting of absolution is a priestly privilege. He looked upon it as a brotherly service which every Christian has the right to practice in an effort to strengthen and comfort the conscience of the penitent.

Forgiveness of sin is not dependent on the merit of contrition, and neither must it be made to depend on satisfaction; it is granted to the faithful exclusively for the sake of the mercy of Christ. The true "satisfaction" is to be found in the suffering and death of Christ, while the demand for making satisfaction is contrary to the meaning of the Gospel, as is also the indulgence system.

In this new interpretation, repentance can thus no longer be designated as a meritorious act. It is rather the fruit of the preaching of Law and Gospel. The judgment of wrath does its work through the Law, by accusing the conscience and by showing man that everything in him is sinful. The Word of forgiveness is proclaimed through the Gospel, which awakens faith in God's mercy and grace and transforms man in such a way that he receives a new mind and turns his eyes from himself to that which Christ is and does. So understood, repentance involves the entire life of the Christian and denotes what happens when Law and Gospel exert their influence and justification by faith is brought about.

c. *Doctrine of justification.* According to Luther there are two kinds of righteousness, an *external* and an *inner.* The former consists of external deeds and is acquired through just conduct. This can also be called civic righteousness, for it concerns man as a member of society, or his conduct in relation to other men. His external life is judged to be either righteous or unrighteous.

Inner righteousness, on the other hand, consists of the purity and perfection of the heart. As such, it cannot be acquired through external deeds — no more than man can make himself to be God. For this righteousness is of God and comes only as a gift, by faith in Jesus Christ. This righteousness is judged not before men but before God. Because man is sinful, he cannot attain to this righteousness by himself. It contradicts all reason and goes beyond anything that can be comprehended or achieved by human effort. This righteousness is acquired through the suffering and death of Christ, and it is attributed to man by faith, quite apart from human merit or worth. God declares sinners to be righteous for the sake of Christ. Such justification is brought about when a man humbles himself before God, recognizes himself to be a sinner, and cries out for the mercy and grace of God. Such a man confesses that he is full of sin, lies, folly, incompetence, and perdition, while God is all that is good. In this faith, and with such prayers, man's heart becomes one with the righteousness and virtue of God. Christ becomes his righteousness, his sanctification, his deliverance. This is the inner righteousness (*justitia ab intra, ex fide, ex gratia*) set forth in accordance with the words of Paul, "For we hold that a man is justified by faith apart from works of the Law." (Rom. 3:28)

We also find, in the Reformation doctrine of justification by faith, that the *concept of faith* itself has been transformed. It is distinctly different from the parallel concept taught by scholastic theology.

In the scholastic tradition, men spoke of faith as something conceivable on the level of reason, which could be acquired through instruction and preaching (*fides acquisita*). This was distinguished from infused faith (*fides infusa*), which is a gift of grace and implies complete adherence to all revealed truth. Luther rejected this distinction: The faith which "comes by preaching" coincides with that which (according to Rom. 3:28) is justifying; it is wholly and completely a gift of God, a "truly infused faith" (*fides vere infusa*). It is not conceivable to the mind of man, and it signifies not only an intellectual adherence to the truths of faith but an actual fellowship with God, in which man places all of his trust in God and looks to Him as the source of all good (cf. the exposition of the First Commandment in the Large Catechism).

Justifying faith, in other words, is not only a historical knowledge of the content of the Gospel; it is the acceptance of the merits of Christ. Faith, therefore, is trust in God's mercy for the sake of Christ. In this connection Luther coined the phrase *fides apprehensiva Christi*. The decisive thing is that the Gospel of Christ's victory over sin and death is received as saving and life-giving truth. "The acquired faith as well as the infused faith of the sophists says of Christ, 'I believe in the Son of God, who suffered and was awakened,' and there it leaves off. But the true faith says, 'I certainly believe in God's Son, who suffered and was resurrected; I am sure that He did all of this for me, for my sins. . . .' This 'for me' or 'for us' — when it is embraced in faith — makes for a true faith; this is different from all other kinds of faith, which only hear of things that have happened" (WA 39 I, 44 ff.). As Luther understood it, faith is not only a mass of knowledge; it is a living power, "which makes Christ active in us, opposing death, sin, and the Law." (Ibid.)

The Lutheran *sola fide* concept must also be understood in the light of what has been said. Also here Luther's opposition to scholasticism lies in the background. In previous years men spoke, on the basis of Gal. 5:6, of a *fides caritate formata* (the Vulgate version) and gave the impression that faith was not alone sufficient for justification. Faith could please God only if it were associated with deeds of love.

Luther demonstrated that the Pauline passage quoted above refers not to justification but to the Christian life as a whole, which is definitely characterized by faith active in love. Justification itself, on the other hand, is solely the work of faith. It takes place not on the basis of human merit but only for the sake of the righteousness of Christ, which has been credited to us. And faith, as we have already said, is the acceptance of Christ's substitutionary deeds as having been carried out for our sake. It makes man one with Christ, so that Christ "lives in his heart by faith." Faith therefore is not an "unformed" function of the soul, which must be perfected by love. It is itself active, a life-giving power, which can only unceasingly do what is good.

In his description of faith Luther referred to the example of Abraham as this is given in Rom. 4: "Abraham believed God, and it was reckoned to him as righteousness." In connection with this, it is customary to speak of an *imputative* justification as characteristic of Reformation theology. The righteousness which is here referred to is not an inherent quality in man. Man is declared to be righteous through God's own decree. And this is done not on the basis of any quality or merit in man himself, but for the sake of Christ *(propter Christum)*. Luther also put it this way, that no one but a sinner can be justified. And with that we come back to where we began: the righteousness under discussion here can only come to man as a gift, an *aliena justitia,* i. e., it is not our own but Christ's righteousness, which is imputed to us by faith.

But this so-called imputation concept must not be interpreted to mean that it refers only to an external form of judgment. For it was precisely in this context (as we saw) that Luther spoke of an "inner righteousness." The verdict which exonerates, which makes a man just, is God's own living and creative Word, which provides the new birth and changes man entirely. Therefore there is no contradiction (as some have wanted to maintain) between the concept of imputation as the basis of justification and the idea of faith as a living, active power. For the Holy Spirit is given with faith, and He works that which is good and through love fulfills the Law.

Many misunderstandings have arisen concerning Luther's doctrine of *faith and works.* For example, it is said that the Lutheran *sola fide* concept implies that good works have lost their rightful significance. A glance at Luther's thinking on the subject would reveal, however, that such conclusions are not at all in agreement with his principles.

Faith and love are related to one another as are Law and Gospel, or as the divine and human natures in Christ. They can certainly be distinguished from one another, but they cannot be separated. The righteousness of faith refers to man in his relation to God *(coram Deo)*. The righteousness of good works or love refers, on the other hand, to man in relation to his neighbor *(coram hominibus)*. These must not be confused in such a way that man will seek to become just in the sight of God on the strength of his good works, nor in such a way that he will attempt to conceal sin with grace. Both would be signs of a false faith. From this it follows that faith and works can be sharply separated, even designated as incompatible opposites; but at the same time it is also true that they are very intimately related.

With respect to justification itself, good works must be as clearly distinguished from faith as possible. For this has to do with faith alone. As Luther expressed it, the Law must not be permitted to force its way up in the conscience. The man who has been crushed by the Law, and recognizes himself to be a sinner, can be raised up only by faith. He must look only to the cross of Christ, and not to the Law or to his own works, as though they could make satisfaction for his misdeeds. On this point, therefore, faith and works are mutually exclusive.

But when one looks upon the actual life of the Christian in its entirety, he can see that faith and works always go together. Faith cannot be apart from works; it constantly does what is good. As a result, we can speak of works in such a way that faith is presupposed by them and included within them. When the Bible, for example, refers to the works of the Law, the basic demand is for faith. For apart from faith no one can fulfill the Law or do what is good. Hence it is that the demand for works itself presupposes faith.

Similarly, one can speak of faith in such a way that good works are included in the very concept of faith. Faith is thus conceived of in a concrete sense, as faith incarnate in the works of love. But this does not mean that love forms faith, as the scholastics said; on the contrary, it is faith that forms love. That is to say, it is faith alone which makes our deeds good. To use another expression, faith is the divine nature of good works. With respect to justification, therefore, faith is spoken of in an abstract manner apart from all works and before all works. But when reference is made to the Christian life as a whole, faith and love belong together and could not be thought of as separate; for faith takes form in love, and love becomes what it is through faith.

d. *Luther's concept of man.* Luther's theological view of man corresponds with his doctrine of justification, but it is sharply at odds with the medieval view of man. It is often said that a "whole man" *(totus homo)* view of man was characteristic of Luther. Instead of the scholastic dualism between body and soul, higher and lower spiritual powers, Luther introduced a concept of wholeness into the theological context. The results of this can be seen in various facets of his theology.

Original sin, as Luther understood it, is not merely the lack of original Godlikeness; it is a real form of corruption, which has set its mark on the whole man. In concrete terms sin is not only *concupiscentia* — conceived of as a negative disposition of the lower powers of the soul — but an evil which effects man in his entirety, including (and indeed above all) the higher powers of the soul.

According to Luther, unbelief is the basic sin, a turning away from God. The first sin, which included all others in itself, was a doubting of

God's Word and a deviation from the divine command
(cf. Gen. 3:1 ff.). In this alienation from God there is present at the
same time an evil desire, a false intention, determined by self-love and
pride, which has left an indelible mark on the will of man. Even the
pious are not without sin — not even when they are at their best. The
judgment which says that man is a sinner involves his entire person,
such as he is before God. If man is judged only in his relationship to
other men, and on the basis of his observable conduct, the import of
original sin may not be apparent. The corruption of sin is congenital,
transmitted from generation to generation by natural propagation, and
is therefore present prior to all experience and all conscious expressions
of the will. As a result, this concept of sin must not be confused with
the use of the term in a moral or legal sense. Luther spoke of original
sin as a hidden evil *(malum absconditum)*, an inscrutable mystery,
which in a secret manner determines the shape of human existence.
One can grasp the fact that he is a sinner in the Biblical sense only in
the light of the Word, and this reality can be kept in mind only in the
knowledge of faith, in confession and prayer.

In some instances Luther's concept of original sin has been interpreted as something which concerns only the God-man relationship,
i. e., that it is a distorted relation to God. But this is not fair to Luther,
for whom original sin meant a real corruption of human nature, involving both body and soul, or the entire man. The depths of this injury
cannot be comprehended by man, inasmuch as we do not know what
human life would be without sin. That it is a concrete form of corruption is also evident from this, that sin is assumed to be inherited along
with our physical birth. "All that is born of father and mother is sin."
Original sin is not simply a condition of guilt, which is removed by
Baptism; it is also a *corruptio naturae*, which does not cease to exert its
influence until the body is destroyed in the grave.

What the *totus homo* view means, therefore, is that man is seen
from the theological point of view in his relationship to God *(coram
Deo)*. And so he is perceived as completely determined by this relationship and not as a composite of various spiritual faculties and powers.
The image of God in man *(imago Dei*, Gen. 1:26), or the original righteousness, does not consist of man's talents and reason, nor of anything
else which now characterizes him as man; it rather refers to man's original perfection and holiness. In a corresponding way, original sin is not

simply an inclination toward evil, attached to the lower spiritual powers (*concupiscentia, fomes*); it is the corruption of man in his entirety.

According to the scholastics, original sin is removed through Baptism. That which remains in the lives of the faithful was said to be merely a vestige of concupiscence, which was not considered to be sin — only a propensity to sin. Luther agreed that the guilt of original sin is certainly removed through Baptism, but the corrupting influence of original sin remains even in those who have been regenerated. The vestiges of sin are in themselves sin. Concupiscence is not merely a force which drives a man to sin; it is in itself sin. This concrete sinfulness gradually abates, however, in those who live under the dominion of the Holy Spirit. A conflict between the Spirit and the flesh begins as soon as a man begins to believe. The faithful are therefore both just and sinful at one and the same time (*simul justus et peccator*). This means, as Luther understood it, not only that sin abates and righteousness increases, but also that the man who has faith in Christ is — that is to say, is reckoned to be — completely righteous, at the same time that he, in his fleshly nature, is completely a sinner. Sin and righteousness are therefore perpetual attributes of the entire man. One is both an "old man" and a "new man" simultaneously. The same person is both "two whole men and one whole man" (*duo toti homines et unus totus homo*).

Free will: Luther's ideas concerning man's free will must be seen in the light of his doctrine of justification. As seen from another point of view, these ideas also give clear expression to his *totus homo* view of man.

In the famous controversial treatise *De servo arbitrio*, which he wrote against Erasmus in 1525, Luther argues as follows: With respect to that which concerns salvation or eternal blessedness, man is completely without a free will; it is entirely a divine quality, which can only be ascribed to God. As Erasmus understood it, man has the capacity to decide to accept or reject grace. Were this not the case, he maintained, the admonitions of Scripture would be meaningless. Luther asserted, on the other hand, that there was absolutely no support for this concept of a free will in Scripture, regardless of how many ecclesiastical authorities might be quoted. Such a free will simply does not exist. It is pure illusion. Salvation depends exclusively on the omnipotent divine will of grace. As far as Scriptural admonitions are concerned, they do not appeal to a free capacity for good; they are rather designed to reveal man's lack of such capacity and, in so doing, his actual condition. This is the function of the Law.

As shown above, the idea of a *meritum de congruo* — natural man's preparation for grace — grew apace during the Middle Ages. This was the tradition that Erasmus perpetuated, even though his own position can best be designated as rationalistic humanism, influenced by late medieval mysticism. In rejecting the Erasmian point of view, Luther turned against the entire psychologizing tendency which characterized the medieval *ordo salutis* and which implied that grace and merit were on the same level.

The merit concept, which was one of the fundamentals of the medieval tradition, was either rejected completely or transformed from the ground up in Reformation theology. If "merit" signifies a good deed, deserving of grace or blessedness in whole or in part, the idea is entirely foreign to Luther's teaching of justification. The Scriptural idea of reward for good works was construed by Luther in a wholly different manner and was not related to the acquisition of salvation. Hence it was that the merit concept itself was altered in the Lutheran point of view.

The freedom of the will which Luther denied was defined by Erasmus as the capacity to associate oneself with that which leads to eternal blessedness or to turn away from it. This freedom refers, therefore, to the ability to do good in the spiritual sense, or the power to choose between good and evil. So if this freedom is denied, this does not involve determinism as it is commonly understood.

Luther drew a sharp line of demarcation between two kingdoms or dominions. The one is subject to reason and involves worldly concerns, while the other involves faith and spiritual concerns. In the former, said Luther, man has a free will; in the latter he does not. Luther therefore spoke of a *libertas in externis*. There is such a thing as natural good, which reason can recognize and choose. But this in no way suggests a modification of the total judgment which says that before God man is a sinner and can be considered righteous only through God's mercy, by faith in Christ. In like manner, the unfree will is something which completely determines man's life and brings him into bondage under sin. It just isn't so, as the scholastics maintained, that grace and free will work together for man's salvation. Man's salvation is the work of grace from first to last.

e. *The doctrine of grace and predestination.* Luther understood the concept of grace in its literal sense. To him it signified God's favor or God's love active in behalf of man's salvation. Unlike the scholastics, he did not think of grace as an infused quality which elevates man's natural goodness to a supernatural level and facilitates virtue. Man is sheer sin, and enmity towards God. Because of this, salvation is entirely a work of grace. It is not accomplished simply because some powers of grace are made available to man; it is God Himself who does it, working directly through His Spirit. In Luther's theology, grace is not delineated above all against the background of man's lack of supernatural good, but against the wrath of God, which condemns man because of sin. The only basis of salvation is the secret of the atonement revealed in the Gospel of Christ. The divine will of grace is combined with God's almighty power and is therefore the only source of the faith which accepts the promises of God — as is the case with all of the good that is found in man.

The connection between grace and God's omnipotence provided the basis for Luther's concept of predestination, which was propounded at greatest length in his book *De servo arbitrio.* Man is not free and is totally unable to contribute to his own salvation; God, on the other hand, is He who works all in all, and with an unalterable necessity impels all that takes place, both good and evil. Did Luther say that God is the source of evil? Yes, as seen from one point of view He is, for nothing is done apart from His willing and without His active cooperation. He is the active and driving force in all things. But the fact that what takes place is evil does not depend on God but on the cooperation of sinful instruments. To illustrate this point, Luther referred to the case of a carpenter who had to work with a poor ax; the results were poor, even though he was a good carpenter. The most difficult problem arises when this idea of God's omnipotence is associated with the doctrine of grace.

If the answer to the question of man's salvation or damnation lies in God's unchangeable power and decree, why does God not permit all men to be saved? Does not the blame for lost souls come to rest upon God Himself, who in His omnipotence permitted men to fall victim to damnation? Luther answered these difficult questions in the following manner:

One must distinguish between what holds true for the hidden God and that which God has revealed in His Word. That the omnipotent God impels and effects even that which is evil is characteristic of the hidden God *(Deus absconditus)*. But the Gospel makes it clear, on the other hand, that God offers His grace to all and that God wants all men to be saved. We are called upon to hold fast to this revelation and not to brood arrogantly over the hidden and inscrutable divine majesty.

Condemnation befalls man as a just punishment for his sin and is therefore a consequence of God's righteousness. But if salvation and damnation are completely in the hands of God, then the question is: Why doesn't God alter the will of those who go lost? His question cannot be answered; the answer has not been revealed. Luther, in this context, distinguished between the light of nature, the light of grace, and the light of glory. There are things that can only be understood in the light of grace, as for example — why do the good suffer while the evil prosper? Such a question cannot be answered solely in the light of nature. By the same token, there are things that are not apparent in the light of faith or grace but will be understood in the light of glory. The mystery of predestination is included in this category. The fact that it is perfectly just for God to permit some people to suffer condemnation will be understandable only in eternity.

f. *Luther's doctrine of the call and his understanding of society.* The word "call" itself *(Beruf, vocatio)* can be used to refer to the call of the Gospel to God's kingdom, as well as to the work one does or the position one holds in our earthly society. It can also designate the factors involved in bringing a man into the office of the ministry, the preaching office. Luther's doctrine of the call refers to the second of these three meanings. In fact, the German word *Beruf*, when used in this sense, is Luther's own creation.

Call and creation go together. It is God, in His sustaining power, who places men in the various callings and positions. There is no difference of rank here, however; the purely secular callings are no less important in the sight of God. In Luther's concept of the call there is a critique of the Roman teaching of the spiritual and secular estates. Those who presume that they are serving God better than others by entering a monastery do violence to God's own order. Instead of serving their neighbors in a genuine calling, they avoid this service and choose their own form of worship. It is not the external form of one's service which determines whether it is good or not; it is faith — which either does or does not precede one's deeds. Because of this, even the humblest tasks are more pleasing to God than all self-chosen "good works" — provided only that they are carried out in faith and with a good conscience. One is not blessed by his works, that is to say, but by faith alone. What, then, is the purpose of the call?

The purpose of the call is to serve one's neighbor. It is a part of this earthly life and is upheld by mutual service as its highest goal. In whatever position a man finds himself, he is to serve his neighbor. Thus it is that God's commands are observed. Within the framework of his calling one finds a superfluity of good deeds to be done. But the call, as seen in this context, does not refer only to wage-earning activity; it is concerned with everything involved in one's situation. A person is called not only to be a farmer or a craftsman or a ruler but also to be a father or mother, son or daughter, etc.

Man cooperates with God in his calling. There he is an instrument for God's sustaining activity. When he fulfills that which belongs to his calling, he is doing something useful for his neighbor, and God thereby reveals His goodness and foresight. We receive good gifts through other men, who execute the tasks implicit in their calling. God works through us in the same way for our neighbor's benefit, when we are faithful in our calling. The Christian need not, therefore, select special tasks for himself in order to increase God's pleasure. He need only carry out those tasks which come to hand through the demands of his calling.

Luther's concept of the call implies two things: (1) that the position and work which each man has is to be looked upon as a divine command, in which man is to seek God's help and obey His will, and (2) that human society is to be shaped by mutual service, in which men serve each other and bring God's gifts to their neighbors by fulfilling their various tasks.

Another consequence of Luther's concept of creation is to be found in his doctrine of the *two realms,* the spiritual and the secular. God exercises His dominion over the human race in different ways: in part through the Word and the sacraments, in part through the authorities and the secular order. The gifts which are needed for man's salvation are imparted in the spiritual realm, while the external order which is necessary for human society (and also for the existence of the church) is upheld through the secular realm.

This distinction must not be confused with modern ideas concerning church and state, in which the state is thought to stand outside the religious sphere, while the church represents the spiritual domain. According to Luther, God rules in both, in the spiritual as well as the secular. The latter is an expression of the ongoing creation, of God's providential care. In some respects both realms are included in God's Word, inasmuch as the secular authority is also constituted by God's word and command. At the same time Luther drew a sharp line of demarcation between the two realms. The spiritual realm is without external power. Its power is exercised by God Himself through the Word and the preaching office. The secular realm is subject to human reason, and its authority is exercised by men who have the power to enforce laws, etc. It is God Himself who is active in both realms, and thus they are united. In the spiritual sphere God works through the Gospel to save men, and in the secular He works through the Law and impels men to live in a certain way, to do the good and avoid the evil, so that their neighbors can be ministered to and general chaos prevented.

Hence we can see that the spiritual realm does not represent a special sphere of power at the side of the secular. Neither is the latter a purely profane area, completely sundered from God. The secular authorities represent God's own power, as it confronts man in visible form in our earthly relationships. Even a completely pagan authority can be used by God to work what is good, to uphold public order and promote human society.

In this connection it must be noted that Luther distinguished between *Person* and *Amt*. God works that which is good through the offices He has established. He impels office bearers to be anxious about the welfare of others, to serve for their benefit. God does this even though the office bearer is not himslf a good man. It is true that evil men can misuse the established order and corrupt the secular realm, but God works through these orders in spite of this; He is independent of man's evil. For even those who are evil can be forced, by the secular powers or by concern for their own good, to execute the tasks of their office and thus minister to their neighbor's welfare.

On the basis of his doctrine of the two realms, Luther opposed both the medieval concept of the church as being superior to the state, and also the political concept of the enthusiasts, who looked upon the state as something foreign to faith and who conceived of man's relation to God in purely spiritual terms (an "inner" experience without "external" implications). The Anabaptists and other representatives of the spiritualistic position were commonly referred to as *Schwarmgeister,* "enthusiasts." One of their principles was that a Christian should not become involved in political activity.

Luther ordinarily divided human interdependence into three broad ranks, *ecclesia, politia,* and *oeconomia,* which correspond in general with the church, the state, and the home respectively. The two latter represent the secular realm, while the church represents the spiritual. The ranks correspond with the callings. One finds his position within one of these three ranks. They overlap, of course, so that one person might be involved in more than one rank *(Stand),* according to the varied relationships in which he finds himself. A man might at the same time be a father, a pastor, and a citizen.

Luther's understanding of *authority* was based on Rom. 13:1: "Let every person be subject to the governing authorities. For there is no authority except from God, and those that exist have been instituted by God." The Christian is thereby obligated to obey even those rulers who do not share his faith. The only exception is found in the words, "We must obey God rather than men" (Acts 5:29). If the authorities should command that which is contrary to God's command or implies a denial of the Christian faith, the Christian must refuse to obey, and suffer instead the punishment meted out to him for the sake of his faith. But Luther did not approve of armed uprisings against the state. Insurrection is contrary to God's order. Even if the cause is just, rebellion is nonetheless reprehensible, and one should rather take his stand with those who are hurt by the rebellion. No subject dare oppose the authorities in a violent manner. There is only one exception: the *Wunderleute* whom God expressly chooses to overturn a regime which is obviously tyrannical or incompetent.

As will be clear from what has been said, Luther's concept of the calling was directed against the medieval monastic system and the distinction between the spiritual and secular estates expressed by this system. In his book *De votis monasticis* (1522) Luther carefully scrutinized and criticized the monkish vows. He came to the conclusion that they are contrary both to God's Word and to reason. The idea that the monk's way of life is superior to and more perfect than ordinary callings is contrary to God's commands, which concern all Christians to the same degree.

Luther's view of society can also be seen in the light of the position which he took vis-à-vis the "enthusiasts." According to the latter, political activity is evil, and Christians ought not to get involved in it. On the contrary, they are called upon to manifest their opposition to earthly society. Even armed opposition was not foreign to this point of view. In the so-called Peasants' War of 1525 a number of these enthusiasts (including Thomas Muenzer) took over the leadership. Luther on the other hand, who had earlier dissociated himself from this group and fought against it and its iconoclasm, violently attacked the peasants and finally urged the princes to use armed force to put down the uprising.

With respect to the exercise of secular power, Luther developed the conviction (especially in the book *Whether Soldiers, Too, May Live in a State of Salvation,* published in 1526) that the Christian can in good conscience serve the state by wielding the sword, for it represents God's own order and is not established or contrived by man himself.

g. *Luther's concept of worship and the sacraments.* In reforming the worship life of the church, Luther (as in so many other matters) had to fight on two fronts. He had to contend not only against Roman abuses on the one hand but also against the radical reforming zeal of the enthusiasts on the other.

Luther maintained that the worship life of the Roman Church deteriorated because of the neglect of the preaching of the Word, which had been replaced by the Mass. This misuse was further compounded by the fact that the Mass was looked upon as having an agreeable effect upon God, rather than being an occasion for fellowship around Word and Sacrament.

Luther intended to retain the continual reading of the Scriptures at daily worship services, but he also felt that the Word should be preached, which is to say, interpreted. "If God's Word is not preached, it would be better if men neither sang nor read or came together," said Luther in *On the Arrangement of the Church Service in a Congregation* (1523). The Lord's Supper should be celebrated every Sunday, or when there are those who wish to receive it. But the daily private Mass of the clergy was abolished.

Current discussion of Luther's concept of worship is, as a rule, dominated by his polemical writings on the subject, his utterances against the Roman Mass. But we must also emphasize the fact that the Reformation brought with it the reanimation of worship concepts of the New Testament and the early church. This is particularly obvious in Luther's earlier presentations on the subject. In *A Sermon Concerning the Most Holy Sacrament* (1519) he pointed to the idea of community as the basic motive of worship. The worship service is the coming together of the congregation, in which a mutual exchange takes place between Christ and the congregation and among the Christians themselves. Our sins are laid on Christ, and His righteousness comes to us. In a similar way, we share the burdens and worries of our fellow Christians and pledge ourselves to bear the cross, at the same time that we receive help and support through our fellowship in the congregation.

It should also be noted that, in spite of all his criticisms of the sacrificial concept of the Mass, Luther by no means completely rejected the idea of sacrifice as having an essential place in the worship service. The mistake in the sacrificial concept of the Mass is that the perfect sacrifice which Christ offered once and for all has been made into a sacrifice continually offered by man. The belief is that in the Mass the priest makes the sacrifice in Christ's stead. As a result the Lord's Supper has come to be thought of as a human achievement and is involved in the works-righteousness context. This is in direct opposition to the meaning of the Lord's Supper. For the Lord's Supper is not a gift we present to God; it is a gift given to us by God, viz., the body and blood of Christ. Therefore it is not a sacrifice in the Roman sacramental sense of the term.

But at the same time the Lord's Supper — and every other worship service — can be called a sacrifice, in so far as we there give ourselves to Christ, presenting our bodies as a living sacrifice (cf. Rom. 12:1). Furthermore, a worship service is a sacrifice of prayer and thanksgiving, given as our answer to God's mercy and His gifts of grace. It can also be called a sacrifice in the sense that Christ, as our intercessor in heaven, offers Himself before God on our behalf. (*A Treatise on the New Testament*, 1520)

During Luther's stay at the Wartburg in 1521–22 his supporters in Wittenberg sought, under the leadership of Karlstadt, to carry out a radical purge of church ceremonies and all liturgical embellishments.

The rationale for this action was provided by the so-called spiritualists or enthusiasts, whom we mentioned earlier. In addition to Karlstadt, Thomas Muenzer was the best known among the leaders of this group. They held that faith and the worship service should be purely spiritual in nature, that no external embellishments were required. It was this point of view which lay behind their iconoclasm and their rejection of all ceremonials. Everything "fleshly" was to be denied, and this included external, material things in general.

As Luther understood it, however, the fleshly is not the external in and of itself, but rather that which has been tainted by the flesh. Similarly, he felt that the spiritual is not the opposite of the external, but that which is permeated by the Spirit of God. If the Word of God is permitted to exert its effect, then ceremonies and pictures can also be consecrated to the edificaton of the congregation. The mistake made by the enthusiasts was that they thought they could achieve their purpose by demolishing pictures, while they set aside and ignored the Word.

The sacraments: In his book *On the Babylonian Captivity of the Church* (1520) Luther broke with the sacramental system of the Roman Church. Of the seven traditional sacraments, Luther designated only two as being genuine sacraments, Baptism and the Lord's Supper. (At the beginning Luther also considered penance to be a sacrament.) Only these, in his estimation, are divinely instituted signs that accompany the divine promise of grace. The fundamental thing in a sacrament is the word of promise connected with the sign. Luther rejected the idea that the sacramental act is effective in itself (the *ex opere operato* concept). That which is effective in the sacraments (as elsewhere) is the divine Word, and not the human act as such. With this, the basis of the entire Roman sacramental cult, including its reserved Host, its Masses for the dead, and other private Masses, was set aside.

Baptism expresses the participation of the Christian in the death and resurrection of Christ. The Christian is to die daily to sin, so that the new man may arise. The essentials of Baptism are water and the Word, used together. At the same time that he rejected the scholastic (Thomistic) concept of an indwelling power in the water, Luther was also sharply critical of the enthusiasts, who disdained the external sign. It is not the water itself which has such a great effect, but the water connected with the Word. But since it is God Himself who instituted the sacramental sign, the external act is God's work and not man's. A baptism provided by an unworthy pastor is nevertheless valid. Neither is the effect of the sacrament dependent on the presence of faith in the one who is baptized. Those who receive Baptism without having faith need not be baptized again if they subsequently come to believe. As a result of this, Luther did not consider it an important question whether a baptized child can be said to have faith. He accepted the traditional answer, that the faith of the sponsors takes the place of the child's faith, but on other occasions expressed the opinion that we must also presuppose faith in the child as the effect of the divine Word. In opposition to the enthusiasts (and Anabaptists) who insisted on adult Baptism, Luther took for granted, upheld, and justified infant Baptism on the ground that Christ's salvation concerns little children as well.

Luther's concept of the Lord's Supper: In his book *On the Babylonian Captivity of the Church* Luther attacked the Roman Catholic doctrine of the Lord's Supper on the three following points: (1) The failure to give the chalice to the laity. This is contrary to the institution of Christ and is based on certain untenable speculations about the whole being found in one of the elements. (2) The doctrine of transubstantiation, the idea that the bread and the wine are altered, that they lose their natural substance. This theory has no support in Scripture. There is no reason to suppose that the bread ceases to be what it is by nature, bread. (3) The sacrifice of the Mass, whereby the Mass is made into a human work and in part profaned to a simple racket *(Geschäft)*. The Lord's Supper is not a feat which men perform to make atonement with God.

Luther explained the meaning of the Lord's Supper on the basis of the Biblical account of its institution. It is Christ's testament to His disciples, in which His gift of grace, the forgiveness of sins, is granted. In Baptism the essentials are the water and the Word with which it is connected. In the Lord's Supper, likewise, the essentials are the physical reception of the elements and the associated words of promise, "given and shed for you for the remission of sins." The Lord's Supper is a sacrament only because of the presence of the Word. Here St. Augustine's statement applies: "The Word comes to the element and makes a sacrament" *(Accedit verbum ad elementum et fit sacramentum)*. The magical implications of the doctrine of transubstantiation are thereby obviated.

Even though Luther rejected transubstantiation, he nevertheless

held to the teaching of the Real Presence in the Sacrament of the Altar. The bread and wine are, in the power of the Word and the divine institution, the true body and blood of Christ, given under the form of the bread and wine. In previous years some of the nominalists, including Pierre d'Ailly, expressed ideas which Luther could accept (the so-called doctrine of consubstantiation). It was said, e. g., that it is actual bread and wine which is distributed in the Lord's Supper, but that Christ's body and blood are also given in, with, and under the external elements — as it appears in the simplest interpretation of the words of institution. How this happens is wholly incomprehensible to reason. Luther's concept of the Real Presence was developed above all in the sacramental controversy of the 1520s. Luther's opponents were in part the enthusiasts, led by Karlstadt, and in part Zwingli and his disciples Oecolampadius and Bucer.

In his writing *Against the Heavenly Prophets* (1525) Luther came out against Karlstadt and his concept of the Lord's Supper. Later Zwingli entered the controversy and published his *Amica exegesis,* which was directed specifically at Luther (1527). A number of smaller treatises were exchanged, and then Luther, in his detailed presentation *A Confession Concerning the Lord's Supper* (1528), gave his final answer to the onslaught of his opponents. In the following year Luther and Zwingli and a few other theologians met at Marburg and discussed this and other matters. It was hoped that an agreement with respect to the Lord's Supper could be brought about and that the German and Swiss Reformers could thus be united. Many points on the Marburg agenda were agreed upon, but the question of the physical presence in the Lord's Supper was passed over intentionally, since the participants were unable to agree on it. The dream of a "pan-Protestant union" thereby came to nought. The so-called Wittenberg Concord of 1536 served as the basis of an external unity for a brief period. This statement was dominated by the Lutheran point of view, which came to prevail in Germany.

Karlstadt and Zwingli represented the symbolical or spiritualistic concept of the Lord's Supper. They said that the external elements are merely symbols of the heavenly, purely spiritual realities to which faith is directed. We cannot, therefore, speak of a material or physical presence but only of a symbolic act, in the performance of which the fellowship of faith with the heavenly Christ is the essential factor. Zwingli interpreted the *est* of the formula of institution as *significat:* "This signifies My body and blood." Luther examined the exegetical support for this interpretation, and he asserted that the word *est* must retain its direct and simple meaning, even though reason is offended thereby. As the statement stands in Scripture, it indicates that the body and blood of Christ are present in the Sacrament not in a figurative manner but as a reality, in their essence. Luther had a somewhat higher opinion of the interpretation set forth by Oecolampadius. He said that the word "body" should be understood figuratively, and not the *est.* The words of institution were thus interpreted to say: "This is a symbol of My body" (*figura corporis mei*). But Luther rejected this also.

This was not simply an argument over words. The underlying points of view were diametrically opposed in their entirety. Zwingli proceeded on the basis of a fundamental dualism between the spiritual and the physical. Faith, he said, can only be directed toward Christ's divine nature. It can therefore have nothing to do with the earthly elements or with Christ's body and blood. He cited, in this connection, the words found in John 6:63: "The flesh is of no avail." The important thing in the Lord's Supper, therefore, is the participation of faith in the heavenly gifts, not the physical eating. Zwingli sought to express this in his symbolical interpretation, as indicated above. Furthermore, he spoke of the words "Christ's body and blood" (in this context) as an *alloeosis,* i. e., a rhetorical figure which implies that what is said about Christ's human nature properly refers to His divine nature.

Luther, on the other hand, most intimately combined the Word (to which faith is directed) and the external elements which are received in the Lord's Supper. They belong together in the power of the words of institution. As a result, the Word and the physical eating are, taken together, the essentials of the Lord's Supper. The presence of Christ is not conditioned by faith. Even the unbelievers who participate in the Lord's Supper receive the sacramental gifts — not as a blessing, to be sure, but as judgment. It is by all means true that the forgiveness of sins comes only by faith, but the "eating" of Christ's body and blood is not only done "spiritually" but in a physical way (*oralis,* with the mouth). At the same time, Christ's body and blood in the Sacrament are not something physical but something spiritual. Luther thereby broke through the philosophical dualism between spirit and matter which lay behind the spiritualistic concept.

In opposition to Zwingli's *alloeosis,* Luther came out in support of a genuine *communicatio idiomatum.* This means that the qualities of the divine and human natures are communicated from the one nature to the other and that they permeate one another on the basis of the unity of Christ's person. The expression "Christ's body and blood" has reference to Christ's humanity. But on the basis of the unity which exists between His divine and human natures, the human nature shares in the qualities of the divine nature and must be most closely related thereto. Faith is therefore directed at Christ the man, and it receives His body and blood in the Lord's Supper, which is, at the same time, the body and blood of the Son of God. This receiving takes place through the physical eating, and not simply as the result of faith's communion in the spiritual sphere.

The idea of the communication of attributes sheds additional light on the question of the Real Presence. Luther sought to explain this idea (to the extent that it can be explained) by referring to the so-called doctrine of ubiquity: Christ is everywhere present as God. And His human nature shares in this quality. Because of this, Christ can be present also as man in the bread and wine given in the Sacrament of the Altar. The origins of this doctrine of ubiquity go back to nominalism, and subsequent Lutheran theology took up the idea of the ubiquity of Christ's human nature, particularly in order to distinguish between its own concept of the Lord's Supper and that of the Reformed tradition.

h. *Luther's doctrine of the church.* In order to understand Luther's concept of the church we ought rather to use the term "the Christian congregation," since the word "church" as used in our day has a connotation which it did not have in Luther's mind.

For Luther, the church *(ecclesia)* was first and foremost the fellowship of believers, which is defined in the Third Article of the creed as "the communion of saints." It is a congregation of all on earth who have faith in Christ. This does not refer to an external association with institutions and offices but to an inner fellowship shared by all who have a common faith and a common hope. As such, the church is an object of faith. Luther's strong emphasis on this spiritual, invisible fellowship as constitutive of the church was something new. The church to him was not the external institution embodied in the person of the pope, but a oneness of the faithful brought about by the Holy Spirit. This fellow-

244

ship is invisible and independent of time and place. For no one can see who it is that has true faith, or know where this faith is found.

But one can also speak of the church in another sense. For it is also an external fellowship, a tangible assembly of persons who gather in a particular building, who belong to a certain parish or diocese, etc. In this sense the church has specific regulations, offices, services, and customs. All who have been baptized, all who have been reached by the preaching of the Word and who confess the Christian faith belong to this external Christendom. Here one cannot draw a line of demarcation between those who really believe and those who are hypocrites.

The first-named fellowship is referred to as the inner, spiritual church or Christendom, while the other is referred to as the external, physical Christendom. They are not to be separated. For the inner, spiritual fellowship is the essential element in the external congregation. It is for the sake of this spiritual fellowship that the congregation is held together. But just as it is wrong for the papists to identify the church with the tangible institution, so is it also wrong to abandon the external fellowship in order to found a congregation only for the saints (as the enthusiasts did). Faith must attach itself to the external signs (the sacraments) and to the external Word, and in like manner it must also seek for true Christian fellowship in the external congregation — insofar as the Word and sacraments are found there. In the interest of clarity one must distinguish between the inner and the external congregation or church, but in the concrete they must not be separated from one another; on the contrary, they must be as closely related as possible.

Luther's concept of the church was clearly expressed in his critique of the papacy and its claims. He believed that the words spoken to Peter, "Upon this rock I will build My church" (Matt. 16), point not to the pope in Rome but to the faith which Peter confessed. At the Leipzig Debate (1519) Luther for the first time attacked the claim of the pope to be the head of Christendom. He asserted that the supports on which this claim was based were false, not only the above-named interpretation of Matt. 16:18 but also the canon law, which provided the basis of papal power. Luther himself made the discovery that the papacy was not nearly as ancient as was commonly believed.

It was customary to refer to the Old Testament description of the Aaronic priesthood as an anticipation of the Roman papacy. Luther repudiated this interpretation. The Old Testament priesthood was abolished in and with Christ. The Old Testament priesthood foreshadowed the coming of Christ, and it was fulfilled in Him.

What are the characteristics of the true church? Luther spoke of three: Baptism, the Lord's Supper, and (above all) the proclamation of the Word. Where the Gospel is preached, there is the true church; and where the Gospel is lacking, so is the true church. The church has its life and being in the Word. The church consists of the fellowship of saints, but it is constituted by the Word and the sacraments. It is through these means that the Holy Spirit works and gathers the Christians of the world. As far as the papacy is concerned, Luther certainly did not feel that it could be juxtaposed with the church. But he recognized that the Gospel was available in the Church of Rome also, in spite of the misuse and neglect of the preaching office; so Christians could be found also there.

If the church is constituted by the Word, then what is the significance of the office of *the ministry*? Luther rejected the cleavage between clergy and laity, between the spiritual estate and the secular, which he found in the Church of Rome. Under the new covenant every Christian is a priest in the sense that he can come into the presence of God. This privilege comes to us through Baptism. But external order demands that certain persons should be chosen to administer the Word and sacraments. In other words, they carry out the priestly task on behalf of the congregation. This is not the only conceivable position to take, however. If it were consistently applied, it would imply that ordination is merely a call to a certain form of service. But there is evidence to show that Luther also thought of ordination as a real consecration to a lifelong divine mission.

In this context Luther distinguished between estate *(Stand)* and office *(Amt)*. The Christian estate, which can be called, in a figurative sense, the priestly estate, is common to all Christians. Because of this, the distinction between the spiritual and secular estates must cease. But the office must be held by certain persons chosen for it, who discharge the responsibility of preaching the Word and administering the sacraments. For Luther there was only one office, the office of the Word or the preaching office. Bishops and teachers belong to this same office, even though they are called to perform other tasks. If the office is to be administered properly, it requires a public call. This comes from the authorities, who are men, and yet it is a call from God.

CHAPTER 22

Melanchthon

Philipp Melanchthon (1497–1560) was not only Luther's foremost disciple and co-worker; he also created an independent variety of Reformation theology. Besides this, he also laid the foundations for higher education in the Protestant Church, not only in the field of theology but also with respect to the philosophical disciplines. It is not without reason that he has been called "the Instructor of Germany" (*Praeceptor Germaniae*).

Melanchthon was only 21 years old when he became professor of Greek at the University of Wittenberg. Under the influence of Luther he gave his wholehearted support to the Reformation and devoted himself more and more to theology, but without giving up his humanistic studies. He became Luther's closest associate, and after Luther's death he was the foremost leader of the Reformation in Germany, even though he gradually became a rather controversial figure in Lutheran circles.

Among Melanchthon's writings his *Loci communes* is theologically the most interesting. It is the Reformation's first book in the field of dogmatics. It was first published in 1521, and Luther praised it highly. Later on Melanchthon reworked the material in the book, and subsequent editions appeared in 1535 and 1543. The third edition was much more detailed than the others. This last edition also revealed the extent to which the author had changed his mind on a number of points since 1521.

Melanchthon was the man who actually wrote the Augsburg Confession. He also wrote the "Apology" to this confession, as well as the Treatise on the Power and Primacy of the Pope, which was appended to the Smalcald Articles. A number of Bible commentaries are also included in his theological bibliography, and also an exposition of the Nicene Creed. His *Examen ordinandorum* was of great help to the young state churches in Germany.

As a writer, Melanchthon did not confine himself to the field of theology. He wrote textbooks for use in a number of philosophical disciplines, and also a commentary on Aristotle. Among other things, he published *Philosophia moralis* (philosophic ethics), *De anima* (pyschology), plus a presentation on dialectics. Because of these writings, Melanchthon's contribution was of decisive significance for the entire range of university instruction in Protestant circles for a long time thereafter.

What was Melanchthon's position relative to Luther? This question was debated even among contemporary theologians, and it is still being discussed in modern research. In some instances Melanchthon has been thought of as a faithful defender and conscientious interpreter of Luther's teachings. On other occasions it has been thought that he distorted the original Reformation theology, that he was basically opposed to Luther's true intentions.

Neither of these interpretations is apt. Melanchthon did not follow Luther on every point. He modified some aspects of Luther's position which he had once supported himself. These changes can be discerned in the various editions of his *Loci*. By nature Melanchthon was by no means a mere "yes man"; he was rather a highly independent individual. He was also studiously active in his support of the Reformation. At the same time, he was an irenic person, who strove for harmony — unlike Luther, who liked a good fight.

Melanchthon's deviations from Luther were not based, therefore, on any lack of understanding of the Reformation's profound message; they were rather the result of his own deliberate choice. He felt that certain basic theological problems should be presented in a different way. What these differences involved will be dealt with in what follows.

Melanchthon's lifework had a stamp which was quite different from Luther's. For while Luther appeared on the stage with prophetic assurance, giving form freely to his ideas, Melanchthon preferred a systematic presentation and thoughtful formulations. He was above all a teacher, while Luther was a prophet. This lack of similarity was of extraordinary value to the Reformation cause. Without Melanchthon's contribution the Reformation would not have had the solidity and breadth which it achieved. It was he who laid the foundation for the combination of theology and scientific education which was characteristic of the Lutheran state churches and universities in former days. He had a high respect for humanistic education and felt that it was definitely necessary to theology. Without such scholarly support, false teachings could easily gain a footing, theology could degenerate into ignorant and confused speculation, and all of Christianity fall into contempt as a result.

The following survey of Melanchthon's theology must be limited to those points on which he went beyond or deviated from Luther.

The *Loci* of 1521 concentrated on Law and Gospel, sin and grace. This was done in accordance with the program set forth in the Foreword: Theology ought not busy itself with metaphysical questions concerning the divine essence or the natures of Christ but with that which concerns the soul's salvation. Only thus can we secure a true knowledge of Christ. Of what good is it if a doctor knows all about the appearance of herbs but knows nothing about their healing powers? Christian knowledge is to know what the Law demands and how a contrite conscience can be restored.

With respect to *the freedom of the will* Melanchthon was initially agreeable to the ideas Luther developed in *De servo arbitrio*. The anthropological considerations were typical of Melanchthon: As far as purely external acts are concerned, man has a certain freedom; the will can regulate our ability to move about. But God's law looks not to the external acts but to the stirrings of the heart. Melanchthon called these "affections," and with respect to them, he said, man is not free. It is not possible for man to influence his own heart. Such a strong affection as hate, for example, can only be altered by a new and stronger affection. That is why man is wholly unfree in the spiritual realm. "The Christian knows that there is nothing over which he has less control than his own heart." This also explains why man is unable to contribute to his own justification. The heart or the affections can be seriously altered only after the Holy Spirit has by faith come to dwell in man, so that the struggle between flesh and spirit begins in him.

Melanchthon also associated himself with other aspects of Luther's "determinism" in the 1521 *Loci*. He justified this not only psychologically but also with the concept of God's omnipotence: since all things happen in accordance with divine predestination, the will is not free. It was on that point, however, that Melanchthon came to deviate from

249

Luther most strongly. By 1530 he began to set forth arguments which, in his estimation, made a doctrine of predestination like that just mentioned impossible.

Alterations with respect to the psychological trend of thought were made in the later editions of the *Loci*. It is true that the Spirit of God alone is able to halt the corrupting influence of original sin and to break the power of the affections, but in reality (said the mature Melanchthon) this is done with the cooperation of the will. For when the Spirit works upon a man through the Word, he can either accept or reject the call (*C. R.* 21, 1078). Conversion results from the cooperation of three factors: the Word, the Holy Spirit, and the human will. In an addendum which first appeared in the *Loci* of 1548, the first edition to be published after Luther's death, this idea was developed even further. Man cannot excuse his inactivity over against the call of grace by saying that there is nothing he can do; for with the support of the Word he can at least pray for God's help. In this context the free will was defined as "the ability to apply oneself to grace" (*facultas applicandi se ad gratiam. C. R.* 21, 659). Here Melanchthon does not wish to express a distinctly Semi-Pelagian point of view. He was convinced that the action of the Word and the Spirit comes first, and that the will is able to act only when it is called through the Word and influenced by the Spirit. But Melanchthon also stressed that man must not stand idle and simply wait for the sudden inspiration of the Spirit. And to this he attached another argument.

Melanchthon also rejected the very *idea of predestination* in the form in which he first presented it. God elects man to salvation and carries out His work of salvation in accordance with His eternal decree. But this cannot mean that God should also predetermine the destruction of evil men. For in such a case God would appear to be the cause of evil, which is inconsistent with God's nature. Therefore the reason why one is chosen and the other is damned must lie with man. The promise is universal. If Saul is rejected but David is accepted, the difference must have its basis in their own behavior. The divine election is a "secret and eternal election," about which we can judge only a posteriori. Those who in faith accept God's mercy for Christ's sake are elected. The call is universal, and if a man is rejected the explanation is to be found in the fact that he rejected the call. One could scarcely say that Melanchthon was a synergist on this question, but he did desire to emphasize the human and volitional aspects of the conversion experience. He also dissociated himself from Luther's "double" predestination concept and from the idea of God's omnipotence as the basis of predestination.

With respect to *the doctrine of justification,* it was Melanchthon who gave precise formulation to the Reformation position, but in doing so he altered to some extent the basic ideas which we find in Luther. This was particularly true of Melanchthon's later work on the subject. In the Apology (1530) Melanchthon was still able to relate faith to an actual *justum fieri,* a justifying of the entire man, at the same time that man is declared just before God's tribunal *(justum reputari).* Later on, however, he fixed the linguistic usage in such a way that justification in the Pauline sense merely signifies a declaration of justification. In this connection we speak of a "forensic" (from "forum," marketplace, place where court is held) justification, since it is thought of as an acquittal before the divine judgment seat. Logically to relate this declaration of justification to actual renewal becomes a difficulty. Melanchthon here introduced a problem which Luther did not discuss. According to the latter, a man participates in the Spirit from the time that he appropriates the merits of Christ to himself by faith. Faith signifies participation in Christ. Regeneration results, simultaneously, from imputation. For the latter is not simply a legalistic act of judgment but also God's life-giving word, which raises man up and gives him the new birth. According to Melanchthon, however, imputation and regeneration are not the same: the former is the attribution of Christ's fulfilling of the Law, which takes place before the heavenly tribunal, while the infusion of the Spirit is something that follows without being organically related thereto. On one occasion — in Melanchthon's dispute with Osiander (about which more will be said later) — this point was of central significance. It then appeared as though Melanchthon's presentation of justification was a veritable defense of the essential Reformation position, at the same time that something of the richness of Luther's point of view had been lost.

Melanchthon described *repentance* as a *mortificatio,* effected by the Law, and a *vivificatio,* effected by the Gospel. The former was thought of as a more or less limited psychological phenomenon. If one adds to this his emphasis on the activity of the will in conversion, his separating of justification and regeneration, his conceiving of repentance as consisting partly of two stages, etc. — then one can speak of the tendency in Melanchthon to anticipate the later *ordo salutis,* with its division of the Christian life into different phases. Melanchthon did not actually teach this kind of *ordo salutis,* however; his statement was a clear and explicit formulation of the evangelical doctrine of repentance, as this was developed during the Reformation.

The Law has a somewhat different position in Melanchthon's theology than in Luther's. The former looked upon the Law as a divine, unchangeable order, to which man is obligated. To the two uses of the Law which Luther referred to, *usus civilis* and *usus theologicus,* Melanchthon added a third, *usus tertius in renatis.* By this he meant that even the regenerate are under obligation to the Law, and in the preaching of the Law find a norm and rule of conduct for their lives. They need the Law for support and guidance, for they are afflicted with weakness and fall easily. (Later Pietism construed this original teaching of the third use of the Law to refer to a special and stricter law, which could only be fulfilled by the faithful — the equivalent, thus, of the Roman Catholic teaching of the evangelical counsels.)

The strong pedagogical strain in Melanchthon's theology has already been mentioned. Associated with this was an emphasis on pure doctrine. This emphasis became very prominent in the older evangelical theology, and the connection between this and the Lutheran concept of faith and the Bible is rather obvious. The increasingly doctrinaire attitude of Melanchthon was revealed among other things in his doctrine of the *church.* He strongly emphasized the visible church *(ecclesia visibilis),* which is made up of those who confess the pure doctrine and use the sacraments. The distinctive mark of the true church, therefore, is not simply the preaching of the Word, but also the pure doctrine. "The visible church is the assembly of those who embrace the Gospel of Christ and use the sacraments rightly. God works in it through the ministry of the Gospel and regenerates many to eternal life. Nevertheless, there are many in this assembly who are not regenerate, but there is agreement on the true doctrine" *(C. R.,* 21, 826). The weight which he attached to the teaching office was also characteristic of Melanchthon's ecclesiology. He divided church members into those who teach and those who listen. Obedience to the teaching office was greatly emphasized. As a result of this, the Lutheran concept of the universal priesthood lost some of its significance.

Melanchthon's formulation of the relationship of the church to the secular authority also provided a prototype for future generations. He taught that the state has assumed both the power functions and the external administration of the church, as well as the responsibility of supporting and protecting the church. The prince was to be *custos utriusque tabulae* — that is, the protector also of faith and the true worship of God. He was thought to be under obligation to the teaching office with respect to that which concerns the administration of the Word and the true doctrine in the congregation.

Reference is often made to Melanchthon's *traditionalism*. This refers to the fact that the ecumenical creeds and the early Christian consensus as a whole received an increasing amount of attention in his theology. He felt that he could not teach that for which support was lacking from the era of the early church. Melanchthon did not believe, however, that tradition is on the same level as Scripture. He rather thought of tradition only as the means whereby the original revelation has come to us, and without which we cannot properly interpret Scripture. Therefore the greatest weight is to be attached to the oldest tradition. Scripture and the properly sifted tradition form a unity. A good example of Melanchthon's strong dependence, on principle, upon the church fathers can be seen in his concept of the Lord's Supper. He was critical of Luther's use of the doctrine of ubiquity in this connection. He could find no support for this interpretation of the Lord's Supper in the old tradition. He held fast to the teaching of the Real Presence, but insisted that it must be understood in another way. The body of Christ is found in heaven, but in the strength of His divine omnipotence He can be present in the Lord's Supper *(multivolipresens)*. His body is not included in the bread, but He is physically present in the use of the Sacrament *(in usu Eucharistiae)* — *with* the bread but not *in* it.

Melanchthon's profound humanistic tendencies were even more significant than his "traditionalism." Philosophical presuppositions played an important role in his theology, not only in the modifications which they gave rise to here and there, but above all in the stamp which they set upon his theology in general. Melanchthon's *method* was clearly influenced by philosophy. In the later editions of his *Loci* he maintained that the theologian, like the scientist, must employ method and order and strive for a clear disposition of the material he is working with. To be sure, rational proofs cannot be given in theology, for it is not based on rational principles but on Scripture as God's Word. But Scripture itself, as well as the confessions of faith, manifest an observable inner orderliness upon which one can construct a theological system. Melanchthon's own *Loci* was designed to follow the order of the history of salvation as presented in Scripture and the creeds. In this as in so many other respects, Melanchthon prefigured subsequent developments in Lutheran theology. His so-called *"loci* method" was used in dogmatic expositions for a long time. Its style was altered, of course, not least of all by the introduction of more and more of the philosophical method. (See the beginning of Ch. 30 below.)

It has long been common in theological research to trace the various tendencies in the subsequent development of Lutheranism back to Melanchthon and his deviations from Luther's theology. This is certainly true to some extent, but we dare not ignore the fact that Melanchthon was much closer to Luther in many ways than were the theologians who have been thought of as Luther's successors. It must be remembered, too, that Lutheran orthodoxy frequently and deliberately rejected and opposed Melanchthon, especially on those points where he had deviated from Luther. This opposition was expressed even during Melanchthon's lifetime, particularly in the controversy which arose between his supporters, the "Philippists," and the so-called "Gnesio-Lutherans."

CHAPTER 23

Zwingli

The contributions of the Swiss reformer Huldreich (Ulrich) Zwingli to the history of theology will require no more than a brief report. His doctrine of the Lord's Supper has already been discussed in connection with Luther's theology.

Zwingli was born in 1484, and after studying in Vienna and Basel (master's degree, 1506), he became pastor in Glarus and later in Maria-Einsiedeln. In 1519 he became "people's priest" *(Leutpriester)* at the Great Minster in Zurich. He was introduced to scholastic theology in its Thomistic form at an early age, but soon went other ways. In 1516 he became acquainted with Erasmus of Rotterdam and was profoundly influenced by his writings. The fact of the matter is that he became a disciple of Erasmus, and at the outset his position coincided with Erasmus' humanistic "reform Christianity." Erasmus held that the people should be "enlightened" through the preaching of the pure Gospel of Christ, above all the ethical principles of the Sermon on the Mount. It was hoped that cult and customs would gradually improve as a result.

But during the years 1519–20 Zwingli's position changed. When he realized that the humanistic program of reform would not attain the desired result, he broke with Erasmus. He also repudiated the Pelagian concept which he found in Erasmus, and taught that man is totally corrupt. Only through the transforming power of Christ can a man be justified.

The reasons for this change to the Reformation point of view have been discussed at length in Zwingli research. Some have believed that it was entirely due to the influence of Luther, whose books Zwingli began to read in 1518. But his own account conflicts with this assumption; according to this, he began to preach the Gospel even before 1518. Furthermore, he firmly insisted that he was not dependent on Luther, nor did he agree with him in all things. The statements in which Zwingli expresses his independence vis-à-vis Luther were conditioned, however, by his desire to keep the Swiss Reformation free of the effects of the Edict of Worms, which outlawed both Luther *and* his supporters. That Luther's writings were of great significance to Zwingli cannot be denied. At the very least they provided an impulse for his practical Reformation activity.

It has become more common, however, to emphasize Zwingli's independence. Furthermore, recently deciphered and published marginal notes taken from books in Zwingli's library have thrown light on another important influence in his life — Augustine. It was from this source, to a large extent, that Zwingli derived his concept of original sin and grace, and it was this which caused him to break with his earlier, humanistic position. Another factor related to his development was the extended plague which Zwingli managed to survive in the fall of 1519 and which created a profound religious crisis in his life.

Under Zwingli's leadership the Zurich reform developed step by step in the years following 1519. This brought with it not only religious change but also a far-reaching social revolution. A particularly strict ethic and a theocratic form of government characterized Zwingli's program of reform.

In spite of his Reformation outlook, Zwingli never altogether gave up his humanistic point of view. His position appears to have been a mixture of antiquity, Renaissance theology, and Reformation elements. As noted, he accepted the Augustinian doctrine of original sin. But he rejected the idea of inherited guilt. Guilt does not appear until the Law has actually been transgressed; it is not inherent in the depraved condition which is handed down from generation to generation. It was also characteristic of Zwingli to say that certain enlightened heathen have come to a saving knowledge through rational means and that they can therefore attain to a state of blessedness just as well as Christians can.

Basic to Zwingli's theology is a metaphysical contrast between spirit and matter. The spirit represents its own sphere and cannot be thought of as a part of what is physical or external. As a result, Zwingli drew a sharp line between the human and the divine in Christ, and he felt that faith refers only to His divine nature. Zwingli did not emphasize the Word as something of great importance. He was of the opinion that faith is awakened not by the external Word but as a result of direct action by God or the Spirit. This conception of the Word influenced Zwingli's understanding of the sacraments, which we touched upon earlier in connection with the Lord's Supper dispute between Zwingli and Luther. As a result, Zwingli did not conceive of either Baptism or the Lord's Supper as means of grace in the proper sense of the term. He did not believe that infant Baptism has any guilt-removing effect. As is evident from what has already been said, Zwingli taught that children are without guilt prior to committing actual sin. With respect to the Lord's Supper, Zwingli did not feel that it provided forgiveness of sin. He rather looked upon this sacrament as a symbolic memorial act.

A large part of Zwingli's writings had to do with practical and political questions. Chief among his theological works was the doctrinal summary *De vera et falsa religione commentarius,* dedicated to King Francis I of France (1525). Among the writings he published concerning the Lord's Supper were *Eine klare Unterrichtung vom Nachtmahl Christi* (1526) and the *Amica exegesis,* which was directed at Luther (1527).

Zwingli became ever more deeply involved in political activity as a result of his efforts to expand his reform movement into other parts of Switzerland. He participated actively in the unsuccessful plan for a European coalition directed against the House of Hapsburg. He also worked zealously for the formation of a unified evangelical state in Switzerland, to be led by Zurich and Bern. The Catholic cantons were to be subdued by force of arms. But even some of Zwingli's own followers opposed this plan, and when an actual civil war finally broke out, the evangelicals were divided and definitely inferior. They were defeated at Kappel in 1531, and Zwingli, who participated in the battle fully armed, was killed. His death on the field of battle strongly underscores the political and nationalistic element in his lifework. It also reveals an attitude toward the work of the Reformation quite different from Luther's.

CHAPTER 24

Calvin

Zwingli's influence remained rather limited. This was not true, however, of the theology of John Calvin, which gradually became definitive for the entire Reformed tradition.

One of Calvin's predecessors was the previously mentioned Martin Bucer, the Strasbourg reformer, who combined elements from Luther as well as from the Biblical humanism of Erasmus in his theology. In the dispute over the Lord's Supper between Luther and Zwingli he took a mediating position. In many respects Bucer foreshadowed the Calvinistic point of view. This was true, for example, of what he taught about predestination and about the glory of God as the purpose of world history. The congregational order he formulated in Strasbourg also reminds us of the one Calvin later developed. Calvin sojourned in Strasbourg during the years 1538–41 and was deeply impressed by Bucer's theology and church polity. Some time later Bucer was in exile in England, and his influence was felt there in the reorganization of the Anglican Church under King Edward VI.

John Calvin, who was born in France in 1509, received a broad education, including studies in the field of law. As far as evangelical theology is concerned, Calvin was largely self-taught; he became acquainted with Luther's ideas chiefly by literary means. Because of his beliefs Calvin was forced to flee from France in 1534; he went to Basel, where in 1536 he brought out a doctrinal manual, the *Institutes of the Christian Religion,* in part designed to defend his brothers in the faith in France. He went to Geneva in that same year and took charge of the Reformation there. Often using harsh measures, Calvin imposed a strict form of discipline on the church in Geneva. He also designed a new congregational order, based on a college of presbyters working in close cooperation with the secular authorities. He died in Geneva in 1564.

Calvin's position was largely completed in the *Institutes* of 1536. But in later editions (1543 and 1559) he expanded the original work into a comprehensive dogmatic presentation, comparable to Melanchthon's *Loci,* but arranged in a more strictly systematic manner. The third edition of 1559 (the last to be edited by Calvin) divided the doctrinal material into four books, which dealt successively with God as Creator, God as Savior, the manner of receiving Christ's grace, and the external means whereby God invites us to and preserves us in the fellowship of Christ (church and sacraments). Besides the *Institutes* Calvin wrote many lesser works, sermons and letters and commentaries on nearly all the books of the Bible.

Although Calvin did in some respects perpetuate the tradition begun by Zwingli and Bucer (not least of all in the field of church polity), we must not disregard the fact that Calvin thought of himself above all as a faithful follower of Luther, as one who represented basically the same point of view as that held by Luther. But as is true of Melanchthon, Calvin's theology bears a stamp different from Luther's and reveals contributions from other sources as well. Some of Calvin's basic concepts will be sketched in what follows.

The idea of *God's glory (la gloire de Dieu)* occupies a central place in Calvin's theology. As he saw it, the glory of God is the goal of all God's plans for the world and for salvation, as well as of human activity. "[God] has established the whole world to this end, that it might be the scene of His glory" (*C. R.,* 36, 294). The lives of Christian people are to serve to increase the glory of God. Absolute subjection to the will of God and obedience to His law are the foundations of the Calvinist faith. The Christian is to demonstrate his faith, and at the same time promote the glory of God, by working industriously at the task to which he has been called and actively cooperating in matters pertaining to the kingdom of God.

Closely associated to the idea of God's glory *(gloria Dei)* in Calvin's mind was the doctrine of *God's providence (providentia Dei):* all that happens is impelled by God's almighty will and by His active cooperation. God's omnipotence also includes human activity, even that which is evil. Is any kind of freedom possible then? Calvin answered by saying that God's providence does not work as external coercion *(coactio externa);* it only means that all that happens stands under a higher necessity. He did not therefore exclude psychological freedom in human activity.

That God is active in evil things that happen must not, according to Calvin, simply be understood as *permissio;* it rather goes back to God's active will, which we are not able to comprehend. God has therefore willed Adam's fall, just as He decides that some men shall be lost and deprives them of His Spirit.

With that we have already touched upon Calvin's concept of *predestination,* which is often referred to as Calvinism's "central doctrine." Just as the entire course of the world stands under God's providence, so also does every man's salvation or damnation depend on God's almighty will and predestination. Or in Calvin's own words: "We call predestination God's eternal decree, whereby He has decided what He will have happen to every man. For not all have been created under the same conditions: some are predestined to eternal life, others to eternal damnation. And inasmuch as a man is created to reach the one goal or the other, we say that he is predestined to life or to death." (*C. R.*, 29, 864 f. — *Institutes*, III, 21, 5)

This, then, is double predestination — both to salvation and to damnation. Calvin emphasized that rejection also depends on God's eternal predestination, a fact which is not to be ignored from the pulpit. Even the damnation and the eternal punishment of evil men serve to glorify God. God is not the source of evil, but He has His secret, inscrutable uses for it. God remains just even in rejecting, but this justice transcends all human norms. For this reason it is incomprehensible; it is a part of God's hidden nature.

Calvin felt that this concept of predestination ought to support rather than destroy one's certainty of his salvation. It becomes clear, in this way, said Calvin, that man's salvation is based not on what he himself does but on an eternal decree. In other words, double predestination in Calvin's thinking (as in Augustine's) is the ultimate guarantee of salvation by grace alone. Furthermore, the eternal decree must be intimately associated with the order of salvation which has been carried into effect in time. The call and justification are definite signs that a man is one of the elect. In a corresponding manner, the rejected have a sign of their condition in the fact that they are excluded from knowledge of Christ or from sanctification.

Calvin's concept of predestination presupposes a divine justice which goes beyond all that man conceives of as just. The divine order cannot be measured by the same gauge as can the order of creation;

neither can it be fathomed by human reason. But Calvin at the same time asserted that there is a distinct connection between divine and human justice. In the work of creation man has a witness to God, and by rational means he can attain to some knowledge of Him — the so-called natural knowledge of God. Similarly, the law which rules in creation is a copy of God's eternal justice. By knowledge of this law, then, man has an insight into God's eternal law and His justice.

At one and the same time, therefore, there is a similarity and a contrast or dissimilarity between the divine and that which is created. This trend of thought, which corresponds to the medieval, Thomist concept of the analogy of being *(analogia entis)*, also contributed to Calvin's doctrine of predestination. The justice which is expressed by the fact that God rejects on the basis of His eternal decree is inscrutable to man and is in opposition to what we otherwise call justice. Nevertheless, this same rejection expresses divine justice and is in agreement with the righteousness of God. That God should stand outside of law altogether (and thus be *exlex*), or that predestination should be decreed in a blindly arbitrary way, is out of the question.

In assigning Calvin his position in the history of theology, the transition between the ideas here presented is an important point to remember. The teaching of double predestination associates Calvin with Luther's theology, while the analogy concept strongly reminds us of the Middle Ages, and above all of the Thomist tradition.

The influence of the analogy concept was responsible for the fact that Calvin's doctrine of predestination was different from Luther's. Calvin also used this doctrine in a different way. He related it to the acquisition of salvation itself, while Luther, in the corresponding situation, emphasized that one should turn away from the hidden God and hold fast to God's revealed will, to the atonement wrought by Christ, which is valid for all.

It is on this point that the Lutheran tradition rejected the Calvinistic doctrine of predestination: in opposition to Calvin's concept of double predestination, Luther referred to the Bible passages which speak of God's universal will to save, or of the reconciliation of the entire world. (Cf. 1 Tim. 2:4; 1 John 2:2)

In his doctrine of predestination, as elsewhere, Calvin proceeded above all on the *Scriptural principle:* theology must set forth what is set down in the Bible. His concept of Biblical inspiration was set forth in terms of the Holy Spirit's dictation, infallibly transmitted through those who wrote down the words of Scripture. Calvin used to be referred to as the originator of the orthodox doctrine of inspiration. This is hardly correct, inasmuch as similar theories were already propounded in the early church. In the later Calvinist tradition the doctrine of inspiration was given a different, more mechanical form than in Lutheran orthodoxy. Whether or not this mechanical doctrine of inspiration can be traced back to Calvin is a disputed question.

The Old Testament had a different position for Calvin than it has in Lutheran theology. Calvin held that the ceremonial aspect of the Mosaic law was abolished in and with the appearance of Christ. But, on the other hand, he taught that the moral law of the Old Testament applies also to Christians. They stand under its obligations and are to arrange their lives in accordance with the injunctions which can be read out of Scripture's proclamation of the Law. Society too is to organize itself according to the principles of Biblical law. To a certain extent, therefore, the Mosaic law was ascribed a permanent validity in Calvin's thinking.

In spite of his attitude toward the Law, Calvin emphasized with great incisiveness that our righteousness before God does not consist of works of the Law, nor in the regeneration which is effected through the Spirit. He criticized both Augustine and Osiander on this point. In his own theology Calvin strongly emphasized the forensic or imputative form of justification.

There was a tendency in Calvin to make sanctification the purpose of justification. Sanctification, in turn, was thought of as a means to increase the glory of God. Man is to live in strict agreement with divine law and thus to testify to his faith and strengthen the certainty that he is one of the elect. It is the Law, therefore, which is the norm of the sanctified life. God's law is eternal and a direct expression of His will. It must therefore concern even those who have been born again, and serve as the norm for their lives. Conformity to God's will is the goal of sanctification.

Calvinistic piety is characterized by strict temperance and by hard work in one's earthly calling. This regimen has been called a "this-worldly asceticism," which has replaced the medieval monastic asceticism for Protestants. In Calvinism a practical, responsible, down-to-earth attitude has been combined with a strong emphasis on the fact that Christians are aliens in this world and that the life beyond is the goal of human existence and the "one thing needful."

Calvin distinguished between a *visible* and an *invisible church*. The latter is made up of the elect. The visible church is constituted by the Word, the sacraments, and church discipline. Congregational order is to follow certain instructions derived from the Bible (including the four offices, pastor, teacher, elder, and deacon). The church also has a *spiritualis jurisdictio*, a careful control of morals and customs. The secular authorities are expected to assist with church discipline. Their task is not only to maintain public order but also to support the interests of true religion. The authorities are God's servants and are subject to the teaching office in all matters relating to religion and morals.

The model church polity which Calvin devised for use in Geneva was characterized by strong organization and a scrupulous supervision of morals and customs. The implacable manner in which those in authority proceeded against heresy was not the result of any despotic will-to-power on Calvin's part, but rather the result of his uncompromising zeal for evangelical truth. The best known (but by no means the only) heresy trial in Calvin's Geneva was the one which condemned Michael Servetus to death because of his refusal to accept the church's confession concerning the Trinity.

Next to predestination, the *doctrine of the Lord's Supper* has been the most controversial issue between Calvinism and Lutheranism. What Calvin objected to in the Lutheran position was above all that the bread is thought of as the body of Christ in a substantial sense, without permitting a figurative mode of expression in the words of institution. Calvin also rejected the idea that the body of Christ is infinite and everywhere present, without local limitations.

At the same time, however, Calvin by no means represented a purely symbolic concept of the Lord's Supper. To him it was actually a matter of participating in the body and blood of Christ. But in view of the fact that the body of Christ is in heaven, locally restricted, it cannot be present in the elements in a physical, "substantial" manner. Nor is a physical presence necessary in the Sacrament. The Spirit of Christ is able to unite the faithful with Christ in heaven. For the Spirit is not limited, and He can bring together that which is widely separated with respect to space. Through the mediation of the Spirit, therefore, the faithful partake of the Lord's flesh and blood, and are thereby brought to life. This *communio* takes place in the Lord's Supper under the symbols of the bread and wine.

As we have already noted, Calvin's basic outlook with respect to the Lord's Supper was different from Luther's. He thought of heaven, where the body of Christ has been since the Ascension, as a definite, restricted place beyond the earthly sphere. The body of Christ cannot partake of the infinity which distinguishes divinity; it is locally restricted. When men speak of the presence of the body of Christ in the Lord's Supper, or of the participation of the faithful in the same, this cannot therefore refer to a physical presence or a physical eating of Christ's body and blood, but only to a spiritual presence or a spiritual eating. It is a matter of the fellowship of faith or the Spirit with the Christ who ascended to heaven.

On the basis of Calvin's assumptions it must be supposed that only the faithful receive the gifts provided in the Lord's Supper *(manducatio fidelium)*. And this partaking occurs through a spiritual eating, i. e., through the fellowship of faith with Christ, symbolized by the sacramental meal *(manducatio spiritualis)*.

Finally, Calvin objected to a literal interpretation of the words of institution. In his own way, Calvin certainly believed in the real presence of Christ in the Lord's Supper, but the elements themselves were thought of only as symbols of the spiritual fellowship or communion which belongs exclusively to the realm of faith.

A sharp distinction between the spiritual and the physical therefore characterizes the Calvinistic point of view, a position which was later expressed in the formula *Finitum non capax infiniti* ("The finite cannot contain the infinite").

CHAPTER 25

Reformed Theology
to and Including
the Synod of Dort, 1618 – 19

Only gradually did John Calvin become the dominant figure in the Christian tradition which is often named after him. The expression "Calvinist," in fact, was coined by the Lutheran opposition during the 16th century, while the church groups which accepted a Calvinist confession usually called themselves "Reformed." Many other theologians in addition to Calvin influenced the development of these Reformed bodies. Unlike the Lutherans, they lacked a common confession. Instead, a number of different confessions were prepared, which were limited to individual countries or areas, as for example the Gallican Confession, the Helvetic Confession, the Westminster Confession (accepted in Scotland), and the Heidelberg Catechism (accepted in the Palatinate). Many of the Reformed theologians were relatively independent of Calvin. Heinrich Bullinger, for example, Zwingli's successor in Zurich, was influenced in particular by Zwingli and by the Wittenberg theologians, and he combined elements from both sources. Furthermore it must be remembered that Melanchthon exerted a profound influence also on the Reformed tradition. A number of his close disciples later on joined Reformed churches. This was the case with Victorinus Strigel, whose name is associated with the synergistic controversy (see below), and Christoph Pezel, who published the writings of Melanchthon and Strigel.

Another theologian who stood very close to Lutheranism was Ursinus, chief among those responsible for the Heidelberg Catechism (1563), the confessional document of the church in the Palatinate.

Thereby he represented a mediating position between Luther and Calvin, the position which characterized the church in the Palatinate. The Heidelberg Catechism propounds the Calvinist concept of the Lord's Supper, but it does not have much to say about the strict teaching of predestination.

Bartholomäus Keckermann, active at the beginning of the 17th century, was also rather independent of Calvin. Most of his contributions were of a philosophical nature. In the field of theology he attempted to apply the so-called analytical method (to start with the goal and then to determine the means of reaching it), which was later adopted by Lutheran orthodoxy. Keckermann was also the first to use the concept "systematic" as the designation for a general description of a scientific discipline.

It was Theodore Beza who perpetuated the pure Calvinist tradition. Beza developed the doctrine of predestination even more stringently than Calvin himself and gave it a more central place in his world view.

But Calvinist orthodoxy is to be found in its strictest form in Franciscus Gomarus. He, like Beza, represented the so-called supralapsarian position, which says that predestination was decided upon without taking the fall of man into consideration. This implies that not only eternal damnation but also the fall into sin was foreordained in God's decree. The infralapsarian position implies that predestation to damnation was decided upon in anticipation of man's fall into sin.

At the Synod of Dort (1618–19), whose decisions became normative for a large part of the Reformed Church, the strict Calvinist point of view was victorious. It was asserted there that a certain number of men have been chosen to salvation in Christ, solely on the basis of God's pleasure. Those included in this number can be sure of their election, for such signs as faith in Christ, a childlike love of God, sorrow for sin, and longing for righteousness are infallible. Of the rejected it was said only that they were passed by when the elect were chosen, and given over to the misery which they brought upon themselves by their own guilt (the infralapsarian position).

The Synod of Dort was assembled to deal with the growing opposition to the Calvinistic doctrine of predestination, which was led by Jacobus Arminius. The Arminian opposition was indeed rejected at Dort, but it nevertheless came to be of great significance. This was true because it absorbed the Socinian movement (of which more will be said later) and also because it anticipated the thought patterns of the age of Enlightenment in many respects. Besides its rejection of the orthodox doctrine of predestination, Arminianism was characterized by a moralistic strain (faith was looked upon as a human achievement) and in later years by its marked rationalizing of theology. The well-known jurist Hugo Grotius developed a similar point of view in his theological writings.

CHAPTER 26

Reformation Theology
in Lutheran Areas
to the Formula of Concord, 1577

OLAVUS PETRI

One of Luther's first disciples was the Swedish reformer Olavus Petri (d. 1552). His disputation was held in Wittenberg in 1518, and from this we can tell that he was an eyewitness to Luther's first appearances as a reformer. In his writings, which were epoch-making for Swedish literature, Petri set forth a clear and independent presentation of the Reformation point of view. His best-known books are *Concerning God's Word and Man's Precepts and Regulations* (1528) and *A Small Book of Sermons* (1530). In his basic ideas he followed Luther, but in the details and the form of his presentation he was independent of him. Petri had also learned from humanism. His pedagogical interest, his insistence upon clarity, and his Biblical argumentation reveal a kinship with the humanist school. This does not mean, however, that he accepted the content of humanist teachings. He accepted Luther's position with respect to the omnipotence of God and the enslavement of man. To justify these beliefs he was content to refer to the Bible: reason must bow before the clear witness of God's Word, even though the consequences of this are seemingly unreasonable in some cases. In a similar situation Luther was more likely to base his arguments on the entirety of the evangelical faith.

Olavus Petri liked to emphasize the unity between faith and works. The true faith must express itself in a new life. If regeneration is lacking, so is the true faith. In controversies with the Uppsala theologian Peder Galle and the Danish reform humanist Paul Helie, Petri developed his position with great clarity. For the most part, however, he sought to attain the goals he set for himself in the service of the Reformation without using polemics.

JOHANNES BRENZ

This man, who is remembered above all as the reformer of Württemberg, was one of Luther's earliest and most faithful supporters. He died in 1570. In the dispute over the Lord's Supper in the 1520s Brenz participated in the defense of the Lutheran position. And when the Calvinist interpretation became more widespread later on, he had further occasion to defend and more fully develop the same point of view. He described the Real Presence as a physical presence (*manducatio oralis* and *manducatio infidelium*). But it was most characteristic of his position on the Lord's Supper to retain and develop Luther's concept of the ubiquity of the body of Christ (which Melanchthon rejected). He used this concept to justify the teaching of the Real Presence. It is not only in heaven (he said) that Christ's human nature shares in the omnipresence and omnipotence of the divine nature; it also did so while He lived on earth. And it is in the power of this ubiquity that Christ's body can be present in the sacramental elements.

With ideas of this kind, Brenz provided the classical form for the way of looking at things which even later and in other contexts gave a certain uniqueness to the theology of Swabia (Württemberg). This theological position is characterized by a Biblical realism which is independent of the rational world view, with a tendency toward mysticism and subtle speculation. Brenz's firm defense of the fundamentals of the Reformation did much to preserve the distinctiveness of genuine Lutheranism. His theology also exerted a strong influence on the Swedish tradition.

BIBLICAL THEOLOGY

An essential but frequently overlooked facet of Reformation theology was the highly developed activity in the field of Biblical theology which was then carried on. This activity provided the basis for the theological work of the Reformation era as well as of the following generations. Some of the better-known books in this field were Matthias Flacius' *Clavis Scripturae sacrae* (1567), a comprehensive examination of Biblical fundamentals, and *Syntagma seu corpus doctrinae Novi Tes-*

tamenti (1558), by Wigand and Judex. The latter is a complete book of dogmatics, based on a simple Bible-theological method, whereby the authors sought to present a collation of the content of Scripture without resorting to the use of philosophical categories.

MELANCHTHON'S DISCIPLES

A stronger attachment to philosophy, as well as to antiquity and Christian tradition, was characteristic of that group of prominent theologians who can be best described as the disciples of Melanchthon. This group included the above-named Victorinus Strigel and Christoph Pezel (who later went over to Calvinism), plus Nikolaus Selneccer.

A mediating position was adopted by Martin Chemnitz (d. 1586), who agreed with Melanchthon on many points but who at the same time was also one of the prime advocates of pure Lutheranism. He also employed a Biblical method. Chemnitz is well known as one of the authors of the Formula of Concord (see below). His writings (e. g., the posthumously published *Loci theologici)* formed the strongest connecting link between the Reformation period and Lutheran orthodoxy. In his book *De duabus naturis in Christo* (1570) Chemnitz presented a detailed, systematic description of the teaching of the communication of attributes. Another exemplary contribution from his pen is the examination of the decisions of the Council of Trent, *Examen concilii tridentini* (1565–73).

THE THEOLOGICAL CONTROVERSIES

a. *General.* The doctrinal disputes which agitated the Lutheran Church during the years following the Reformation have often been thought of as more or less fruitless word-battles. But a more careful evaluation will show that — in most cases, at any rate — these disputes concerned significant doctrinal questions, which necessarily came to the fore as men sought to give more precise form to the message of the Reformation. Some of these controversies involved questions which later proved to be of no importance, but on the whole the intra-Lutheran doctrinal disputes led to a deeper understanding of the Lutheran doctrine of justification and to a more precise delineation of its consequences.

The many different controversies can be more easily surveyed if one will bear in mind that a great number of them are directly related to one another and refer to central questions concerning salvation or the acquisition of salvation. The so-called first antinomian controversy concerned the preaching of repentance. The synergistic controversy had to do with the process involved in the conversion experience. The meaning of justification was debated in the Osiandrian controversy, while the Majoristic and the second antinomian controversies concerned the question of good works and the third use of the Law.

b. *The controversy concerning Agricola's antinomianism.* Johann Agricola came to Wittenberg from Eisleben ca. 1537 and asserted that the Law ought not be preached among Christians, but only the Gospel. The comfort of the Gospel should be preached first, and only then might people be frightened by God's wrath. In this connection Agricola made a highly unusual distinction between wrath and law. He referred to Rom. 2:4, where we are told that "God's kindness is meant to lead you to repentance." With this in mind, Agricola maintained that men should be aroused to contrition and repentance only through the Gospel — through the preaching of Christ's suffering. Luther looked upon Agricola's thesis as a grave misinterpretation of his doctrine and became involved in the struggle himself (in a number of disputations with the antinomians, as well as in the treatise *Wider die Antinomer,* 1539). Luther pointed out that the contrition and grief which is associated with repentance can only be awakened by the Law, which reveals sin. Hence the Law must be proclaimed. The Law is everything that reveals sin, wrath, and death. And to the extent that the Christian is always a sinner, he remains subject to the operation of the Law, which is designed to put the old man to death. Agricola's antinomian views did not exert any great influence at the time, but similar ideas have been put into practice in Lutheran circles since that time — for example, in the group which had its center at Herrnhut.

c. *The problem of synergism.* The so-called synergistic controversy of the 1550s and 1560s traced its origins from the statements of certain "Philippists" to the effect that the will could be said to cooperate to some extent in the conversion experience. The major opponents were Flacius and Strigel, who gave this matter a thorough analysis at the Weimar Disputation of 1560. According to Strigel the will, in conversion, continues to function in its natural way. It is simply transformed from an evil will to a good will. But Flacius asserted that the natural will is entirely unable to assist in conversion. It does not merely remain passive; it actively resists grace. Because of this, a completely new will, a "new man," must be created, while the old will is restrained and coerced by the grace of God. This debate — which led to no tangible result — was obscured by the fact that the opposing sides held stubbornly to the question of the cooperation of the will (synergism), while as a matter of fact another problem was also involved. For Strigel proceeded on the basis of a philosophically conceived theory of the will, while Flacius — although with strange expressions — supported the Biblical concept of the new creation (the new man). Strigel's main point was that conversion, as a progressive experience, always takes place on the level of the human will. Flacius maintained, on the other hand, that the first stage of the conversion experience (or "the first conversion," as he put it) is wholly the result of grace, and that the human will, which is naturally depraved, is so far removed from doing what is good that it rather resists the grace of God.

Flacius' controversial teaching of original sin also became involved in this same debate. Strigel, who held that man does not receive a new will (in a substantial sense) in conversion, also asserted that the essence of man was not lost in the fall into sin. He was therefore able to describe original sin as an "accident." But Flacius felt that this represented a modification of the sin concept, and so he opposed Strigel on this point as well. According to Flacius, original sin is a "substance," or rather, something congruent with man's substantial form (forma substantialis). Basically, Flacius desired to defend the Biblical and Lutheran totus homo view of man (by which original sin concerns the whole man, just as regeneration implies the appearance of a "new man"), but he transformed this trend of thought into an (even philosophically) unsatisfactory theory which was generally repudiated by theologians and cast the shadow of heresy over its author.

d. *The rejection of Osiander's doctrine of justification.* Andreas Osiander (remembered as a leader of the Reformation in Nürnberg, later pastor in Königsberg) in a debate in 1550 set forth certain ideas concerning justification which were obviously foreign to the current interpretation. Osiander believed that our justification cannot be provided by the atoning work wrought by Christ many hundreds of years ago. It must rather be related to the Christ who dwells within us, i. e., to the divine nature which is imparted to us through the acceptance of the

Gospel. What Osiander objected to, in other words, was the undiluted imputation concept. He taught that we become just not through an external imputation but by the fact that Christ dwells in us as an "inner Word." The Atonement is only the necessary prerequisite for this experience, given once and for all time.

Osiander's critics (above all, Melanchthon and Flacius) insisted that the concept of "justification," as used in the Bible, means "to declare just." Justification by faith is possible because of Christ's superabundant fulfilling of the Law, imputed to us. This is an *aliena justitia,* located outside of us *(extra nos).* One must carefully distinguish between this and the first stages of regeneration, which come into being as a result of the indwelling Spirit and which are not the basis of justification.

The undiluted imputation idea and its related forensic concept of the Atonement made it hard to grasp the connection between justification and regeneration. But as a result of the Osiandrian controversy the original Reformation idea that it is the *sinner* who is justified and that justification by faith consists of the forgiveness of sin (and not of inherent qualities) was strongly affirmed. In his own way Osiander had intended to express some facets of Luther's theology which had otherwise been ignored, but he confused Reformation concepts with speculations derived from the Cabala and mysticism (the inner Word). The current Lutheran interpretation of justification was more firmly established as a result of the dispute with Osiander. The tendency to distinguish between imputation and regeneration and to think of the Atonement solely in legalistic categories was strengthened.

e. *The Majoristic controversy* made no essential contribution to the theological discussion. Georg Major, one of Melanchthon's followers, defended the proposition that "good works are necessary to salvation." The Gnesio-Lutherans looked upon this as an example of works righteousness, and they replied (as they had in the Osiandrian controversy) by drawing a sharp line of demarcation between justification (which precedes all works) and regeneration. One of Major's most zealous opponents, Nikolaus von Amsdorf, advocated the opposite thesis, that "good works are harmful to salvation." It is obvious that both propositions were poorly formulated and left room for numerous misunderstandings. Major did not mean that good works are necessary for justification; he only meant to say that they must accompany faith — that faith would cease without them. Hence good works are necessary to preserve faith. Against this it was pointed out that justification is not preserved by works but only by faith, which is to say, by returning to grace.

Amsdorf intended to give expression to the Lutheran *sola fide* concept when he set forth his thesis. The way he did this, however, served to obscure the ineluctable connection between faith and works. The chief results of this controversy were that in the future many of the ambiguous formulations used in the debate were avoided and that conditions were provided for a clearer definition of the place of good works within the context of the doctrine of justification.

f. *The second antinomian controversy* was chiefly concerned with the question of the third use of the Law. Some of the so-called Gnesio-Lutherans — Amsdorf, Poach, and Otto — maintained that neither justification nor the new life is regulated by the Law, but that both are elevated above the legal order. The justified man does not therefore stand under the Law; he freely fulfills its commands. This is not antinomianism in the strict sense of the term, since these men did not question the preaching of the Law or deny the function of the Law in producing knowledge of sin. They simply desired to sharpen the contrast between the Gospel as a gift of grace and the Law as something to which men are obligated. Those who opposed them said that a denial of the third use of the Law involved a diminution of the Law's status, and they therefore called it antinomianism. The problem was settled in such a way that the idea of a third use of the Law was commonly accepted. This implies that the concept of the Law is understood in the widest sense as a designation for God's will in general, and not simply as an expression for an obligatory order. The point was also made that the regenerated are not only "righteous" but also "sinners," and because of this require the guidance and nurture of the Law.

g. *The dispute over adiaphora.* In the interest of attaining unity between the different confessions, Melanchthon conceded that the Lutherans could reintroduce a number of discarded ceremonies. These were, as seen from the Lutheran point of view, "adiaphora" — things indifferent to faith and conscience. The Leipzig Interim of 1548, a confessional document accepted for a time by some Lutheran churches, elaborated this point of view. The stricter Lutherans, however, looked upon this as an act of treason against the evangelical faith. These reinstituted ceremonies were certainly adiaphora; but when enemies of the Gospel insisted on their use as a necessary thing, then their acceptance implied a denial of evangelical freedom. In a situation which involved one's confession or the freedom of the Gospel, nothing could be thought of as an adiaphoron. Flacius said, "When confession and offense are involved, nothing is an adiaphoron" *(In casu confessionis et scandali nihil est adiaphoron)*. The harsh words spoken by Paul to Peter in the situation recorded in Gal. 2 were used as a comparison. Melanchthon later recognized that he had been in error on this question.

h. *The controversy over the Lord's Supper.* The Calvinistic concept of the Lord's Supper was attacked in 1552 by the Lutheran theologian Joachim Westphal of Hamburg. This led to a thorough debate on the Sacrament between Lutherans and Calvinists. Among the Lutherans who took part was the above-mentioned Johannes Brenz, who upheld the conservative Lutheran position and set forth anew the concepts of ubiquity and of the communication of attributes as arguments in support of a literal and realistic interpretation of the words of institution.

Melanchthon and his disciples, who dominated the faculty in Wittenberg at this time, did not at the outset become involved in this dispute. After Melanchthon died, however, the Lord's Supper became the most decisive point of controversy between the Philippists and the Gnesio-Lutherans. The Wittenberg theologians felt that the Real Presence ought not be explained with the help of the ubiquity doctrine. They were opposed in this by Martin Chemnitz and by Jakob Andreä of Württemberg. When an anonymous statement written by one of Melanchthon's followers appeared in 1574 and set forth the Reformed implications of Melanchthon's doctrine of the Lord's Supper, the Elector took action against the Wittenberg theologians. The so-called Torgau Articles condemned the Calvinist point of view. The Philippists on the Wittenberg faculty were replaced in the 1570s by conservative Lutheran theologians, and so-called Crypto-Calvinism was suppressed.

CHAPTER 27

The Formula of Concord

The controversy over the Lord's Supper had shown that the Philippist position was inconsistent with genuine Lutheranism. As a result of this, the long-standing desire to unite the Lutheran churches around a common confession was finally realized. The work on this project, which was supported by a number of evangelical princes (there were political implications in this too), eventually led to the creation of the so-called Formula of Concord, which was accepted by most Lutheran churches. This statement presented the Lutheran position in sharp contrast to Calvinism. It also excluded the specific Philippist point of view, something which in no way contradicts the fact that the Formula of Concord was constructed to a large extent on Melanchthon's interpretation of the Reformation. It is only on those points where Melanchthon deviated from Luther that the Formula of Concord takes distinct exception to the former's position.

The *Schwäbische Konkordie* of 1574, written by Jakob Andreä of Tübingen, formed the basis for the Formula of Concord. Andreä's work was subsequently revised by Martin Chemnitz and others, and as a result a common doctrinal statement was accepted in Württemberg and Saxony (*Schwäbisch-Sächsische Konkordie*, 1575). This statement in turn was revised some more by a group of Württemberg theologians (the Maulbronner Formula). At a theological conference called by Elector August of Saxony and held in Torgau in 1576, a report (called the *Torgisches Buch*) based on the two last-named statements was sent to the various regional churches for their judgment. At a later convention, held at the cloister of Bergen near Magdeburg, the *Torgisches Buch* was given a new form in the light of the opinions received. The theologians present signed this confessional document and sent it to the Elector. It was called the *Bergisches Buch* or the Formula of Concord, and it was subsequently signed by princes, clergymen, and theologians from the various regional churches and accepted by about two thirds of the estates of the *Reich* which had already accepted the Augsburg Confession. The Formula of Concord consists of a detailed section (Solid Declaration) and a briefer version (Epitome); the latter is based on an extract which Jakob Andreä made from the *Torgisches Buch*.

Why was this formula devised? To settle, in a manner consistent with Scripture and evangelical teachings, the doctrinal disputes which had arisen among Lutherans. The Flacian position with respect to original sin was rejected, as was Osiander's doctrine of justification and Amsdorf's allegedly antinomian concept of good works and the third use of the Law. The synergistic tendencies among the Philippists were likewise repudiated. The pure Lutheran position on the Lord's supper, as developed by Brenz and Chemnitz, won the day. Luther's point of view with respect to predestination was finally modified, insofar as Luther's ideas concerning God's omnipotence and hidden will in connection with the doctrine of election were passed by.

Through the formation of the Formula of Concord the ground was prepared for a uniform collection of confessional statements by the different Lutheran church bodies. This was accomplished in the year 1580 with the publication of the Book of Concord. This includes, in addition to the Formula of Concord, the following statements: the three ancient creeds, the Augsburg Confession and its Apology, the Smalcald Articles, the Treatise on the Power and Primacy of the Pope, and Luther's two catechisms. The Book of Concord replaced the collections of doctrinal statements *(corpora doctrinae)* which had been used previously in the various regional churches (for example, the *Corpus Philippicum* of 1560, accepted in Saxony, Denmark, and elsewhere). As an anthology of Lutheran confessional statements, the significance of the Book of Concord gradually came to be recognized even outside the circle of German Lutheranism. In Sweden an edict promulgated in 1663 recommended that pastors study it. In Denmark and Norway, however, it was not officially recognized, since the authorities there did not wish to bind themselves to the Formula of Concord.

Within the Book of Concord the Augsburg Confession enjoys a unique position as the basic Lutheran confessional statement of the Reformation era. The "C. A." takes its place there alongside the three ancient creeds. According to the Formula of Concord's own clearly expressed purpose, it had no intention of supplying new material to supersede the Augsburg Confession. On the other hand, in agreement with the Augsburg Confession and in accordance with the Word of God, the Formula of Concord was designed to provide a clear and fundamental analysis of some of the disputed questions which had arisen between 1530 and the 1570s.

The theological content of the Formula of Concord will in some degree be evident from the following survey of the chief questions treated therein.

In the vital *Introduction*, reference is made to the Scriptures as the only norm and rule to be used in all doctrinal questions. Mention is made here of the Augsburg Confession as "the creed of our time," but it is also emphasized that all creeds and confessional statements are only a testimony of faith. They show how the Biblical doctrine has been preserved and how the Holy Scriptures have been interpreted in different times and in the light of different questions.

I. *Concerning original sin:* Against Flacius (whose name is not mentioned) and his supporters, a distinction is made between human nature and original sin. This is justified by saying that the former is created, redeemed, and shall one day be brought back from the dead. This can not be said about original sin, which is nevertheless a profound corruption that will not be separated from human nature until the resurrection.

II. *Concerning free will:* With respect to the function of the human will in spiritual matters, the Formula of Concord rejected Pelagianism in all its forms. The cooperation of the will in the conversion experience (synergism) is similarly repudiated. The "Enthusiasts" who claimed that conversion takes place by a direct illumination, without the use of the means of grace, received the same treatment.

III. *Concerning the righteousness of faith before God:* In regard to the chief question at issue in the Osiandrian controversy, it was made clear that Christ is our Righteousness, which is to say that God forgives our sins only for the sake of Christ's perfect obedience, without respect to our works or to the regeneration accomplished through the Spirit. At the same time, however, true faith is always combined with good works, love, and hope.

IV. *Concerning good works:* Both Major's thesis ("Good works are necessary for salvation") and Amsdorf's thesis ("Good works are harmful to salvation") were rejected. Man's good works do not help to preserve him in the faith. Good works are only a witness to faith and to the indwelling Spirit. Antinomianism, which held that the Law should not be preached among Christians, was also rejected in this article.

V. *Concerning Law and Gospel:* The antinomian problem is also in the background here. Is the Gospel only a proclamation of grace, or is it also a proclamation of repentance, which rebukes unbelief? The implication here is that the Law is not able to unmask unbelief. In reply, the Formula asserts that Law and Gospel must be carefully distinguished: Everything that rebukes sin is Law, while the Gospel preaches nothing but the promise of faith and seeks only to raise up and encourage.

VI. *Concerning the third use of the Law:* The problem involved in the second antinomian controversy is dealt with in this article. These are the three uses of the Law: to maintain public order, to lead men to a knowledge of sin, and to provide a norm for Christian conduct. The same law applies both to the regenerate and the unregenerate. It must be preached with power also among the faithful, inasmuch as the flesh continually opposes the Spirit in their lives. The one difference is that the unregenerate do what the Law demands only when they are coerced (and then it is done reluctantly), while the faithful, to the extent that they are born again (as "new men"), willingly fulfill the Law and do what the Law can never enforce.

VII. *Concerning the Lord's Supper:* In opposition to the so-called "sacramentarians," of whom there were two kinds — those who denied the Real Presence and those who held "that this presence exists spiritually, by faith" — this article expounds the Lutheran position as handed down by Chemnitz and Brenz. There is a physical presence, not of a spatial nature but a sacramental, supernatural presence in the strength of Christ's power to be wherever He desires to be, even corporeally *(multivolipresens)*. Because of this, the partaking of Christ's body and blood which the Lord's Supper provides is not simply the participation of faith in the heavenly Christ (cf. Calvinism) but a reception with the mouth, "though not in the Capernaitic manner but in a supernatural and heavenly manner" *(manducatio oralis)*. Furthermore, Christ's body and blood are received not only by the faithful and worthy but also by the unfaithful and unworthy, "though not for solace and life but to judgment and damnation, if they do not repent and if they are not converted" *(manducatio indignorum et infidelium)*. "This mystery is revealed in God's Word and is comprehensible only to faith." Article VII rejects the symbolical, Zwinglian concept as well as the Calvinist and Crypto-Calvinist points of view.

VIII. *Concerning the person of Christ:* The Christological discussion had emerged directly from the Lord's Supper controversy. The doctrine of a genuine communication of attributes *(communicatio idiomatum)* was developed in opposition to the "sacramentarians." The divine and human natures share in one another's qualities not only in name but in actual fact. God is not only called man; He is man. Human nature has been raised to God's right hand and shares in divine omnipotence. In the Solid Declaration three varieties of *communicatio idiomatum* are identified: (1) The attributes which belong to one nature also belong to the Person, who is simultaneously divine and human. (For example, we say that God's Son suffered and died, even though suffering and death are characteristic of the human nature only.) (2) The offices of Christ (Redeemer and Mediator, for example) are exercised not merely in, with, and through the one nature but in, with, and through both natures. (3) The human nature has received divine majesty, glory, and power, which transcend its original attributes. The divine nature, however, has not been changed (since God is unchangeable) by its union with the human nature; its attributes have neither been diminished nor increased.

It is by virtue of the human nature's participation in divine majesty that Christ (even according to His human nature) can be with His own perpetually, or be present in the Sacrament of the Altar. With respect to the subject of Christology the Formula of Concord also appended a Catalog of Testimonies from the Bible and from the church fathers.

IX. *Concerning Christ's descent into hell:* This article ignores the difficult question of how this descent took place. It affirms the belief that Christ conquered the power of death and the dominion of the devil and saved the faithful from both. That is the essential point made in this connection.

X. *Concerning churchly ceremonies which are called adiaphora:* This question, which was posited by the Augsburg Interim, was answered thus: In times of persecution, when a clear confession is required, or when evangelical freedom is in danger, one cannot give ground to the opposition even in trivial matters.

XI. *Concerning God's eternal foreknowledge and election:* It was asserted, in opposition to Calvinism's double predestination, that eternal election refers only to those who, through faith in Christ, will gain salvation. The promises of the Gospel and the preaching of repentance are universal. The condemnation of the ungodly results from the fact that they despise the Word or cast it away. Because of this, their own evil, and not God's decree, is responsible for their fate. The Pelagian concept, which holds that election is conditioned by man's behavior, was also rejected. "For God has chosen us in Christ, not only before we did something that was good, but even before we were born — yes, this was done even before the foundations of the world were laid." (Solid Declaration, 88)

The final article (XII) of the Formula of Concord provides a brief description of certain sects which did not accept the Augsburg Confession, the Anabaptists, the Schwenkfelders, the Anti-Trinitarians, whose teachings were rejected as opposed to God's Word and the confession.

CHAPTER 28

The Counter-Reformation: Roman Catholic Theology

The development of scholastic theology continued within the Roman Catholic Church through the 16th century and a large part of the 17th, but under new conditions. Paris was no longer the main center of theological education; other seats of learning, such as Salamanca in Spain and Coimbra in Portugal, which remained largely untouched by the newer streams of thought, took its place. A vital factor in all of this was the organization of two new religious orders, the Society of Jesus (Jesuits) and the reformed Carmelites.

Among the Dominican theologians Cardinal Cajetan of Italy (d. 1534) assumed a prominent position. He participated in the discussions concerning Luther and the Reformation but is probably best known for his commentary on Thomas Aquinas' *Summa theologica* (which was reprinted in the official publication of this work, the *Leonina* edition of 1882 ff. Generally speaking, the theology of Thomas Aquinas was used more and more as the basis of instruction during this time. His *Summa theologica* replaced Peter Lombard's *Sentences* as the dogmatic handbook. The Dominican school at Salamanca became the chief promoter of the Thomist tradition. (Cf. Dominicus Soto, d. 1560, and Melchior Cano, d. 1560, authors of *Loci theologici*, the first of its kind.)

Among the theologians who were engaged in a direct way in the controversy with the Reformers (chiefly Luther) were Johann Eck (*Enchiridion locorum communium adversus Lutheranos*, 1525), and Peter Canisius (Jesuit, d. 1597), leader of the German Counter-Reformation.

The decisive event which took place in the Roman Catholic Church during the time of the Counter-Reformation was the council which assembled at Trent on Dec. 13, 1545, and continued (in three different phases with long time intervals) until Dec. 4, 1563. (A total of 25 sessions were held.) The Council of Trent formed the terminus of certain trends in the medieval development and was of great significance for the future, inasmuch as it fixed Roman Catholic doctrine and practice in the new situation brought about by the Reformation. Among the crucial Tridentine decisions which affected Roman Catholic doctrine and practice, we are chiefly interested here in the decretal of the fourth session concerning the canonical Scriptures and the decretal of the seventh session concerning justification.

The scope of the Biblical canon was established at Trent (the apocryphal books of the Old Testament period were included), and the Latin "Vulgate" translation was declared to be the authentic version (a normative edition came out in 1590). But in addition to the canonical Scriptures, the Council of Trent also accepted, as being equally valuable for the determination of dogma, the "traditions" which originated with Christ or the apostles and which were preserved in the church through the years. These were "received and honored with the same piety and reverence" as the Scriptures (*pari pietatis affectu ac reverentia suscipit et veneratur*). It was concluded that these traditions, as defined by Trent, were "dictated by the Holy Spirit" just as the canonical Scriptures were. The question concerning the relationship between Scripture and tradition (are they two parallel sources, or can tradition be thought of as being included in some way in the Scriptures?) has been thoroughly discussed in recent years. The Tridentine interpretation suggested, however, that this was a question of two parallel norms of faith, an attitude which was clearly different from the Scripture principle of the Reformation.

The Tridentine doctrine of justification was constructed on the basis of two fundamental concepts, both of which sharply indicate the disparity between the Roman Catholic and the evangelical doctrine of salvation: partly the idea that the human will cooperates with the grace of God in securing salvation and partly the claim that good works are necessary for the preservation of righteousness and for the final possession of eternal life.

On the questions in controversy between Thomism (which was influenced by Augustine) and Scotism (which was tinged with Semi-

Pelagian views) it was possible to avoid taking a definite position. A certain preparation was said to be necessary for justification, but nothing was stated about whether or not this is meritorious. What is involved? Accepting the inviting grace and cooperating in those acts which follow the invitation and precede baptism (repentance, love to God, faith in revelation, etc.). In agreement with Thomism it is assumed that the inviting grace is the first step in conversion, but Trent at the same time attached significance to the cooperation of the will and to the preparatory acts. What the Reformers said about complete assurance was rejected ("this vain confidence, remote from all piety"). Instead it is asserted that one can never know with certainty that he possesses the grace of God and that to remain in grace and grow in it he must fulfill the commands of God and the church. The passage "Faith without works is dead" is quoted in this connection. Eternal life is described at one and the same time as a gift of grace, made available through Christ, and as a reward for one's own merits. The doctrines that justification consists of forgiveness of sins and that the gift of eternal life is provided exclusively for Christ's sake are anathematized above all else.

If justification is looked upon, essentially, as the infusion of grace, and if this is thought to take place through the sacraments, then it is only natural that the Tridentine decisions concerning justification should have been followed by deliberations concerning the doctrine of the sacraments. The fifth session, and various others that followed, issued decretals related to this question. As a matter of fact, the doctrine of the sacraments assumed a dominating position throughout the entire remainder of the council. Many of the points of doctrine which have been thought of ever since as specifically characteristic of the Roman Catholic Church were given their definitive formulation at Trent. For example, the teaching of transubstantiation (at the 13th session); the use of the confessional (at the 14th session); the doctrine of the sacrifice of the Mass (at the 22d session); and the adoration of saints and relics, plus the teaching of purgatory and indulgences (at the 25th session).

After the Council of Trent, scholastic theology blossomed forth again for an entire century. A new element was introduced by the philosophy of humanism, with its insistence on a return to the ancient sources. A renewed study of Aristotle and other philosophers of antiquity resulted from this program. For the most part, however, the old orders perpetuated their theological traditions. Thomist theology exercised the greatest influence. Scotism was perpetuated chiefly among the Franciscans. The new Jesuit order was eclectic in nature. It was also most open-minded about the new philosophy. Extended controversies were carried on between the Jesuits and the Thomists.

One of the Jesuits who conveyed the humanistic scholasticism of Spain to Germany was Gregory of Valencia (d. 1603, professor at Ingolstadt). As a result of his efforts, Roman scholasticism was revived in Germany. Most prominent among the Jesuit theologians, as well as among the newer scholastics in general, was Francisco Suarez (d. 1617, active in Salamanca). His combining of scholastic theology and Neo-Aristotelian metaphysics made a significant contribution to theological education at that time. His textbook in the field of metaphysics, *Disputationes metaphysicae,* was also widely used among Protestants. As a result of his labors, Suarez became one of the precursors of the Neo-Aristotelian school in Germany (about which more will be said later on).

Among the polemical theologians, the Jesuit Robert Bellarmine (d. 1621, cardinal) stood out above the rest. His book, *Disputationes de controversiis christianae fidei* (1586–93), dealt with Protestant objections point by point. Because of it, even more fundamental and comprehensive rebuttals appeared from the Protestant side. (For example, Johann Gerhard's *Confessio catholica,* 1634–37; see below.)

A significant facet of Roman Catholic theology — not least of all in more recent times — has been the literature of mysticism. As was true of scholasticism, Catholic mysticism in the 16th century was above all a product of Spain. The founder of the Jesuit order, Ignatius Loyola (d. 1556), exerted a strong influence on Roman Catholic piety, primarily through his *Spiritual Exercises,* a handbook designed for the discipline of the spiritual life. Most prominent among the mystics of that age were Theresa de Jesus (d. 1582) and Juan de la Cruz ("John of the Cross," d. 1591), who together organized the so-called "Barefoot Carmelite" order. St. Theresa, who is also well known for her literary achievements, described the experiences of the mystics with profound psychological insight. John of the Cross, employing theological insight provided by Thomas Aquinas, has given us the classical Roman Catholic presentation of the psychology and metaphysics of mysticism. He has been referred to as "the teacher of Catholic mysticism" (Grabmann).

One of the opponents of the prevailing scholasticism, with its Pelagian tendencies and its emphasis on merit, was the Belgian theologian Michael Baius (d. 1589, chancellor of the University of Louvain). He went back to the Bible and to Augustine, and taught that man is incapable of good, rejecting at the same time the meritorious nature of good works. In 1567 Pope Pius V condemned 76 items in Baius' writings.

Baius' critique of scholasticism reappeared with renewed strength in the form of "Jansenism." Cornelius Jansen (d. 1638, professor at Louvain and bishop of Ypres) concluded, as the result of his exhaustive study of the writings of Augustine, that scholastic theology had fallen away from the ancient ecclesiastical tradition. In his major work, *Augustine,* published in 1640, he presented the Augustinian concept of grace and predestination in its strictest form. He wrote that the human will is completely depraved and subject to concupiscence. Only the gift of grace can enable man to do good works.

Augustinian theology also played a fundamental role in the reform movement which had its center in the monastery at Port Royal. In the 1640s Antoine Arnauld was the leader of this movement, which was strongly opposed by the Jesuits. The pope condemned some facets of the Port Royal theology, which was allegedly repeating Jansenist ideas. Among those who became involved in the struggle was Blaise Pascal (d. 1662), who identified himself with the Jansenists. In his well-known *Provincial Letters* (1656–57) Pascal directed a sharp and brilliantly executed attack on the Pelagian concept of grace and on the casuistry of Jesuit ethics with its neglect of the conscience.

Even though it was violently attacked by the Jesuits, the Jansenist movement continued its activity for a long time, and was brought to an end only by degrees. The monastery at Port Royal was destroyed in 1709–10, and in the papal bull "Unigenitus" (1713) the Jansenist point of view was condemned anew. The revealing criticism directed at the Jesuits from this source (particularly in the *Provincial Letters),* however, turned out to be one of the causes of the spreading opposition to Jesuit activity. As a result, the Jesuits were forbidden to function in France in 1764.

One of the major developments in the Roman Catholic Church from the middle of the 17th century on into the 19th century was the progressive disintegration of scholastic theology. How did this happen? The Jansenist movement, whose criticisms were motivated by a deep concern for the church, contributed to this decline, as well as the newer philosophy and, later on, the spirit of the Enlightenment.

CHAPTER 29

The Reformation
and Post-Reformation Theology
in England

The course of the Reformation in England was entirely different from what it was on the continent and in the countries of the North. Although the theologians who led the development there during its decisive phase were strongly influenced by the continental Reformers, the Church of England nevertheless received a unique character, both with respect to theology and polity. It is different from both the Lutheran and the Reformed church bodies.

King Henry VIII, whose political maneuvers freed England from the domination of the pope and led to the recognition of the king as the supreme head of the Church of England, was very conservative in theological matters. As a result, the opponents of the papal church in England, who were led by such churchmen as William Tyndale and Thomas Cranmer, were given very little room in which to operate. Tyndale, who is remembered for his translation of the Bible into English (1526), had met Luther and was impressed by his writings. He felt that the distribution of the English Bible was the best way to counteract the false beliefs of the Church of Rome. In his teachings about man and salvation Tyndale represented the conservative Lutheran and Augustinian point of view. Tyndale's translation of the Bible was not appreciated in England, and he suffered a martyr's death for his Reformation convictions (1536).

Thomas Cranmer, who became the primate of the Church of England in 1533, was the theological leader of the Reformation there. He stood behind the publication of the Book of Common Prayer (1549) and the Forty-two Articles of 1553 (later revised to the Thirty-nine Articles). In spite of the far-reaching concessions to traditional church life during the reign of Henry VIII, Cranmer nevertheless prepared the way for the Protestant breakthrough which took place under King Edward VI (1547–1553). With the assistance of Martin Bucer (see above, p. 259) and others, the Book of Common Prayer was revised in such a way that it conformed more nearly to the Protestant position (the edition of 1552). The Forty-two Articles were linked to the confessional writings of the continent, not least of all to the Augsburg Confession, and were clearly distinguished thereby from the doctrinal position of the Church of Rome.

Cranmer felt that the doctrine of transubstantiation was the root of the heresy and superstition then found in the life of the church. In opposition to this doctrine, he set forth a concept of the Lord's Supper which came very close to the Calvinist position. Since the Ascension, Cranmer said, the body of Christ is located in a certain place in heaven and cannot therefore be present in the bread at the Lord's Supper. So when it is said that those who receive the Sacrament worthily and in faith "eat the body of Christ," this must be understood as figurative language. It is a spiritual "eating," which takes place exclusively by faith and can also take place apart from the Sacrament. To a large extent this was the view of the Sacrament which was later sanctioned in the Thirty-nine Articles. (Art. IV, XXVIII, XXIX; see below)

Thomas Cranmer, under whose aegis the Church of England developed into an independent episcopal church under royal supremacy, and who contributed much to the doctrinal position of this church body, was put to death in the Catholic reaction under "bloody" Queen Mary (1556). When face-to-face with his martyr's death, he gave courageous proof of having strong principles, a quality which was often lacking in his ecclesiastical statesmanship.

During the reign of Queen Elizabeth I (1558–1603), the Church of England was consolidated for the most part in accordance with the orientation provided earlier by the Protestant churchmen. The Book of Common Prayer accepted in 1559 was in basic agreement with the evangelical edition of 1552. The Forty-two Articles were transformed into the Thirty-nine Articles in 1563. In this confessional document of the Anglican Church we find traces of dependence upon the evangelical

Christianity of the continent as well as traces of Anglicanism's own uniqueness and independence. The Holy Bible is said to include all that is necessary for salvation, so that nothing which does not have its source there can be forced on anyone as an article of faith. The Roman Catholic principle of tradition was thereby rejected. The apocryphal books were not accepted as a part of the canon and as a source of doctrine; the Old Testament apocrypha, however, were recommended for use in the churches, for teaching and guidance (Art. VI). With respect to original sin as the corruption of nature (Art. IX), and the inability of the will to believe and to do works that are pleasing to God (Art. X), the Anglican confessional position follows the strict Augustinian point of view, and it accepts the Lutheran doctrine of justification by faith alone. The Roman Catholic teaching about good works preceding justification as a *meritum de congruo* was repudiated in favor of the Augustinian view that all works apart from grace are sin (Art. XIII). Predestination is set forth as election to salvation. There is therefore no recognition of "double" predestination; the Calvinist doctrine on this point was carefully avoided (Art. XVII).

The church is defined (as in Augustine) as a fellowship of believers in which God's pure Word is preached and the sacraments are rightly administered according to Christ's command (Art. XIX). Authority is ascribed to the church both with respect to ceremonies and to doctrinal controversies. It may not, however, prescribe something contrary to the Scriptures, whose witness and preserver the church is. The traditions and ceremonies of the church are not thought of as having been given once and for all in the Bible; they may be altered from time to time. Every national church has the right, therefore, to change or to discard such ceremonies and rites, as long as such action does not violate Scripture. On the other hand, no individual has the right to change the traditions and ceremonies of the church on the basis of his own private judgment, as long as these are not opposed to God's Word. (Art. XXXIV)

As indicated above, the Lutheran teaching of the ubiquity of Christ was excluded by the statements in Art. IV, and Christ's presence in the Lord's Supper was described in accordance with the following Calvinistic formulation: "The Body of Christ is given, taken, and eaten, in the Supper, only after an heavenly and spiritual manner. And the mean[s] whereby the Body of Christ is received and eaten in the Supper, is faith." (Art. XXVIII)

The Thirty-nine Articles affirm the supremacy of royal power over the Church of England. It is emphasized, however, that the king is not to concern himself with the service of the Word or the administration of the sacraments but only with the external control of the church. Under Elizabeth I the designation "Supreme Head" was changed to "Supreme Governor."

The position adopted by the Anglican Church can be described as a course midway between Rome and Geneva. The "Elizabethan Settlement" in religious matters elicited opposition from two sources, from Roman Catholicism and from Puritanism. Against the former, John Jewel, bishop of Salisbury, wrote his *Apology for the Church of England* (1562). He emphasized the connection between the Anglican Church and the original church of the apostles. Rome, he said, condemned Protestantism at the Council of Trent without giving it a fair hearing. If the Protestants were actually heretical, they should have been overcome by appealing to the Scriptures.

The foremost leaders of the Puritan movement during the reign of Elizabeth, Thomas Cartwright and Walter Travers, had both resided in Geneva, where they had been impressed by Calvinist church polity. It was their desire to introduce Calvinist ideas into the government of the reorganized church in England. So the movement they represented was also called Presbyterianism, which referred to that branch of Puritanism which hoped to replace the power of the bishops in the Church of England with an authority exercised by consistories and synods, composed of pastors and elders. The Puritans did not want to recognize the episcopal system which had been established under Edward VI and Elizabeth I (the Established Church). The basic idea in the Presbyterian program was that the Holy Scriptures, as God's Word, must provide the only source of guidance both for Christian conduct as well as for the ordinances and ceremonies of the church. Christians expect to find explicit instructions in the Bible which govern their actions in various situations, and by the same token it was felt that the Bible also provides a definite pattern for the organization of the church. It was also believed that this Scriptural church order was identical with the one formed on the basis of similar presuppositions in Geneva. It was, in principle, unchangeable, inasmuch as it was allegedly based on God's Word.

Among those who opposed Cartwright was John Whitgift, later archbishop of Canterbury, who defended the existing church order. The church, said Whitgift, is free to adjust external ceremonies and practices according to the time and the circumstances; it is not obligated to follow an order given once and for all in the Scriptures.

The Presbyterian program was set forth in an anonymous writing on church discipline in 1574, written by Walter Travers, a pastor who later served in the legal school, "The Temple," in London. There he engaged in a theological dispute with Richard Hooker, the Master of the Temple (and later pastor in Kent, d. 1600), who represented the Anglican position. As a result of his dispute with Travers, Hooker was prompted to examine the entire question of proper church order, which he did in a huge book, *The Laws of Ecclesiastical Polity*. This famous work, the first five volumes of which appeared between 1594 and 1597, is unsurpassed as a learned and sagacious defense of the Anglican system. Hooker's book, which is still used today as a standard work for the training of Anglican priests, is distinguished by its thorough analysis of the subject, its unfailing moderation, and its discrete judgments. It has exerted great influence also upon political thought in England.

It was clear to Hooker as well as to his opponents that church polity — like all human systems — must rest on divine authority. This is not to say, however, that church polity can be derived in every detail from Biblical instructions and examples. To seek a pattern for ecclesiastical ordinances and ceremonies in the Bible is to demand too much of it. The "perfection" of the Bible must be understood in terms of its designated purpose — to provide the knowledge which is necessary for human salvation. But a church order which is valid for all times cannot be derived from the Bible. The legal order which ought to exist in the church as well as in all human relationships rests on other ground. God has given man natural law, which coincides with the judgments of reason, and which provides man with an innate understanding of what is right and wrong. There is no one church order which is valid for all time; but the church, on the basis of Biblical examples and instructions, as well as on the basis of the wisdom expressed in tradition, must establish a reasonable form of church polity.

Hooker used the first four volumes of *The Laws of Ecclesiastical Polity* to present the essential basis of the Anglican position. In Vol. V he describes the actual development of the rites and ordinances of the church. Vols. VI, VII, and VIII were published long after Hooker's death, and whether they are completely authentic is a much-disputed question. Hooker's own position is reliably reflected only in the first five volumes.

The Presbyterians felt that the English state church was a compromise with Romanism, and they desired a "reformation of the Reformation." They wanted to accomplish this purpose within the framework of the state church and in concert with the authorities. But some of the Puritans were more radical and wanted to carry out a reformation without depending on the state or the hierarchy. As they saw it, the Christian congregation (consisting only of the truly faithful) is the only governing power within the church. The "holy people" themselves represent the authority of Christ. As a result, each local congregation ought to attend to its own affairs by itself, without the interference of secular or ecclesiastical authorities. Laymen and clergy have different functions, but there is no difference of rank between them. This democratic ideal for the church — which is usually called Congregationalism or Independency — was outlined by Robert Browne, who fled to Holland in 1582 in order to escape persecution (but later rejoined the state church), and by Henry Barrowe, who suffered martyrdom in 1593 because of his Congregational convictions.

The Baptist Church in England, whose leader was a certain John Smyth, grew out of Congregationalism as a distinct, separatistic movement. The first Baptist congregation in England was founded by Thomas Helwys in 1612. (Smyth had organized a congregation in Amsterdam before this.) The English Baptists were related to the Anabaptists on the continent. They were distinguished among other things by their strong insistence on freedom of conscience and on religious tolerance. Religion was said to be a matter between God and the individual, and as a result the interference of the authorities could not be tolerated. Dissenters of all varieties rejected the Book of Common Prayer as well as the enforcement of a fixed, legally prescribed liturgy. This became one of the major points at issue between the Anglicans and the Nonconformists.

Anglican theology developed during the 17th century on the ground prepared by Richard Hooker in *The laws of Ecclesiastical Polity*. The question of church order played a prominent role in this development, just as it did in Hooker's book. The individuality of the Anglican position became clear as a result of its struggle with Rome and, above all, with Puritanism. Its signature is a firm adherence to the episcopal tradition and the state church system, avoiding the extremes of both. In regard to ceremonies, the following words are found in the Preface to the Book of Common Prayer of 1662: "It has been the wisdom of the Church of England ever since the first compiling of her Publick Liturgy, to keep the mean between the extremes, of too much stiffness in refusing, and of too much easiness in admitting any variation from it."

Chief among those who opposed Puritanism was William Laud (archbishop of Canterbury from 1633), who is well known for his unscrupulous use of power in the struggle to enforce conformity to church order. Theologically speaking, Laud dissociated himself not only from Puritanic polity but also from the strict Calvinism with which Puritanism was often related. He accepted the Arminian view of predestination and conceded a certain freedom in the doctrinal area, which he coupled with an implacable strictness in the observance of ritual. The Puritans, on the other hand, usually combined a strict observance of doctrine with freedom in regard to the order of worship.

The great revolution which struck England in the 1640s brought with it a radical alteration in the ecclesiastical situation. The Presbyterians dominated the scene first, during the era of the Long Parliament, and then the Independents took over during the Cromwell regime. William Laud was imprisoned and, after a lengthy trial, put to death in 1645. King Charles I, the foremost supporter of the Anglican Church, suffered the same fate in 1649. Both of these men, and not least of all King Charles, thought of themselves as martyrs for the Anglican Church, and many of their contemporaries agreed. The Restoration of 1660 did not bring about a settlement of the religious disputes (as many had hoped). Genuine Anglicanism gained the most from the Savoy Conference of 1661, which had been called to adjust ecclesiastical affairs, and the revised Book of Common Prayer of 1662 stands out as the conclusion of the development in which the uniqueness of Anglicanism was chiseled out in the face of a harsh fate and violent disputes with non-Anglicans. Among the many prominent Anglican theologians of the 17th century, attention is called (in addition to those already named) to James Ussher (d. 1656) and John Pearson (d. 1686). Pearson's *Exposition of the Creed* is an exemplary example of Anglican dogmatic literature.

During the 17th century, Anglican theology departed further and further from the norms of orthodox Calvinism. Calvin was still highly thought of by the majority of the theologians, and a number of Anglicans participated in the Synod of Dort and accepted its strict position on predestination, but this was not the case as a rule. As we noted in speaking of William Laud, Arminianism exerted no small influence in English theology. Presbyterians dominated the Westminster Synod (1643), where the Westminster Confession was accepted. This doctrinal statement has been binding on the Presbyterian Church in England ever since. Most prominent among the Presbyterian theologians of this period was Richard Baxter, who is best known for his inspirational writings, which were circulated even in Lutheran areas (cf. *The Saints' Everlasting Rest,* 1650). One of the unfortunate results of the ecclesiastical politics of the Restoration was that the Presbyterians were driven out of the Anglican state church to make common cause with the Independents. This development served to widen the social and theological gap between the Anglicans and the Presbyterians. After the Glorious Revolution (1688–89) no less than 400 Anglican clergymen refused, for reasons of principle, to swear allegiance to the new king, William III, who was not, in their view, legally enthroned. These "nonjurors" were relieved of their offices, and the church was weakened as a result. This became particularly noticeable in the church's confrontation with deism and other rationalistic tendencies in the years that followed.

Among the more radical Puritans of the age were the poet John Milton (*Paradise Lost,* 1667), and John Bunyan (a Baptist; *Pilgrim's Progress,* 1678), whose names ought to be remembered also in connection with 17th-century English theology.

CHAPTER 30

Lutheran Orthodoxy

GENERAL CHARACTERISTICS

Lutheran orthodoxy, whose classical period began about the year 1600, was an extension of the tradition represented above all by the Lutheran confessional writings (the Book of Concord, 1580) and by the theologians (such as the previously mentioned Wigand and Chemnitz) who more thoroughly developed a corresponding point of view. The name of Aegidius Hunnius (d. 1592, teacher in Marburg) should also be included among the major precursors of the orthodox position.

In spite of its profound loyalty to the universal church and to the Lutheran tradition, classical orthodoxy nevertheless denotes a fresh beginning, not least of all with respect to its erudite reworking of theology. The new orientation which Lutheran orthodoxy represents can be associated with the philosophical school known as Neo-Aristotelianism. This school originated in certain south European seats of learning (Padua, Coimbra), but it secured a footing in the Protestant universities of Germany by the end of the 16th century. Here it gave birth to a Protestant scholastic metaphysics which in many respects provided the scientific presuppositions for the theology and science of that period. The scientific program of this metaphysics involved the revivification of Aristotelian metaphysics, coupled with the demand for a more radical revision of scientific principles. This scholastic metaphysics had in part a purely humanistic bent, as, for example, in the case of Cornelius Martini of Helmstedt, but at certain Lutheran universities it was combined with the orthodox Lutheran position, as, for example, in the case of Balthasar Meisner and Jakob Martini (both active in Wittenberg), and (later on) Christopher Scheibler in Giessen and the theologian Abraham Calov.

The influence exerted by scholastic philosophy upon orthodox Lutheran theology cannot be determined in any simple way, inasmuch as a sharp distinction was made between theology and philosophy. Even on this point the attempt was made (in principle, at least) to hold fast to the Reformation position. It was not, therefore, a question of a direct takeover of metaphysical concepts, or of the insertion of theology into a metaphysical system — something which would conflict with its own assumptions. At the same time, however, Neo-Aristotelian philosophy did play an important role in many ways in the theological development of that period. Its influence can be characterized from the following points of view:

Scholastic metaphysics placed the universal concepts of the world and of reality in clear formulae. It defined the intellectual assumptions of contemporary science in conceptual terms — assumptions which to a large extent also served as the basis of theological activity. The parallelism between Lutheran orthodoxy and scholastic philosophy is to be seen also in the fact that both flourished at the same time. Furthermore, both were superseded by other currents of thought at about the same time (early 18th century). The world view of scholastic philosophy was distinguished among other things by the Aristotelian concept of knowledge (one proceeds from external reality — both sensuous and supersensual — as the primary and immediate reality) as well as by the Aristotelian view of form (it is the form of things, and not their substance, which provides the reality accessible to knowledge). As a result, this point of view detached itself both from idealism and from the mechanical concept of the world. The acceptance of scholastic philosophy by theology was facilitated by the fact that the former based its universal concept of the world on a religious principle: it is God who is the highest reality (the absolute actuality or form) and also the ground and goal of all other reality.

Neo-Aristotelianism also gave rise to a thorough revision of the scientific method, a fact which influenced theological exposition as well. The leading philosopher in this sphere was Jacob Zabarella (teacher in Padua, d. 1589), who felt that there were only two ways to present a given proposition in all branches of science. He called the first *ordo compositivus,* which proceeds from principles to conclusions. The other is the *ordo resolutivus,* which begins with the goal in view and then sets forth ways to reach this goal. It was felt at the time, however, that theology, since it was outside the scientific sphere, was not bound to use either of these methods. Yet they were used to some extent also in theological exposition, as for example in the development of the Scriptural principle as the foundation of theology, and above all in the acceptance of the so-called analytical method. Attempts were being made as early as the beginning of the 17th century to orient the presentation of theology according to the method which was applicable to the so-called practical sciences, i. e., the above-named *ordo resolutivus*. A Lutheran, Balthasar Mentzer, and a Reformed theologian by the name of Keckermann were among those who made this attempt. They began with the belief that God is the eternal goal, and then proceeded to deal with the doctrine of man, the subject of theology, and finally with the means whereby man can attain eternal blessedness. This analytical method was generally accepted in Lutheran circles later on (cf. Calixtus and Calov) and replaced the older so-called "loci" method. The analytical method was an attempt to present theology in a more standardized form than was previously the case, i. e., to present it as a doctrine of salvation and of the means whereby this salvation can be attained. Also the theological treatises which employed this method, however, at the same time followed the order of the history of salvation, which is independent of philosophical methods. Theological developments in the 17th century led to an ever stricter systematic reworking of the enormous amount of material inherited from the older Lutheran tradition. The works of the later orthodox dogmaticians were often characterized by an endless number of artificial distinctions.

To the extent that it was accepted by theology, German scholastic philosophy served to strengthen the intellectual strain which characterized Lutheran orthodoxy. It also promoted a more pronounced scientific treatment of theological questions. By its use of philosophy, Lutheran orthodoxy was, in a way, provided with better means of preserving and passing on the Biblical and Reformation inheritance. It was not until this philosophical element was surrendered that the orthodox structure of theology began to seem to many to be a formalism alien to the essence of Christianity.

The orthodox exposition of doctrine rested primarily on arguments derived from the Bible. Similarly, a continuing study of the Scriptures formed the basis for theological education. The attachment to contemporary scholastic philosophy did not imply any fundamental confusion of the principles of faith and reason. It was agreed that the conceptual apparatus of philosophy should function only in the defense of faith or in the explanation of theological questions in the academic context. With respect to the content of doctrine, every rational argument must give way before the testimony of Scripture. On this point Lutheran orthodoxy dissociated itself both from medieval scholasticism and from contemporary Reformed orthodoxy, in which attempts were made (to some extent) to harmonize the content of revelation with the arguments of reason. Keckermann felt, for example, that the doctrine of the Trinity could be demonstrated philosophically, but the Lutherans disagreed. Their ideal was what Balthasar Meisner called a *sobria philosophia,* i. e., a sober philosophy, which humbly subjects itself to the testimony of revealed truth.

But at the same time that dogmatic works were based on Scripture as the only foundation (the Scripture principle), the interpretation of the Bible was influenced in turn by the dogmatic view of the whole and by the doctrinaire attitude. The first attempts to interpret the Bible historically (in the modern sense of the term) were certainly made during the 17th century — not within the orthodox Lutheran tradition, however, but in other circles. The Dutch jurist and theologian Hugo Grotius was one who anticipated the modern point of view on this matter.

As already noted, orthodox Lutheran dogmatic expositions followed the order of the history of salvation: Creation, the Fall, Redemption, and the Last Things are the major points which always appear in such presentations. The doctrine of the Word and the doctrine of God are set forth first. The usual order in the various "loci" typically included the following: (1) the Holy Scriptures, (2) the Trinity (the doctrine of God, of Christ, of the Holy Spirit), (3) Creation, (4) Providence, (5) Predestination, (6) the Image of God, (7) the Fall of Man, (8) Sin, (9) Free Will, (10) the Law, (11) the Gospel, (12) Repentance, (13) Faith (justification), (14) Good Works, (15) the Sacraments, (16) the Church, (17) the Three Estates, and (18) the Last Things.

What we have here is an objective form of theology, quite different from the modern method of dogmatic exposition. Theology was then defined as a "teaching about God and divine things." Revelation, as codified in Scripture, provided the point of departure, and not faith as

302

something within the soul. Theology was usually conceived of as a "practical" discipline, but that meant only that it was designed for practical application, and not that it had its basis in the experience of faith. This point of view was first altered by Pietism.

The Scriptural principle excluded the principle of traditionalism (which looks upon tradition as the standard). But that fact notwithstanding, the weight of tradition assumed a very prominent place within orthodox theology. Gerhard's ideal was an "evangelical-catholic theology," a Reformation point of view, that is, which can be found in the theological tradition preserved throughout all the centuries of Christian history. The dogmatics of classical orthodoxy was characterized by a copious use of the material provided by patristic sources and (to a lesser degree) scholastic theology. Augustine exerted by far the strongest influence in this area.

With respect to its versatile comprehension of theological material and the breadth of its knowledge of the Bible, Lutheran orthodoxy marks the high point in the entire history of theology. And it was not only the contemporary tradition or the next preceding tradition which provided the material for the great Lutheran doctrinal expositions of the 17th century, but to an even greater extent it was the Bible and patristic sources.

The method employed was quite different from the one used by dogmaticians today. It was not felt that theology had to be presented in a uniform way, by placing an emphasis on certain basic ideas. On the contrary, the dogmaticians of the 17th century believed that it was their task to reproduce the infinite richness of the Biblical revelation. As a result of this attitude, their minds were open to all of the details in the tradition which had been handed down, but this method also led to an endless division of questions and to a difficulty in distinguishing between the essential and the non-essential. Attempts were made to systematize this effort, but they were not successful. For example, the analytical method was an attempt to arrange the entire doctrinal exposition under a single point of view: How shall man reach his highest goal, eternal blessedness? A similar tendency can be seen in the concept of the so-called fundamental articles: only one part of the content of faith could be said to be necessary to salvation, while other portions of doctrine are only of secondary importance.

REPRESENTATIVES OF LUTHERAN ORTHODOXY;
ITS STAGES OF DEVELOPMENT

Properly speaking, the era of Lutheran orthodoxy ranged over the entire 17th century, but one can distinguish between the classical period in the first half of the century and a later phase which began with the Peace of Westphalia (1648). This latter period was characterized by a struggle against syncretism and a rigorous systematizing of the Lutheran tradition, as well as by a more doctrinaire attitude.

The chief representatives of the older, classical orthodoxy were Leonhard Hutter (d. 1616, teacher in Wittenberg) and Johann Gerhard (d. 1637, Hutter's disciple, active for the most part in Jena). Hutter's concise treatment of dogmatics, *Compendium locorum theologicorum, ex Scripturis Sacris et Libro Concordiae collectum* (1610), to a large extent replaced Melanchthon's *Loci* as a textbook.

Gerhard, the foremost dogmatician of Lutheran orthodoxy, continued to build on the Reformation tradition (chiefly on the basis of Chemnitz' work), but he also laid the foundation for the theological activity which followed. The best known of his writings is the *Loci theologici* (1610–25), which is a comprehensive treatment of the evangelical doctrinal position, based on a particularly wide range of material. His *Confessio catholica* (1633–37) sought to refute the objections of contemporary Roman Catholic theology with quotations taken from the Church of Rome's own tradition. Gerhard also wrote Bible commentaries, devotional works such as the popular *Meditationes sacrae* (1606), homiletical treatises (*Postilla*, 1613), disputations, and a detailed exposition of the ethics of the life of faith, *Schola pietatis* (1621).

Nikolaus Hunnius (d. 1643) is best known for his theory of the fundamental articles — the idea that only certain points of doctrine, and not the entire content of Scripture, ought to be looked upon as necessary to salvation and as constituting the theological position. Hunnius' summary of the doctrine of faith, *Epitome credendorum* (1625), has been widely used.

Matthias Hafenreffer of Tübingen was also active during this period. His *Compendium doctrinae coelestis*, an abridged edition of his *Loci* of the year 1600, was still being used as a textbook a hundred years later (in Sweden, for example).

A somewhat divergent position was represented by the prominent

Helmstedt theologian Georg Calixtus (d. 1656), who believed that the different confessions could be united on the basis of the *consensus quinquesaecularis,* the oldest Christian tradition, recognized by all as a foundation of doctrine. This so-called syncretistic concept was further developed by his followers, members of the "Helmstedt school." The struggle against syncretism left a definite mark on Lutheran orthodoxy in the latter part of the 17th century.

The chief opponent of syncretism was Abraham Calov (d. 1686, professor in Wittenberg), who perpetuated the tradition associated with Gerhard but who also accentuated these ideas in a doctrinaire and polemical manner. His magnum opus was the voluminous *Systema locorum theologicorum* (1655–77). Other dogmatic works of the latter part of the 17th century were similarly characterized by a more strongly systematic reworking of the orthodox tradition, as well as by an increasingly incisive logical definition of the various doctrinal problems. In this category we find Johann Friedrich König's *Theologia positiva acroamatica* (1661), and Johann Andreas Quenstedt's *Theologia didactico-polemica* (1685). A more concise treatment can be seen in Johann Wilhelm Baier's *Compendium* (1686).

David Hollaz' *Examen theologico-acroamaticum* (1707) is usually referred to as the last great doctrinal system produced by Lutheran orthodoxy. The influence of Pietism can be noted in this work, but it is at the same time a meticulous presentation of the orthodox Lutheran tradition.

The theology of northern Europe was closely related to that of Germany in this period. In Sweden the older orthodoxy was represented by Olaus Martini, Johannes Rudbeck, and Paulinus Gothus (*Ethica Christiana,* 1617–30), and in Denmark by Jesper Brochmand, whose comprehensive *Systema universae theologiae* (1633) won great respect. Somewhat later on, Swedish theology was represented by Johannes Matthiae, who set forth syncretistic ideas, and by Olaus Laurelius, who defended the strict orthodox position.

The following summary of some major ideas of orthodox dogmatics is based primarily on the older, classical orthodoxy, as represented by Leonhard Hutter and Johann Gerhard. Later treatises in the field of dogmatics are rather different in many respects.

CHIEF CHARACTERISTICS OF ORTHODOX
LUTHERAN THEOLOGY

a. *The Holy Scriptures; the Word as a means of grace.* As we have already noted, the Holy Scriptures were looked upon as theology's only "principle," or as its fundamental presupposition. This meant that the teachings of the Bible were to be followed even when they seemed to oppose reason, as well as when they seemed to contradict ecclesiastical tradition.

The Holy Scriptures were equated with the Word of God. The idea of an oral apostolic tradition, preserved by the clergy, was rejected. The Bible certainly evolved out of an original, oral proclamation, but for the present church it is the only authentic source of the prophetic and apostolic witness. The Roman Catholic principle of tradition was thereby repudiated.

When God's Word is equated with Holy Scripture, this assumes that the external Word or "letter" is not thought of as something external to the underlying meaning, but that the concept of "Scripture" refers to the inner (meaning, content) as well as to the external, of which the inner or the "formal" (to use the philosophic terminology of the time) is basic. The Aristotelian conception of form supplied the orthodox view of Scripture with a quality lacking in the Biblicism of later years, which frequently ascribed divine dignity to a rational, literal interpretation.

The formation of the doctrine of inspiration can be seen in connection with this. That Scripture is the Word of God is based on the fact that it is divinely inspired. This signified, in the older orthodox tradition, that prophets and apostles were entrusted with a divine mission to take down and to pass on in writing the message which they had received from God and had first proclaimed orally. By virtue of this mission the divine Word has been preserved in Scripture without error or deficiency. Scripture is therefore an infallible norm for Christian faith and conduct, and the judge in all doctrinal controversy *(norma fidei, judex controversiarum).*

When reference is made to Scripture's "perfection" or "sufficiency," this means that Scripture, as the *only* theological principle, includes all that one needs to know to be saved — "that Scripture fully and perfectly instructs us concerning all things necessary for attaining salvation." (Gerhard, *Loci,* Cotta ed., II, 286a)

The general rule applied to the exegesis of Scripture was that Scripture is clear in itself *(per se evidens)* and can therefore serve as its own interpreter *(sui ipsius interpres)*. This follows from what has already been said, for if Scripture is the *only* and *sufficient* norm of faith, then its content must be accessible to understanding, insofar as this content is necessary for faith. Difficult passages should be interpreted with the help of clearer ones. As a general rule, interpretation must agree with the analogy of faith, i. e., with the doctrine of faith as clearly set forth in Scripture. Great weight was attached to the literal interpretation. There can be only one original meaning, *sensus literalis*. Allegorical expositions were also recognized, but they were looked upon as a posteriori figurative applications — unless they were intended by the text itself, as was thought to be the case in the Song of Solomon, thus constituting its original *sensus literalis*. This concept did not imply a historical interpretation in the modern sense, but it rather pointed, in general, to the meaning originally intended by the Holy Spirit. Typology or allegory was looked upon (even where suggested by the text itself) as an application and not as an original "mystical" meaning in the text. In later orthodoxy, reference was made to a real *duplex sensus,* i. e., a literal and a mystical meaning in one and the same text.

A controversy which took place in the 1620s throws considerable light on the concept of Scripture. The question involved concerned the effectiveness of the Word and the relation between the Word and the Spirit. Hermann Rahtmann (pastor in Danzig) had said (referring, in part, to Johann Arndt) that the Word in itself would only be a dead letter. A man can be converted only with the cooperation of the Spirit. Rahtmann thus distinguished between the external Word and the inner Word, the latter being identical with the power of the Spirit. As he saw it, the fact that so few are influenced by preaching can be explained in no other way. The orthodox theologians, including Gerhard, were critical of this trend of thought. They maintained that just as the Word is in itself inspired and full of divine authority, so also does it have the power to bring a man to conversion. The Spirit is therefore directly related to the Word, and He constantly uses the Word as a means through which to do His work. It was also asserted — as the ultimate consequence of this — that the Word possesses its spiritual effectiveness even before it is used *(extra usum)*. But this brought them, in a way, into an untenable position, since the efficacy of the Word always presupposes its use. The conclusion was comprehensible, however, if seen in association with the Aristotelian conception of form, which was employed here. According to this, "the Word" is not so many letters or a book (the Bible), but living content. The position taken in the dispute with Rahtmann was simply a consequence of the doctrine of the Word's authority and inspiration. The rejection of spiritualism was a basic characteristic of the orthodox tradition. The Spirit does not work beside the Word or independently of it, but in and with the divine Word as it is heard or read.

b. *The doctrine of God.* In some ways the entire orthodox dogmatic position constitutes a "doctrine of God." The doctrine of Creation and the order of salvation are connected to the exposition of God's being (the Trinity, Christology, etc.) as a description of God's will, manifested in His work. Reference is also made to God as theology's "principle of being" *(principium essendi):* to the extent that He has revealed Himself, God is Himself the cause of our knowledge of Him. Just as the things of the world around us influence the intellect and thereby elicit sensuous and conceptual knowledge, so also is God's manifestation of Himself — His emergence in His words and works — the direct cause of our knowledge of Him. This basic idea was a common assumption in orthodox theology.

A distinction was made between natural and supernatural knowledge of God. The latter is that given once through the prophets and apostles, now to be found in the Holy Scriptures. The former is in part congenital, in part acquired *(notitia insita et acquisita).* The *congenital* knowledge of God was looked upon as an insight put into the heart of man at the time of Creation; after the Fall this was reduced to weak reminiscences of the original, perfect light which once illuminated the soul. It merely includes the idea that God is, that He is almighty, etc. — examples of which can be found in heathen forms of worship (cf. Rom. 1:19). To this must be added the conscience, which is also a congenital faculty, enabling man to distinguish between right and wrong (cf. Rom. 2:14-15). A conception of God can also be found in this, indirectly, inasmuch as the natural knowledge of the Law *(lex naturae)* presupposes the question: Who established this law? The accusations of the conscience, while they may be vague or suppressed, nevertheless convey the realization that there is someone who punishes evil deeds. The *acquired* knowledge of God is that which is attained through inferences based on our observations of created things. On this point the "proofs" of the existence of God which were developed by the medieval scholastics were by and large taken over — e. g., the "causal" proof (the chain of causes presupposes an ultimate or first cause) and the "teleological" proof (the appearance of a certain purposefulness in creation presupposes that someone conceived of the purposes in question). It ought to be noted that the natural knowledge of God was thought of as a part of revelation — in keeping with the idea (mentioned above) that all our knowledge of God has its basis in the fact that God has revealed Himself, either through the work of creation or through the Word.

This natural knowledge of God has been vitiated, and it is entirely insufficient for achieving salvation. Since it is largely limited to an insight into the fact that God is, our knowledge of what God is like — knowledge of His nature and attributes — must be secured above all from the Holy Scriptures. Teachings about the attributes of God are, for the most part, a systematic exposition of what the Bible tells us about Him. This method does not provide us with an adequate knowledge of God — for "God dwells in a light to which no one can come" — it merely supplies us with certain lessons which are necessary to faith and are adapted to our ability to comprehend. A distinction is made between the *inner* attributes, those that are intrinsic to divinity in itself (e. g., that the being of God is spiritual and invisible, eternal and everywhere present), and the *external* attributes, those that appear in relation to creation (e. g., God's omnipotence, righteousness, and truthfulness). The very division into attributes is in itself an adaptation to our imperfect ability to understand: the fact of the matter is that God's qualities are not accidental, but identical with His nature. God, for example, is not simply "truthful" but "Truthfulness itself" *(ipsa veritas)*. It has often been said that the orthodox position with respect to the attributes of God is just so much abstract speculation, a learned embellishment of the Christian faith. But this is a misunderstanding, for these doctrinal statements give expression, in many cases, to fundamental concepts which are necessary assumptions for theology in general. The concept of divine omnipotence, for example, provides the background for the trust in providence which is characteristic of Lutheran piety, and the concept of righteousness is fundamental to the doctrine of the Atonement.

The doctrine of the Trinity was developed in association with the patristic tradition, above all the *Symbolum quicunque* (the Athanasian Creed). Special weight was attached to the evidence of Scripture. Reference was made to the creation account in the Old Testament, for example, where we are told about God's Word and about God's Spirit, which "hovered over the waters." In the New Testament, reference was made to the description of Jesus' baptism (Matt. 3:16-17) or to the command to baptize (Matt. 28:19). The following are some of the fundamental points of view presented: The intratrinitarian distinctions between the Persons lie in the fact that the Father is neither begotten nor created (ἀγεννησία), the Son is begotten of the Father (γεννησία), and the Spirit is neither begotten nor created but proceeds from the Father and the Son (ἐκπόρευσις). With respect to Creation, the Persons can be distinguished by the fact that Creation is first of all ascribed to the Father, redemption to the Son, and sanctification to the Spirit. At the same time, however, all three Persons cooperate in these activities; the external work of the Trinity is indivisible.

The Scriptural evidence of the divinity of the Son and the Spirit was elaborated with great care, not least of all because it provided the Lutherans with one of their main arguments in the struggle with Socinianism (on which more will follow).

Christology was set forth as a "doctrine of Christ's Person and work." In agreement with the formulation of the ancient church, Christ was spoken of as "true God" and "true man." The crucial question had to do with how the union of the two "natures" in the one person is to be understood. The teaching of the *unio personalis* became, therefore, the central point in Lutheran Christology. The figures that were used in an attempt to illustrate this union were not satisfactory. It was suggested, for example, that it could be illustrated by the union of body and soul, or by the glowing iron which is a union of iron and fire. Christology does not, as a matter of fact, suggest that two elements have blended together to form a third; it rather asserts that Christ is simultaneously God and man. The body of Christ is not to be found apart from the Logos, the divine nature, and the Logos (subsequent to the Incarnation) is not to be found apart from the body of Christ. On this point the Lutherans disagreed with the Calvinists, who maintained that the body of Christ is confined to heaven, while Christ as spirit is everywhere present and therefore exists also apart from the body (an idea expressed by the term *extra calvinisticum*).

The *unio personalis* concept indicates that God and man have united in Christ in such a way that they form one person. That "the Word became flesh" must not, however, be understood as an alteration of the flesh into divine nature. Neither has divinity simply manifested itself in bodily form — as though this were a temporary form of revelation (comparable to the Old Testament accounts which tell us how God revealed Himself in human form). But the *unio personalis* implies that the Logos, the Second Person of the Godhead, assumed to Himself the "person" (or hypostasis) of the human nature. In other words, orthodox Lutheranism accepted the ideas which were given their classical expression by John of Damascus (enhypostasis theology), with the exception of some of his Platonic points of view.

As a result of holding to the *unio personalis,* the Lutherans also taught a *communicatio naturarum* and a *communicatio idiomatum.* "Communication of natures" refers to the fact that the divine and human natures stand in the closest communion with one another, that the divine nature permeates and perfects the human, and at the same time that the latter imparts itself to the divine. Because of this communion between the two natures, what is true of the one can be predicated of the other. One can say, for example, "God's Son is man" or, "The man Jesus is God." At the same time, however, both natures remain separate and distinct; the divine nature is not transformed into the human, nor the human into the divine.

The "communication of attributes" concept, which was borrowed from an earlier tradition, expressed similar convictions. As a consequence of the *communicatio naturarum,* the different attributes which distinguish the natures also belong to Christ as a person and therefore also interact upon one another in the most intimate manner. The one nature shares in the attributes of the other, and both natures share in the attributes of the person. The various instances of *communicatio idiomatum* which can be seen in the Biblical picture of Christ are limited, however, to three kinds, or genera (cf. the Formula of Concord).

The first, *genus idiomaticum,* implies that the attributes of one nature can also be ascribed to the whole person of Christ. So when it is said of Jesus Christ, for example, that He is "the same yesterday and today and forever," this means that a divine attribute is ascribed to Him; or when it is said that "Christ is born of the Virgin Mary," "Christ is of David's seed," then a human attribute is ascribed to Him. The same is true when human attributes are ascribed to Christ as God, as when we read, "They crucified the Lord of glory" (1 Cor. 2:8). The second kind, *genus majestaticum,* implies that the divine nature imparts its majesty and glory to the human nature, without itself sharing in the suffering of the flesh. This can be illustrated from the words, "All authority in heaven and on earth has been given to Me" (Matt. 28:18), or from John 6:51 ff., where it is said that to eat the body of Christ will enable a man to "live forever." There is no reciprocity in such a case, however, for while divine qualities can be said to be communicated to the human nature, human qualities are not communicated to the divine nature, which is unchangeable and eternal. The doctrine of the ubiquity of the body of Christ belongs to this genus. The third kind, *genus apotelesmaticum,* concerns the deeds performed by Christ. Each of the natures was active in these according to its own peculiarities, while the other nature also participated. So when we read that "Christ died for our sins" or that "Christ teaches" or that "He gave Himself as an offering to God," such statements belong to this genus.

The distinction between our Lord's "state of humiliation" and His "state of exaltation" is given a certain significance in the light of this *communicatio* doctrine. The former refers to Jesus' life on earth; the latter to His condition following the death on the cross, including His descent into hell, His resurrection, His ascension, and His being seated on the right hand of the Father. About the year 1620 two theological schools (Tübingen and Giessen) became involved in a dispute concerning Christ's divine attributes during the state of humiliation. Some argued that He possessed these attributes even then, but that He hid His majesty (κρύψις); this was the Tübingen position. The Giessen theologians, on the other hand, asserted that Christ actually laid aside His divine attributes during this period, divested Himself of His majesty (κένωσις). This arcane question was not settled conclusively, but neither did it lead to a deeper schism. It was agreed that Christ certainly did possess His divine majesty throughout His entire life on earth, but that He did not always make use of it.

The Protestant tradition (Calvin, Gerhard) was the first to refer to *Christ's threefold office* (as prophet, priest, and king), thereby providing a summary description of Christ's work as mediator and Lord. This concept, which is supported by many passages in Scripture, holds that as "king" Christ reigns over the faithful and all creation, that as "priest" He presented the perfect sacrifice for the sins of the world and now intercedes for His own, and also that as "prophet" He proclaimed God's eternal decree of salvation and continually works in the congregation through the office of the Word.

The kingly office was originally thought of as Christ's dominion over the faithful, protecting the church on earth, but in the orthodox Lutheran tradition (beginning with Gerhard) this concept also came to include His authority over all creation. Reference is made to the "kingdom of power," extending over heaven and earth; the "kingdom of grace," which coincides with Christ's activity in the congregation; and the "kingdom of glory," the glorious kingdom which is to come.

The priestly office, the office of the high priest, includes Christ's work of reconciliation — His fulfilling of the Law and His substitutionary suffering *(obedientia activa et passiva)*, the complete redemption of the human race, and the satisfaction He made for the sins of the world *(satisfactio vicaria)*. Christ's continued intercession for man before the Father also belongs to this office *(intercessio)*.

The prophetic office involves the message brought by Christ, His institution of the office of the Word and of the sacraments, plus the work which He will carry out in the church through the preaching office until His return. These three offices do not refer to separate stages of Christ's work; they rather designate different facets of the ongoing work of salvation.

c. *Creation and man's fall.* The work of Creation (in six days) was based exclusively upon God's free decision. The one Triune God brought forth out of nothing *(ex nihilo)* all that there is, both visible and invisible. There was a time when matter did not exist. But at the time of Creation God first brought forth an unformed mass, out of which the visible world was subsequently given form and order. The creation was, from the beginning, good; its evil and defective aspects have come in by degrees. God created the world for His glory, but also for man's good.

Man — the crown of creation and an "epitome" of the universe, a "microcosm" — was created in God's "image" and "likeness" (Gen. 1:26). These Biblical terms are interpreted as two expressions of the same reality. The likeness of God, *imago Dei*, is defined (partly in connection with Eph. 4:24) as an original, native form of righteousness and holiness. This signifies the perfection and harmony of a whole man: in his understanding, wisdom, and knowledge of God; in his will, righteousness, and conformity to God's law. To this must be added immortality. This original condition was "natural," i. e., given in and with creation and not a supernatural gift.

The Fall — man's transgression of God's command, induced by the devil's guile — brought about the loss of original righteousness *(justitia originalis)*. As a result of this — since perfection was "natural" — man was totally corrupted. And because of the unity of the race, this corruption has been transmitted from generation to generation via physical birth. In place of the original righteousness, a condition of guilt *(reatus)* and an inclination toward evil *(concupiscentia)* have entered in through "original sin" *(peccatum originis)*. Man stands under the wrath of God; unless he is regenerated, he is subject to temporal and eternal punishment. Death is directly related to sin. Death did not, therefore, reign over man at the beginning; it was not a part of man's nature at creation but has come as a result of his transgression. Life presupposes righteousness, that is, an inner harmony between spiritual and physical powers, and an unbroken relationship to God.

There is a scrupulous parallel between the original righteousness or perfection, the corruption which entered through the Fall (original sin), and the new creation which comes into being through Word and Sacrament. The life which was lost through Adam's fall is born anew through faith in Christ's atoning work.

d. *Providence and predestination.* The orthodox concept of providence is directly related to the doctrine of creation, and forms a necessary complement thereto. As seen from one point of view, providence (providentia) is nothing other than *creatio continuata*, continued creation. God did not only create things in the beginning; He also preserves them in their continued existence. Apart from this preservation *(conservatio)* they would be unable to exist or work in accordance with their nature. "Created things do not subsist by their own power, but 'God upholds the universe by His word of power,' Heb. 1:3" (Gerhard, *Loci,* Cotta ed., IV, 83a). The existence of men and things, their movement and activity, presupposes God's perpetual creative and sustaining cooperation. It is God who enables the sun to rise, who gives bread its nourishing power, herbs their ability to heal, etc. Without this continued cooperation things would lack their natural effectiveness.

Similarly all that happens, all events — with preservation of man's freedom of will and of natural causes — are completely subject to God's direct guidance and supervision; nothing takes place apart from His will. Furthermore, He directs everything to the goal He has selected. In God's care of creation, man occupies the foremost place. God's purposes for man (who is an "epitome of the world") form the center of the course of world history, particularly the goal which has been established for the faithful in the order of salvation. Here we can apply the well-known words, "In everything God works for good with those who love Him" (Rom. 8:28). God's active management of events is referred to as *gubernatio,* in distinction from *conservatio.*

As seen from another point of view, providence also includes the foreknowledge *(praescientia)* of God, which means, to speak more precisely, that God, dwelling in a perpetual "now," sees all and knows all. Because God is eternal, the boundaries of time are abrogated for Him. God's active will to care for the world and man is intimately associated with His foreknowledge — the eternal decision concerning all that subsequently happens in time.

In the later orthodox tradition the doctrine of providence — as was true of so many other points of doctrine — was divided into many different concepts and definitions, and as a result the general picture was quickly obscured. There can be no doubt, however, about the essential significance of this doctrine for the Lutheran position taken as a whole. It has influenced both individual piety and the general world view to a like extent.

But how is God related to evil? This question has posed problems of particular difficulty. The Calvinistic concept, which taught that God preordained and carried out evil in accordance with His hidden will, was rejected by the Lutherans. As Melanchthon said, we cannot conceive of God having two contradictory wills. And yet it can be said that God is actively involved in evil deeds in many different ways: He upholds man and man's natural abilities while evil is being done; He permits evil to happen; He abandons those who do evil; and finally, He sets limits thereto according to His free pleasure and can turn evil to good. When God "hardened the heart of Pharoah," this was not the result of "predestination" to evil; it was punishment for Pharoah's impenitence.

And with that we have touched upon the problem of predestination. Lutheran orthodoxy solved this in general agreement with the Formula of Concord. It was said that predestination, or election, refers only to those who come to believe in Christ and who remain in this faith to the end. God chose them for eternal life in Christ prior to the creation of the world. On the other hand, reprobation concerns those who persist in unbelief and impenitence to the end. They receive the just judgment of eternal death. This too is based on an eternal "decree."

But neither of these decrees is unconditioned: Election is carried through for Christ's sake and is based on the fact that God foresees who will remain faithful to the end (*ex praevisa fide*). Reprobation, on the other hand, is based on the fact that God foresees who will remain impenitent to the end.

The orthodox Lutheran doctrine of predestination adhered to what might be called an imperfect, logically incomplete theory: On the one hand, God alone is the source of man's salvation (which lies in predestination), while on the other, it is not God but man's own evil which leads to rejection. The question of God's omnipotence was deliberately omitted in this context, which suggests that justice was not done to the ideas which Luther set forth in his *De servo arbitrio*. On the other hand, however, the Calvinistic concept of double predestination was clearly repudiated.

e. *Free will*. The doctrine "Of Free Will" (*De libero arbitrio*) played an important role in the dogmatic structure of orthodox Lutheranism. But it must be said that the question concerning the relation of the will to predestination was not dealt with here in a specific way (which is rather surprising); the dogmaticians rather emphasized the synergistic problem, which involves the question of whether or not the human will is able to cooperate in spiritual things prior to or in the experience of conversion. This question was answered by saying that man, in specific respects, lacks free will. He is in bondage (*servum arbitrium*) through sin and is therefore unable to do good spiritually; he cannot, as a result, cooperate in his conversion. Hence the position set down in the Formula of Concord was accepted, and the point of view enunciated by Melanchthon was rejected (together with the grosser forms of synergism).

In the dogmatic locus *De libero arbitrio* this question was placed in a broader context. The problem of determinism was not really dealt with, nor the psychological problem of the function and nature of the will (even though such problems are touched upon tangentially here and there). The subject is rather this: the wholeness of man as seen in the context of the order of salvation. In agreement with Augustine and the medieval tradition reference is made to man "before the Fall," "after the Fall but before conversion," to "the regenerate man," and finally to "man after the resurrection." The freedom of the will in relation to its ability to do what is good in a spiritual sense is categorized in these various stages: In his original condition man was free to do good, as a result of his native righteousness; after the Fall the condition described above prevails — man is completely unable to do what is good; through regeneration man's freedom is partially restored, so that he can cooperate with grace and fight against sin; the condition of the consummation implies final release from the thraldom of sin.

The question in this context did not concern freedom as a psychological fact (i. e., whether or not the volitional act has a "voluntary" character), but it rather concerned freedom in relation to the object chosen. On this point a distinction was drawn between physical things *(res corporales),* i. e., the "lower hemisphere" or "social good," and spiritual things *(res spirituales),* i. e., true fear of God, pure love, and so on. With respect to the former it was said that a certain amount of freedom remained even after the Fall. Man can, to a certain degree, bring about external, civil righteousness. But with respect to the latter, freedom (as already noted) was entirely lost — which means that man is unable to cooperate in his salvation or produce what is good before God.

f. *Law and Gospel; repentance.* We have already spoken of the Word as a means of grace. The function of the divine Word in the order of salvation is further elucidated by the doctrine of Law and Gospel. It is by virtue of the operation of Law and Gospel — and only through this — that man can be converted and pass over from death and wrath to life. This is also called repentance *(poenitentia).*

What is the Law? In answer to this question, the definition suggested by Melanchthon was accepted: the Law is an "eternal and unchangeable wisdom and rule for righteousness with God." This *lex aeterna* is reflected in the righteousness of the first man, and subsequently in the Decalog given at Sinai. It not only demands external deeds but that man agrees in all things with the will of God *(lex spiritualis).* This is the Law which Christ fulfilled in a perfect way through His obedience and which provides the pattern for the pious and holy life of the Christian estate in this world, as well as for the perfection which we anticipate in the life to come.

Because man is unable to fulfill the Law's demands, it is not a rule for the conduct of his life. Instead, the Law serves to reveal sin, to accuse man, and to condemn all who are not released from the curse of the Law by the grace made available through Christ's atonement. Forgiveness is pronounced through the Gospel, which, unlike the Law, is not known to human reason; it is only revealed through God's Word, spoken to prophets and apostles. The Gospel, as a proclamation of Christ's complete redemption, is a consoling and edifying message. The idea that the Gospel also accuses man of sin, thus supplementing the Law, was rejected. In the strict sense of the term, the Law is the word which threatens, accuses, and condemns, while the Gospel comforts, edifies, and saves.

The evangelical concept of *repentance* was developed in direct connection with the doctrine of Law and Gospel. Repentance was placed side by side with conversion, the experience whereby faith is ignited and man passes over from wrath to grace. Since it was believed that this could be done only through the Word, it was only logical to define repentance as the effect of the operation of Law and Gospel on man. Instead of saying that penance consists of contrition, confession, and satisfaction (as was done in the Middle Ages), it was said that the decisive experience in repentance consists of contrition and faith. The former results from the Law, the latter from the Gospel. By providing man with an insight into sin and into the wrath of God, the Law drives him to repentance. The Gospel, on the other hand, brings the assurance of the forgiveness of sin for Christ's sake, which comforts the contrite conscience. The fruits of this faith are good works and the amendment of life. In the interest of clarity, the belief that good works play a role in repentance was rejected. In the strict sense, repentance consists only of contrition and faith.

In later orthodoxy these ideas concerning evangelical repentance were replaced and supplemented by a detailed discussion of the various acts whereby the Holy Spirit "applies" salvation to the individual (reference was made to the *gratia Spiritus Sancti applicatrix*). Included among the facets of this *ordo salutis* were the following: the call *(vocatio)*, illumination, regeneration and conversion, renewal *(renovatio)*, and the mystical union. This doctrine of the "order of grace" traced its origins far back in time — back to the Augustinian concept of grace. But it was the dogmaticians of late Lutheran orthodoxy who first gave this concept its distinctive form. It subsequently became a cardinal aspect of the theology of Pietism. The orthodox exposition emphasized, however, that the different concepts do not designate different stages which must be passed through. Such concepts as justification, conversion, and regeneration can be distinguished only in a logical sense, so that different aspects of the same experience might be illuminated.

g. *Faith and works.* The faith which is the "instrument" for justification *(fides justificans)* was described as *notitia, assensus,* and *fiducia* (in contrast to *fides historica,* the mere acceptance of the facts of faith). The knowledge *(notitia)* of faith refers to the divine Word set down in Scripture, which the believer assents to *(assensus)*. As confidence *(fiducia)* faith directs itself to the divine grace promised in Christ.

Justification and regeneration are included in faith. Both refer to the forgiveness of sin, not to the actual transformation which is a result of faith *(renovatio)*. In later orthodoxy reference was made in this connection to the mystical union as the acme of faith. When a man is born again, a "substantial" union takes place between God and the soul; the Holy Trinity comes to dwell within the believer.

The fruit of faith is good works. Renewal or the "new obedience" implies the beginning of the transformation of man into conformity with the image in which he was once created. Man's deeds are good when they are in conformity with God's law, but since no one can fulfill the Law, it is only because of faith that an act can be said to be good in the true sense. For it is because of faith that the faults which continue to inhere in man can be covered over, so that he can be reckoned as just before the judgment seat of God. Only those acts which originate in faith and a good conscience are good. The model for the exposition of Christian ethics was above all the Decalog, as interpreted in accordance with contemporary assumptions.

The purpose of good works is to glorify God and to promote the welfare of one's neighbor. Man is not declared just because of his good works, for he is justified only by the faith which holds fast to Christ's atonement and to the mercy of God revealed therein.

The connection between faith and works is that the latter are the fruit of faith. That faith must be accompanied by an actual renewal is revealed in this, that it will be lost through "sins against conscience." Such "conscious" transgressions indicate that renewal is lacking. When this is true, faith cannot be present either.

h. *The sacraments, the church, and the last things.* Baptism and the Lord's Supper were looked upon as precise counterparts of the "sacraments" of the Old Testament, circumcision and the Passover. The latter are referred to as prototypes of the coming Messiah, while the New Testament sacraments set forth the Christ revealed in the flesh, i. e., the reality foretold in the prophecies of the Old Testament *(figura — veritas; umbra — corpus)*. In spite of this difference, however, the purpose and the meaning was and is the same in both cases: to convey the heavenly gifts, promised in the words of institution, and to apply to the individual the promise of the forgiveness of sin, which belongs to the Gospel. This promise was first given in the Old Testament, although it is presented there in a "shadowy," more imperfect way than in the New Testament, which bears witness to the incarnate Christ. Participation in His atoning work, in His body and blood, is the spiritual gift *(res coelestis)* which, in the power of the words of promise, is provided in, with, and under the external signs — the water in Baptism and the bread and wine in the Lord's Supper. The presence of Christ in the Lord's Supper was interpreted in essential agreement with the point of view represented by the more conservative Lutherans (Brenz, Chemnitz) and by the Formula of Concord.

The church was defined in accordance with Reformation presuppositions as *eine heilige Gemeine,* "the congregation of saints and believers," in which the divine Word is preached in purity and the sacraments are properly administered. This congregation, which extends throughout the world and is united by the bonds of love, includes all who profess the Gospel and the sacraments. Among them are those who belong to the church only in an external way, as well as those who are true believers. Hence a distinction was made between the visible fellowship — the church as an external organization — and the invisible fellowship of those who are true and living members of the church. But until the Day of Judgment the latter group cannot be distinguished outwardly from those who are Christian in name only. The criteria which determine whether the church as such is true or false are, above all, the proper preaching of the Word and the proper administration of the sacraments.

The orthodox Lutheran ecclesiology is distinguished by its emphasis on the whole church, which is quite different from the fellowship concept which was introduced into Protestant theology later on. "The church," or the congregation, is not simply the sum of a group of individuals brought together around a certain object; it is rather an organic unity, into which the individuals are placed as members in one another's service. The concept of the church as then held also taught that the aim of spiritual and secular agencies is to sustain one and the same external fellowship, whether this be the family, the congregation, or the nation. It is within these natural groups or associations that the church comes into being, to the extent that they are leavened by the inner, invisible fellowship of the Spirit, *communio sanctorum*. Within the church (in the wider sense) there are three distinct orders or estates: the preaching office *(ordo ecclesiasticus)*, the political estate or authority *(ordo politicus)*, and the domestic estate, constituted through marriage *(ordo oeconomicus)*. The first of these is designed to bring man to eternal blessedness; the second, to maintain order and to protect society; the third, to increase the race and provide mutual support.

The order of salvation, which had its beginning in time, will also terminate in time. Yet it has its goal in that which lies beyond the boundaries of time, in eternal life. *Eschatology*, the doctrine of the last things, has an important place in orthodox dogmatics. The end of man (a microcosm) is death, when the body is separated from the soul and disintegrates in the grave. At the end of time, on the "Last Day," the resurrection of the dead will take place, followed by the final judgment, when each one shall be confronted again by the deeds of his life on earth. And just as man's life ends in death, so also shall the entire present world (the macrocosm) go to meet its doom. This will be accomplished by fire, which shall destroy and consume everything *(consummatio mundi)*. In the eternal existence, which shall follow the end of time, those who did evil will receive eternal death, and those who did good will receive eternal life. On the basis of these major concepts, developed on Biblical grounds, it was felt that the world order as well as the order of salvation would soon reach their final stages.

THE STRUGGLE AGAINST SOCINIANISM

The 16th century witnessed the upsurge of an antitrinitarian point of view which had its origins in Italy. In Transylvania and Poland, which were not reached by ecclesiastical persecution, organized congregations were established in which this point of view was upheld. In Poland a number of divided groups were united by Fausto Sozzini (in Latin, Socinus; d. 1604), who also became the foremost theologian of this movement. By the middle of the 17th century "Socinianism" was forbidden in Poland, and its organized existence came to an end soon thereafter. In the history of theology, however, this movement played a significant role: Socinianism, by its radical criticism of accepted dogma, prepared the way for the rationalistic theology of the Age of Enlightenment and also foreshadowed the modern concept of religion in many respects.

The rejection of the Socinian position played an important part in the orthodox Lutheran tradition. Based as it was in many ways on the heritage of late medieval nominalism and Renaissance humanism, Socinianism insisted that dogma or the content of Scripture — whose authority was accepted in a formal way — must be justified before the bar of sound human understanding. As a result the Socinians repudiated those doctrines which were thought to be opposed to reason. In their exposition of Scripture they established rational intelligibility and moral utility as the basic criteria.

Socinianism was, of course, antitrinitarian: the divinity of Christ and of the Holy Spirit was denied. Christ was looked upon as a mere man with a prophetic mission. The Holy Spirit was thought of as nothing more than a divine "power." The Bible passages which said otherwise were radically reinterpreted. In opposition to these rationalistic tendencies, orthodox theologians vigorously asserted the Scriptural principle as the basis of their theology; the Socinians, as a matter of fact, considered reason to be the ultimate norm.

With respect to their anthropology the Socinians were Pelagian. Adam was not created to be immortal; the likeness of God in man, which was not lost in the Fall, merely consists of a certain dominion over creation. Original sin was denied, and man was said to have a free will with which to obey God. "The help of grace" was conceived of only as an expression for the threats and promises included in sermons. On all of these points, orthodox theology — as is evident from the previous sections — was implacably opposed to Socinianism.

It was the doctrine of the Atonement, however, which was probably the most controversial point involved in this dispute. Socinus and his followers attacked the orthodox idea of satisfaction from the ground up. They maintained that the righteousness of God does not demand atonement for sin. Righteousness is only something that characterizes God's outward acts; it is not an "essential" quality, or one that is a part of His nature. God, of His free will and in "absolute goodness," can forgive and bestow eternal life upon all who believe and strive to live in innocence. As a logical consequence of this the Socinians denied that Christ's obedience has any substitutionary value and that His death provided satisfaction for man's guilt. The death of Christ on the cross merely proved that Jesus was obedient, and the Resurrection confirmed His divine mission. The Bible passages which speak of atonement, redemption, etc., were freely reinterpreted. Christ's work consisted only of this, that He showed man how to live a better life before God. In this we find "atonement."

In refuting these ideas, the orthodox theologians set forth the following principles: There is an "essential" righteousness in God, according to which sinful man must be punished. But because He is also merciful, God desires to spare the human race. Thus it was that Christ came to bring merit and make satisfaction. The punishment which sin deserves has been transferred to Christ; as a result, God can receive sinners by grace without violating His righteousness. Hence we have this "wonderful combination of divine righteousness and mercy" (Gerhard, *Loci*, VII, 47b). Christ was set forth as the Mediator between God and man, who has freed us from the curse of the Law, from God's wrath, and from eternal judgment. He is the Redeemer, the "Atonement for our sins." Because of this, Christ is referred to as *causa meritoria justificationis*, the One who works our justification through His merit. His death was a *satisfactio vicaria*.

In this matter as well as on many other points — one could also mention the doctrine of the sacraments, for the Socinians also denied the regenerating effect of infant Baptism and the Real Presence of Christ in the Lord's Supper — Socinianism appeared as a rationalistic critique of dogma. In somewhat different forms, and under more favorable conditions, this critique was frequently repeated in the new era which began with Pietism and the Enlightenment. Various characteristics of the modern Protestant interpretation of Christianity were already fully formed in Socinianism.

CHAPTER 31

Pietism

PIETISM'S PLACE IN THE HISTORY OF THEOLOGY

The Pietist movement, which penetrated Lutheran territory in the latter part of the 17th century and contributed to the diminution or the internal transformation of the orthodox Lutheran tradition, was not simply a reaction against certain weaknesses in the church life of the time; it was rather a new theological position, which was based on a new concept of reality and which bore within itself the seeds of the modern point of view. But how was Pietism related to the tradition that preceded it and that which followed? Scholars are still debating this question. Certain points of view shall be mentioned in the following.

To the extent that Pietism insisted on a living piety and revealed the insufficiency of objective theological knowledge, it had many precursors among the earlier Lutherans, such as Johann Arndt and Johann Gerhard at the beginning of the 17th century and Theophil Grossgebauer and Heinrich Müller (both in Rostock) in the latter half of the century. The fact of the matter is that the leading orthodox theologians were well aware of theology's practical purpose, just as they also commonly insisted on the improvement of morals and manners. Many of the strictly orthodox also reacted in a positive way to the recommendations for reform which Spener set forth in his *Pia desideria,* 1675 (trans. Theodore G. Tappert; Philadelphia: Fortress Press, 1964).

At the same time, however, Pietism revealed a number of new tendencies which were contradictory to the fundamental presuppositions of orthodox theology. These new ideas gradually became more apparent. The violent and long-lasting controversies between the representatives of orthodoxy and the Pietists clearly reveal the profound disparity between these two points of view.

Where did Pietism's new ideas come from? Various sources (even beyond Lutheranism) have been suggested, such as Roman Catholic mysticism, certain facets of Reformed theology, such as Grotius' and Coccejus' principles of Biblical interpretation, the preaching of Labadie, and the so-called precisianism of Holland. Another possibility, commonly overlooked, is Socinianism. But it ought to be remembered in this connection that a new trend of thought cannot always be entirely explained in the light of what has gone before. A trend may rather represent something basically new, whose origins are hidden.

What about the relationship between Pietism and subsequent tendencies? This question has often been answered by saying that in essence Pietism remained attached to the orthodox Lutheran position, while the Enlightenment denotes the breakthrough of the new age. In more recent years, however, scholars have emphasized the close connection between Pietism and the Enlightenment. In spite of the fact that it commonly rejected the new philosophical tendencies of the 18th century, Pietism itself helped to prepare the ground in many respects for the new ways of thinking. Pietism included a number of different tendencies, however; some of these were akin to rationalistic thought (e. g., radical Pietism), while others stood closer to the orthodox Lutheran tradition (e. g., the so-called Württemberg Pietism).

SPENER'S THEOLOGY

Pietism's foremost theologian, and its founder within Lutheran ranks, was Philipp Jakob Spener (1635–1705, from 1691 dean in Berlin). He transmitted the Pietist point of view only in a very modest form. He sought to retain the orthodox doctrinal basis without alteration. But the questions he dealt with, and not least of all his very method of presentation, manifested a new theological spirit and a new way of thinking.

In his book *Pia desideria* (1675) Spener set forth a number of recommended reforms designed to deal with the state of decay into which the church had fallen. He suggested, for example, that the Bible be studied more commonly. To serve this end, he recommended the organization of associations for the promotion of piety *(collegia pietatis)*. The universal priesthood was to be exercised through mutual admonition and soul care. He also expressed a desire for a reform of the study of theology: the dialectical method should be replaced by the reading of the Bible and inspirational literature.

Lutheran Pietism appeared first of all as a reform movement with practical goals in view, but it gradually came to exert a transforming effect on theological activity and the general outlook as well. Spener published his theological point of view chiefly in the large collection entitled *Theologische Bedenken,* I–IV (1700 and the following years) and in *Die evangelische Glaubenslehre in einem Jahrgang der Predigten* (1688).

The new way of thinking was expressed in *epistemology*. According to Spener, experience is the ground of all certainty, both on the natural level and on the level of revelation. As a result the personal experience of the pious is the ground of certainty for theological knowledge. Only the regenerate Christian can be a true theologian and possess real knowledge of revealed truth. Spener distinguished between physical and spiritual knowledge. The former he looked upon as dead knowledge, which even the unregenerate can attain. The doctrine of faith is therefore accessible, without the aid of the Spirit, as sheer external knowledge; but if it is to be acquired in the true sense of the term, one must have a personal experience and be born again through the Spirit. These ideas are based on presuppositions which are completely different from those found among the orthodox. The latter believed that, under any circumstances, insight into revealed truth requires the illumination of the Holy Spirit. The Pietists answered that such knowledge could be acquired even by nonbelievers; since by the light of the Spirit the orthodox meant the light which is found in the Word itself, the true doctrine could therefore be proclaimed even by an unregenerate teacher. — In the light of the foregoing, it is not surprising that Spener was criticized by the orthodox for separating the Word and the Spirit, and that Pietism was sometimes looked upon as a recrudescence of Rahtmann's position. (See above, pp. 307–308)

Spener's new orientation with respect to the concept of faith and the doctrine of justification provides us with similar examples. As Spener understood it, faith is not simply knowledge and confidence (*notitia, assensus,* and *fiducia*); it is at the same time a living power, out of which the actual experience of renewal proceeds. One is certainly not justified by this power or virtue, but if it is not present, then faith cannot justify either, since it then is not a living faith. Between historical faith and justifying faith there is therefore a "dead faith" *(fides mortua),* which can receive the true doctrine but cannot justify.

Major emphasis was placed on regeneration, which Spener thought of as the granting of a new life. Justification is the fruit of regeneration. The doctrine of imputation was therefore replaced by the idea that justification and sanctification form a unity. This unity is expressed by the term "regeneration" (or "new birth"), which no longer — as in the older tradition — coincides with the concept of the forgiveness of sins but designates an inner transformation which in turn is the source of the new life that characterizes the Christian man.

The same thing can also be expressed in this way, that according to Spener justification is directly related to the indwelling Christ. Faith is thus not simply the acceptance of the merits of Christ; it must also cause Christ to dwell in the believer's heart. Some Pietists began to say of themselves, as a result, "I am Christ"; Spener himself did not approve of this, however. The idea of a personal union with Christ was not new, of course — orthodoxy spoke of the *unio mystica* as a fruit of faith — but what was new here was that Spener conceived of this inner transformation as the essential basic aspect of faith and expanded the concept of justification to include the inner new creation as well.

The contrast between orthodoxy and Pietism has often been described as a contrast between doctrine and life. Even though this is rather misleading and scarcely touches upon the actual differences, it is correct to the extent that Pietism did place strong emphasis on the sanctified life as a testimony to the true faith. This was in accord with the teachings of orthodox Lutheranism, but a new feature was expressed in terms of a negative attitude toward life in this world. Dying to the world was to manifest itself in the avoidance of all worldliness, of all pleasure and amusement. Spener did not hold that a Christian could live a perfect life in this world, but he did believe that there are those who could attain freedom from all intentional sin. As a rule the Pietist point of view led to a more or less bifurcated ethic: stricter demands were made on Christians than on men in general.

Spener's sharp criticism of the unsatisfactory state of the contemporary church was combined with an optimistic view of the church's future. He did not share the belief of the more radical, millenarian Pietists concerning a future 1,000-year earthly kingdom, but he did foresee a period of great success for the church, in which the Jews would be converted on a universal scale and the papacy would fall. Spener deviated sharply from the older tradition in holding these views, for the latter anticipated the imminent end of the world, plus a progressive degeneration of and an increasing opposition to the Christian church.

CHARACTERISTICS OF PIETISM

In spite of Spener's conservative attitude and his basic adherence to the orthodox Lutheran doctrinal tradition, a profound reorientation revealed itself on many points.

The theology of Pietism concentrated on the question of salvation. Most interest was given to those questions which are directly related to the order of salvation and to the individual's conversion or conduct of life. The metaphysical questions were written off, as well as the traditional philosophical substructure. Spener was critical of Aristotelian philosophy, and he rejected its use in the field of theology. The canonical authority of the Old Testament was clearly acknowledged, but the Old Testament was subordinated to the New Testament, because the truth revealed in the former was thought to be of a more peripheral nature. The Halle Pietists even began to criticize certain parts of the Old Testament as being contrary to morality.

Another characteristic was that subjective events were taken to be the point of departure. The role of experience as the ground of certainty has already been emphasized. Inner spiritual phenomena and individual experiences elicited the greatest interest and provided the focus for theological discussion.

Here we can see a new attitude toward theological questions. Orthodoxy had proceeded on the basis of objective reality and grounded the certainty of theological knowledge on the Scriptural principle, which was thought of as self-evident and, so to speak, self-creative of the knowledge that theology deals with. Pietism, on the other hand, proceeded on the basis of experience; it looked upon the experience of the individual as being fundamental to religious knowledge or insight. Pietistic theological exposition came to deal primarily with empirical religious events, just as it was assumed that theological knowledge could not be acquired apart from the experience of regeneration (the new birth).

Thus it was that conservative Pietism inaugurated, in a variety of ways, the modern way of thinking in the field of theology and ecclesiology. In its subjective concept of knowledge and in its interest in morality and the empirical facts of religion, Pietism bore within itself tendencies which came into full bloom in the thought world of the Enlightenment, in the secular area as well as in the theological sphere.

HALLE PIETISM

Of decisive importance for the development of Pietism was the fact that the newly formed university in Halle filled several of its faculty positions with men of the Pietist persuasion. August Hermann Francke (d. 1727) came there to teach in 1692, for example, and he went on to become the leader of Pietism in his era and the founder of the famous orphanage in Halle. Other theologians with the same convictions were Joachim Justus Breithaupt, Johann Anastasius Freylinghausen, and Joachim Lange, all of whom taught at Halle. Johann Jakob Rambach (d. 1735), who was active in Giessen, exerted great influence as a preacher and interpreter of the Bible.

The science of theology was thoroughly altered by the Halle Pietists. Theological activity in Halle was dominated by a study of the Bible which was designed to serve practical, inspirational goals. To accomplish this, the very method of interpretation was simplified. The older concept of a single, literal meaning of a given passage of Scripture was gradually abandoned; it was supplanted by a double or sometimes a triple meaning — literal, spiritual, and mystical (Rambach). This system made it easier to explain those parts of the Old Testament which were considered offensive. Dogmatic studies were reduced to insignificance. The men of Halle were satisfied with a concise reiteration of the orthodox doctrinal system, qualified by the deviations introduced by Spener. The philosophical conceptual apparatus was rejected.

The Halle Pietists diverged from Spener's position in certain distinctive ways, particularly with respect to their teaching about the repentance struggle and their legalistic attitude toward the world. While Spener held that God dealt with different men in different ways in conversion, Francke asserted the rule that the Christian should be able to point to a distinct, demarcated conversion experience, preceded by an inner crisis (the repentance struggle) evoked by the preaching of the Law. In this condition, man is brought to the point where he decides to break with the world and begin a new life. Then it is that the gift of faith is bestowed on him, and it is through this faith that he receives forgiveness of sin.

The new conduct of life, which is the fruit of faith, is characterized by stringent self-examination and the suppression of natural affections. Every detail of life is to be directed by the Holy Spirit, or by the new affections of faith. That which is natural is looked upon, as a result, as being intrinsically sinful. The pious Christian will avoid worldly pleasures and amusements. Dancing, playing, and going to the theater were considered sinful. — On this point, too, Spener had refrained from providing legalistic instructions.

RADICAL PIETISM

Conservative Pietism was followed by a radical trend which was related to the enthusiasts of the Reformation period as well as to Socinianism. Here, as often elsewhere, a fanatic, mystical religiosity was combined with a rationalistic critique of church doctrine. The influence of Jakob Boehme's theosophical philosophy is readily discernible in certain instances (e. g., Dippel; see below).

Johann Wilhelm Petersen (d.1727) represented the pronounced chiliastic point of view. The reference to Christ's 1,000-year reign in Rev. 20 was not interpreted, as in the older tradition, by referring to the church's domination of the world from the time of Constantine to the papacy of Gregory VII. Petersen rather interpreted this, in the Jewish manner, as a prophecy concerning a future kingdom — in which the faithful shall reign with Christ for 1,000 years. Spener did not reject the millennial point of view altogether, but (as noted above) he had his own somewhat different interpretation.

Gottfried Arnold (d. 1714) can also be included among the radical Pietists. He wrote the well-known *Unparteyische Kirchen- und Ketzergeschichte* (1699–1700), in which he set himself above all confessions (*unparteyisch* — "impartial") in his description of church history and criticized them in a supercilious manner. As he saw it, true Christianity was almost always preserved and passed on by the sects.

The most distinctive of the radical Pietists was Johann Konrad Dippel (d. 1734). He was particularly critical of the orthodox doctrine of the Atonement. According to Dippel, satisfaction is contrary to God's love, which simply overlooks sin and re-creates the heart. Every facet of religion is immanent, or subjective, said he. As was true of Boehme, Dippel taught that all things will be restored. He also accepted the chiliastic position. The 1,000-year reign appeared to him as a release from

331

the domination of church and state. Dippel's point of view, which was published in *Vera demonstratio evangelica* (1729), evoked violent controversies, even in Sweden, where he lived for a time.

HERRNHUTISM

While radical Pietism usually appeared in the form of temporary fanatical movements or privately held ideas, the "United Brethren" organization, founded by Count Nikolaus von Zinzendorf in 1727, developed into a permanent group. In contrast to radical Pietism, the Herrnhut movement thought well of the church. It was based on the Augsburg Confession, but its supporters did not feel that the distinctions made between the various communions were essential. As a result, one did not have to be a Lutheran to be welcome in Herrnhut; members of other confessional groups were also received.

Von Zinzendorf centered his entire theology around one point: the feeling of fellowship with Christ, achieved through contemplation of the cross. As far as he was concerned, theology had no connection with philosophy or with general education; neither did he accept any natural knowledge of God. Knowledge of God comes only from the Crucified One. All the rest is heathen speculation. This theology of the cross was completely subjective and highly emotional. By virtue of one's contemplation of the cross, of the blood and the wounds, one comes to feel that Christ's struggle and suffering release us from punishment and unite us with Him who was sent to be our Savior, who is also Father and Creator.

The Herrnhuters did not refer to the repentance struggle induced by the Law, as did the older Pietists. The entire conversion experience was replaced by the experience of the cross and the Atonement. The preaching of the cross in the evangelical manner was the one and only thing that mattered. An antinomian attitude characterized this position.

But in spite of their hyperevangelical tendency, there was no talk in Herrnhut (as there was among the radical Pietists) about abolishing the orthodox doctrine of the Atonement. Christ's substitutionary suffering and His redemption from sin was to be found, on the contrary, at the very center of the Herrnhut faith.

The way in which the Atonement was set forth by the Herrnhuters was quite different, however, from the older tradition. The emphasis was placed on the emotional *experience* of Christ's suffering. Subjectivism was carried to an extreme. The relationship of the Christian to God and Christ was described in terms of human intimacy, frequently in a way we find distasteful and offensive today.

At the same time that the Herrnhut movement undoubtedly sought to do justice to one of Lutheranism's basic ideas, it was, through its subjective emphasis, strongly conditioned by the era in which it appeared. Its piety was of an effeminate and sentimental nature. The Herrnhut movement was opposed not only by the orthodox but by the conservative Pietists (e. g., Bengel) as well.

WÜRTTEMBERG PIETISM

Johann Albrecht Bengel (d. 1752) and Magnus Friedrich Roos (d. 1803), both well-known in Sweden as authors of inspirational literature, were the leaders of the Württemberg branch of Pietism. This group was closely related to the church, and it clung more faithfully to the orthodox heritage than other branches of Pietism.

Bengel's greatest contributions were made in the field of Biblical studies. His publication of the Greek New Testament, in which he divided the manuscripts in groups according to their place of origin, provided the basis for modern textual criticism. The commentary which became his most extensively used work, *Gnomon Novi Testamenti,* is distinguished for its acute observations and a profound analysis of textual details. The ideal for which Bengel strove was a concrete, historical interpretation free from all philosophical or doctrinaire formalism. In his exegesis of the Book of Revelation he attempted to set forth a prophetical interpretation of history. He even asserted that the end of the world could be expected in the year 1836.

Roos was a member of the Bengel school with respect to Biblical exegesis, and he was essentially orthodox in doctrine. His position was also influenced by the basic principles of Pietism, as well as by the struggle against contemporary rationalism. The best known of his writings is *Christliches Hausbuch,* which, together with several more of his books, was translated into Swedish. These books were particularly popular among the Swedes who were followers of Henrick Schartau.

THE CONTROVERSY OVER PIETISM

It was not long after its appearance that the Pietist movement encountered the violent opposition of orthodox theologians. Pietism was criticized for nourishing all kinds of heresy and for watering down the pure doctrine as a result of its indifferentism. A great number of polemical treatises were exchanged in the decades just before and after the year 1700. Among those who attacked the Pietist position were several members of the faculty in Wittenberg, as well as Benedikt Carpzov of Leipzig and Johann Friedrich Mayer of Greifswald (d. 1712, held in high regard by King Charles XII of Sweden). These critics found in Pietism a Platonic tendency, a *schwärmerisch* attitude toward the Word and sacraments, plus an "Osiandrian" doctrine of justification. Many other controversial questions were discussed. We have referred to some of the major points in previous sections: the questions of the efficacious power of the Word, of the relation between the Word and the Spirit, of *theologia regenitorum*, of *fides mortua*, of the legalistic concept of sanctification (the negative attitude toward nature and toward adiaphora). The so-called terministic dispute was elicited by the fact that a number of Pietists set forth the idea that in the case of certain ungodly men the period of grace or the possibility of conversion could cease even before they died *(terminus gratiae)*. The millennial hope entertained by some Pietists was also included in the list of controversial questions.

The most incisive confrontation between the Pietist and the orthodox points of view was the doctrinal dispute between Valentin Ernst Löscher (d. 1749, general superintendent in Dresden) and the Halle theologian Joachim Lange. The former, in his *Timotheus Verinus* (1711–17), presented a searching criticism of Pietism from the orthodox vantage point, but he also extended the hand of reconciliation at the same time. Lange replied with a vehement and factually inferior polemic. Löscher did not feel, however, that he was simply fighting against a temporary phenomenon, whose defects one could easily establish; he rather believed that Pietism represented a new spirit of the times, whose tendencies in the direction of "enthusiasm" and indifferentism threatened to destroy the very assumptions of orthodox thought from within. His critique did not achieve the intended goal.

Pietism's subjective, anthropocentric attitude dissolved the objective concept of reality as expressed in the old scholastic philosophy and in orthodox Lutheran theology. Or as Löscher put it in his judgment of Pietism: the external practice of religion *(habitus religionis)* was transformed into religion and salvation itself.

CHAPTER 32

The Enlightenment

GENERAL BACKGROUND

It can be said, speaking in general terms, that the age of the Enlightenment on the European continent coincided with the 18th century. A profound scientific and cultural transformation took place during this time, a transformation which completely altered the conditions under which theological activity was carried on.

The roots of this age and its ideas are to be found in Renaissance humanism and Socinianism, as well as in the deism of 17th-century England. The philosophical systems which began to replace the older philosophical structure in the latter half of the 17th century (Descartes, Leibniz, Locke) also helped to prepare the ground for the Enlightenment. New discoveries and theories in the field of natural science (Newton) and in the field of jurisprudence (Grotius, Pufendorf) also contributed to the development of the more modern point of view, which became increasingly widespread during the 18th century. In the theological area, Pietism served to promote this same development in some ways.

The epoch we are now discussing marks the emergence of the modern period. A new world view forced its way into a dominating position in the cultural sphere, and new intellectual assumptions grew apace. In order to understand the import of this radical change, it is desirable to compare it at certain points with the older tradition and its scientific principles.

Philosophical thought was transformed from the ground up, through the great philosophical systems as well as through the new scholastic philosophy which replaced Aristotelian scholasticism at the German universities in the 18th century (Thomasius, Wolff).

The metaphysical concept of substantial forms was replaced by an empirical and atomistic concept of reality. Previously the world of the spirit, epitomized in God *(ens supremum),* was considered the highest and the primary reality. But not so in the age of the Enlightenment, when the eyes of men were turned toward the empirically conceived material world with all its diversity. The older objective philosophy was replaced by a practical and utilitarian form of wisdom, whose primary objective was to teach man to understand and control his environment and to enjoy happiness in this world (the so-called philosophy of moderation).

Older forms of thought proceeded from the object — metaphysics sought for an objective knowledge of the deepest meaning of reality. The new philosophy began with the subject, which was considered primary in the search for knowledge. Self-consciousness and inner experience were looked upon as the most obvious and fundamental factors — immediately at hand for the thinking and feeling subject. The tendency toward rationalistic thought was thereby given: attempts were made to explain the world on the basis of the principles of human reason.

One of the most important prerequisites of the age of the Enlightenment, and therefore for modern thought as well, was the new *concept of learning.* Philosophy was no longer regarded as the handmaiden of theology *(ancilla theologiae).* Learning was freed from its dependence on theology and scholastic metaphysics and was based instead on the observations of experience and on rational principles. Thus it was, beginning already in the 17th century, that the so-called natural system of knowledge — based on the idea that humanistic erudition, religion and morals, law and politics, can be grounded on distinct rational principles common to all men in all ages — began to develop. This rational knowledge was thought of as being autonomous, immediately accessible and fully evident to all, without having been obscured by original sin.

Even more profound, perhaps, was the change which took place in the field of natural science. Scholars now began to apply the mechanical-mathematical method and proceeded more than ever before on the basis of empirical observation.

This new natural science brought with it an altered *picture of the world.* The empirical investigation of the world came to be of primary interest. It was not until the 18th century that the conception of the solar system which Copernicus set forth in the 16th century was generally accepted. The earth was no longer looked upon as the center of things, and man, in this new perspective, became nothing more than a speck of dust in the universe — at the same time that he controlled the universe through his reason. The Aristotelian conception of form was replaced by a mechanical-atomistic explanation of the world. Life consists of unalterable space, things are compounded of particles which exert a mechanical influence upon one another and fill out space. No longer did men think of substantial forms as the basic elements in the edifice of the universe; they rather thought solely in terms of material entities. A basic contrast between matter and spirit, sensuous and supersensual, was one of the results of this mechanical explanation of nature. This was quite far removed not only from the older scholastic metaphysics but also from the original Lutheran view of the world (with its *finitum capax infiniti*).

Behind this new understanding of the world was the conviction that human reason is competent to survey and control its environment, to establish laws for the events of life as well as rules for human society. A rationalistic explanation of nature and a rationalistic doctrine of morality came to the fore as consequences of this new attitude. The Enlightenment was characterized by its naive faith in man and his possibilities.

In the field of *jurisprudence* new ideas were broached by Hugo Grotius (d. 1645) and Samuel von Pufendorf (d. 1694), which have provided the basis for the modern concept of natural rights. The older Protestant tradition also spoke of natural rights or a natural law. But this referred to the knowledge of right and wrong which was put into man's heart at the time of creation, weak vestiges of which remain even after the Fall. The idea of natural law was therefore involved in the context of revelation and of the Biblical view of man. The natural rights of the age of Enlightenment were emancipated from this. They were rather based on the belief that distinct principles of law are imbedded in human reason and that these form a common basis for the public administration of law. Morality, therefore, was based on autonomous reason. The tie between revelation and natural law was cut.

A similar change took place with respect to *the concept of the state.* While the Lutheran tradition looked upon authority as a divine institution, commissioned to be "the protector of both tables of the Law" *(custos utriusque tabulae),* men such as Thomas Hobbes conceived the idea of a secular state, based on human forbearance, designed to promote the *salus publica* — the general welfare. In the state governed by an absolutist prince, political considerations were placed above the ecclesiastical, and the church lost its independence. The new concept of the state was similarly based on an optimistic faith in reason; it was believed that man was able to adjust political matters in such a way that the common good would be served.

Quite a long time passed before the Enlightenment began seriously to affect the field of *theology*. It was not until the latter part of the 18th century that neology, or a rationalistic theology, began to appear among German Protestants. Even before this, however, the general shift in the way of thinking had left obvious traces in this area as well.

The most influential of the new ideas introduced into the theology of the Enlightenment was the concept of natural religion. This was first developed in 17th-century English deism. In his book *De veritate* (1625) Herbert of Cherbury set forth the idea that there is a natural religion, common to all men and independent of revelation, through which man can be blessed even apart from knowledge of revelation. He thought of Christ as a wise teacher and above all as an example in virtue. The meaning of natural religion was presented in the five following propositions: there is a God, a highest being; this highest being ought to be worshiped and served; this worship consists above all in piety and virtue; deviations from virtue (sin) must be repented, and if there is repentance, there will be forgiveness; the evil will be punished and the good will be rewarded in a life to come. The idea that the doctrines of "God, virtue, and immortality" form a summary of religion, much cherished during the age of the Enlightenment, was already present here.

During the 18th century, deism appeared in a more radical form. This can be seen, for example, in Matthew Tindal's well-known book *Christianity as Old as the Creation* (1730), as well as in the philosophers of the French Enlightenment and in German rationalism (e. g., in the *Wolfenbüttel Fragments*, written by Reimarus and published by Lessing).

The culture of the Enlightenment was distinguished by its increasing secularization. The new form of natural science pointed toward an immanent explanation of the world. A secular culture developed, independent of church and confessions. The state was similarly released from its religious purposes and from its connection with the Christian confessions.

The process of secularization did not, however, signify a rejection of Christianity or of religion, but it did bring about a profound alteration of the prerequisites for Christian theology and preaching.

This change revealed itself in (among other things) the following tendencies, which exerted a profound affect on the theology of the Enlightenment.

1. Theology came to be more or less dependent on philosophy and rational thought. Even in those presentations where the author did not wish to go so far as to replace revelation with natural religion, intending rather to stand fully within the Christian tradition, it was not uncommon to find rational arguments placed alongside revelation on an equal basis. The demand that reason be subjected to the testimony of Scripture was replaced by the firm belief that revelation and rational principles are in complete harmony, plus the desire to legitimize revelation in the presence of reason.

2. Parallel with theology's rationalizing was its tendency to moralize. Morality is a more immediate concern than religion to the modern, rational view of life. The promotion of good morals was looked upon as Christianity's main objective, and ethical content as its very essence.

3. The idea that religion was based in particular on principles imbedded in human reason supported an individualistic conception: religion became an individual, private matter, its certainty based on a person's own experiences.

4. A basic characteristic of the theology of the Enlightenment was the tendency to "humanize" Christianity, to accommodate it to an anthropocentric frame. Theology was expected to promote human welfare, and theological truth was expected to harmonize with commonly recognized rational principles. This-worldly goals predominated: earthly happiness and a rational morality were the primary benefits that men expected from religion.

ENGLISH THEOLOGY IN THE AGE OF THE ENLIGHTENMENT

The thought pattern of the modern age began to influence English theology at an early date: by the end of the 17th century it came to dominate a point of view which was called "latitudinarianism." Its representatives believed that revelation was in full accord with reason and the religious principles discerned therein. Unlike the deists, they did not desire to replace traditional Christianity with natural religion, but they did feel that revealed religion had its best support in reason. Faith was looked upon as a conviction based on rational considerations. Religious truth cannot be "proved," but moral certainty can be attained, partly on the basis of the assumption that the Bible is a reliable source and that the miracles confirm its authority. One of the chief spokesmen of this influential branch of English theology was John Tillotson (1630–94), famous as a preacher, after 1691 archbishop of Canterbury. The ideas of the latitudinarians were neither radical nor subversive. They were different in that they were independent of the reasoning of scholastic metaphysics and also because of their serene confidence in the belief that the Christian faith can be supported by rational arguments. The latitudinarians held that, in the final analysis, the decisive proof for faith is to be found in an upright conduct of life. For them the moral aspect was superior to the religious.

A kindred spirit can be noted in the contribution which the great philosopher John Locke (1632–1704) made to the question of faith and knowledge. Locke made a clear distinction between revelation and reason, and asserted that the propositions of faith rest on completely different ground than the truths of reason. Direct revelation, such as that which came to the prophets and apostles, involves a certainty equal to that associated with evident knowledge. We cannot expect to receive a direct revelation, however; revelation is mediated to us through language and human understanding. Because of this, the Christian faith, as we comprehend it, must always be judged to a certain extent by reason, and it can be accepted only if it is not contrary to the evident principles of reason. In his book *The Reasonableness of Christianity* (1693) Locke sought to present a pure Biblical Christianity, independent of the later theology and of the creeds of the church. He did not deny the doctrine of the Trinity, but he endeavored to find the Biblical equivalents of its terms. In Locke we find the prototype of two tendencies which came to be characteristic of the theology of the Enlightenment in England: the first was the desire to exhibit the reasonableness of Christianity, and the second, to reproduce what was considered to be an uncorrupted form of Biblical doctrine.

At the side of latitudinarianism, which was moderate in its attitude and strove to retain the essentials of the Christian tradition, radical deism appeared in new forms, developing in a manner consistent with the ideas set forth earlier by Herbert of Cherbury (see above). A book published by John Toland in 1696, *Christianity not Mysterious,* attempted to excerpt from Christianity certain simple, basic dogmas about God and immortality, which were referred to as the essential and rational elements thereof. The "mysterious" elements of the Christian faith, on the other hand, ought to be repudiated. In the book by Matthew Tindal mentioned above, *Christianity as Old as the Creation* (1730), the thesis was set forth that the Gospel was simply a reiteration of the original, natural religion. Its content is essentially the proclamation of a pure and moral life, which promotes God's glory and man's happiness. The thesis concerning a rational religion was thereby combined with the idea that morality is the end and purpose of religion. This reductive Christianity, which was excerpted from the gospels, was said to be identical with the natural religion of reason, and therefore the form of religion best equipped to encourage morality and happiness.

Among those who came out against the deists was Joseph Butler (1692–1752, bishop of Durham), who published his famous apologetic work, *The Analogy of Religion, Natural and Revealed, to the Constitution and Course of Nature,* in 1736. Butler's analogy presupposed faith in a supreme Creator of the world. It was not, therefore, directed against atheism, but it sought to manifest the probability of faith and its consistency with reason for those who already recognize God as creator. In opposition to the deists, Butler asserted the necessity of revelation; natural religion does not by any means make revelation superfluous.

The main argument in the part of Butler's book which deals with revealed religion is this: If we admit that Scripture has come to us from the God who is the Creator of nature, then we can expect to find in the truths of faith something of the same structure — and of the same difficulty to explain in its totality — as we find in the natural order. This is what Butler called an analogy between religion and the world of nature. He did not suggest that such an analogy can be found everywhere; the examples are at best sporadic. But to him this was sufficient. We cannot expect to have exact proof of the claims of faith. Probability is the highest goal we can reach in this respect, and a demonstration of probability is what Butler sought to establish through a detailed proof of the analogy which exists between nature and religion. He was in

341

many ways very close to the deist position on the affinity between natural religion and Christianity, but unlike the deists he wanted to defend also the specific Christian revelation.

One major point concerned the doctrine of the Atonement. The deists considered the Atonement to be superfluous, inasmuch as God's mercy ought to be sufficient in itself to forgive the sins of those who repent. But Butler asserted that Christ's substitutionary suffering is the ground of forgiveness, and he showed that one can find analogies even to this in the world around us. Butler's encounter with deism was not without its contradictions, but one can discern in his work the contours of a new concept of revelation. During the 19th century Butler's influence on English theology became even greater than it was while he was alive.

The struggle against deism occupied an important place in 18th-century English theology. It was soon overshadowed, however, by another factor — the victorious progress of the Methodist movement, beginning at the end of the 1730s. This is not the place to describe the history of Methodism, or its effect on church and society; we shall only take note of its theological contours.

John Wesley (1703–91) was a priest in the state church of England, and early became one of the leaders of a high-church movement at Oxford. On his mother's side he also had connections with the latitudinarian (broad church) and Socinian tradition; furthermore, he had, during a two-year stint as a missionary in the colony of Georgia, come under the direct influence of the Herrnhut point of view. As a result of his association with Herrnhutism, Wesley was convinced that trust in the merits of Christ forms the sole basis of man's salvation, a doctrine which he found confirmed in the homilies produced within the Church of England during the time of the Reformation. His conversion (1738), which proved to be the point of departure for the Methodist awakening, was described by Wesley as a suddenly aroused inner certainty of forgiveness of sins through faith in Christ alone. This occurred under the impact of Luther's *Preface to Romans.* Wesley's brother Charles had experienced a similar conversion, prompted by his study of Luther's commentary on Galatians.

Justification by faith alone was the crux of John Wesley's preaching after his conversion. He therefore broke with an idea that was prevalent in Anglican theology, viz., that good works are the goal of faith, and a necessary qualification for salvation. The clergy of Wesley's time were generally unacquainted with the doctrine of justification by faith alone. Wesley insisted that sanctification must not be confused with justification. It is the fruit of faith. It is characteristic of Methodism that the new birth is not attributed to Baptism but to justification, which is associated with conversion or the conscious enkindling of faith.

Wesley sought to avoid controversy as long as possible. His entire message was designed to awaken people to lives of active faith and holiness. It was natural, therefore, that his interest in doctrinal dispute would be minor. In spite of this, however, a number of rather profound differences of opinion gradually arose even within Methodism. Wesley subsequently developed the doctrine of faith and works in a direction which led him further away from the Reformation point of view and closer to the current English conception. He maintained that works are a necessary condition for justification. As a result of this, he came into conflict with the conservative Calvinists, who held fast to the belief that the merits of Christ are the sole ground of human salvation.

The teaching of predestination also became controversial. Wesley proclaimed universal grace in the Arminian manner and vehemently opposed the idea of divine reprobation. George Whitefield, with the Wesley brothers the foremost leader of the Methodist movement, followed the strict Calvinist tradition and preached double predestination. Because of these antithetical opinions, Methodism was divided into two factions.

Methodism would appear to provide the greatest contrast to the general theological thought of the Enlightenment with its expressed interest in rational arguments and a harmonious combination of philosophy and religion. Methodism answered the questions raised by deism in a way completely different, e. g., from Butler's dispassionate analogy. But just in its reaction against rationalism, Methodism was not without connection with the general development of thought in the English Church during the age of the Enlightenment.

TRANSITIONAL THEOLOGY

This designation serves to group together a number of German theologians of the first part of the 18th century who combined a conservative attitude toward the older Lutheran tradition with the philosophical position of the early Enlightenment and the theology of Pietism. In contrast to the bona fide Pietists, these men were deeply interested in systematic and historical theology, and they made significant contributions in these areas.

Johann Franz Buddeus (d. 1729, professor in Halle and Jena) was also active as a philosopher and sought, in several widely used textbooks, to replace Aristotelian scholastic philosophy with an "eclectic" philosophy. Buddeus stressed in particular the practical use of knowledge; metaphysics was limited to an explanation of certain concepts useful to theology; an empirical attitude is evident in his works. Parallels can be found in the writings of Christian Thomasius (d. 1728, professor in Halle), who was the first to give philosophic expression to the spirit of the new age.

In Buddeus' theology (cf. *Institutiones theologiae dogmaticae,* 1723) the orthodox Lutheran tradition was permeated by a new ferment. Practical ends were strongly emphasized: the goal of theology was thought to be the presentation of that which sinful man needs to know in order to be saved. Natural religion was placed at the side of revelation; it was held that in man's innermost being there is the ability to perceive and know God as the highest good. Even the truth of revelation must be legitimized before this natural knowledge of God (which is not only theoretical but above all practical, volitional). Revelation cannot contain anything that is contrary to natural religion; it can only supplement it.

Buddeus strove to understand theology in an empirical-historical manner. He was the first to write the history of the Old Testament period and the apostolic age. One of his foremost disciples in this area was Johann Georg Walch, well-known as a church historian and as a publisher of Luther's works.

Other "transitional theologians" should also be mentioned. Christoph Matthäus Pfaff (d. 1760, professor in Tübingen and Giessen) was influenced both by Pietism and by the deistic concept of a natural religion of reason, before which revelation must be legitimized. Johann Lorenz von Mosheim (d. 1755, professor in Helmstedt and Göttingen) applied the new scientific ideas to the field of theology. His *Institutiones historiae ecclesiasticae Novi Testamenti* (1726 and 1737) treated the history of the church from the point of view of secular history. The same historical point of view is applied to the Bible, whose truths must be scientifically presented by dogmatics.

THEOLOGICAL WOLFFIANISM

Christian Wolff (d. 1754, professor of mathematics and later also of philosophy at Halle and Marburg) sought to construct a rational scholastic philosophical system, using mathematics as a model. He formed his metaphysics not only on the law of contradiction (the same thing cannot be and not be at the same time) but also Leibniz' "principle of sufficient reason" ("All that exists must have a sufficient rational basis" and "Nothing exists apart from a sufficient rational basis"). While the older scholastic philosophy treated the diversity of existence in a more empirical fashion, Wolff's so-called demonstration method strove to describe things in such a way that one attribute is derived from another in a strictly logical relationship. Learning must be based on clear and distinct concepts; nothing should be set forth without proof — this was one of Wolff's basic principles.

When compared to transitional theology, Wolffianism represents a return to a more objective point of view. Independent of practical goals and subjective experience, theology, said Wolff, forms a logically consequent system, open to rational argumentation. This philosophy strongly influenced theological activity for several decades beginning with the 1720s and it also set the standards for contemporary education. The Pietists and some others opposed it on the grounds that it was a dangerous form of rationalism, but others felt that it provided the solution to the problem of learning even in the field of theology.

Among those who sought to apply Wolff's method in the area of dogmatics were Israel Gottlieb Canz (d. 1753, professor in Tübingen) and Jakob Carpov (d. 1768; *Theologia revelata methodo scientifica adornata*, 1737–65).

One of the foremost systematicians in the middle of the 18th century was Sigmund Jakob Baumgarten (d. 1757, professor at Halle), who was profoundly influenced by Wolffianism but at the same time continued the tradition stemming from orthodoxy and Pietism. His *Evangelische Glaubenslehre* (1759–60), the first major dogmatics written in German, was characterized by a sober rationality and a scrupulously logical division of the material. Harmony between reason and revelation was taken for granted; the very natural knowledge of God which we possess leads to the idea of a special revelation, and the rational proofs for the truth of Scripture convince us that the Bible is the source of this revelation.

The content of Scripture supplements natural religion. Baumgarten insisted on making a free, scientific investigation. He stood halfway between the older 18th-century tradition and neology proper, for which he prepared the way in certain respects — without, however, intending to deviate from the pure Lutheran doctrine.

NEOLOGY

This term denotes the stage in the theological development of the age of Enlightenment when English deism secured a foothold in the cultural life of Germany and when ideas typical of the Enlightenment began to permeate Protestant theology.

While Wolffianism desired to defend traditional church doctrine with the aid of reason, neology represents the transition to a conscious critique of *dogmas*. The doctrines of original sin and the Trinity, plus the Christology of traditional theology, were rejected with particular emphasis. These dogmas were attacked by the use of the historical method, the application of which had now begun. Christian dogma was looked upon as a variable factor inserted into historical development. Because of this, its content was relativized. It was subjected to the historical point of view, which led to a separation between dogma itself and contemporary theology.

Perhaps the most far-reaching change was that the same historical point of view was applied to the *Scriptures*. The Bible was inserted into the framework of human development. The Old Testament was separated from the New Testament as something belonging on a lower level. The content of the Bible was exposed to criticism on the basis of modern norms.

Both Wolffianism and neology held fast to the necessity of revelation. But whereas the former largely accepted dogma (having related it to logical, mathematical thought), neology proceeded on the basis of an expanded concept of reason. Feeling *(das Gemüt)* and moral consciousness were given the major emphasis. The concept of reason was thought to include these facets of man's spiritual equipment also. Religion was evaluated according to its practical benefit and according to "spiritual need." Dogma was considered to be largely ineffective, even downright harmful, with respect to morality. As a result it was severely reduced or reinterpreted.

The "moralistic psychologizing" of neology was combined with an optimistic view of man. The doctrine of original sin was thought to be contradictory to the idea of human value. There was no fall into sin. Man must be awakened to an understanding of his inherent goodness. The doctrine of the Trinity and the traditional Christology were also exposed to a thorough criticism. Christ was not looked upon as God's Son; it was rather said that He was the Savior sent by the Father. All references to atonement and satisfaction were expunged; the Spirit was thought of only as a power to do good.

Most prominent of the neologians was Johann Friedrich Wilhelm Jerusalem (d. 1789). As early as 1745 he criticized the teaching of original sin from the pulpit, and he gradually developed a position consistent with the new ideas mentioned above. He finally published his point of view in a book entitled *Observations Concerning the Major Truths of Religion* (1769–79). Other neologians included Johann Joachim Spalding (d. 1804), Johann Gottlieb Toellner (d. 1774), and Johann Christoph Döderlein (d. 1792).

Neology must be distinguished from naturalism, which corresponded to English deism. Like the deists, the naturalists disputed the necessity of revelation and desired to replace it with a natural religion.

Although the essentials of neology were derived from earlier sources, it nevertheless deserves its name, "the new teaching," for it was in this school that the modern spirit came to expression as a complete theological point of view. From this point on it is possible to speak of the "new Protestantism" as a dominating force in contrast to the "older Protestantism."

Johann Salomo Semler (d. 1791, professor in Halle) was another prominent leader of this school. He did much to promote the development of neology through the application of his historicocritical method, which he directed toward the Bible as well as the history of dogma. He was in some respects critical of the new ideas, however, and he was decidedly opposed to the naturalism of Karl Friedrich Bahrdt and Hermann Samuel Reimarus. Semler was most closely related to Baumgarten and sought (in spite of his radical new ideas) to retain a connection with the older Lutheranism. He felt, in fact, that he could quote Luther in support of his position. Because of this mediatory attitude his position is in many respects unclear and compromised.

Semler's major contribution was his application of the historicocritical method. It was his desire to renew theology and to release it from the bonds of dogma on the basis of an unbiased critique. For Semler, historical perspective was a means of release from dogma.

It was Semler who laid the foundation for the history of dogma as a special discipline. He was also one of the first Bible critics, inasmuch as he also applied the critical method of historical research to the Scriptures. He assumed that there is a distinct difference between the Old Testament and the New. To him the canon was simply the collection of writings which the church had accepted. He did not recognize any original canonical authority. The content of Scripture is to be judged with a moralistic measuring rod. The so-called literary criticism of the New Testament can be traced back to Semler's research — for example, his examination of the language of the Johannine literature.

In order to explain the lack of agreement between the New Testament and the moralistic religion which he used as a measuring rod, Semler assumed that Jesus and the apostles consciously adapted themselves to the ideas of their time (the so-called accommodation theory). Christianity can and ought therefore be developed over and beyond the Biblical position (this is its "perfectability"). Revelation does not coincide with Scripture. That which is essential therein are the basic truths which refer directly to man's moral improvement and can bring about ethical results (God as Father, Jesus as teacher, the Holy Spirit as the source of a new character).

Semler's attempt to set forth the new ideas without wholly rejecting the older tradition was expressed in the distinction he drew between *theology* and *religion,* and between *private* and *public religion.* He did not juxtapose theology with Biblical doctrine or with the content of revelation, as had been done earlier; to him, theology was merely the factual knowledge which theological professors discuss. Theology is, therefore, a human, historical consideration, changeable in content, depending on the time, place, and religious parties. In contrast to theology is religion, which denotes the living piety which coincides with the universal religious consciousness but at the same time is based on the Christian revelation. Vis-à-vis religion, theology has a historicocritical function. The close connection between theology and the faith of the church, which characterized the older tradition, was replaced by Semler with a sharp line of demarcation.

Semler also distinguished between private and public religion. While the individual has to realize his own religious feelings (in association with his moral consciousness), society, for the sake of public order and uniform religious practice, must hold fast to a certain confession and to certain doctrines, which do not entirely correspond to the intentions of individual piety.

So as Semler described it, the development of theology is not a sudden overthrow of the old and existing, but a cautious reform and a gradual perfection of the same.

In spite of the lack of clarity which characterized Semler's position, his ideas were of profound importance for subsequent developments. Friedrich Schleiermacher (see below) was, in many respects, Semler's chief heir. It was he, for example, who perpetuated the idea of the historical development of church doctrine. Semler and Schleiermacher were also united with each other (and with neology in general) by their freedom from the authority of Scripture in the earlier sense, by their critique of dogma, as well as by their subjective analysis of religion.

Johann August Ernesti (d. 1781, professor in Leipzig) was more conservative than Semler. His major contributions were made in the field of hermeneutics. It was his conviction that a historical-grammatical interpretation of Scripture should form the basis of theological activity. The interpretation of the Bible was placed on the same level with other interpretation. Work in the field of philology formed the point of departure. Ernesti's goal was an exegesis free from dogma. He did not recognize Pietism's demand concerning the personal piety of the interpreter. In spite of his conservative attitude, Ernesti was critical of traditional theology, and he rejected (among other things) the orthodox teaching of Christ's three offices.

RATIONALISM AND SUPERNATURALISM

The entire point of view of the age of Enlightenment is sometimes referred to as rationalism, but this is a somewhat crude generalization, inasmuch as the question of reason and revelation was solved in many different ways within various movements during this period. It is more proper, on the other hand, to reserve the designation "rationalism" for the concept which held that the religion of revelation includes and by degrees develops into a religion based entirely on reason. (Unlike deism, rationalism did not ignore the Christian heritage altogether.) Such rationalist ideas were expressed as early as in the 1770s by Gotthold Ephraim Lessing (d. 1781). They were characteristic of his opposition to both orthodoxy and neology. For also neology believed that the propositions of natural religion were guaranteed by revelation, while Lessing looked upon revelation as a vanquished stage: its content could be transformed into rational truth. Hence he opposed neology as well.

Theological rationalism in refined form is also to be found in Immanuel Kant's (d. 1804) book *Religion innerhalb der Grenzen der blossen Vernunft*, 1793 (trans. Theodore M. Greene and Hoyt H. Hudson, *Religion Within the Limits of Reason Alone*; New York: Harper Torchbook, 1960). According to Kant's own distinction, rationalism is different from naturalism (radical deism) in that it does not deny revelation. It does insist, however, that the moralistic religion of reason is the only necessary religion. The most important facet of the religious experience is the change of character whereby the "radical evil" in man is overcome and the good is brought forth. This is accomplished through punishment and repentance. The church, Christianity, can provide the impulse which leads to such salvation. Its teachings ought to be interpreted in accordance with moral ideas, which are alone universal and consistent with the religion of reason. Kant broke with the eudaemonism of the Enlightenment: he placed the absolute ethical demand in the primary position, and not happiness. On the other hand, he retained its Pelagian doctrine of salvation and its moralistic concept of religion. The deistic emphasis on God, virtue, and immortality had a firm place in his theory.

The foremost dogmatician of rationalism was Julius August Ludwig Wegscheider *(Institutiones theologiae Christianae*, 1815). He either rejected or misinterpreted the basic teachings of Christianity; miracles, as well as everything supernatural, were repudiated; conversion was thought of in a Pelagian sense; the sacraments were interpreted symbolically. Wegscheider explained the resurrection of Christ as a resuscitation from an "apparent death," and he asserted that the death of Christ symbolizes the fact that sacrifices have ceased. He did not accept the Atonement, and maintained that the Ascension was a fairy tale. The concept of original sin was rejected as a somber illusion, repentance was said to be man's own work, Baptism was classified as a ceremony of dedication, and the Lord's Supper as a memorial feast. — Karl Gottlieb Bretschneider stood somewhat closer to the doctrines of the church (cf. his *Handbuch der christlichen Dogmatik*, 1814).

Rationalism was deliberately opposed by *supernaturalism,* which was based on the necessity of revelation and the authority of Scripture. As the name implies, there were those who desired to defend the supernatural, that in Christianity which reason cannot comprehend. Both rationalism and supernaturalism had this trait in common, however: an intellectual concept of religion. The substance of religion was set forth in terms of doctrinal propositions, some of which are imbedded in man's reason, some of which have been given through revelation only. Also supernaturalism was characterized by a sober rationality. Attempts were made to prove the credibility of Scripture and to defend the content of revelation on the basis of rational argument. Representatives of this trend of thought included Gottlob Christian Storr (d. 1805, active in Tübingen) and Franz Volkmar Reinhard (d. 1812).

The contrast between rationalism and supernaturalism — which in fact was bridged over by a variety of mediating tendencies — was brought to an end as a result of Schleiermacher's new concept of religion. The influence of Romanticism, with its newly awakened sense of the historical in religion, plus its interest in the immediate and the transcendental, also contributed to this same end. When men ceased to think of religion as a collection of doctrines, and thought of it rather as an element in the personal life of the soul, the alternative between rationalism and supernaturalism was no longer relevant, for both could be united into a uniform point of view. Religion was no longer thought of in terms of morality and metaphysics but as an independent manifestation of man's spiritual life.

CHAPTER 33

Nineteenth-Century Developments

SCHLEIERMACHER

Friedrich Schleiermacher (d. 1834, professor in Berlin from 1810) was educated in a Moravian milieu, but he broke with the Herrnhut faith when he was 19. In his earlier writings, above all in the famous *Reden über die Religion an die Gebildeten unter ihren Verächtern*, 1800 (trans. John Oman, *On Religion: Speeches to Its Cultured Despisers;* New York: Harper Torchbook, 1958) he associated himself with Romanticism and gave expression to its newly awakened feeling for the religious.

One of Schleiermacher's greatest contributions to the history of theology was his attempt to describe the uniqueness of religion as a function of the human soul. In opposition to rationalism, he asserted in his *Reden* that religion does not consist of intellectual or moralistic elements; it rather refers to an independent area in the life of the spirit. Religion is not knowing or doing, but "the immediate consciousness of the universal existence of all finite things within the infinite and through the infinite, of all temporal things within the eternal and through the eternal" *(das unmittelbare Bewusstsein von dem allgemeinen Sein alles Endlichen im Unendlichen und durch das Unendliche, alles Zeitlichen im Ewigen und durch das Ewige).* He defined religion in the *Reden* as "intuition of the universe." In this immediate consciousness of oneness with all that is, man experiences the divine. The idea of God therefore coincides with a feeling of universal unity and identity with the infinite. This feeling was assumed to be inherent in the soul of man.

In *Der Christliche Glaube*, 1820–22 (trans. *Christian Faith;* New York: Harper Torchbooks 108 and 109) Schleiermacher's major work in the field of dogmatics, religion was defined as "the absolute feeling of dependence" *(das schlechthinige Abhängigkeitsgefühl).* The word "feeling" *(Gefühl)* was not used in the ordinary sense in this context, but to refer to something which is a part of the immediate self-consciousness. Man senses that he is absolutely dependent on the infinite. Therein lies religion — and it is this feeling of dependence which characterizes man as spirit.

It would be erroneous to think of this concept of religion as being purely subjective. Schleiermacher rather sought, in this context, to put an end to the contrast between subjective and objective: that which is ultimately human coincides with the divine or the infinite. In his innermost being and immediate self-consciousness, man experiences himself as being identical with the all. The objective and the subjective merge into one.

It can also be said of this concept of religion, on the other hand, that it abolishes all dualism: God and the world are thought of, in the final analysis, as identical. There was a pantheistic strain in Schleiermacher, particularly in the *Reden.* Evil cannot be conceived of as something hostile to God. The idea of a devil or of evil spirits was rejected. The spirit is supreme in man and cannot be thought of as something evil. Schleiermacher's point of view was, therefore, monistic.

Christianity was to Schleiermacher the highest if not the only expression of this religious consciousness. According to a definition provided in *Der Christliche Glaube,* Christianity is "a monotheistic form of piety of a teleological variety, in which all refers to the salvation brought to completion through Jesus of Nazareth" (11). In this context, salvation denotes that devout self-consciousness (the feeling of absolute dependence) has been realized. There was therefore a direct connection between Schleiermacher's general concept of religion and his understanding of the essence of Christianity.

This does not mean, however, as some have thought, that the entire Christian doctrine of faith can be deduced from this feeling of absolute dependence. The doctrine of faith is not based solely on universal principles. According to Schleiermacher, Christian dogma has both a historical and a speculative element. Theology presupposes an empirically discernible fellowship of faith, which is called the Christian church, and it is the function of dogmatics to describe the doctrine of faith as found in the church at a given point in time. Therefore the field of dogmatics is also included in historical theology. In his own dogmatics, *Der Christ-*

liche Glaube, Schleiermacher intended to set forth the faith as it was then found in the evangelical church. The speculative element in dogmatic theology is found in this, that the claims of faith constantly lead back to the feeling of absolute dependence and therefore to the concept of religion which is derived from universal rational science (or "ethics," in Schleiermacher's usage).

The claims of faith do not represent objective knowledge; they are, rather, expressions of devout self-consciousness. They do not describe the object of faith; they describe the personal function of faith. The Christian articles of faith are legitimized by the fact that they correspond to the devout Christian consciousness of faith, or to the Christian's inner experience (61, 1). The task of dogmatics is not to set forth the claims of faith but merely to give historical expression to the concept of faith as it is actually to be found within the church as a whole or within a certain branch of the church.

On the basis of these principles, Schleiermacher built up a uniform system, which included the various branches of theology and religion. *Ethics* is the speculative exposition of rational science which parallels natural science. Within ethics we find the universal definition of the concept of religion. The concrete description of the religions of mankind is provided in *the philosophy of religion. Theology,* the science which is required for the guidance of the church, is divided into philosophical, practical, and historical theology. The first of these (which, in turn, is divided into apologetics and polemics) is designed to present the essence and uniqueness of Christianity. *Dogmatics,* which is included in historical theology, describes the Christian faith as it appears at a given time or in a certain church body.

In *Der Christliche Glaube* (1820–22, 2d ed. 1830), we find Schleiermacher's own presentation of evangelical doctrine. The characteristic ideas of this book, which was epoch-making in its time, must be looked at here at several points:

1. In the doctrine of God, Schleiermacher generally concurred in the philosophic assumptions. The consciousness of God is involved in devout self-consciousness. To sense that one is absolutely dependent is the same as to be conscious of standing in relation to God (4). In this immediate self-consciousness the being of God coincides with man's own being. The question of the existence of God becomes irrelevant.

Dogmatics need only consider the consciousness of God, which coincides with devout self-consciousness.

The doctrines of *creation* and *preservation* are treated in a corresponding manner as expressions which show that God and the natural context are one. The world is absolutely dependent on God. This is implicit in the idea of creation, which therefore does not refer to an event in time. The doctrine of providence expresses the consciousness that man's dependence on nature coincides with his dependence on God. The concept of divine intervention, of miracles or of revelation in the true sense of the term, was rejected. As already indicated in another context, this view of creation cannot be combined with the idea of an evil spiritual power. As a result, no reality or influence can be ascribed to the devil.

2. The Christian teaching of *sin* similarly caused some trouble for Schleiermacher. Sin is related to the feeling of mental discomfort which is always present in the devout consciousness of God, since this is impeded by sensuality. Sin can be described, therefore, as the flesh in opposition to the spirit; it is this struggle which hampers the consciousness of God. On the other hand, the idea that sin is a transgression of God's law was rejected. Schleiermacher did not put sin into the field of the will but into that of the pious feelings. One cannot speak of a fall or say that sin originated in a voluntary act. Sin was thought of as being in man originally. It is implicit in the fact that the sense of dependence is not yet complete. The concept of original sin was repudiated as inadequate. Schleiermacher thought of original sin in terms of humanity's common and original sinfulness or inability to do what is good.

The concept of sin lost its ethical character in Schleiermacher's theology. He thought of sin not only as something evil but as something included in the consciousness of God — the necessary presupposition for the need of salvation and thereby also for the development of a superior consciousness of God. The consciousness of sin is a lower stage in the development of the good. The contrast between God and sin is eliminated. Schleiermacher assumed it to be part of God's own order that the consciousness of sin must precede salvation. Sin is undeveloped nature. It is not contrary to creation; it is a part of it. Schleiermacher's idea of sin represents an attempt to harmonize the Christian concept with the monistic view of the world from which he proceeded.

3. Schleiermacher described *salvation* as the transition to a superior consciousness of God, unhampered by sensuality, which can be realized in the Christian congregation through faith in Jesus Christ. Jesus had a perfect consciousness of God, the power and blessedness of which He imparts to human nature. Christ is the second Adam, the prototype of the new humanity. His unimpaired consciousness of God denotes the fulfillment of creation. From the very beginning, human nature has been inclined toward this unity with God, but it could not be realized because of the presence of sin in man. The influence exerted upon man by the person of Christ is of the same kind as other spiritual power. One cannot therefore speak of atonement in the proper sense of the term. (Schleiermacher did use the word *Versöhnung*, but with an entirely different meaning; it referred particularly to the blessedness conferred by Christ). Christ's work — or His suffering, death, and resurrection — has no bearing on salvation, but only His person, which represents the perfect consciousness of God. Neither was forgiveness of sin looked upon as the substance of salvation; the only thing that matters is the transformation of man with the subsequent improvement of his religious feelings. No significance can be ascribed to Christ's suffering on the cross in this context. The Passion story serves only as an exemplary illustration of perseverance in suffering. Schleiermacher looked upon the Resurrection as resuscitation from an apparent death, and he referred to the Ascension as Christ's actual death. Salvation refers only to "God being in Christ" *(das Sein Gottes in Christo)* and to the posthumous impact of His person — not to Christ's death and resurrection.

4. In Schleiermacher's *Christology* we find a projection of his general concept of God-man relationships. The unity of the divine and the human received its perfect expression in the person of Christ. The person of Christ certainly denotes an improvement over humanity as it was prior to His coming, but at the same time He only represents the highest development of that which is human. Creation and salvation are only separate stages in one and the same natural process. Schleiermacher did not recognize any history of salvation. His reinterpretation of the Gospel of Christ's death and resurrection has already been touched upon. In this transformation of Christology into a philosophy-of-religion concept, Schleiermacher's theology reminds us of Gnosticism. His neglect of Christ's death and resurrection is, for example, something he had in common with the Gnostics.

The same unity of the divine and the human which we see in a person in Christ can also be found in a fellowship, in the church. The church is the direct continuation of Christ's appearance; it represents the new humanity, for which Christ is the prototype. Schleiermacher did not, however, accept the idea of Christ's dominion over the world. Man is related to Christ only in his own inner life and in the fellowship of the church.

5. The doctrine of the *Trinity* was not emphasized by Schleiermacher as it was by Hegel (see below). The former did not feel that this doctrine gave any direct expression to the devout self-consciousness of the Christian. Schleiermacher recommended a radical alteration of the doctrine of the Trinity as taught by the church. He identified himself most intimately with the Sabellian point of view (see above, pp. 71–72). God is one indivisible substance. The Son and the Spirit are merely forms of revelation for this substance. The Holy Spirit is identified with the public spirit which animates the fellowship of believers.

6. The *eschatological* statements do not apply to devout self-consciousness any more than the doctrine of the Trinity, inasmuch as they refer to a future event. Schleiermacher did mention them at the end of *Der Christliche Glaube,* however; he called them "prophetic teachings." The idea of eternal damnation was repudiated as being inconsistent with Christian feelings. Schleiermacher rather accepted and proclaimed the teaching of universal restoration, accomplished in the power of salvation. This opinion was most consistent with his naturalistic reinterpretation of the history of salvation and his monistic world view.

7. *Der Christliche Glaube* has strikingly little connection with the *Scriptures.* This was justified on principle: it was Schleiermacher's intention to describe faith as it occurs in religious experience, and in this endeavor the Scriptures are allowed to speak only when they express the same consciousness of faith.

According to Schleiermacher, only the New Testament is normative. The Old Testament is found in the canon only because of its historical connection with the New Testament. But it does not serve to express the Christian spirit, and it therefore lacks proper doctrinal authority.

The New Testament was certainly thought of as normative, but

Schleiermacher searched its contents above all to find material that coincided with the devout consciousness of the Christian. The true doctrine is that which succeeds in maintaining itself through development. It has been said that Schleiermacher replaced the principle of Scripture with an "evolutionary principle of tradition." The consciousness of faith existing in the church is the final authority. The Bible is placed on the same level with the Christian tradition, although it enjoys chronological priority and actually contains the most significant description of religious experience.

The authority of Scripture cannot serve as the basis for faith; it rather assumes that faith is already present. The idea of Scripture's self-evidence or of the ability of the Word to create faith was eliminated.

Revelation, in this context, was synonymous with devout self-consciousness, which denotes God's presence in man.

The general concept of religion was therefore placed above the Scriptures and the Word. The use of Scriptural proof in dogmatics is justified only if this intimates that a certain doctrinal proposition stands out as a legitimate expression of Christian piety.

Schleiermacher's theological system represents a thorough transformation of traditional dogmatics. It was an attempt to lay a new foundation for the science of theology. As a result of Schleiermacher's efforts, theology came to be looked upon as a science, on the same level as the secular branches of learning. Dogmatics became a historically descriptive exposition of devout Christian self-consciousness. In opposition to rationalism and supernaturalism, religion was depicted as a distinct sphere at the side of the intellectual and moral spheres. Theological statements, as expressions of religious feelings, have their own unique character.

But even though Schleiermacher brought theology to a place of eminence in contemporary culture and discovered new ways of solving its scholarly problems, his system of doctrine — as judged purely on the basis of content — was essentially alien to the evangelical doctrine of faith. His dogmatics, based as it was on the theory of immediate self-consciousness as the foundation of religion, in reality led to a gnostic, monistic system, whose connection with historic Christianity did not prevent the reinterpretation and distortion of essential elements in the Christian faith.

Even though Schleiermacher had few personal disciples, the significance of his theology has been exceedingly widespread, not only in the 19th century (when a number of theological schools were influenced by him to a greater or lesser degree) but in our own century as well.

A thorough but sometimes misleading critique of Schleiermacher's position has come from the ranks of the dialectical theologians (Barth, Brunner), who have attempted to break with the entire tradition of which he was the originator and chief representative.

HEGEL AND SPECULATIVE THEOLOGY

Georg Wilhelm Friedrich Hegel (d. 1831, professor in Berlin from 1818), German idealism's most influential philosopher, played a significant role also in the history of theology by virtue of his religious and philosophical principles and his extensive impact on 19th-century theology and historical research.

Hegel came out against Schleiermacher and the Romantics, for whom religion manifested itself in immediate intuition and in a sense of the absolute. According to Hegel, religion (like the life of the mind in general) appears above all in the form of man's thoughts or concepts. Feeling is the lowest expression of consciousness, while thought — that which distinguishes man from the animals — is the highest. "If God reveals Himself to man, He does so essentially for man as a thinking being . . . animals do not have any religion." Hegel's system provided room for the scholarly and speculative aspects of theology. The difference between him and Schleiermacher can be accounted for in part on the basis of their diverse religious backgrounds: for whereas the latter came out of the Herrnhut milieu, Hegel was brought up in an "old Protestant" environment (in Swabia).

For Hegel, concept or scientific thought coincided with reality. Truth is to be found in the system which gives expression to those thoughts which, having been contemplated, become conscious of themselves. This is also called *Der Geist* — the spirit. The spirit is the absolute, the only reality.

The ideal reality, according to Hegel, is not a static form-world as in Platonic idealism, but one which also includes spatial reality and historical development. It was characteristic of Hegel to insert historical development into his system — and this was probably his foremost philosophical contribution. He combined philosophical speculation with a profound understanding of historical reality.

The absolute, the true reality, and fully developed knowledge always include a progression which Hegel assumed to be of a dialectical, logical variety, at the same time that he also understood it to be a historical change. Hence it was that Hegel based his system on the so-called dialectical method: every concept points beyond itself to another, opposite concept; the opposition is resolved in a higher unity. This progression (from thesis to antithesis to synthesis) forms the pattern for the development of ideas as well as for the course of history. It also provides the basis for the universal system in which Hegel sought to summarize both knowledge and reality.

The absolute appears as pure conception. It is this which constitutes *logic*, the first part of philosophy. But the absolute is transformed into its opposite, *das Anderssein* — the individual, the particular, the "thing-ish." This aspect of knowledge is treated under the heading of *natural philosophy*. Finally, the absolute reverts to a consciousness of itself and becomes spirit. The philosophy of the spirit is divided into the doctrine of the subjective spirit (anthropology; phenomenology, i. e., the teaching of the development of consciousness and knowledge; psychology), of the objective spirit (morality, law, politics), and of the absolute spirit (art, religion, and philosophy).

There is complete harmony between religion and philosophy in the Hegelian system. Both have the same object, the absolute. Christianity is the final stage in the development of religion. Its counterpart in the field of philosophy is the Hegelian system (according to Hegel).

Hegel presented Christianity as the absolute religion. He felt that the dialectical method was to be found in the doctrine of the Trinity. Divinity has developed in three stages. God is in His eternal idea (the Father's kingdom), He reveals Himself in finitude, in consciousness, and in action (the Son's kingdom), and then reverts to Himself in unity with the finite in the congregation (the Spirit's kingdom).

Hegel's influence extended far beyond those who called themselves "Hegelians." His dialectical method has, for example, exerted a strong influence on the writing of both sacred and secular history and has also contributed new ideas to the presentation of the history of dogma.

During Hegel's lifetime there were those who looked upon his system as the ultimate solution of theological problems. It was thought that the entire field of theology might be reconciled to the most advanced education of that day on the basis of this system. Christian teachings were inserted into the Hegelian framework. Revelation was placed on the same level with the absolute spirit, with speculative knowledge — which was looked upon at the same time as God's own knowledge and the human spirit's knowledge of the absolute.

Among the representatives of this orthodox Hegelianism (commonly referred to as "speculative theology") were Karl Daub (d. 1836, professor in Heidelberg) and Philipp Konrad Marheineke (d. 1846, professor in Berlin.) The latter was critical of Schleiermacher, whose description of religion he considered one-sided. To the Hegelians, religion was not merely life and feeling but, above all, knowledge of the truth. Hegelian philosophy was looked upon as the scientific form for the presentation of the Christian faith.

Hegelianism, however, also gave rise to a tendency which drew conclusions entirely different from Hegel's. This was the so-called Hegelian "left," represented (among others) by David Friedrich Strauss (d. 1874), who, in his *Das Leben Jesu* (1835 f.), set forth the Gospel message as a myth. At the center of religious faith he replaced the person of Christ with "the idea of humanity." Strauss felt that Christological statements ought to be referred to this collective concept, in view of the fact that the historical Jesus was only an ordinary man, a teacher of morality and religion.

Another member of the Hegelian "left" was the philosopher Ludwig Feuerbach (d. 1872). His concept of religion as a factor in human life devolved into a specific denial of the existence of God. God, said he, is merely the sum and substance of human qualities, and faith in God is the result of man's wishful thinking.

RESTORATION THEOLOGY

In the 1830s and 1840s a process of change began, the effects of which are felt even in our own time. The golden age of Romanticism and German idealism had ended by then. New ideologies burgeoned forth, socialism and materialism, which took an entirely different position vis-à-vis religion. As a result of their influence the rationalistic interpretation of Christianity increased once again.

At the same time the economic and political alteration of society was taking place — a transformation designated by the terms industrial-

362

ism and liberalism. The patriarchal order began to dissolve, and the modern welfare state came into being with both new political ideals and greatly altered social conditions.

No less extensive were the changes made in the scientific (scholarly) field. Modern natural science, the exact writing of history, the division of universal education as a result of strict specialization, the advance of technology — these are some of the phenomena which characterize the epoch which began at this time. This epoch confronted theology with the task of solving — under new conditions — the question of Christianity and culture, of science and religion, a task which has scarcely been taken care of satisfactorily even in our own day.

Many solutions were attempted in the period of time with which we are now chiefly concerned. It was characteristic of these attempts that they either reached back to the older tradition, in order thus to preserve church doctrine intact (restoration theology), or else they subjected themselves entirely to the spirit of the age and thereby surrendered certain fundamental aspects of the Christian faith ("free" or "liberal" theology). The kind of synthesis between Christianity and culture which we find in Hegel and Schleiermacher could no longer be reached. Uniformity in theology and church life was lost, as was the uniformity of cultural life in general.

Die Erweckung ("the Awakening"), the revival movement which was already developing at the beginning of the century, can be classified with restoration theology — i. e., the tendencies to attain theological goals primarily by turning back to the older, prerationalistic tradition. *Die Erweckung* was an heir of the older Pietism, above all in its Württemberg form, but it was also related to the newly awakened religious interest of Romanticism and German idealism. Its proponents were pleased to claim Luther as a patron (the Reformation jubilee of 1817 served to actualize Reformation ideas), but no importance was attached to the difference between Lutheran and Reformed theology. The influence of the Awakening upon church life in general was of more significance than the contributions it made to systematic theology. This movement was more interested in historical theology and Biblical erudition than it was in dogmatics.

The major spokesmen for what was called "repristination theology" were Ernst Wilhelm Hengstenberg (d. 1869) and Friedrich Adolf Philippi (d. 1882; *Kirchliche Glaubenslehre,* 1854–79, in six volumes).

This school was concerned about the resuscitation of old Protestant theology, which was considered an adequate (and for the evangelical church the normative) interpretation of the Bible and the confessions. The application of modern science to theology was rejected, as well as the idealistic transformation of Christianity. Repristination theology exerted a great influence on church life, and its attempts to make the older tradition vital and living were in many respects fruitful both for the contemporary church and theology. Its achievements were limited, however, by its lack of attention to Luther's theology and also by reason of the fact that its leaders seemed to ignore the difference between the intellectual assumptions of the old Protestant period and of the 19th century. They instinctively accepted the world view of their own age and thereby fell into contradictions. A genuine repristination proved to be impossible. The older Lutheran position was denied at several points. The distinction between Lutheranism and Calvinism was considered unimportant. Hengstenberg therefore championed the cause of unionism. But as a result of its strong opposition to Pietism and the Enlightenment, as well as to Schleiermacher and idealism, repristination theology did assist in keeping the older Lutheran tradition alive during the 19th century. It should also be mentioned that Hengstenberg tried to restore the Old Testament to its place in the life of the church. Heinrich Schmid's widely used summary of old Lutheran theology, *Die Dogmatik der evangelisch-lutherischen Kirche*, 1843 (trans. Charles A. Hay and Henry E. Jacobs, *Doctrinal Theology of the Evangelical Lutheran Church;* Minneapolis: Augsburg Publishing House), is another example of the efforts put forth by the repristination theologians.

"New Lutheranism" was similar to repristination theology, but it is usually referred to as a separate tendency. It too was strongly confessional and sharply opposed to the spirit of the new age. The new Lutherans rejected the dominant subjective interpretation of religion and sought for a palpable, objective reality which could guarantee Christianity's truth and its continued existence. This objective foundation was found, not in the Word and in faith as in the older Protestantism, but in the church, which was looked upon as an "institution" through which the gifts of salvation are bestowed upon man generation after generation.

Friedrich Julius Stahl (d. 1861), a lawyer, provided the legal basis for this new concept of the church. In his view church and state are divinely established institutions into which the individual is placed and to whose authority he is obligated to subject himself. Among the theologians and churchmen who interpreted and sought to give practical application to high-church ideas concerning the church, the clerical office, and the confessions were Theodor Kliefoth (d. 1895; *Acht Bücher von der Kirche,* 1854), Wilhelm Löhe (d. 1872, founder of the institutions at Neuendettelsau), and August Friedrich Christian Vilmar (d. 1868). The sacraments were strongly emphasized as the church's objective foundation, partly at the expense of the doctrine of the Word and of faith.

With respect to the church question, and other facets of Christian life, the intention was to revitalize what was considered the original Lutheran position (hence the name, "new Lutheranism") and not simply to go back to orthodoxy, as the repristination theologians did. The new Lutherans were strongly opposed to the Reformed tradition, as well as to the burgeoning free-church tendency. Furthermore, they emphasized the unity of the visible and the invisible church (the objective institution and the spiritual fellowship of the true believers) and criticized the Pietists for distinguishing between the two. In doing this they gave expression to a Lutheran idea. In the development of their ecclesiology, however, the new Lutherans accepted to some extent ideas which were not characteristic of original Lutheranism. The church and the sacraments were looked upon as institutional ordinances, to a certain degree independent of the Word.

The conservative tendency also brought with it a renewed demand to base theology on the Bible. A unique form of Biblical theology was created by Johann Tobias Beck (d. 1878, professor in Tübingen). He combined the older Württemberg tradition of Bengel and Oetinger with a strong infusion of idealistic philosophy. Beck's theology was distinguished by a marked speculative tendency. The content of the Bible was thought of as a divine conceptual system, uniform in nature, which brings to us the living power of the Holy Spirit and the supernatural realities of the kingdom of God. This Beckian Biblicism has exerted a great influence, in Finland for example.

In Sweden a position closely related to German new Lutheranism was developed by a group of Lundensian theologians, including Ebbe Gustaf Bring (d. 1884), Wilhelm Flensburg (d. 1897), and Anton Niklas Sundberg (d. 1900). Their sounding board was a journal called *Svensk Kyrkotidning* ("Swedish Church News"), published from 1855 to 1863.

The Grundtvig movement in Denmark, which was of great significance for both church and culture, can also be included under "restoration" tendencies, even though it was unique in many ways, both in comparison with contemporary developments and otherwise. Nikolai Frederik Severin Grundtvig (1783–1872) was influenced by the rationalism of the Enlightenment and later on by Romanticism and German idealism. He also became interested in Nordic mythology at an early age, and this came to play an important role in his symbol formation and in his theological development. There was a period in his life when he was a staunch supporter of Lutheran orthodoxy, but his strong historical sense caused him to doubt the orthodox doctrine of inspiration. He made what he himself called the "marvelous discovery" that the foundation of the Christian faith is not to be found in the Scriptures (viewed as written words), but in the living Word in the church, in the sacraments and in the confession used in connection with Baptism. It was on this basis that Grundtvig developed his concept of the church. The ideal, as he saw it, is a free state church, which can embrace various points of view without organizational coercion or compulsion of belief. Grundtvig held that the original, popular form of religiosity, symbolized by Nordic mythology, prepared the way for the coming of Christianity. In his mind, Christian and national elements were combined into one.

Grundtvig was inspired at many points by the theology of Irenaeus. This influence is reflected, for example, in the central position accorded the confession of faith, as well as in the dominant importance of such categories as "death-life" (instead of "guilt-forgiveness") and "creation-restoration" in his teaching of salvation. Grundtvig was opposed to the doctrine of original sin as then taught, and he believed that man retained a likeness of God which could form a connecting link with Christian instruction and upbringing.

MEDIATING THEOLOGY; THE CHRISTOLOGICAL QUESTION

The tradition which began with Schleiermacher was carried on in particular by the tendency which is usually referred to as mediating theology. The appearance of this tendency can be dated from the year 1827, when the journal entitled *Theologische Studien und Kritiken* was founded. Its stated program was to mediate between Biblical faith and the modern scientific spirit. But at the same time that this theological school sought to mediate between Christianity and science, it also attempted to mediate between various schools of thought as well. Schleiermacher was the guiding light *par excellence,* but there were close ties with the older tradition too, as well as with the Awakening and at times also with Hegel.

The chief spokesmen for this school were such Schleiermacher disciples as Karl Immanuel Nitzsch (d. 1868; his *System der Christlichen Lehre,* 1829, was one of the most widely used dogmatics books of the day) and August Detler Christian Twesten (d. 1876). Mention should also be made of Isaak August Dorner (d. 1884), who with the aid of Hegelian thought forms attempted to present a new exposition of Christology (*Entwicklungsgeschichte der Lehre von der Person Christi,* 1839 ff.).

Dorner found it difficult to combine the picture of the historical Jesus, as created by modern research, and the old doctrine of the two natures, and this formed the background of his Christological study. He rejected the idea of the "enhypostasis" (see above, pp. 103–105) and taught that the human nature is an independent person. The divinity of Christ was thought of in this context as a gradually developing unity with the Father. Generally speaking, this concept represented a surrender of the traditional view of the Incarnation. If the divinity of Christ is set forth in terms of His fellowship with God — as a representative and prototype of humanity — this is no longer a question of a Logos who became man, or of a true "God-man."

Another attempt to solve the Christological problem is found in what is called *kenoticism.* This was championed above all by the Erlangen theologian Gottfried Thomasius (d. 1875; *Christi Person und Werk,* 1852–61). He was highly critical of Dorner, and in contrast to the latter held fast to the traditional teaching of the two natures. Thomasius' basic idea was that when the Logos became man, He divested Himself *(kenosis)* of all that exceeds human consciousness and laid aside the divine attributes which indicate relationship to the world (omnipotence, omnipresence, etc.). When He was glorified, Christ took these back. In this way the attempt was made to do justice to Christ's humanity and also retain the old categories. It must be noted, however, that this kenosis doctrine deviated from the older tradition in certain respects. In classical Christology it is not the divine Logos who is said to have divested Himself; rather it is believed that the human nature with which the Logos was united in Christ refrained from using the divine attributes. These remained with Christ during His earthly life, however, in the divine person.

This kenoticist concept clearly illustrates the problem which pervaded all of 19th-century theology: How can the ancient categories of Christian doctrine be combined with the modern point of view? This problem was revealed in the fact that even the conservative and churchly tendencies found it hard to maintain the older tradition intact.

Another of the mediating theologians was a Dane, Hans Lassen Martensen (d. 1884; his *Dogmatik,* 1849, was used for a long time as a textbook in higher education, also in Sweden). Martensen accepted the kenoticist Christology, which he developed in a masterful way. He was influenced not only by Schleiermacher but also by Hegel and by a theosophical mysticism which set its mark especially on his view of the sacraments.

The most distinctive representative of this school was Richard Rothe (d. 1867), who, with assistance from Schleiermacher and Hegel, built up a complete philosophy of religion as set forth in his *Theologische Ethik* (1845–48). He went beyond the boundaries of mediating theology and actually stood closer to the point of view of liberal theology.

THE ERLANGEN SCHOOL

An independent theological principle was worked out by the so-called Erlangen theologians, who were otherwise most closely associated with the confessional group. The founder of this school was Adolf Harless (d. 1879), who based his theology to a large extent on Luther studies. He also developed the characteristic principle of the Erlangen method, which held that the content of Scripture and the individual Christian's personal experience of salvation correspond with one another.

Johann Christian Konrad von Hofmann (d. 1877), the best known of the Erlangen theologians, made his greatest contributions in the field of Biblical interpretation. His magnum opus, *Weissagung und Erfüllung* (1841–44), sought to show that prophecy does not only include a foretelling or a presentiment but a profound interpretation of the contemporary situation, based on the fact that history points beyond itself to that which will one day be fulfilled. All of Scripture was interpreted as a uniform history of salvation, in which the Old Testament points forward to Christ, and the New Testament points forward to the consummation. In another great work, *Der Schriftbeweis* (1852–56), Hofmann set forth the fundamentals of his theological method.

According to Hofmann, a theological system can be tested on the basis of the three objective factors which form the foundation of theological statements. These are: the experience of the new birth, the church, and the Holy Scriptures. Hofmann himself was particularly devoted to the Scriptural test. A system must be in harmony with the history of salvation as presented in the Scriptures. Essentially the method Hofmann outlined amounts to this: the fact of the new birth concludes the history of salvation, which is implied in it. The testimony of experience and Scripture must mutually support each other at all times. The trend of thought is approximately this: that which makes a man a Christian is a fact immediately accessible to theology, viz., the personal fellowship between God and man, mediated through Jesus Christ. Cf. Hofmann's famous saying: "I as a Christian am the most fitting material for me as a theologian" *(Ich der Christ bin mir dem Theologen eigenster Stoff meiner Wissenschaft)*. This fact involves the entire history of salvation as described in the Bible — the eternal as the presupposition of the historical and the temporal from creation to fulfillment. The validity of this argument, which for the most part was scarcely advocated even by Hofmann himself, has been sharply questioned.

The experiential and subjective basis of Hofmann's method brought him into close contact with both the Awakening and the theology of Schleiermacher. Of greater significance for posterity was his work in the field of Biblical theology, in which he associated with the Württemberg school (Bengel, Beck). His interpretation of Scripture was distinguished above all by the application of the point of view of the history of salvation. In general, Hofmann's theology marked the transition from a more philosophical and speculative theology to one more thoroughly conditioned by historical perspective.

Hofmann attempted to replace the orthodox doctrine of salvation with a new theory: The death of Christ, said he, was only the demonstration of an obedience and love which conquers sin and death. An atonement in the true sense was out of the question. This attitude elicited strong opposition, even among theologians of kindred spirit. In order to defend his theory, Hofmann sought to show that Luther, in contrast to later Lutheranism, supported a corresponding point of view.

This attempt to show how Luther's theology was different from subsequent Lutheranism can be considered, to some extent, the beginning of modern Luther research. Theodosius Harnack wrote his famous book *Luthers Theologie* (1862–86) in opposition to these tendencies.

In general the Erlangen school adopted a conservative position that was strongly attached to the older tradition. G. Thomasius, whose kenoticist concept was touched upon earlier, provides us with a good example of this in his *Die Christliche Dogmengeschichte* (1874–76). He described the theology of the Formula of Concord as the conclusive summit of the history of dogma, to which all prior doctrinal developments pointed.

KIERKEGAARD

Kierkegaard's significance for modern theological developments is sufficient justification for us to devote a special section of this history of 19th-century theology to his ideas.

Søren Kierkegaard (1813–55) was thoroughly trained in aesthetics and philosophy. He was also trained in theology, but he never occupied any position in the church; he devoted himself exclusively to his authorship. His brilliant, creative literary power was placed in the service of an incisive critique of ideas, concerned above all with Romanticism and the Hegelian system, both of which were, according to Kierkegaard, expressions of an attitude which did not touch the true seriousness of life and the existential decision which is necessary if man is to "find himself in his eternal validity." As an author, Kierkegaard's chief objective was to describe what real Christianity is. "Thus all [my] activity as an author concerns this: within Christendom to be a Christian." During his first literary period, which ended with the writing of his *Concluding Unscientific Postscript* (1846), he sought to depict the way to the Christian "stage" of life as this is confronted by other ideals, which he called the aesthetic and the ethical stages. In the later period, Kierkegaard's concept of the religious ideal became increasingly acute, and he accused the contemporary church of treason vis-à-vis original, New Testament Christianity. He finally came to present Christianity above all as the imitation of Christ in the tribulation of obedience and loneliness.

Some of the main ideas in Kierkegaard's critique of contemporary speculative philosophy and of the spirit of the church can be illustrated by an explication of certain basic categories which he used over and over again, and through a description of the "stages" which, as he saw it, were characteristic of the development of man's life. In what follows we shall pay particular attention to Kierkegaard's concepts of "existence" and "the individual" — two of his basic categories.

What Kierkegaard meant by "existence" is perhaps most evident in the description he provided of the "stages" of life in such works as *Either — Or* (1843) and *Stages on Life's Way* (1845).

The three "stages" — the aesthetic, the ethical, and the religious — do not refer so much to a personal, individual development as they do to three distinct points of view or attitudes about life. The primary aim in this entire presentation of the stages is to determine as carefully as possible what it means to be a Christian. If one does not presuppose this point of view, he cannot understand Kierkegaard's description of man or his concept of "existence." It is at this point that modern existentialist philosophy is radically different from its presumed master.

The various points of view are not described with the use of abstract formulae; Kierkegaard rather does this by reflecting them in the lives of different fictitious individuals who appear in his pseudonymous writings (John the Seducer, Assessor Wilhelm, Anti-Climacus, etc.). By stepping back in favor of these various pseudonyms, Kierkegaard intended to bring the reader in an indirect way into an existential situation involving a concrete decision. Kierkegaard sought, through the use of this method — comparable to the "intellectual midwifery" of Socrates — to get away from objective thought and historical observation, which he did not wish to reject in themselves but which he considered of no value in delineating the nature of Christianity. This ought to be added, that we have hereby merely touched upon one of Kierkegaard's reasons for using pseudonyms. The problem they pose has been thoroughly discussed by Kierkegaard scholars, and it has been shown that a number of other factors prompted Kierkegaard to publish some of his writings in this manner.

The *aesthetic* stage is characteristic of the superficial epicure, who lives exclusively for visible, temporal, and incidental goals and who judges life from the vantage point of beauty. The aesthetic man is alien to ethical decision, "the choice." Furthermore, since he is limited to the external and finite elements of life, he is unable to relate the eternal to the temporal — that is, to find a synthesis between time and eternity, which is characteristic of Christianity. The speculative individual, who by means of objective thought flees from situations in which he must make a choice, is also found on the aesthetic level.

The *ethical* stage begins to exist when a man enters into a relationship with the absolute — when he is confronted by God's unconditioned demand in "the choice" between good and evil. The ethical does not consist of certain reasonable, universal regulations — as Hegel said — but of an absolute demand on the conscience, which confronts the individual with an "either — or." In this ethical "choice" the individual finds himself "in his eternal validity." He either achieves or he misses the destiny which is God's will for his life. In *Fear and Trembling* (1843) Kierkegaard sets forth Abraham's offering of Isaac as an example of a man in a situation where he must make a choice. Abraham's faith was such that he could humbly obey the divine demand, even though it was contrary to all that was reasonable.

The ethical — unfulfillable — demand forces man to consider his own life with a seriousness which is marked by the eternal weight of choice. This in turn induces within him a condition of remorse or repentance, for he can see that he does not meet the eternal demands adequately. And then it is that the ethical stage leads directly over to the religious stage, with which it partially coincides. For in and with the "ethical" decision, man becomes conscious of God. It is repentance — the knowledge of guilt — which distinguishes the religious stage from the ethical.

Kierkegaard distinguished between a general religious attitude ("religiosity A") and the true Christian stage ("religiosity B"). The latter consists of Christ's revelation (God in time), of a consciousness of *sin* (a consciousness of total sinfulness as over against a general consciousness of *guilt*), and of faith in the forgiveness of sin in the power of Christ's atonement.

Within the Christian (the paradox-religious) stage the synthesis between eternity and time, which is man's lot in life, is realized. To die away from the immediacy of the aesthetic in "the moment" — i. e., in the ever-present now, where eternity impinges on time — to become nothing before God and, cognizant of one's own nothingness before the eternal demands, to grasp the Christ who is present in faith — this is to realize "the synthesis," to live in existence.

It is on the basis of this concept of existence — understood either in

372

its general character or in its specific Christian sense — that one must understand Kierkegaard's statement that "subjectivity is truth." Objective thought, or speculation, is a flight from existence, from decision. Knowledge arrives at the truth only when it is related to an individual's existence, to the thinking subject's own decision, to the synthesis between the finite and the infinite. This is not, therefore, a question of "subjectivism" in the usual sense. True knowledge presupposes that the individual stands in an existential relationship to his object. Kierkegaard's description of the Christian's relationship to God is the best illustration of what he means by this. He does not refer to a general, philosophical theory of existential knowledge. When Kierkegaard spoke of "the existential," he was thinking above all of the synthesis between the temporal and the eternal — "the passionately infinite interest in one's personal eternal salvation" — which is faith's prerequisite.

Kierkegaard often emphasized the fact that in his writings he turned to "the individual." The ethical-religious decision applies to the individual only. The masses, or the human race in general, do not form a link between the individual and the absolute. Christianity is realized only in the faith of the individual. Christ is the One who is always present, with whom the man of faith becomes "contemporaneous," not by reaching back in history to the Christ who walked on earth but by becoming one with Him and receiving His presence in "the moment," in the present situation. "Contemporaneousness" is therefore one of the main concepts used in describing the Christian faith (as, e. g., in *Training in Christianity*, 1850).

The Christian life is characterized by "imitation," by which Kierkegaard meant not an *imitatio* in the medieval sense but an emulation of Christ in the suffering of reconciliation and in conquering love. (Cf. *The Works of Love*, 1847, and *Training in Christianity*)

In the midst of his bitter controversy with the church, which formed the dramatic end of Kierkegaard's literary activity, he emphasized more and more the necessity of offense. The hatred and persecution of the world are inevitable in the life of the Christian. The demand for "imitation" was carried to the extreme. In *The Moment* (1855) Kierkegaard expressed his conviction that the "official" Christianity of the time was a scandalous falsification, that New Testament Christianity no longer existed. Anyone who wanted to be a Christian had to make a radical break with the existing church; this, as Kierkegaard saw it, was an unavoidable demand. Scholarly opinions of Kierkegaard's last, violent attack on the existing church have been varied in nature. In some respects it seems that this critique was consistent with his earlier ideas, but we cannot overlook the indications of pathological one-sidedness which colored the struggle in which he invested his last measure of strength.

Kierkegaard's influence was not great during his lifetime. His ideas were too markedly different from the major tendencies of his age to be utilized in contemporary education. But in our present century, and particularly in the past several decades, Kierkegaard's writings have had an unusually wide distribution. This is due in part to the fact that so-called "existentialist philosophy" has made use of the Danish thinker's legacy. But this is not all, for also in theology (not least of all in America) serious attempts have been made to go back to the richly seminal sources which Kierkegaard's books provide. It it true in some ways that Kierkegaard's work is without parallel not only in the 19th century but in the entire history of theology.

RITSCHL AND HIS DISCIPLES

A "liberal" or broad-minded Protestantism appeared in many different forms and in a variety of contexts during the 19th century. Its origins can be traced back in most instances to the deistic and rationalistic opinions of the Enlightenment. Most of the representatives of this liberal school were men who sought to apply the critical historical point of view in the field of theology, including the above-mentioned D. F. Strauss and also Ferdinand Christian Baur (d. 1860, professor in Tübingen). Both of these men applied historical criticism to the Bible, and Baur was also influential as a historian of dogma.

A "liberal" theology which was to some degree new and unique was developed in the latter part of the 19th century and in the early years of the present century by Albrecht Ritschl (d. 1889, professor in Göttingen) and his followers.

Ritschl was closely related to both Kant and Schleiermacher. He located the essence of religion not in the feeling of absolute dependence but rather in the distinctive ideas of the religious fellowship, which refer to the alteration of the will and to the promotion of human salvation or blessedness. Ritschl did not accept revelation in the real meaning of the term. "Revelation," in his opinion, is the same as positive religion. The "Christian religion" is attached to the Christian congregation and to the person of Jesus. The sole task of theology is to describe man's fellowship with God as this is expressed in historical Christianity.

Ritschl intended to put firm scholarly ground under theology and to guarantee its position against the attacks of materialistic natural science. In doing so, he resorted to positive religion and regarded it as historical fact. Dogmatics was used to supply a historical description of faith.

In opposition to those who said that Christianity is concerned only with the salvation imparted in Jesus Christ, Ritschl emphasized that we have to deal with *two* dominant basic ideas: Christianity can be compared to an "ellipse, which is controlled by two foci." As Ritschl put it, Christianity is just as much concerned about the common ethical goal, *the kingdom of God*, as it is about the salvation of the individual.

Ethical considerations were decisive for Ritschl. The function of religion is chiefly to promote and bring into being the kingdom of God — man's destination as conceived in ethical categories.

Salvation, which Ritschl defines as "justification" *(Rechtfertigung)* or "forgiveness of sin," restores the ethical freedom impeded by sin. Through faith man's disturbed relation to God is transformed into confidence and sonship. This results in an inner change of will: man comes to acknowledge God's will and is thereby predisposed to do what is good. This inner transformation is what Ritschl called "reconciliation" *(Versöhnung)*. It, in turn, results in good deeds. Salvation is not, therefore, concerned only with the blessedness of the individual; it also refers to a common ethical objective, the realization of the kingdom of God, which is man's highest good.

If one so desires, he can assign "salvation" to religion and "the kingdom of God" to ethics, but in doing so it must be remembered that, according to Ritschl, religion and ethics are interrelated and interact upon one another. One can rather say that the religious is subordinate to the ethical, although both are included as the two "foci" in what Ritschl called the Christian religion.

The traditional doctrines were pruned considerably or reinterpreted to harmonize with the basic "ethical" or "spiritual" ideas which were thought to contain the essential meaning of revelation. Ritschl did not conceive of sin as universal corruption, a condition of guilt before God; he rather thought of it as isolated deviations from the good, resulting from insufficient knowledge of the common welfare, which is simultaneously the ethical good. The *ethical freedom* which is a part of man's natural endowment must therefore be strengthened and perfected. This is accomplished through the new relation to God which is available to man by faith in Christ and His salvation.

Christ can be called God only in a figurative sense: His divinity exists in the unity of His will with God, in the perfect fellowship with God which He manifested in His obedience to God's call. Christ's suffering and death are simply the ultimate proof of this obedience. They are important for salvation only as examples of the obedience through which Christ can bring others into the same relationship with God the Father in which He stands (*Unterricht in der christlichen Religion,* 42). References to substitutionary or propitiatory suffering of punishment were rejected. According to Ritschl, God is love, period; wrath, revenge, or judgment are alien to His nature. Punishment and discipline are used only to educate man.

The task of theology, as Ritschl saw it, consists in bringing traditional Christianity into harmony with contemporary man's "world consciousness." Religion is not designed to explain the world, or to make theoretical, metaphysical judgments; it can only make value judgments. The goal is a "Christian philosophy," which fully satisfies the demand for a perfect, moral and spiritual religion.

Ritschl set forth his system primarily in the huge work entitled *Die christliche Lehre von der Rechtfertigung und Versöhnung,* I–III, 1870–74 (Vol. III includes the principle exposition). A brief summary can be found in his *Unterricht in der christlichen Religion,* 1875.

In his writings Ritschl gave expression to a sober, bourgeois form of religion, which was quite consistent with the cultural attitude of his day. In his rational and practical approach to religion he is strongly reminiscent of Socinianism and other similar forms of rationalism. While he underscored the ethical seriousness of Christianity, he reduced its content to a world view and an ethical system. The widespread influence which Ritschl's ideas enjoyed can be explained not so much in terms of their depth and originality as by their ability to satisfy the general spirit of the times and to actualize the problems which then confronted theological thought.

Chief among Ritschl's followers was Wilhelm Herrmann (d. 1922, professor in Marburg, influential also in Sweden), who deepened and completed Ritschl's ideas in many respects. He drew a much sharper distinction between theology and metaphysics than Ritschl did. Herrmann asserted that statements of faith are judgments which are directly involved in the personal experience of God, and as a result they are on a different level than are all philosophical and metaphysical pronouncements. Religious and philosophical judgments were said to be incompatible. Herrmann concentrated the entire meaning of Christianity in the revelation of Jesus Christ. While Ritschl deduced the meaning of faith from out of this revelation in a more rational and dispassionate manner, Herrmann emphasized the personal experience of the Christ-figure as the basis of faith. Religious reality becomes transparent to man only after he has come to recognize his own impotence and guilt in the light of the ethical imperatives. The man who is serious about these ethical imperatives is inwardly "subdued" by the influence of the person of Jesus and is thereby brought to faith. The concept of a general revelation was repudiated. The connecting link between natural man and the Christian faith is ethical in nature. Herrmann's best-known works are *Der Verkehr des Christen mit Gott* (1886) and *Ethik* (1901).

The well-known historian of dogma Adolf von Harnack (d. 1930, professor in Berlin) must also be numbered among the followers of Ritschl. His theological contribution is considered in a subsequent section, under "The Theology of the Early 20th Century."

ENGLISH THEOLOGY IN THE 19TH CENTURY

Three factors above all dominated the development of English theology during the 19th century: the high-church Oxford Movement, the indigenous philosophical tradition (characterized by a synthesis between Platonism and Christianity), and the increasing influence of historical criticism.

The Oxford Movement was inspired by a group of theologians in Oxford. Among them was John Keble (1792–1866), whose famous sermon of 1833 on "the national apostasy" was sharply critical of the liberal parliamentary politics of that era, which involved itself in ecclesiastical matters and on the strength of a secularized ideal of the state threatened the independence of the church. This sermon is usually considered the Oxford Movement's point of departure. Among its chief representatives (in addition to Keble) were Edward Pusey (1800–82) and John Henry Newman (1801–90). It was Newman who published the "Tracts for the Times" (beginning in 1833), in which the high-church program was developed, in part with a strong Romanist tendency.

Apostolic succession was set forth as being fundamental to the office of the ministry. The concept of the church and the sacraments was also developed in a manner consistent with the Roman pattern. In Tract No. 90 (published in 1841) Newman attempted to prove that the Thirty-nine Articles could be interpreted in such a way that they harmonized with the decisions of the Council of Trent. The original purpose of the Oxford Movement was to so emphasize the Catholic aspect of the Anglican Church that this communion would be revitalized as a result, but Newman and after him also other theologians interpreted this in such a way that they went over to the Church of Rome (Newman in 1845). The movement continued, however, and gradually became a more general Anglo-Catholic tendency, which has exerted a decisive influence on English church life and theology in modern times. Traditionalism is one of its characteristic features. Its theological program includes a return to the theology of the early church and to the classical Anglican theology of the 16th and 17th centuries. It is because of this, not least of all, that a study of the church fathers has come to have a central place in English theology. A comprehensive publishing program has also been carried through as a result of high-church initiative (cf. the "Library of Anglo-Catholic Theology," 88 vols., 1841–66).

Samuel Taylor Coleridge (1772–1834), poet and philosopher, also exerted an extensive influence on English theology, in spite of the fragmentary nature of his philosophical and theological works. Influenced by German Romanticism and idealism, as well as by the Platonizing tradition in England (the Cambridge Platonists of the 17th and 18th centuries), Coleridge opposed deism and created a synthesis between theology and philosophy. Religion for him was a spiritual, mystical reality, into which reason could penetrate ever more deeply by virtue of its participation in the divine nature. Coleridge seems to have oscillated between pantheism and a more orthodox position. On the basis of his reflections upon the distinction between philosophy and theology he expanded the horizons of theology and created an alternative to the negative attitude vis-à vis Christianity held by the deists and the utilitarians.

Under the influence of Coleridge and others Frederick Denison

Maurice (1805–72) continued the Platonizing of English theology. His theological position was described as a "Christianized Platonism," the center of which was formed by the combination of the divine and the highest in humanity, manifested in Christ, "the Son of God and the Son of Man." This combination bases itself on the love of God and expresses itself in a similar way in the Logos which dwells in every man. This Logos is the source of a progressive revelation, which was brought to perfection in Christ. Maurice interpreted "eternity" (eternal life, eternal punishment) not in temporal but in qualitative categories; this aroused strong opposition, and Maurice lost his Oxford professorship as a result. Maurice represented a Christian idealism which did not deny the historical truth of Christianity but which appealed above all to the heart, to the highest in humanity.

It was the above-named S. T. Coleridge who more than anyone else introduced the historical criticism of the Bible into English theology (it had originated in Germany). He recommended that the Bible be studied as an ordinary book. At the outset such tendencies elicited opposition, both among high-churchmen and evangelicals, but the critical view gradually became entrenched. The new theories of evolution set forth by Charles Darwin (*On the Origin of Species,* 1859) and Herbert Spencer were not without significance in this regard, in spite of the fact that they met with strong resistance within theological circles for many years.

Liberal ideas were manifested in *Essays and Reviews* (1860), which championed the right of free research in the field of theology and upheld the demand for the historical criticism of the Bible. Even more important in this connection was the publication of the anthology entitled *Lux mundi* (1889). This did not emanate from liberal circles but was the decisive expression of the fact that even high-church Anglicans accepted historical criticism as an indispensable prerequisite in the study of theology. The stated purpose of this collection of essays was to "bring the Christian confession of faith into its proper relation to the modern development of our scientific, historical, and critical knowledge, and to modern problems in politics and ethics."

The publisher of *Lux mundi* was Charles Gore (1853–1932), a representative of high-church Anglicanism who sought to combine its principles of authority with an acceptance of scientific norms in theology. Gore worked out his position in connection with a series of lectures on the Incarnation. It was due not least of all to his influence that Anglican theology has placed the Incarnation at its center. This is different from the evangelical point of view, for example, in which the Atonement is to be found at the center. Characteristic of Gore was his kenosis doctrine: Christ, he said, laid His divine attributes aside at the time of the Incarnation and subjected Himself to human limitations. There is a certain connection between this idea and Gore's attempt to combine the divine authority of Scripture with a critical view of the Bible. As a result of Gore's influence, the high-church tendency developed along new, more modernistic lines, and he became the leader of what has been referred to as liberal high churchliness. (Cf. R. Ekström, *The Theology of Charles Gore,* 1944.)

ROMAN CATHOLIC THEOLOGY IN THE 19TH CENTURY

After a period of decline brought about by the Enlightenment, the Roman Catholic Church (like the Protestant Church) was awakened to a new interest in church and theology with the dawning of the 19th century. This interest was aroused and promoted among other things by the spirit of Romanticism. The medieval church, which was so severely criticized during the Enlightenment, was now looked upon with admiration and appreciation.

With respect to the renewal of Roman theology in the 19th century, the so-called Tübingen school made a pioneering contribution. Its foremost representative was Johann Adam Möhler (d. 1838), well-known among other things for his *Symbolik,* an incisive confrontation with Protestant theology. This school was above all interested in historical theology. Because of this, it also prepared the way for a new and deeper understanding of the patristic and medieval traditions.

The classical tradition of Roman Catholic doctrine has been based on a positive appreciation of rational knowledge as a prerequisite for the knowledge of faith. During the 19th century two tendencies appeared which represented a contrasting point of view. *Traditionalism* looked upon revelation and faith as the source not only of religious knowledge but also of natural knowledge (within metaphysics and morality). *Ontologism,* which was represented by Henri Maret (d. 1884) and others, and which found its prototype in the Augustinian tradition, assumed that there is an intuitive knowledge of God which forms the basis of all knowledge of truth. Both of these positions were rejected by official decree, the former in 1840 and 1855 and the latter in 1861.

The question of reason and revelation was answered in a completely different way by the school of thought which became dominant in the middle of the 19th century — neoscholasticism, also known as Neo-Thomism. As a result of the influence of a number of Italian and French theologians — as well as of the Tübingen school in Germany and the outstanding German theologian Joseph Kleutgen (d. 1893) — medieval scholasticism became the center of interest not only within historical theology but also in the field of dogmatics. Confirmation of the dominating position which this tendency enjoyed can be found in Leo XIII's encyclical *Aeterni Patris* (1879), in which the philosophy of Thomas Aquinas is enjoined as a basic study for higher education within the church. Thus it is in modern Roman Catholic theology that this medieval theologian stands out as the teacher of the church *par excellence*. It is prescribed in the church's canon law (*Codex iuris canonici*, can. 1366) that study and instruction in both philosophy and theology at Catholic educational institutions must be consistent with the ideas and principles of Thomas Aquinas.

The writings of Matthias Joseph Scheeben (d. 1888), who was probably the major Roman Catholic dogmatician of the 19th century, also testify to the importance then accorded to the classical tradition, both the church fathers and medieval scholasticism. Scheeben based his dogmatics on these sources and sought in an independent and profound analysis to breathe new life into the inheritance received from this older tradition. Scheeben gave particular emphasis to the distinction between Christian faith and that which is merely rational or natural. It was in this connection that he coined the expression "supernature," by which he referred to that in Christian doctrine which is transcendental and inaccessible to reason (*Die Mysterien des Christentums*, 1865 [trans. Cyril Vollert, *Mysteries of Christianity;* St. Louis: Herder, 1946]).

In the bull *Ineffabilis Deus* (1854) Pius IX proclaimed the dogma of "the Virgin Mary's immaculate conception," i. e., the dogma which teaches that Mary, through a special privilege, was preserved from the taint of original sin. This declaration, which was a concession to the popular adoration of Mary, brought to light a new concept of the nature of dogmatic pronouncements, since the otherwise self-evident demand for a Biblical or apostolic basis was set aside. This proclamation of a new dogma presupposed that the highest official in the church has the power to authorize new dogmas that are binding on the church. At the First Vatican Council (1869–70), which the Church of Rome reckons to be the Twentieth Ecumenical Council, this teaching was confirmed and proclaimed in the dogma of papal infallibility: When the pope speaks in his office and defines a teaching concerning faith or morals which is valid for the entire church, he possesses the infallibility which the Savior promised to His church.

In the "Syllabus of Errors," published in 1864, Pius IX condemned such modern phenomena as pantheism and rationalism, socialism and indifferentism, as well as the critical and agnostic philosophies. Similar judgments were expressed upon various facets of the modern point of view on several occasions. This development continued and intensified during the long and (as seen from the point of view of dogmatics) fateful struggle against modernism at the end of the 19th century and the beginning of this century. Modernism was a widespread movement, whose representatives sought in a variety of ways to combine the Roman Catholic faith with modern culture. In doing so, they advocated historical criticism with regard to the Bible, turned against the dominant scholastic influence in the field of philosophy, and sought to introduce a modern philosophical point of view. One of the centers in which these new ideas were nurtured was the Institute Catholique in Paris, where Alfred Loisy (d. 1940) worked for a time as a teacher and carried on a program of critical Biblical research. In an encyclical *Providentissimus Deus* (1893) Leo XIII indeed underlined the importance of erudition in the study of the Bible, but he warned against the critical view of history which Loisy defended. Loisy was relieved of his office, but he continued to plead modernism's cause, as for example in his little book *L'evangile et l'eglise* (1903), in which he attacked A. von Harnack's *Das Wesen des Christentums* (see below). Loisy defended the cultus and dogmas of the church against Harnack but indicated at the same time that these could not be traced back to the Gospel; they are a later creation, he said, expressive of a necessary development within the congregation which resulted from the unfulfilled parousia. Loisy's book was placed on the index, and he was excommunicated in 1908.

The climax of the church's struggle with modernism was reached with the publication of Pius X's bull *Pascendi Dominici gregis* (1907), in which the pope exposed the many different tendencies and concepts in the movement to an incisive analysis and declared them to be heretical. In the same spirit it was decided in 1910 that all priests and teachers should register a confession of the Catholic faith with its repudiation of the false teachings of modernism (the antimodernist oath).

In spite of the original rejection of Biblical criticism, the scientific approach to the Bible has gained ground in Roman Catholic circles just as it has within other communions. The bull *Providentissimus Deus* (1893) recommended the scientific treatment of the Bible within certain limits. Fifty years later the comparable encyclical *Divino afflante Spiritu* (1943) made far-reaching concessions to scientific, critical views. A few years later, however, the bull *Humani generis* (1950) sharply rejected the new form of modernism which, it was felt, threatened the Catholic faith.

The Roman Catholic concept of tradition, like the attitude toward Biblical criticism, has undergone obvious changes in recent years. This development can be traced back into the previous century. In post-Tridentine theology, tradition was understood to be a source of revelation parallel to the Scriptures, different from and yet supplementary to the apostolic testimony which was written down in the Bible. But the intensified contact with the theology of the early church and of the Middle Ages during the 19th century led to a fresh interpretation of the meaning of tradition. The pioneers in this matter were the above-named J. A. Möhler and M. J. Scheeben, together with Cardinal Newman. These men looked upon Scripture and tradition as an organic unity and understood the latter to be a dynamic factor which includes the entire teaching office of the church. Scripture, too, is tradition as seen from a certain point of view. It was emphasized that Scripture could not be interpreted without tradition, but tradition was no longer looked upon as a new source of revelation at the side of Scripture; it was now being thought of as a continuous development of revelation. This new attitude toward tradition has not yet resulted in any official doctrinal decisions, but it does provide an important presupposition for theological discussion in our day, not least for confrontation with the position of the evangelical churches.

REVIVAL MOVEMENTS IN THE 19TH CENTURY

Extensive revival movements developed during the last half of the 19th century, particularly in the Anglo-Saxon world but also in the

Scandinavian countries. The task of describing the development of these movements and their leading personalities properly belongs to the sphere of the church historian. In the present context we shall content ourselves with a survey of a number of the basic ideological aspects of the revival movements.

When speaking of revival movements in the broad sense of the term, it would be possible to include such phenomena as Grundtvigianism in Denmark and the Oxford Movement in England. As a general rule, however, the term has a more limited connotation. But even among the more typical "awakenings" there is a marked difference between those that developed out of a free-church matrix (which we shall investigate with care in this study) and the awakenings which took place strictly within the church — those that emerged from within the context of existing ecclesiastical organizations and which took shape while remaining loyal to their rules and regulations.

Among the various churchly awakenings of this period were Schartauism in Sweden (Henrik Schartau, associate pastor in Lund, d. 1825); Haugeism in Norway (Hans Nielsen Hauge, lay preacher, d. 1824); *Die Erweckung* in Germany (see above, pp. 373–74); and also a number of other Lutheran revivals in Finland and Sweden, with such leaders as Paavo Ruotsalainen (d. 1852), Fredrik Gabriel Hedberg (d. 1893), and Lars Levi Laestadius (d. 1861).

An intermediate position between the earlier Pietist awakening and the free-church movement of the 19th century was assumed by the so-called "new evangelical" movement within the church. In Sweden this was associated with the name of Carl Olof Rosenius (lay preacher; author; editor of *The Pietist*, 1842–68; d. 1868). Rosenius' preaching was influenced above all by Luther, but he was also conditioned by the Pietism within the Church of Sweden and by Herrnhutism, which had a strong foothold in the village in northern Sweden where he grew up. But in addition to this, Rosenius was also under the influence of contemporary Methodist and Reformed preaching. And in spite of his repudiation of separatism he thereby formed an ideological connecting link between certain facets of churchly revivalism and the free-church movements which we shall now proceed to describe.

The Baptist movement, which in the previous century burgeoned forth even in Lutheran territory, can be traced to the Baptist Church in England and America. The Anabaptists of the Reformation era and the

Mennonites of Holland were the original precursors. (The Mennonites were named for Menno Simons, a Dutch priest of the 16th century.)

Another branch of the 19th-century awakening developed under the influence of English Methodism and was supported by men from that group. New Methodist church bodies came into being as a result — e. g., in the Scandinavian countries.

The widespread American revival of the 19th century had a direct antecedent in the "Great Awakening" which began in 1734, led by the prominent theologian and preacher Jonathan Edwards (Congregationalist, d. 1758). Among the principal leaders of the 19th-century revival were Charles Grandison Finney (active in Great Britain as well as in America, d. 1875), and another American preacher who was much like him, Dwight Lyman Moody (d. 1899). Moody and his Methodist song leader, Ira David Sankey (d. 1908), also visited Great Britain a number of times and promoted huge revival campaigns there. The energetic Baptist preacher Charles Haddon Spurgeon (d. 1892), whose base of operations was the Metropolitan Tabernacle in London, also exerted a powerful influence on the revival movement, far beyond the confines of his own church group.

In the North the first Baptist congregations were organized in the middle of the 19th century (Denmark, 1839; Sweden, 1848; Finland, 1856; Norway, 1860). And even though the Methodist persuasion had had sympathizers and adherents in Scandinavia before this, the first Methodist congregations were not formed until somewhat later (Norway, 1856; Denmark, 1859; Sweden, 1868; Finland, 1884). Of great significance for this development was the 12 years which Methodist minister George Scott spent in Stockholm as a preacher (1830—42). C. O. Rosenius was deeply influenced by Scott and found in him an example for his own preaching.

The Swedish Mission Covenant (founded in 1878), which was intended from the outset to be a missionary society, actually developed into a free-church denomination of the Congregationalist type. Its doctrinal position was determined for the most part by Paul Peter Waldenström (d. 1917), who was its foremost leader for many years.

As far as outlook and structure are concerned, the free-church revival movements referred to above displayed a large number of common characteristics. The unique nature of the theology of revival can probably be best seen if one undertakes to study what the revivalists taught concerning (1) regeneration and sanctification, (2) the church and its organization, and (3) the sacraments.

1. In its doctrine of justification, Methodism (as previously indicated) was indebted above all to Lutheranism. As a result, it defined justification as the forgiveness of sins and as the imputation of the righteousness of Christ. In other denominations, however, justification was as a rule equated with regeneration and was therefore described as an obvious change in a person's attitude. "Justification" must mean that a man actually is "made just," and this was presumed to require an inner transformation.

In the early 1870s the previously mentioned Waldenström set forth the idea that the Atonement, in its New Testament sense, could not involve the propitiation of the Father by the Son, inasmuch as God is the fullness of unchangeable love. Instead, said Waldenström, "atonement" (or "reconciliation") refers to a change of mind in man. This point of view, which represented a sharp break with the traditional doctrine of the Atonement, elicited a stormy debate during the ensuing years. Over against Waldenström's concept of the Atonement, with its emphasis on man's moral transformation ("subjective" atonement), stood the current ecclesiastical position that God's righteous wrath over man's sin had been averted by Christ's sacrifice ("objective" atonement). Waldenström based his doctrine of the atonement on certain patterns of speech which he noted in the New Testament — "it is written" was the argument to which he constantly reverted — but his ideas were also in harmony with the powerful liberal tradition of the 19th century; they were the result of the rational and moralizing interpretation of Christianity which he represented.

Ongoing growth in holiness (or sanctification), conceived of as the continuation of regeneration (the transformation which is the result of justification), is the one point which is most frequently stressed in the theology and preaching of revivalism. The Christian is obligated to live in a manner consistent with Christ's new law, which is looked upon not only as an explanation and reiteration of the law given at the time of creation, or of the universally valid law incorporated in the Ten Commandments, but as a superior ethical order which can be followed only by the faithful. Sanctification is based on justification by faith, but it is also, in turn, the presupposition for achieving salvation, just as it is also the prerequisite of continued membership in a Christian congregation.

2. As is true of the doctrine of sanctification, the free-church revival movements also possess, in certain respects at least, a uniform position with respect to the church and its functions: The church is a tangible fellowship of believers. Only those who have declared their faith and their willingness to live in holiness are accepted as members of such congregations.

The external organization of the church can, on the other hand, be varied. Methodism has a definite order for the reception of members, and it also forms an international church body with a strictly regulated organization.

But other revivalist groups, such as the Baptists and the Swedish Mission Covenant, are in principle congregationalist, which is to say that they proceed on the assumption that every local congregation is independent and represents the church of Christ. All believers are welcome in such congregations, but all unbelievers ought to be excluded. And just as the individual members are to live in holiness, struggling against the flesh with the help of the Holy Spirit, so too should the congregation grow in holiness and by strict church discipline exclude those who live in unbelief or who openly break the rules of the congregation.

3. As far as the sacraments are concerned, divergent opinions and practices have developed.

The Baptists see Baptism as only a symbolic act whereby the Christian confesses his faith and is received into the congregation. The demand for adult Baptism resulted from this concept. The significance attached to Baptism varies from one Baptist group to another, but neither Baptism nor the Lord's Supper is thought of as a means of grace by which forgiveness of sin is mediated.

This Reformed point of view can also be discerned in other free-church revival groups. Waldenström, on the other hand, took a position which was distinctly at variance with the Baptist, symbolic concept of the sacraments. In spite of this, however, a variety of opinions and practices has prevailed within the Swedish Mission Covenant.

The observer on the modern scene can see that many shifts have taken place with respect to doctrinal presuppositions and that the differences between the large denominations and the free churches are not as sharply drawn as they once were. This can be explained in some instances by a leveling down of doctrine, but there are other reasons too. There is on both sides an ongoing attempt to give a simpler and more factual explanation of the fundamentals of the Christian faith. Because of this the old controversies have become obsolescent. Ecumenical dialog between the established churches and the free churches is one of the contemporary results. The discussions in England between the Methodist Church and the Anglican Church, which are directed toward complete unity within the near future, are perhaps the foremost example of this activity.

CHAPTER 34

The Theology
of the Early 20th Century;
Contemporary Trends

HARNACK, KÄHLER, AND BILLING

Adolf von Harnack (d. 1930), who was referred to above as a disciple of Albrecht Ritschl, made his mark above all as a church historian, with primary emphasis on the history of dogma. He dominated this area in his own lifetime and mastered the vast field of patristics and exegetics as no one else has ever done. His best known work, *Lehrbuch der Dogmengeschichte* (I–III, 1886–90, several later editions; trans. *History of Dogma*, ed. Neil Buchanan; New York: Russell & Russell, 1958) was the mature fruit of his many-sided historical research.

In a famous lecture series held in Berlin in 1900, published later under the title *Das Wesen des Christentums* (trans. Thomas Bailey Saunders, *What Is Christianity?* Toronto: McClelland, 1958), Harnack sought to present a summary of what he considered the essence of the Gospel. If Wilhelm Herrmann (see above, pp. 376–77) emphasized above all an inner, personal experience of Jesus, who becomes real to man through the proclamation of the Bible, Harnack put greater stress on Christianity as a historical phenomenon. The timeless element in its message, the real substance of the Christian faith, is the same as Jesus' original teaching, which can be derived from a reading of the gospels. The process of extracting the doctrinal content of a given document was, to Harnack, a purely historical task, and he looked upon the gospels as being for the most part authentic texts. Harnack summarized the proclamation or Gospel of Jesus under the three following headings, each of which could be thought of as containing the entire Gospel:

1. The kingdom of God revealed as a present reality in the heart of man.

2. God as Father, and man's absolute value.

3. The higher righteousness proclaimed by Jesus, i. e., the law of love.

This "simple teaching of Jesus" was derived from the gospels by the application of the historical method. One could look upon this as a concentrate of the loftiest, ideal religious truths. Harnack thereby anchored Christianity in history but at the same time presented it as a timeless, universally valid religion. He drew a sharp distinction between Christian dogma and the original Gospel, and looked upon the former as a later development, conditioned by Greek philosophy. He referred to dogma as a "creation of the Hellenic spirit on the soil of the Gospel."

Harnack's concept of Christianity, like Herrmann's, was characterized by a strong interest in apologetics. In a time when it seemed as though Christian dogma was being undermined by science, there were those who desired to set forth that which, independent of all scientific criticism, can be thought of as permanent and unchanging in the Christian message. The unusual thing was that Harnack's historical interpretation of Christianity was refuted at many points by the very exegetical and patristic research which was done during the first decades of the 20th century.

Of what importance to the Christian faith is the history which the scientific study of the Bible has confided to us? This was one of the most burning questions confronting theology at the turn of the century. As we have already seen, Herrmann and Harnack, who were both disciples of Ritschl and members of the liberal school of thought, arrived at different answers. For Herrmann the ground of faith lay in the attitude of trust which comes into being when the picture of Jesus' inner life is made real to a person through the words of the Bible. He therefore pointed from the historical to the timeless experience of a personal confrontation with Christ. For Harnack Christianity was above all a historical reality. Through the science of history one can find the Gospel, Jesus' original proclamation, which, in its historical setting, is simultaneously a timeless truth, representing the ideal religion.

In the year 1892 Martin Kähler (professor in Halle, d. 1912) published a small book entitled *Der sogenannte historische Jesus und der geschichtliche biblische Christus* (trans. Carl E. Braaten, *The So-called Historical Jesus and the Historic, Biblical Christ;* Philadelphia: Fortress Press, 1964). In this work Kähler approached the problem of faith and history in a way that presaged new trends in the field of theology. Kähler rejected the attempts of liberal theologians to construct a picture of the historical Jesus. Such efforts result in a falsification, inasmuch as the extant sources — above all, the gospels — were not designed to present a biography of Jesus in the modern sense of the term. They were rather intended to provide the foundation for the church's proclamation of Christ. The purpose of the gospels was not to present a scholarly description of a person but to promote the proclamation that would establish the church and create faith. The Christ of faith is identical with the historical *(geschichtlich)* Christ to whom the Bible bears witness. Kähler distinguished between *historisch* and *geschichtlich* in this context. By the former, he referred to that which the modern science of history incorporates into its supply of naked facts. The latter word, on the other hand, was employed with reference to the historical in its significance for humanity or for man in our time. According to Kähler, faith relates not only to the historical but also to something "beyond history," i. e., to the eternal, which is decisive for man's salvation and is revealed in the historical events to which the Bible bears witness.

Kähler's book has retained its significance right up to the present time. His point of view was the portent of a number of theological tendencies which have since been asserted with great cogency. The exegetes of the so-called "form criticism" school, for example, took up the idea that the very nature of the Gospel was designed to serve its proclamation and was determined by the preaching about Christ which was current in the Christian community. This insight also gave shape to the basic idea of so-called "kerygmatic" theology, represented by Karl Barth and his many disciples.

There was an idealistic facet in Kähler's thinking, for example his emphasis on that which is "beyond history." In itself, this term could be interpreted as pointing exclusively to the transcendental, the eternal — that which lies "over" history. This is not the case, however. Kähler said that what is important for the Christian faith can be found precisely within the context of history, in the historical Christ of the Bible *(totus Christus),* and not merely in His inner life (as Herrmann claimed) or in certain timeless religious concepts contained in His preaching, as Harnack asserted.

The historical criticism of the Bible — which had begun long before this but did not become the dominant theological method until the end of the 19th century — might have seemed inimical to the Christian faith, insofar as this felt itself bound to a timeless and unchanging doctrine, given once and for all time in the Bible, and insofar as the Bible in its entirety was looked upon as containing pronouncements of an absolute kind. The solution of the problems raised by this new criticism of the Bible was a major concern for theologians active at the turn of the century. We have already noted how Martin Kähler sought to answer one of the questions involved by insisting that the so-called "historical" Jesus was a modern falsification. The actual, Biblical Christ is the Christ who is proclaimed abroad, who is living and present in the Christian congregation. The Christ in whom Christians believe and the Christ to whom the gospels bear witness is one and the same. A historical "critique" of the texts can never go back any further than to the original "testimonies to the faith," and these must be looked upon as elements in the preaching of the first congregations.

Similar problems were also taken up by Einar Billing (professor at Uppsala, bishop of Västerås, d. 1939), who clearly demonstrated that the Biblical revelation is linked up with historical facts, with God's treatment of His people and with the life of Jesus, and not, as in the case of Greek wisdom, with a universal concept of knowledge. Even though the contrast between Greek thought and the Bible is not as fundamental or as significant as some have claimed, Billing's discovery of what was later referred to as the "dynamic" concept of revelation in the Bible was of enduring value. This concept not only served to alter the way in which men look upon the Bible but also the manner in which the task of theology is understood. If our contact with the divine and eternal is brought about, according to the Bible, by God's own involvement in history, and not via some timeless knowledge of eternal truths, then it follows that it cannot be the function of theology to present Christianity as a logically impeccable system; theology must in some way do justice to the historical and dynamic elements in the Biblical revelation.

Billing came to be a prominent figure in modern Swedish theology for other reasons as well. On the strength of a learned examination into

Luther's doctrine of the state (1900) he became the progenitor of modern Luther research in Sweden, a school which came to dominate Swedish theology in the 1920s and 1930s, even to a great extent in the systematic area. This "Luther renaissance," as it is usually called, has made a significant contribution to Protestant theology in the 20th century. For Luther research has grown correspondingly on the continent as well, led by such church historians as Karl Holl and Heinrich Boehmer and by such systematicians as Carl Stange, Rudolf Hermann, and Paul Althaus.

In the discussion concerning the nature of the church, Billing developed (in a number of significant contributions) what he referred to as "the religiously motivated folk-church idea." This idea was based on the territorial character of the Church of Sweden. All of Sweden is divided into parishes, and Billing asserted that such a system does much to give expression to the universality of the proclamation of grace. The church has the responsibility of preaching the Gospel to the entire nation. The religiously motivated folk church, said Billing, is not bound to the apparatus of a "state church" — and neither was his idea of the church based on the concept of a universal religiosity which is to form the foundation of the Christian proclamation. Billing's ecclesiology was clearly directed against the free-church tendency with its concept of the church as an exclusive gathering of believers. The folk-church idea as set forth by Billing did not, however, clarify such matters as church discipline and the role of the Confessions as the basis of church fellowship.

THE HISTORY OF RELIGIONS SCHOOL

When Adolf von Harnack gave his lectures on "What Is Christianity?" he asserted that a universally valid presentation of the Christian religion could be made on the basis of a purely historical examination of Jesus' original message. Contemporaneous research in the exegetical field revealed another tendency, however, which appeared to contradict the presuppositions of Harnack and of liberal theology. This tendency emerged from certain theologians who were referred to as the history of religions (or comparative religions) school.

If one investigates the history of early Christianity by applying the historical method, one will find not a universal religion but a series of ideas and assumptions which are so alien to modern ways of thinking that they cannot be successfully transferred to our time and incorporated into our religious instruction.

Most of these foreign elements in early Christianity are of an eschatological and apocalyptic nature. Jesus and His disciples took these over from the Judaism of New Testament times. In a book on the kingdom of God concept in the preaching of Jesus (*Die Predigt Jesu vom Reich Gottes*, 1892), a young German scholar by the name of Johannes Weiss demonstrated, in a purely exegetical manner, that Jesus' preaching of the kingdom of God envisioned a coming, eschatological reign of God, which was to become a reality at the imminent end of the present age.

This view represented a serious challenge to the liberal concept of the kingdom of God (as, e. g., in Ritschl; see above, pp. 374–76). The liberal school conceived of the kingdom of God as an entity in the present world, brought into reality by faith and increasingly manifested in the Christian community.

Johannes Weiss and his co-workers pointed out those Oriental and late-Jewish elements in early Christianity which are so foreign to the modern age. Interest in the historical context of religion then began, and Christianity came to be looked upon as a link in the development which resulted in part from ancient Oriental and in part from Hellenistic-Jewish religious history. But is it possible to accept this interpretation and yet insist that Christianity is a religion which is suited to the modern age and which satisfies modern religious needs? This became a real problem for the history of religions school. This school was sustained by a strong scholarly interest, and it helped to discredit many of the illusions which liberal theology entertained when it sought to adapt the Christian faith to modern thinking.

From a scholarly view the history of religions school was of great importance; it clarified the uniqueness of Christianity at many points. It was precisely against this background of a deepened study of the history of religions that it appeared particularly meaningful to investigate and describe Christianity in its historical uniqueness, without adapting it to modern rationalistic assumptions. The history of religions school did a great deal of valuable preliminary work in this area, even though it did not in itself reach any definite results of essential importance to the future. And a number of the men in this school finally ended up by espousing the concepts of liberal theology, especially when they were confronted with the task of presenting the actual message of Christianity.

The reason for this lack of the expected results lay perhaps above all in the fact that the picture which was given of the historical development of religion was to a large extent an invention, alien to the texts under examination. The stated purpose was not in keeping with Christianity's own view of its original documents: the purpose was not to understand the distinctive nature of these texts but to use them as the basis for the construction of a history of the religion of Israel and of early Christianity. In this program lay both the strength and the weakness of the history of religions school.

Weiss's discovery that the kingdom of God in the preaching of Jesus was a future reality, waiting beyond this present age, was taken up and built upon by Albert Schweitzer (d. 1965) in a book entitled *Von Reimarus zu Wrede* (1906; later editions were called *Die Geschichte der Leben-Jesu-Forschung;* trans. William Montgomery, *The Quest of the Historical Jesus;* New York: Macmillan, 1961). In this study Schweitzer interpreted Jesus' entire career (and not merely some of His utterances) as being designed to achieve one purpose: to hasten the downfall of the present world order and thus call forth the kingdom of God.

When the expectations concerning the return of Jesus and the imminent breakthrough of the kingdom of God were not fulfilled, the content of the Christian message was gradually altered. All of the church's doctrine, like the proclamation of the New Testament, must be understood in the light of this eschatological upheaval which was originally expected but then failed to appear.

Schweitzer's thesis — referred to as the thesis of "consistent eschatology" — was built on an inadequate exegetical foundation and has subsequently been abandoned by scholars. But it aroused a lively discussion when first broached, and as a result it achieved major significance. Schweitzer emphasized as clearly as possible that Jesus' purported original message was not something which could be applied in modern times; it belonged to an apocalyptic milieu which is alien to man today.

Schweitzer's own understanding of Christianity as an existential religion had no relationship to the results of his own research into early Christianity. On the other hand, he selected a number of ideas out of German idealism and humanism and made the concept of "reverence for life" *(Ehrfurcht vor dem Leben)* the basis of his religious life.

Schweitzer was the most radical representative of the history of religions school, but there were many other prominent scholars who implemented its basic principles in their work. Among these were Hermann Gunkel (d. 1932), who, among other things, made a significant contribution to the history of Old Testament literature in a commentary on Genesis (1901), and Wilhelm Bousset (d. 1920), who investigated the Christ concept of the ancient church, using the new history of religion as a point of departure. This was done in his book *Kyrios Christos: Geschichte des Christusglaubens von den Anfängen des Christentums bis auf Irenäus* (1913).

The contributions made by the history of religions school in the area of Biblical research also inspired a strong new interest in universal religious history (Nathan Söderblom; Eduard Lehmann), as well as in the psychology of religion (cf. William James, *The Varieties of Religious Experience*, 1902, which came to be normative for modern empirical research in the field of religion).

A front-rank historian and philosopher of religion, who can also be considered a representative of the history of religions school, was Ernst Troeltsch (professor at Heidelberg and elsewhere, d. 1923). Troeltsch based his conclusions on a radical historical interpretation of Christianity. Christianity cannot be understood as the absolute religion, he said, but only as the historically highest form of the religion of personality development. Troeltsch wrestled with the problem of revelation and history. For him, this was a major question: How can one accept a consistent historical interpretation of Christianity and at the same time assert its salvatory power and its role in current preaching? Troeltsch sought to find a cultural synthesis and contemplated the concept of a natural religion. According to his view, all value judgments, religious as well as moral, are based on certain evident presuppositions in human reason (the religious a priori).

The significance of personal freedom and decision-making was clearly recognized by Troeltsch, but he could never solve the problem of relating this to the critical, empirically inductive view of history. In all of this, however, he anticipated later developments and pointed to tendencies which subsequently came forth with incomparable potency. This was true, for example, of the emphasis placed on Christianity as a proclaimed message which confronts the individual with the necessity of making a decision right here and now (dialectical theology), and also of the continued discussion concerning the justification of the historical interpretation of Christianity and its importance to theology.

The contributions made by the history of religions school to the sphere of systematic theology were of little value to the future and have been, for the most part, long since forgotten. But the methodology and the pure historical research of this group have proved to be of lasting significance.

DIALECTICAL THEOLOGY

Immediately after the end of the first World War a commentary on Paul's Letter to the Romans (*Der Römerbrief,* 1919, the Foreword, 1918) was published by a Swiss pastor by the name of Karl Barth (b. 1886, professor in Basel since 1935). In this book Barth lodged a sharp protest not only against contemporary theology but against the entire tradition which began to take shape with Schleiermacher and which anchored Christianity in human experience and looked upon faith as an element in the spiritual life of man. *Der Römerbrief* was also a protest against those schools which had transmuted theology into a science of religion and had held the historicocritical analysis of the Bible to be the only possible interpretation. Barth brought out a second edition a few years later (1922; the Foreword, 1921; sixth ed. trans. Edwyn C. Hoskyns, *Epistle to the Romans;* Oxford University Press, 1933), and this completely revised version can be considered the beginning of the new school which subsequently came to be known as dialectical theology. The man who worked most intimately with Barth in this school was Eduard Thurneysen (b. 1888, pastor in Switzerland and later professor in Basel). Other kindred spirits were Emil Brunner, like Barth a Reformed theologian (professor in Zurich, d. 1966), and the Lutheran theologian Friedrich Gogarten (b. 1887, professor in Göttingen since 1935).

During the 1930s Barth and Brunner came to a parting of the ways, and Gogarten too came to have reservations about Barthian theology. From that point on it became impossible to refer to dialectical theology as a unified entity.

For our present purposes we shall direct our attention to a number of basic ideas treated in the Barthian literature. In addition to the previously mentioned *Römerbrief,* Barth's enormous productivity has resulted in the publication of such significant works as *Das Wort Gottes und die Theologie,* 1925 (trans. Douglas Horton, *The Word of God and the Word of Man;* New York: Harper Torchbook, 1957), a collection of propositions which throw considerable light on the early phases of dialectical theology; *Christliche Dogmatik — Prolegomena,* 1927 (the first, unfinished version of his dogmatics); *Fides quaerens intellectum,* 1931 (trans. Dan W. Robertson, *Fides quaerens intellectum;* New York: Meridian, 1962), a commentary on the theology of Anselm; *Kirchliche Dogmatik,* 1932 ff. (trans. *Church Dogmatics,* ed. G. W. Bromiley and T. F. Torrance; Edinburgh: T. & T. Clark), the huge and as yet incomplete dogmatics, the 12th volume of which [Part IV, 3, 2] appeared in 1959.

Barth has also written on political questions. He was one of the leaders of the "confessing church" in Nazi Germany, and was ejected from that country in 1934. The so-called Barmen Declaration — which served the church as a confessional document in its struggle with Hitlerism — was based on Barth's theology and was, to a large extent, the product of his pen. In subsequent years Barth has urged the church to reveal a greater spirit of openness vis-à-vis communism (*Eine Schweizer Stimme,* 1945).

In a notable contribution to the Baptism controversy (*Die kirchliche Lehre von der Taufe,* 1934; trans. *The Teaching of the Church Regarding Baptism;* Chicago: Alec R. Allenson, 1956) Barth, using the Reformed tradition as a point of departure, repudiated infant Baptism and recommended adult Baptism.

Dialectical theology was one of the results of the culture crisis which followed upon the conclusion of World War I; it involved, among other things, a violent reaction against the theology of the history of religions school. Barth did not reject the historicocritical interpretation of the Bible in itself, but he felt that it failed to accomplish its purpose because it occupied itself with peripheral concerns and ignored the real issues in the texts under consideration. As he made clear in *Der Römerbrief,* Barth intended to replace the mere philological and historical interpretation with a profounder "dialectical" exposition of the Biblical material itself. He found his examples primarily in the classical Christian tradition, as, for example, in Luther and Calvin. Barth's interpretation of the Bible is not, however, a mere carbon copy of the Reformers' work; the dialectic which he has found in the Bible is not, as in Luther, a contrast between God's wrath and God's grace, between the sin of man and the righteousness provided by God; it is rather a fundamental contrast between eternity and time, between God as God and man as man. "If I have a 'system,' it is that, to the highest possible degree, I keep my attention upon both the positive and negative significance of what Kierkegaard called 'the infinite qualitative difference' between time and eternity. 'God is in heaven, and you are on earth.' The relation of this God to this man, and the relation of this man to this God is for me both the theme of the Bible and the sum and substance of philosophy" (*Der Römerbrief*, Foreword to the second edition).

The application of this fundamental concept has, as a rule, resulted in the abnegation of the human, thereby making way for divine revelation, for the "wholly other," which is revealed through God's Word to those who in a spirit of humility are receptive to God's acts and the message of the church.

Barth's understanding of revelation — or the Word of God (which he treated in the first two volumes of his *Kirchliche Dogmatik*, 1932—38) — is conditioned from beginning to end by the contrast between time and eternity. This presupposition forms an element of idealism in Barth's theology, which otherwise takes the form of a protest against the idealistic tradition. "Eternity" in this context does not suggest a prolongation of time, or eternity in the Biblical sense of a new age. As Barth uses it, the term rather refers to the purely transcendental, which has nothing in common with time and which therefore can be equally present in every age. The God-man relationship is conceived of as a direct parallel to the contrast between eternity and time.

God's Word and God's acts can never, therefore, be identified with human words or the historical events recorded in the Bible, but must rather be looked upon as purely transcendental. As far as theology is concerned, this suggests — among other things — that all so-called natural theology must be denied. The divine implies the negation of the human and can never be thought of as being implanted in human nature or even as having any point of contact with it. Furthermore, Barth came to look upon the Bible and the history of salvation as mere analogies to the transcendent Word and acts of God and as a witness *(Zeugnis)* to these. The preached and written Word — which alone spans the breach between God and man — does nothing more than to point *(hinweisen)* to the true divine revelation, viz., the Word of God in its absolute and transcendent sense.

In this we can see the basis for Barth's use of the so-called dialectic method — by which one places different points of view in opposition to one another, in order that they might mutually cast light upon the matter in question. Barth insists that we are unable to clarify or give expression to the content of divine revelation by using direct statements, which would constitute a "dogmatic" approach. This can only be done, he believes, on the basis of a permanent confrontation of contrasting statements. In this way, one can achieve a balance between statements which affirm and statements which deny a given assertion. One thereby questions the answers and answers the questions. "There remains only . . . to relate both, positive and negative, to each other. To clarify the yes by the no and the no by the yes, without delaying more than a moment in a fixed yes or no; thus, for example, to speak of the glory of God in creation only to pass immediately to emphasizing God's complete concealment from our eyes in nature, to speak of death and the transitory quality of this life only to remember the majesty of the wholly other life which meets us in that very death." (*Das Wort Gottes und die Theologie,* p. 172)

The idea that the proclamation, or the kerygma, forms the point of departure for theology is fundamental in Barth's thinking, and many other modern theologians have borrowed this idea, including some who are otherwise far removed from the dialectical school.

Barth was himself a parish pastor when he made his debut as an author in the field of theology, and he feels that theology ought to serve the needs of the preaching function exclusively. Or, more specifically, he would say that the task of theology is to test and to guide the preaching function in a critical manner. This is above all the task of dogmatics, which Barth defines in the following words: "Dogmatics as a theological discipline is the scientific self-criticism of the Christian church concerning the content of its distinctive language about God." (*Kirchliche Dogmatik,* I, 1, 1)

Proclamation assumes a central position not only as the presupposition of theological activity but also because it serves as the point at which God's Word confronts the listening congregation today. Thus it is that the divine-human encounter continues to take place, leading to decision and faith. Many modern theologians have combined this basic concept with existential philosophy, as, for example, in the Bultmann school. We hear a lot in our day about a "kerygmatic" theology, which is distinguished from a more historically oriented one and from the kind of theology which is content to provide a descriptive or critical analysis of the Christian tradition.

Barth's concept of the Word of God leads us to his Christology. God's Word, according to Barth, confronts man not only in the proclaimed message, but this points back to the written Word (the Bible), which provides the norms for preaching and the criterion against which preaching must be tested. Does this, then, mean that Scripture is the Word of God? Not in the direct sense, according to Barth — but Scripture, in its turn, refers to the "revealed" Word, viz., to the hidden God's appearance in Christ. The Bible "bears witness" to the revelation which occurred with the coming of Christ. To "bear witness" *(bezeugen)* in this context means "to point in a definite direction beyond one's self to something other" *(Kirchliche Dogmatik, I, 1, 14)*. The divine may not in any respect be put on the same level with anything temporal or human; the latter can therefore merely "point" to the former.

The chasm between God and man has been bridged over at one point, however, and that was in the Incarnation, which means that God's eternal Word chose to assume human nature, and did so in Jesus Christ. This was an expression of God's sovereign freedom, an act which occurred exclusively as a result of the exercise of divine freedom. Barth finds this illustrated in the Virgin Birth: the miracle of the Incarnation took place without any human cooperation.

The Christology which Barth develops from these premises occupies a central position in his dogmatics. Since no contact between the divine and human is possible apart from the Incarnation, the result is that all questions in the field of dogmatics are referred back to Christology. The relationship between God and man — the basic theme of theology (see above) — has been set forth in Christ in an exemplary manner. In Him we see reflected both God's dealings with man and man's obedience and elevation to the likeness of God. Creation has no significance other than to prefigure the act of God which was realized in Christ. Barth's doctrine of the church, and his ethics as well, were also developed in accordance with his Christology; it is assumed that both serve to explicate the relationship between God and man which is illustrated in Christ's person and work.

The manner in which Barth relates the teaching of predestination to his Christology is especially illuminating. Like the Reformed tradition to which he belongs, Barth accepts the concept of a double predestination. But the term "predestination" does not mean, according to Barth, that some men have been chosen to be saved and others to be lost; it refers, instead, to Christ, who at one and the same time represents God's choice and rejection of man. The fate which befell Christ reflects an eternal inner-Trinitarian process by which God chose the Son, and in Him the human race, in that He rejected the Son and permitted Him to submit Himself to death in order that He might be raised up to eternal glory in and through the Resurrection. Predestination is therefore an eternal decision made by God, implying that men — all men — are admitted to salvation, while God Himself, in the form of the Son, takes damnation upon Himself.

This implies, according to Barth's interpretation, that the New Testament report concerning Jesus of Nazareth is not in and by itself a message of salvation, but only a reference to — or an image of — something which took place in the eternal sphere as a process within the Godhead. Salvation is universal and, practically speaking, is conceived of as a transcendent occurrence to which the proclaimed Word can only be a witness (Zeugnis).

Barth looks upon the death and resurrection of Jesus as an analogy of an eternal process in which God rejects and chooses the Son. In the light of this interpretation, the earthly life of Jesus is, for the most part, relegated to a subordinate role. The rejection of Christ by God the Father is not made clear until the time of His death, whereas the Resurrection depicts His eternal election.

At the same time, that which occurred in the life of Christ serves as a paradigm for the salvation of all mankind. By gaining insight into eternal salvation, man comes to participate therein. This insight comes to man through the preaching of the Gospel of Christ, through the proclaimed Word.

Barth's Christology finally results, therefore, in a kind of speculative doctrine of universal salvation. If one compares this concept with the variety of views held in the early history of Christianity, one discovers that Barth's position is rather unusual: it contains both docetic and Nestorian tendencies. It is docetic insofar as it suggests that the Gospel message is but an illustration of an inner-Trinitarian event, exclusively divine in nature, and it is Nestorian insofar as the humanity of Christ is never identified with His divinity but is conceived of only as an analogy thereto. Or — to put it another way — the historical (the New Testament witness to Christ), which Barth takes very seriously in itself, is thought to have meaning only insofar as it gives expression to what Barth calls *die Urgeschichte*, i. e., the timeless event within the Godhead, the Father's dealings with the Son.

The "Christocentric" facet of Barth's theology involves the complete repudiation of every form of "natural" theology. As early as in his commentary on Romans, Barth attacked human religiosity (or natural religion), which is based solely on human experience and considers religion to be one aspect of this experience. All that is human must become as nothing in the presence of the divine Word, which comes "straight down from above" and thus invades human existence and confronts man with the need of making a decision.

When Emil Brunner asserted in *Natur und Gnade* (1934) that there must nevertheless be a point of contact in natural man for the proclaimed Word if man is to be influenced thereby, Barth responded with a categorical no. In a statement entitled *Nein* (1934) Barth dissociated himself not only from natural theology in its traditional form (the idea that man has a certain knowledge of God and also a natural insight concerning right and wrong) but also from Brunner's concept of a "point of contact." This controversy led Barth and Brunner to a parting of the ways. But Barth's rejection of "natural theology" made a strong impact on contemporary theology anyway, even outside of the dialectical school. It was given expression, for example, in the Barmen Declaration of 1934.

When Barth began writing theology, he said that he was basing his work on ideas derived from Kierkegaard and Dostoevski, among others. In an earlier phase of his development he also related himself directly to contemporary existential philosophy, but he subsequently in *Christliche Dogmatik* (1927) dissociated himself from every type of philosophy. Just as the proclaimed Word is in itself able to awaken understanding in those who hear it, without assuming that there is some kind of a point of contact in the hearers, so, said Barth, ought one cultivate a theology of the Word without seeking for any contacts with philosophical doctrines and systems.

Barth's doctrine of the Word and his Christology correspond to one another meticulously as one can tell from the structure of his ideas. God's Word confronts us in Holy Scripture, but Scripture is not, in a real sense, God's Word; it only witnesses thereto and points us to the eternal Word of God. By the same token, the Christ of history is neither God's Son nor the Son of Man in the proper sense. He rather "illustrates," and presents as by analogy, the deeds of the eternal Son of God and provides the pattern for man's role vis-à-vis God. One can even go so far as to say that Christ — as a historical person — did not actually work out our salvation within the context of time, but that He only bears witness to *(bezeugt)* and proclaims the eternal salvation whose reality is found in God's decree. (Cf. Regin Prenter in *Studia theologica,* XI, 1957, 1 ff.)

As a result of this, Barth's view of salvation emphasizes knowledge: Christ's death and resurrection have made known to man that eternal salvation which consists in that the Father first rejected and then elevated the Son. Those who recognize this have been reconciled to God. The history of salvation as recorded in the Bible is only a reflection of the eternal "history of salvation." One learns to know the latter through the former, and it is thus, says Barth, that reconciliation takes place. Forgiveness of sin, justification, provides an analogy to and represents here in time that eternal salvation which alone forms the basis and the proper object of faith.

PAUL TILLICH

In the work of Paul Tillich (d. 1965) we find a theological system which is related to Barthianism in some respects but which is nevertheless structured in an entirely different way. Although born in Germany (where he taught at Frankfurt am Main and elsewhere), Tillich exerted his greatest influence in the United States (where he taught at Harvard and elsewhere).

Tillich proceeded on the basis of an older German philosophical tradition and combined this, in his eclectic system, with insight from existentialism and from Edmund Husserl and other philosophers. He was both a theologian and a philosopher of religion; the major problem dealt with in his books concerned the relationship between theology and philosophy, between revelation and empirical reality, as well as between theology and culture.

Ever since Kierkegaard's concentrated attack on the Hegelian system, the philosophy of idealism and the type of thought that is based on actual human experience have come into focus as incompatible opposites. The uniqueness of Tillich's work can be seen in that while he constructed his system in a strictly idealistic manner, he also incorporated into it an "existential analysis" by which he sought to utilize stimuli from existential thought. It must be said, however, that what Tillich has written about the human situation in relation to life's ultimate questions (or about man's "existence") appears to be the exact counterpart of the content of his system. This would seem to suggest that the system is the dominant factor — that which determines the content of the existential analysis.

According to Tillich, that which forms our "ultimate concern" is the object of theology. In order to determine what this is, he employed the terminology of the old ontology: our ultimate concern is that which determines our "being or nonbeing." God, who is "Being itself," is the answer to man's ultimate questions. Man's own situation is alien in relation to actual reality. But inasmuch as God has entered into human existence, He gives man the possibility of discovering his destiny as the New Being, which is realized in Christ.

Tillich's system is based, therefore, on a kind of ontology, which, it is assumed, provides the absolute answer to the questions which men raise as a result of their sense of alienation. The assumption that question and answer, system and existential analysis, are correlated one to the other is the essence of the methodological approach which Tillich applies above all.

The substance of Christian dogma is included in Tillich's system, but its genuine character has in some way been lost in the process. It has been thoroughly reinterpreted and reduced to symbols which are used to illustrate man's transition from a condition of alienation to the New Being. The fact that the union between God and man, between being and existence, is illustrated in the New Testament's picture of Jesus of Nazareth is a coincidence. It could also be symbolized in another way. The historicity of Jesus' earthly life, His death and resurrection, lack significance in the context of the system (cf. K. Hamilton, *The System and the Gospel*, 1963).

In a situation which has been colored both by the existentialism of Kierkegaard and by insight into Christianity's historical basis, Tillich's theological system may appear to be a dated remnant from an older idealistic tradition. But behind his confidence in a system of absolutes, and behind his metaphysical speculations, lies an apologetic interest — to present Christianity as the way out of the confusion of the present age, enabling men to experience a sense of wholeness, which, according to this same system, is the answer to man's deepest needs.

Tillich has also sought, at the same time, to create a cultural synthesis, whereby humanism and Christianity could be brought together in complete harmony. In this respect his theology stands in sharp contrast to Barthianism. Tillich's greatest theological work is his *Systematic Theology* (I and II, 1951 and 1957). A large part of his work was done in the field of the philosophy of religion.

RUDOLPH BULTMANN; THE DEBATE ON KERYGMA AND HISTORY

An intensive theological debate was touched off in 1941 when the famous exegete Rudolph Bultmann (b. 1884, professor at Marburg) published a small volume entitled *Neues Testament und Mythologie* (which was one section of a larger work, *Offenbarung und Heilsgeschehen*). Numerous contributions were inserted into the discussion which followed, written by both theologians and scientists. The so-called Bultmann debate has involved a number of primary questions both in exegetical and systematic theology, and it constitutes one of the most important elements in the theological development of the postwar era.

In the above-named volume Bultmann asserted that the New Testament world view, together with its conception of demons and supernatural acts, of miracles, of the preexistence of Jesus, of the cataclysms of the last days, etc., is incompatible with modern man's concept of reality. Bultmann refers to these elements in the New Testament as "mythological." How shall these be interpreted? What ought the man with a modern education make of these? This is the problem as Bultmann sees it.

It is clear that in Bultmann's view the mythological elements in the New Testament are not merely peripheral in nature — they also involve the essentials of the Christian faith. Because of this, it is not a satisfactory solution to do as liberal theology did, and merely eliminate the mythical in order to preserve the basic moral and religious ideas in the Bible. Neither can one make a *sacrificium intellectus* and accept the mythical as such, simply because it is found in the Bible. That would be repugnant to intellectual honesty and turn faith into a human achievement. Thus it was that Bultmann's presentation resulted in a demand for the "demythologization" *(Entmythologisierung)* of the New

Testament message. By using this term — which has so often elicited misunderstanding — Bultmann does not suggest that the mythological should be excised, but rather that it should be interpreted in accordance with its original purpose. When this is done, Bultmann says, the mythical element will fall of its own weight.

According to Bultmann, the demand for demythologizing is actually made by the myths themselves, inasmuch as they are not intended to describe external events or facts but rather to say something about human existence. They are to be interpreted anthropologically, not cosmologically — or, to use another of Bultmann's own expressions, the demand for the correct understanding of the myths, by a process of demythologization, can be met only through an "existential interpretation."

This implies that the message's reference to the human situation, and its summons to man to reach a decision, is placed at the very center. Bultmann combines fundamental kerygmatic-theological concepts with points of view which he has deliberately extracted from contemporary existentialist philosophy, whose chief German spokesman, Martin Heidegger, was for a time Bultmann's colleague at Marburg.

In this philosophy Bultmann finds a view of man which in essence agrees with the New Testament's view. In his natural environment, man is subject to the powers of this world, to temporal interests, to the things he has at his disposal. His true destiny is to be found in release from this dependence, so that he can devote himself to the future without those feelings of anxiety which follow him as long as he is held captive by the temporal. This alteration in the human situation can take place through the message about Christ, who by His death represents the dying away from this world, becoming thereby the source of a new form of existence. The kerygma, the message of Christ's death and triumph over death, offers the possibility of altering man's existence; this is realized in the decision of faith, which is man's answer to the appeal of the kerygma.

Such, in rough outline form, is the concept of human existence from which Bultmann proceeds. The existential interpretation is designed to describe the conditions of human existence and the possibilities which man has of altering his existence and becoming free. The goal is to provide man with a new understanding of himself (Selbstverständnis).

What Bultmann has intended to do thereby is to utilize the content of the Gospel by presenting it in a form which corresponds to modern man's understanding of himself and his situation. As he sees it, the anthropology of existentialist philosophy not only represents the modern concept of reality; it also is in agreement with the New Testament's own primary goal.

In some of his earlier works (e. g., *Jesus*, 1926) Bultmann — in harmony with the form criticism school — had emphasized that the gospels were not designed to provide a biography of Jesus but to present Jesus' own message and that of the first Christian congregations. This attitude was in keeping with the basic concept of kerygmatic theology: it is through the proclaimed Word that man is confronted by the need for making a decision, and it is thus that he experiences the transition from unfaith to faith. The Word confronts man as a divine address, and not as so much factual information or as religious ideas.

Bultmann combines ideas from both form criticism and kerygmatic theology, and adds to them the anthropology of existentialist philosophy. It is against this background that he sets forth the demand for an existentialist interpretation of the New Testament.

Since 1941 Bultmann has further developed his theories and has provided a philosophical justification of his anthropology and his method of Bible interpretation (cf. *Glauben und Verstehen,* an anthology which presents Bultmann's own theses in Vols. I–III, and *Kerygma und Mythos* [trans. *Kerygma and Myth,* ed. Hans W. Bartsch; New York: Harper Torchbook, 1961] I ff., which provides an ongoing documentation of the Bultmann debate).

It has already been made clear that Bultmann's program stands in sharp contrast to that of liberal theology with its attempts to create a picture of the historical Jesus. In certain other ways, however, Bultmann stands rather near to the liberal tradition. That is true, for example, with respect to his use of the myth concept, which, in fact, remains unclear in his argumentation. This lack of clarity has colored the discussion of "demythologizing." In the light of modern scholarship, "myth" denotes something which is unacceptable, and one cannot but wonder if this is a plausible basis for determining what makes for an adequate interpretation of Biblical texts.

An even more important facet of the Bultmann program is that which speaks of the existential interpretation. As many critics have pointed out, this approach rejects as unessential the gospels' claim of factual information and eyewitness testimony. As far as Bultmann is concerned, the kerygma has a historical anchoring only insofar as it goes back to the person and message of Jesus. The substance of the kerygma, he feels, is independent of historical facts. The death and resurrection of Christ are of significance only in the sense that they symbolize the alteration of human existence which is offered as a possibility in the kerygma. Bultmann, by the way, acknowledges the Crucifixion as a historical event, but not the Resurrection. The statements concerning the Resurrection are merely expressive of the fact that so much significance was attached to the death of Christ by His faithful disciples, whose lives had undergone a decisive alteration.

Many of Bultmann's own followers have in recent years dissociated themselves from these extreme conclusions and have more strongly emphasized the connection between the Jesus of history and the Christ of the kerygma. Bultmann himself, however, has retained the centrality of his existential interpretation, which implies that the question of the historicity of the individual events related in the gospels is not important. What is important is what the reports — be they mythical or factual — have to say about human existence, and the extent to which they can awaken man to making a decision.

Bultmann's consistent utilization of ideas drawn from kerygmatic theology and existentialist philosophy has actualized as never before in the history of theology the question concerning the importance of historical evidence to the Christian faith. A large number of prominent contemporary theologians have devoted themselves to this problem, which has been treated on an exegetical basis as well as from the point of view of the history of philosophy.

One of the clearest and most basic alternatives to Bultmannism has been set forth by the Swiss exegete Oscar Cullmann (b. 1902, professor at Basel and Paris). Immediately following World War II Cullmann published a work entitled *Christus und die Zeit*, 1946 (trans. Floyd V. Filson, *Christ and Time;* Philadelphia: Westminster Press, 1964). This study was not directly involved in the ongoing debate; it rather examined, in a purely historical manner, the early Christian concept of time and set this against the Gnostic system of salvation. As it turned out, however, Cullmann's conclusions were entirely opposed to the interpretation of the Bible recommended by the Bultmann school.

Cullmann demonstrated, among other things, that the Biblical description of the passing of time from Creation to Fulfillment (the history of salvation) presupposes a linear concept of time (in contrast to the cyclical scheme of the Gnostics) and that this view of history is basic to the New Testament. The unique event which is suggested or described in various ways is set forth as being decisive in the Gospel message. Those details which constitute the cardinal facts in the history of salvation also form the foundation for the salvation of mankind. According to the New Testament, the death and resurrection of Christ are at the very center of world history, which will reach fulfillment at the time of Christ's second coming, when the world will be judged and the kingdom of God brought to completion.

This concept of time came into conflict with the Gnostic doctrine of salvation in the first centuries of Christian history. The Gnostic doctrine was set forth as a timeless message, in which reference was made not to past events as the basis of salvation but to certain general religious ideas, presented in mythological form.

In a later work, *Heil als Geschichte* (1965), Cullmann confronted the results of his research with Bultmann's theology and examined more carefully the role played by historical facts in the faith and salvation of the individual according to the New Testament point of view. Cullmann's major emphasis here is that the reference to historical facts which is included in the Christian confession does not suggest a disinterested objectivizing of the Christian faith; these facts are rather related to the certainty that they are of immediate relevance to the existence of individual men, inasmuch as faith implies that the destiny of individual lives is involved in the history of salvation as presented in the Bible. An "existential interpretation" — for which the reliability of historical evidence is of no significance and for which the history of salvation means nothing — is, on the other hand, synonymous with the transformation of Christianity into a Gnostic or idealistic system of salvation.

The present discussion of kerygma and history touches upon questions which are of vital importance for the entire interpretation of Christianity. As Cullmann has shown, this discussion at a number of points actualizes differences of opinion which were already current in New Testament times and which have recurred in different forms throughout the history of theology.

Index of Persons

411

Index of Subjects